CITIES IN SPACE: CITY AS PLACE

CITIES IN SPACE: CITY AS PLACE

DAVID T. HERBERT

Professor of Geography,
University College of Swansea

and

COLIN J. THOMAS

Lecturer in Geography
University College of Swansea

David Fulton Publishers
London

David Fulton Publishers Ltd
2 Barbon Close, Great Ormond Street, London WC1N 3JX

First published in Great Britain by
John Wiley & Sons Ltd 1982, titled *Urban Geography: A First Approach*
(Reprinted 1986 & 1988)

This edition published in Great Britain by
David Fulton Publishers 1990

British Library Cataloguing in Publication Data

Herbert, David *1935- Dec. 24-*
  Cities in Space: City as Place
  1. Urban regions. Geographical features
  I. Title   II. Thomas, Colin J.
  910.021732

  ISBN 1-85346-109-1 (*Paper*)
      1-85346-138-5 (*Cloth*)

Typeset by Chapterhouse, The Cloisters, Formby
Printed and bound in Great Britain by
Biddles Ltd, Guildford and King's Lynn

Contents

Preface

The teaching of urban geography is an important component of degree schemes in Geography and has also found a place at earlier stages of the curriculum as both schools and examination boards accept the value of obtaining a better understanding of the urban environments in which most of us live. An urban geography offers a wider vision of that urban environment than most other disciplinary approaches and reflects the concern of geographers with both cities in space and city as place. Geographers have studied the urban system in which cities are regarded as points or locations in space with complex patterns of interaction and also the urban place where the focus is upon the city as territory with internal structure and processes of movement and change. That both urban system and urban place are products of the societies within which they are located, and that those societies are integral parts of a global system, has become a truism that geographers readily accept. This book is designed to provide a broad introduction to the study of urban geography as part of a discipline which has experienced rapid change in the past two decades, and also to demonstrate ways in which geographers have become far more involved in the more general, interdisciplinary fields of urban studies. It is sometimes observed that as urban geographers have become more immersed in the concepts and methodologies of the social sciences they are less devoted to the 'fetishism of space' and more to the social processes which underpin spatial outcomes. As with all texts this will reveal some of the particular interests of its authors but it aims to include all those topics and ideas judged to be important at this point in time. It also seeks to discuss these topics and ideas in sufficient depth to give them meaning and comprehensibility rather than resort to the inventory approach which includes all but explains little. This aims to be an academic text in the proper sense of the word but one that is legible to a wide range of readers. Whereas the book does not seek to be dismissive of any of the tried and trusted topics of study to which urban geography owes a considerable debt, it does wish to recognise that there are some of these traditional concerns which no longer warrant the kind of prominence which they have previously been given. Urban geography is a dynamic field of study and there are topics now with which it was not associated some decades ago. It is proper that these should receive recognition.

As the topical coverage of urban geography has extended and changed in its emphases so has the form of the conceptual bases upon which the analysis of these topics rests. For students it is perhaps this range of conceptual positions and methodologies which raises the greatest challenges rather than the innovative topics. One option exercised by the writers of urban geography has been to follow a single methodological perspective. As Badcock's *Unfairly Structured Cities* adopts a political economy approach, for example, so Walmsley's *Urban Living* is more firmly wedded to a behavioural-humanist stance. Such books are obviously valuable but the approach in this text is purposefully more catholic. The aim is to identify and discuss the various methodological positions adopted by geographers in the study of the city and to evaluate the contributions which they have made. The object is balance rather than bias, using the latter term in a non-pejorative sense. Geographers are making many and varied contributions to urban studies and a general text should record these and present them to the student in a clear and balanced way. Urban geographers, by writing as geographers but without the self-imposed constraints of an abiding concern within space and pattern, are making significant impact upon the social sciences; it is a research record which we can be justly proud to portray.

This book was conceived as a joint authorship and has been carried through in those terms. It was first published in 1982 as a larger text under the title *Urban Geography: A First Approach* but has been changed considerably in both format and content for this new version. It is a revision which takes note both of reactions to the earlier book and also updates the text to take account of the continuing rapid rate of change during the 1980s. The book was produced at the Department of Geography, University College of Swansea and we have benefited as previously from the excellent level of support services available. Mr Geinor Lewis and Mrs Nicola Jones provided the new and amended illustrations, Alan Cutliffe undertook the photographic work and Mrs Merle Prentice committed her considerable enthusiasms and energies to the typing of the manuscript. To all of these and other colleagues, our thanks. Our families have had to put up with the byproducts of our commitment to a major piece of writing; these are roles with which they are by now well familiar but we are nevertheless, as always, grateful to them for their forbearance.

DAVID HERBERT
COLIN THOMAS
November 1989

Department of Geography
University College of Swansea

List of Figures

CHAPTER 1

The Development of Urban Geography

Until comparatively recently, geographers lagged significantly behind other disciplines in the serious study of the city. Griffith Taylor could still state in the 1940s that urban geography was in its infancy, at a time when many classic urban studies had already been written. This delay reflected the broader directions which the development of geography had taken. Geographers had been strongly influenced by natural science paradigms, indeed Taylor had written in his own *Urban Geography* that he was centrally interested in the relationship between man and environment. Most geographers saw the city as being less attractive than rural or regional landscapes for the development of that theme. The early urban geographers, therefore, focused on the few distinctive themes which reflected the disciplinary context from which they arose:

- **Site and situation** studies were concerned with the physical qualities of the land over which urban settlements had developed and their position in more general location terms.

- **Urban settlement patterns** focused on the spatial distribution of towns and cities, the network of urban places and forms of connectivity within that network, and the notion of hinterland or market area around each urban place.

- **Urban morphology and growth**: the internal structure of the town or city was studied through its morphology or physical fabric, the types of buildings, layout of streets, and general town plan were depicted with close attention to detail and to the historical phases of urban growth.

- **The city in history and in regional settings**: the urban settlement has a long record in history and a diversity of forms in different parts of the world, change over time and cultural variations were clear components of early urban geographies.

These themes reflected the concerns of geography as a discipline and served to make urban geography distinctive from urban sociology or urban anthropology. Griffith Taylor used the terms 'infantile, juvenile, mature, and senile' to characterise stages of urban growth, he also classified towns by site and situation – 'cities at hills, cities at mountain passes' – and developed

1

examples from different parts of the world. Dickinson saw the determination of site and situation as being the first task of the geographer in urban study. This mode of analysis had its critics, however, and Crowe had earlier used town studies as examples of geographers concentrating upon inanimate objects of landscape rather than upon people and movement. An example of perhaps the last of the early urban geographies was Smailes's *Geography of Towns*. Inevitably it reflected the author's own particular interests but its topical themes of the origins and bases of towns, settings, towns and cultures, towns and regions and morphology, place it in this early group.

Without doubt several of the dominant themes of the early urban geographies survive and remain important albeit in much modified form. We no longer dwell on site and situation in any advanced text but urban morphology remains a significant issue which still receives attention. Urban change over time and regional differences in the forms and processes of urbanisation are too clearly facts of the real world to be ignored and the whole field of urban system studies is the inheritor of the town and region themes. All of these will find their full and proper place in the text which follows as part of a modern urban geography.

Before leaving this introductory comment on the development of urban geography, it is worth noting the fact that the past four decades have witnessed significant change in the role of urban studies in geography. Taylor (1949) stated:

> It is rather surprising that there is so little regular study of the characteristics of urban geography.

but by the middle 1950s this had changed and Mayer (1954) could say:

> One of the most rapidly developing fields of geography post World War II has been urban studies.

The first edition of this book (Herbert and Thomas, 1982) contains the statement:

> Whereas in the early 1950s a separate course on urban geography . . . was quite exceptional, today the *absence* of such a course would be equally remarkable.

These statements testify to a growth of urban geography which still retains momentum and shows new characteristics. Firstly, and in part reflecting the heightened interest in cities, specialisms have developed within urban studies. A basic urban geography course is typically followed by separate courses such as urban-social geography, the urban economy, urban services or ethnic areas within cities; in many ways the literature reflects this focusing of interest around specific themes. Secondly, geographers in common with other social scientists have found that there are many issues for which it is not necessary to regard the city as a discrete phenomenon. Unemployment or social deprivation, for example, are strongly associated with cities but not of necessity. They are essentially societal problems which find expression in urban places. Again,

Figure 1.1   Topics in urban geography

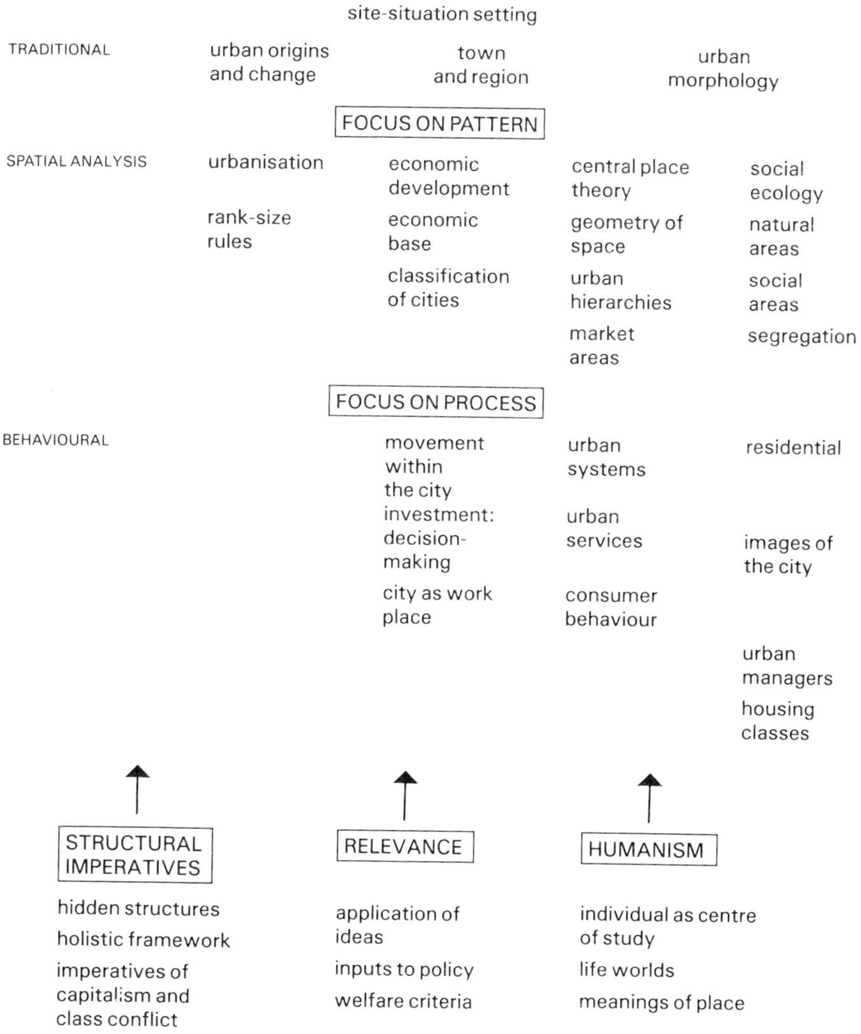

site-situation setting

TRADITIONAL	urban origins and change	town and region		urban morphology	

FOCUS ON PATTERN

SPATIAL ANALYSIS	urbanisation	economic development	central place theory	social ecology
	rank-size rules	economic base	geometry of space	natural areas
		classification of cities	urban hierarchies	social areas
			market areas	segregation

FOCUS ON PROCESS

BEHAVIOURAL		movement within the city	urban systems	residential
		investment: decision-making	urban services	images of the city
		city as work place	consumer behaviour	
				urban managers
				housing classes

↑
STRUCTURAL IMPERATIVES

hidden structures
holistic framework
imperatives of
capitalism and
class conflict

↑
RELEVANCE

application of
ideas
inputs to policy
welfare criteria

↑
HUMANISM

individual as centre
of study
life worlds
meanings of place

where the focus is a specific issue, like deprivation, the disciplinary boundary is not necessarily a central concern. There has been a decided shift away from 'spatial chauvinism' or the tendency to emphasise space to the exclusion of other key dimensions. These are issues to which we shall return but for the moment they serve to underline the continuing change in the ways in which geographers study cities and the place of urban studies within the discipline.

A further point on the development of urban geography over the past four decades is that the subject matter has changed considerably. Topics which rose rapidly to pre-eminence during the 1960s are little regarded in the 1980s: 'births' and 'deaths' within urban geography have been numerous. To a large extent these reflect broader trends affecting both geography itself and the social sciences as a whole. The plethora of CBD delimitation studies of the 1960s, for example, reflected a pre-occupation with land-use and the notion of definable 'segments' of urban space; a 1980s survey of urban financial services would be much more concerned with process and interaction within a world economy. Again, central place theory was tailor-made for a positivist geography intent on model-building and law-generating, consumer behaviour was by contrast a response to a stronger focus on decision-making and behaviouralism. Figure 1.1 summarises this change. Traditional urban geographies gave way to studies with much stronger awareness of people in the urban system though in the spatial analysis age of the 1960s they were treated in objective mechanistic ways. The topics of the 1960s, rank-size rules, economic base studies, urban hierarchies and social areas were new, but reflected the thrust towards modelling, quantification and generalisation of largely static structures. With the advent of behaviouralism, there was a stronger focus on processes, movement and decision-making in the 1970s. Also, since that time, the awareness of structuralism, the need for relevance and re-awakened interest in humanism have brought new forms of urban geography. Again, this is a thumb-nail sketch which will be amplified in the text which follows, but the main point here is that the 'new' urban geography is itself a 'movable feast' which contains older and newer subject matter and a widening range of perspectives from which this may be viewed.

Definitions

Issues of definitions, though seemingly tedious, are very necessary. Besides their obvious role of clarifying basic terms, they often throw light on the subject matter with which they are concerned. One necessary definition is that of urban

Figure 1.2   Sub-disciplines of human geography

	Topic:			
	Historical	Economic activities	Social institutions	Political institutions
Sub-discipline:				
Historical geography	*			
Economic geography		*		
Social geography			*	
Political geography				*
Urban geography	*	*	*	*
Rural geography	*	*	*	*

geography. We can approach it by following the rationale that a definition must take the form of a geographical approach to the study of urban places. Definitions of geography abound, as for example:

> That discipline that seeks to describe and interpret the variable character from place to place of the earth as the world of man. (Johnston, 1980)

Most consistently geography has three main benchmarks in its concerns with space, place and environment/people interaction. These tend to be constants though the significance of any one may be heightened by a particular perspective or 'paradigm'; *space*, for example, was central to the positive science of spatial analysis whilst *place* is the key concept for a subjective, humanistic approach. With these considerations in mind a working definition of urban geography could be:

> Urban geography studies the patterns and processes which occur among and within urban places; the objective form which these take, the subjective manner in which they are interpreted, and their mode of origin at both local and societal scales.

Among the sub-divisions of human geography, urban geography, along with rural geography, sits somewhat uneasily. Figure 1.2 exemplifies this in a simplified way. Whereas economic geography and social geography are distinguished by thematic concerns, urban geography has an area concern. Frey commented on this type of issue with the suggestion that geography considered both single elements or *topics* which could be studied systematically or assemblages of *areas* which could be studied regionally. As an area or place-derived field of study, urban geography has some 'danger' of a catholicity of interest, but in fact the urban studies which approximate regional geographies of specific cities have become exceptional and the dominant focus is upon economic, social and political themes as applied to urban places. This kind of discussion, though worth stating, has become somewhat *passé*. Adjectival geographies of the kind classified above are less used than the more specialised topical fields. For the moment we can profitably turn to another definitional problem – what is meant by the term 'urban'.

The word 'urban' is in itself adjectival and needs either to be allied with another word such as place or settlement, or else to be substituted by town or city. We can arrive at definitions but the problem arises because all these words – urban, city, town – tend to be time-specific and culture-specific; they evoke

Figure 1.3 Definitions of urban

Definitions:	
Urban	population size, population densities; economic functions: market, central place urbanism or life style in the city
Urban place	continuous built-up area with minimum size criterion; functionally-linked contiguous areas, with labour flows or journey to work as principal indices

different meanings at different historical periods and in different parts of the world. British use of the term 'city', for example, is historical and legal, American use of the term has far more ubiquity. Whatever way we approach definition, this diversity becomes evident as we can demonstrate by reviewing some of the attempts to define urban using population size, urban functions, and the concept of urbanism (see Figure 1.3).

Population size

Undeniably, urban places are *larger*, so the point at which the rural village becomes a town or city should be identifiable at some point along the population-size continuum of settlements. Difficulties arise because this *point* seems to vary over both time and space. For several Scandinavian countries, including Denmark and Sweden, any settlement which has more than 200 inhabitants is classed as urban in the national census; a settlement of at least 1000 inhabitants forms the required threshold in Canada, but 2500 is the minimum for the United States. Many countries impose much higher thresholds on resident population before a classification of urban can be obtained; Greece, for example, stipulates 10,000 inhabitants, whilst Japan requires 30,000. From examples such as these, the diversity is initially confusing, but on a global scale there is some measure of logic and comprehensibility. We are reminded that population-size and indeed 'urban' may well be relative criteria which are best judged within their societal contexts. Given the physical geography of Scandinavia, for example, and the ways in which its settlement patterns have evolved over time, a settlement with over 200 permanent inhabitants may well be regarded as urban. In a country like Japan, on the other hand, with a relatively limited land area and considerable population pressure, virtually all settlements may exceed such a low threshold and a high figure such as 30,000 may provide the only realistic line of demarcation. By no means all of the inconsistencies in population-size thresholds for urban can be explained in these ways, but there are grounds for recognising some order in the apparent diversity. In addition to size, *density* of population is sometimes used as a criterion with the assumption that urban places have typically higher densities threshold.

Urban functions

Most official censuses adopt a population-size definition of urban, largely in response to the fact that it is simple and that an information base of statistics is readily available. It is widely acknowledged, however, that there are more telling criteria. Plato acknowledged this in *The Republic* when he stated that:

> The origin of a city is, in my opinion, due to the fact that no one of us is sufficient for himself, but each is in need of many things.

He developed his argument:

> Then the workers of our city must not only make enough for home consumption; they must also produce goods of the number and kinds required by other people?
>
> We shall need merchants . . . a market place, and money as a token for the sake of exchange.
>
> We give the name of shopkeepers, do we not, to those who serve as buyers and sellers in their stations at the market place, but the name of merchants to those who travel from city to city.

Plato goes on to develop the argument in terms of other needs of the city such as doctors, education, laws and justice but his definition clearly revolves around functions and activities contained within the city. Urban places, then, have functions which distinguish them from rural settlements, functions that are various but have at least two significant qualities. Firstly, they are non-agricultural in character and, secondly, they may well be primarily concerned with the exchange rather than with the production of goods. On the first of these qualities, arguments revolve around notions of the 'economic base' of a settlement or the dominant activities which are conducted within its environs. Rural settlements possess activities but these are exclusively concerned with land as a resource and with agricultural production. A simple definition of urban, based upon activities, is therefore one which expresses dominance of non-agricultural functions. Such a criterion, combined with a population-size criterion, is employed in Israel, where a settlement must have in excess of two-thirds of its labour force engaged in non-agricultural work to be classed as urban. Similarly, in India, a qualification of over 75 per cent of the adult male population in non-agricultural work is used.

Reference to an 'economic-base' approach, based upon dominant activities, opens up a considerable range of possible definitions of urban. It is clear that over time a large number of settlements has emerged with specialised functions which are certainly not rural and to which the term urban could properly be applied. The administrative function, often with political connotations, has one of the longest historical tenures and was frequently designated to settlements which were established to control or administer regions of a country. Greek and Roman cities are early examples of administrative/political centres in a tradition which has been carried through to modern capital cities such as Canberra, Ottawa, and Brasilia. Early urban places were often multifunctional with religion, defence and culture amongst their primary roles. Religion has provided a key specialist function for many urban places from the religious centres of the Middle East and Southern Asia to the cathedral cities of medieval Europe. Although there were craft and mining-dominated urban settlements in the ancient and medieval worlds, the manufacturing centre only really dominated settlement evolution with the progress of industrialisation in Europe in the later eighteenth and nineteenth centuries. Industrialisation has undoubtedly created a large number of settlements which are urban. Distinguished by size, density and dominance of industrial employment they were, in Britain at least, the new towns of the nineteenth century.

Single-function settlements, whether they are religious or cultural centres or manufacturing towns, may persist in their original roles over long periods of time. As cities develop, however, they are more likely to add to these original roles or even replace them. These are changes which may well have the effect of consolidating urban status.

The activities conducted in a settlement are clearly of importance in defining its character and the economic-base approach has a valid contribution to make in this context. A stronger line of enquiry relating to a definition of urban in terms of economic functions, however, has focused upon the functions of distribution and exchange and the marketing role of urban places. Pirenne, in his well-known study of the emergence of urban settlement in medieval Europe, placed great emphasis upon the town as a market place; his central thesis, as Jones suggests, was that the city is a 'community of merchants'. This emphasis upon the economic functions of marketing and exchange, became explicit in the ways in which urban geographers defined central places and the urban 'hierarchy'. Dickinson emphasised the roles of urban places as institutional centres for a surrounding territory or hinterland; the demand for services calls the urban settlement into being and, once established, it extends a network of functional relationships over the region. Work stimulated by Christaller's central place theory made this centrality or nodality status of urban places explicit. Most of the empirical work on central place studies has focused upon economic services, particularly retail and wholesale trade, which are the most tangible and easily measured. Urban geographers and others, however, have retained an awareness of the significance of non-economic institutions and services in affording urban status to settlements; as Mumford has suggested, the city should not be over-regarded as an aggregate of economic functions; it is above all a seat of institutions in the service of the region, it is art, culture, and as political purposes. It was in these latter roles that early cities could be most clearly identified.

Urbanism

A further strand in the definitional debate has developed in the context of sociology and is often associated with Louis Wirth's statement on urbanism as a way of life; a statement which continues to attract discussion and elaboration. Wirth argued that urban places can be distinguished by the lifestyles of their inhabitants. Affected by qualtities of population size, density and heterogeneity which typify 'urban' settlements, the 'urbanite' becomes distinguishable from the 'ruralite'. Relative anonymity and a paucity of face-to-face relationships were seen as the hallmarks of an urban lifestyle, and this type of hypothesis found support in the theories of contrast which were developed in anthropological studies. Tönnies, Weber, and Redfield were amongst those who postulated rural-urban contrasts such as sacred-secular, traditional-rational, and personal-impersonal. Such contrasts cannot be sustained in empirical studies and the general concept now has limited credibility. Lewis made a detailed re-examination of Redfield's work in Tepoztlan and found that factors other than place were of central relevance in understanding societal differences. There is, suggests Lewis, a 'culture of poverty' which unites poor urbanites and rural peasants throughout the Third World. Other studies have confirmed this and Abu-Lughod has shown that particular districts of Cairo were populated by migrants from specific rural areas, whose values and lifestyles, derived from those areas, were perpetuated in an urban setting. Differences were fewer between urban and rural than between rich and poor.

These studies are frequently quoted in the literature, but the evidence from Third World countries on this issue remains somewhat ambiguous. Clearly there are no consistent, measurable, abrupt changes of attitudes and values between 'urban' and 'rural' populations, and in many ways the vast 'armies' of poor urban dwellers have more in common with their rural counterparts than with the professional and business elites who occupy the same cities. The more telling question, however, is whether poor urbanites in, for example, one Latin American city begin to resemble poor urbanites in another more closely than the rural peasants of the same region. There is some sense in believing that this may be so. The whole rhythm and content of life in urban places is different from that in rural areas and this difference may well deepen with length of urban residence. Key factors in this process include the mechanisms of urban-rural relationships, the efficacy of transport and communication networks and the form of spatial diffusion processes; in many Third World situations these factors may well operate to the effect that urban places are places apart and their populations, over time, become distinctive.

Critiques of Wirth's urbanism and of the theories of contrast have followed rather different paths in studies of Europe and North America. Numerous studies have demonstrated that social cohesiveness and face-to-face relationships exist within localities in cities; urban neighbourhoods or communities serve as the territories for such interaction. As general features, therefore, anonymity and impersonality do not serve to distinguish urban places. It is now also evident that the progress of Western urbanisation has reduced urban-rural differences to a point at which they become almost meaningless. Transport and communication networks have become so efficient that a place of residence loses some of its significance as a formative influence upon attitudes, values and behaviour. Certainly some traditional differences remain and there continue to be residual and distinctive rural enclaves, but urbanisation has generally become a pervasive societal process. A related and more general point, which will be pursued in a different context, is that all settlements are merely outcomes of more general societal forces; the form of the outcome is less important than the nature of the forces.

Evidence of lifestyle difference between urban and rural places is particularly ambiguous. There are qualifications to be made over both space and time which suggests that contrasts may be more real at some stages of societal development than at others. Urban-rural differences are blurred and almost meaningless in some advanced Western societies; a similar position seems to exist, though for different reasons, in some Third World societies which have experienced recent and large-scale rural-to-urban migration. There are points along the continuum of urban development, however, at which urban places, in some generalised ways, do exhibit distinctive characteristics.

Urban places

These various approaches to urban definition have not brought us to a consensus view; with hindsight it was almost inevitable that the result would be inconclusive. The meaning and reality of urban and urban places will vary considerably over both time and space; a town or city is a physical concentration of people and buildings, but it also has economic, social and political qualities which are specific to the cultural context within which it emerges. The strongest contemporary focus is less concerned with defining urban as a quality than with defining urban place as an entity. Two central objectives of this approach are, firstly, to recognise the reality of urban *regions*, comprising city and hinterland, as meaningful functional units; and, secondly, to provide a framework of standardised urban units which will make the tasks of comparative analysis easier. Simmons and Bourne (1978) demonstrate that by the mid-1970s, most countries had adopted some notion of an 'extended' city to measure urbanisation. This, defined normally on the bases of minimum population size, density and journey-to-work area, is labelled a standard metropolitan statistical area (SMSA) in the United States; a census metropolitan area (CMA) in Canada; and a labour-market area in Sweden.

The concept of the extended urban area has been pioneered by the United States Bureau of Census since 1910 and its modern definition as SMSA summarises the key features of recent research and comprises:

(1) Either one central city with a total population of 50,000 or more, or two contiguous cities constituting a single community with a combined population of 50,000 and a minimum population of 15,000 for the smaller of the two.
(2) The remainder of the county to which the central city belongs.
(3) Adjacent counties, if
    (a) 75 per cent or more of the labour force is non-agricultural;
    (b) at least 15 per cent of workers in the outlying county work in the central county, or 25 per cent of workers in that county live in the central county, i.e. there are significant journey-to-work links between areas;
    (c) at least 50 per cent of residents in a county meet density requirements *or* non-agricultural employment thresholds.

This definition (see Simmons and Bourne, 1978) has been stated in some detail because it does include measures of population size, centrality and economic functions. It is standardised across the United States so comparative analyses are possible, and it forms a useful study-base because it does approximate the services and labour catchment area of the central city.

British attempts to define urban places have followed similar lines. The Standard Metropolitan Labour Area (SMLA) consisted of a core together with a metropolitan ring and had a population of more than 70,000. Amongst criteria for a 'core' are job densities over 5 per acre (13.75 per hectare) and more than 20,000 jobs in total. An SMLA 'ring' consists of contiguous administrative areas sending at least 15 per cent of their labour force to work in the 'core'. A development of this system was produced by the Centre for Urban and Regional Development Studies (CURDS). They gave the term 'Core' to a continuous built-up area containing a concentration of employment and retailing activities. To each Core is attached its primary commuting field or 'Ring' from which at least 15 per cent of those employed travel to work in the Core and more to that Core than to any other. Core plus Ring forms the Daily Urban System and to this is allocated the Outer Areas which are districts most closely linked to them in commuting terms. Local labour market area (or LLMA) is the given term for the whole 'urban place'. In 1981, 61.6 per cent of the British population lived in Cores, 26.6 per cent in Rings and 6.6 per cent in Outer Areas. In the context of complex international variations of data availability, Cheshire and Hay (1989) have developed the conceptually similar functional urban regions (FURs) to compare changing patterns of urbanisation throughout Western Europe.

These recent researches are concerned with defining urban places rather than what is urban. They are furthermore concerned with larger urban places and the thresholds adopted exclude many small towns and cities. It is, however, a line of research which has witnessed high levels of cooperation between academic researchers and various departments of government which have a common interest in monitoring urban change and in providing standardised recording units for comparative analysis. Whereas the question of defining urban can remain a topic for academic debate with no pressing need for resolution, the question of defining urban places has practical implications and of necessity *some* answer must be found.

Urban geography and urban studies

In many ways the identification of urban geography is a division of convenience rather than either a reflection of academic meaning or of the way in which society is structured. The city, however defined, has no monopoly of social problems, economic disadvantage, or more general population attributes. Most of the subject matter which we study has a societal rather than an urban frame of reference. Herbert and Johnston made the distinction between problems *in* and problems *of* the city. Problems *in* the city were in fact general problems affecting society as a whole: they appear to be urban simply because they cluster in urban places. Poverty, for example, is evident in many cities; we can often identify urban poverty areas, but it is by no means exclusively an urban problem. The concentration of poverty in cities simply reflects the numbers and densities of people, it is not created by the urban place *per se*. The causes of poverty lie in economic or socio-political structures rather than in spatial structures. It can be argued, though with some difficulty, that there are also problems *of* the city brought about by, or exaggerated in some way by the urban conditions in which they occur. Are there forms of urban densities, for example, or built environments which create their own problems? Are there neighbourhood effects particular to cities?

This kind of issue on the distinction between problems in and of the city also finds expression in the distinction made between *people policies* and *place policies*. The former would focus policies on people wherever they live and is therefore aspatial, the latter focuses on places and affects all people who live in particular areas. Examples of these will occur later in the text and need not be laboured here, suffice to say the point does demonstrate that the focus on urban geography cannot be fully justified in terms of the uniqueness of urban place.

A further point is that although an urban geography has central concerns with space, place and the urban environment, geographers have moved considerably from any kind of obsession with spatial patterns and distributions for their own sake. Modern urban geography has an awareness of broad and deep-rooted social processes and with current 'policy climates'. The focus on urban place ensures that the distinctive perspective of urban geography emerges but the essential task is to understand the phenomenon rather than to show its immediate association with geographical space. Recent trends have moved urban geographers closer to the multi-disciplinary fields of urban studies and Short (1984) expressed the position well when he suggested that urban geography identifies the city as a useful object of analysis but not one which is independent from the nature of the wider society. The task is to identify and explain those features which distinguish cities but also to see these as integral parts of the societies in which they are placed.

Human geography contains a number of competing perspectives and 'paradigms' and our view is that a text of this kind should reflect all of these and their contribution to different areas of urban geography. The 'triad' of perspectives: positivism, structuralism and humanism are discussed below. Our main concerns can be summarised as the need:

(1) to demonstrate the essential continuity of much urban geography and the ways in which traditional themes retain their significance;
(2) to be aware of the dynamic nature of the city and its components of change and process;
(3) to see the city as part of society and the place where features, issues and conflicts are often thrown into sharpest focus;
(4) to see the city as work-place, market-place and home for many millions of people;
(5) to recognise both the problems of cities and the ways in which urban policies can be evolved which contribute towards their solution.

Modern perspectives

Modern perspectives can be conveniently summarised under the broad headings of positivism, humanism and structuralism. Whilst these perspectives are not necessarily mutually exclusive, they are certainly not complementary and some texts in urban geography have been written more specifically towards one or other of them. Walmsley's (1988) book *Urban Living* for example is more strongly directed towards behavioural and humanistic methods than most whereas Badcock's (1984) *Unfairly Structured Cities* is centred to a large extent around a political economy perspective. This text is rather more eclectic in the sense that it uses good analysis from different theoretical stances to illustrate particular aspects of the city. Here, the nature of these different perspectives will be briefly identified as part of this general introduction and will be developed into rather more detail in Chapter 5, where they take their place among theories of the city.

Positivism

Positivism was proposed by Comte in the 1820s to distinguish science from religion and received its fullest expression in the school of logical positivism known as the Vienna Circle in the 1930s. The positivist method seeks to explain events in the natural world by showing that understanding of a single event can be deduced from certain general statements or theories which contain one or more universal laws. Positivism became translated into geography as spatial analysis, the study of human activities which result from:

> ... the operation of universal processes of decision-making whose characteristics could be identified by a combination of modelling, observation and statistical analysis of the outcomes of those decisions. (Johnston, 1980)

This kind of work had a number of distinctive characteristics:

- It focused on general laws rather than exceptional cases.
- It used numerical methods and was quantitative.
- It had predictive power and could be used in public policy.

Two statements can be made about the conditions under which these characteristics became translated into urban geography as spatial analysis. Firstly, many of the ideas were derived from other disciplines and reflected the more general impact of normative, scientific approaches on the social sciences. Secondly, although one can find examples of generalisations in human geography from much earlier periods, the discipline in practice was centrally concerned with exceptionalism and stood in sharp contrast, for example, with the search for general laws in several branches of physical geography. From the isolated examples, such as Christaller, Weber, and Lösch, a much more general shift towards a nomothetic discipline, in which the search for laws and models was a central concern, was one highly significant change in the contemporary period and one which struck traditional geography at its very core. Associated with this shift was a much greater emphasis on quantitative analysis and statistics, an emphasis which both added a 'degree of difficulty' to the new paradigm and better equipped geographers for the development of a new methodology.

Schaefer's plea for a move away from exceptionalism was a significant single event; more important in the longer term was the systematic development of spatial analysis by other American-based geographers, notably Garrison and Berry. Based initially at Seattle, the interests of this group were very much with spatial laws of two main kinds. The first were concerned with the patterns of points on the earth's surface, of which the main examples were clearly urban places; the second were of flows of goods and people, based upon a view of humans as exceptionally rational beings who reacted to the various costs of moving from one place to another by keeping them at a minimum. Their main stimuli were clearly from economics, both those provided by Christaller's central place theory and those from regional scientist-economists such as Isard, Lösch, Dunn, Greenhut and Ponsard. Their work was strongly mathematical, focusing, for example, upon operational models developed in linear programming, though they also adopted statistical procedures to present their morphological and associational laws and to test their notions about the economic rationality of men. Urban geography proved especially amenable to the impact of this move towards increased quantification, and the role of Brian Berry, who promoted the analysis of settlement patterns and sought spatial order in size and location of towns and cities, villages and hamlets, neighbourhood and regional centres, was considerable. Urban geography had some additional advantage in that the rediscovery of central place theory (a process helped by Baskin's 1966 translation of Christaller) provided a comprehensive spatial model, which, both as a whole and in its many individual facets, provided a rich testing ground for many elements of an emerging quantitative methodology with all the assumptions of normative behaviour and a positivist-scientific approach. Dacey's use of nearest-neighbour analysis in Wisconsin to test distributions of central places, and Berry and Garrison's calculation of threshold populations were two of the best-known early studies.

The new methods of spatial analysis were by no means confined to central place studies. They were applied to classifications of settlements, to examination of urban population sizes, and to the analysis of population densities within cities. On internal urban structure, a considerable amount of research was aimed at the comprehension of land-use and associated land-value gradients. Of the various texts, that by Haggett (1965) was amongst the most influential, and the application of models as a general panacea reached its height in Chorley and Haggett's work (1967). During the early 1960s interest in urban geography had shifted significantly towards social aspects of city life. This shift became associated with the increasing influence of spatial analysis and gave quantification and model-building a new and vigorous platform.

Research focused upon the classification of residential areas within cities and the issue of residential segregation. As multi-variate statistical techniques and the use of high-speed computers were developed, factorial ecology became the most widely adopted methodology. Much of this thrust towards quantification, though synonymous with positivist ideas, was data-based and coincided with the availability of census small area statistics.

As the methodology of spatial analysis was extended and made more precise, it became more scientific with greater use of symbolic language and the formulation of mathematical models. Doubts began to grow as analyses became more sophisticated but yet remained descriptive, while optimising solutions served the needs of suppliers rather than consumers. With its emphasis on the geometry of space, spatial analysis produced theories based on mechanistic assumptions of human decision-making. These involved the concept of 'economic man', a perfectly rational being whose location decisions were based on perfect knowledge, optimisation of opportunities and minimisation of costs. These latter themes stimulated the development of behavioural approaches still adhering to positive theory, but centred on processes rather than on patterns. More general reactions to the shortcomings of a positive science approach led to the introduction of other perspectives. It is important to stress, however, that despite these shortcomings positivism and spatial analysis gave urban geography an important methodology and perspective which it retains.

Humanism

Humanism was in many ways a reaction against positivism and its tendency to ignore human agency. Humanistic geographers looked to different philosophies such as phenomenology, which evokes the subjective description of the life-worlds of human experience. The absolutism of scientific thought is rejected and idealism and mental activity is accorded a primary explanatory role independent of the material order (Jackson and Smith, 1984). For humanistic geographers, an essential question concerned an understanding of the processes by which shared meanings within groups developed, the inter-subjectivity which imbued places with special values:

> People come together in time and space . . . they recognise each other . . . out of their daily taken-for-granted impersonal dynamics, these spaces of activities evolve a sense of place that each person does his small part in creating and sustaining. (Seamon, 1979)

For humanism the key was the meanings of place rather than the geometry of space, 'man' was a central figure rather than an anonymous component of a model or law. As a perspective, the priorities and methods of humanism are vastly different from those of positivism.

Structuralism

As it entered geography, the structuralist approach was also in many ways a reaction against positive science and spatial analysis. Structuralism is first and foremost a theory of society but its entry into urban geography had the more pragmatic catalysts of civil disorder and public unease in the late 1960s. In these pragmatic terms it developed the lack of relevance in spatial analysis:

> There is a clear disparity between the sophisticated theoretical and methodological framework we are using and our ability to say anything really meaningful about events as they unfold around us. (Harvey, 1973)

In relation to social science theory, structuralism is a generic term but two meanings in particular have assumed significance:

(1) Relationships amongst component parts are more significant than the individual parts themselves.
(2) All human actions are underlain by 'hidden structures' which influence and condition these actions. Explanations, therefore, cannot be found in observed phenomena or spatial outcomes but must be sought in the general structures to which these relate.

These general themes have been dominant and the notion of hidden structures particularly so. One source of such hidden structures may lie in the cultural/symbolic traditions; structural symbolists talk of the 'rules of the mind' which govern actions and are embedded in the mores of a society. Of the structuralism which derives from the political economy, that which relates to Marxist theory has been the most pervasive. According to Marx, every society is built upon an economic base which contains the mode of production and exchange. From this economic base or structure develops a super-structure of social and political institutions (legal systems, religions, customs). Economic bases may vary over time and space but in the modern world it is the capitalist system which dominates and provides the structural imperatives. Modern Marxism is far from being a single perspective and there are divergent views on issues such as the relative significance and autonomy of base and superstructure and on the role of human agency. Harvey for example, recognises the duality of the worker as an *object* for capital and as a living, creative *subject*: a duality unresolved in Marxist theory. Marxism's basic divisions of labour and capital, workers and bourgeoisie and the concept of class as a collectivity and class struggle have all been subjected to revisionist writing. As we will see in Chapter 3, some modern writers have taken Weber's view and have interpreted class differently from Marx. These are issues of structuralism, some of which will be dealt with more fully in the text; for the moment, however, it serves as a generic term for a highly influential set of approaches within modern urban geography and the triad of positivism, humanism and structuralism sets the broad parameters for the content of the chapters which follow.

CHAPTER 2

The Emergence of the Urban System

Urban origins

There are problems in the definition of what is urban, and similarly there are considerable difficulties in establishing the beginnings in time and place of the first urban settlements. The two issues are not unconnected and scholars from a variety of disciplines continue to find them questions for debate and new research. Much of the available evidence for very early forms of settlement is archaeological and goes back several millennia in time. In most of the detailed site investigations the scale and sophistication of the built environment, with its accumulation of artifacts, leaves little margin for doubt of the existence of an urban centre. Other evidence, particularly of smaller settlements, is contentious, however, and uncertainty remains. Archaeological evidence is often characterised by its unevenness. Some parts of the world have revealed little or no evidence of early cities but a number of reasons could explain this. Lack of evidence may confirm that cities did not exist, but it is also possible that insufficient proof has survived in recognisable form. Detailed archaeological investigation is extremely expensive and time-consuming, and many of the major investigations were completed before the advent of major technological advances such as remote sensing and dating techniques. Without such studies only generalised statements are possible on parts of the world thought to have experienced early urbanisation. McGee (1967) for example, can only suggest that the origins of south-east Asian cities are obscure and seem related to the diffusion of Chinese and Indian forms of political organisations in the first century AD. Again, even where very detailed evidence is available, as for Catal Huyuk in Anatolia, it is typically restricted to one site and cannot easily be generalised to encompass regional systems of settlements.

As with most urban topics, and particularly those which have been a focus of attention from other disciplines, the literature is voluminous. Though primarily a 'historical' question in a narrow disciplinary sense it is one which has received close and scholarly attentions by some geographers. In what inevitably must be a summary which does scant justice to the debate at large, some prominence will be given to their views. Carter (1977; 1983) has offered detailed and perceptive reviews of the theories of urban origins, whilst contrasted analytical insights have been suggested by Wheatley (1971) and Harvey (1973).

17

The 'traditional' theory of urban origins

There is an established theory of the origins of cities, mostly associated with Childe, to which most scholars would subscribe in part at least, which might be termed the ecological or environmental theory – though the terms do less than justice to the breadth of Childe's thesis. One basic tenet is that the emergence of cities was consequential to a process of agricultural change. A neolithic revolution which advanced society from a stage of primitive hunting and gathering to one of food producing was the necessary precondition for the emergence of towns. Domestication and cultivation led first to more permanent settlements, the neolithic villages. An increase in carrying capacity of the land and a rise in population gave more villages but also freed some of the community from the rhythm of agriculture and the new seasonality allowed for some periods of lower activity. There is evidence, according to Jones, that the standard Mayan plot could produce twice as much corn as was necessary to support an average family unit. The freedom from agriculture gave conditions under which specialisations could develop, producing initially perhaps only priests, leaders and craftsmen but eventually a class of merchants.

The ecological or environmental thesis of urban origins requires favourable conditions of the natural environment of physical geography. The projected sequence of events is most likely to occur in those parts of the world favoured with topography, soils, water supply, and climate which make agricultural 'revolution' more possible. Some would argue that these natural conditions have to be matched by an advanced level of human endeavour through which critical changes in agriculture may be achieved.

Most writers would accept, in general terms at least, the part of Childe's thesis which suggests that agricultural surplus is the catalyst for change which leads to urban development. Mumford extends the notion of surplus back in time to the cave painters of the upper Paleolithic period. These specialists, perhaps with some religious roles, were released from the primary function of hunting and gathering by an abundance of game and thus exhibit some of the first strands of an urban tradition. A key question has been not the fact of surplus but the way in which it became the basis of city civilisations, how the city became the locus for people and activities not tied to agricultural production. Before considering that and other questions relating to surplus, however, it is useful to note that one viewpoint exists which disputes the basic tenet of agricultural change leading via surplus to cities. Jacobs (1969) has argued that transition from rural to urban does not bear close investigation either in terms of some archaeological evidence, or from modern interpretations of the relative roles of cities and countryside. Using the evidence of Catal Huyuk, an early Anatolian city, she argues that the city was the first form of settlement in the region and that change in rural areas was subsequent to it. Catal Huyuk was a mining centre in a previously unsettled area; it was in response to demand generated from the city and to innovations originating in the city that any significant changes in the rural area occurred. Jacobs extends the thesis by arguing that rural areas have rarely been sources of invention, innovation, and change; cities much more typically fill those roles. The argument has some force but doubtful generality. Modern examples may be found of mining centres in uninhabited areas which provide a stimulus, though often temporary, to local agricultural change; they tend to be exceptions rather than rules, however. Again, although cities have stronger records as centres of innovation, rural areas have not been devoid of such roles. It is reasonable to assume that changes that only affect rural areas, and that are part of a long process of evolution in settlement and economy, will originate within those areas. The case of Catal Huyuk then is valid but exceptional.

There are other more general criticisms of the Childe thesis. Friedmann and Wulff (1976), for example, discount the term urban 'revolution'. The development of urban civilisations occupied a very long period of time, counted in hundreds of centuries, and took various and distinctive forms in different parts of the world. A more considerable debate surrounds the issue of *where* the nuclear areas of cities really were. The issue has two parts. Firstly, there is the basic question of the locations of the earliest urban civilisations; secondly, there is the related question of whether some areas were primary and others were derived – whether there was independent development or diffusion. Listings of the early urban civilisations do vary but have nevertheless, a significant common core. Sjoberg included Egypt, Mesopotamia, and the Indus valley with later nuclear areas in North China and Middle America. Braidwood and Willey concluded that south-west Asia, Meso-America, Peru, India and China had urban civilisations by the beginning of the Christian period. Wheatley (1971) suggests seven areas of independent or primary urbanisation: Mesopotamia, the Indus valley, the Nile valley, the North China plain, Meso-America, the central Andes, and south west Nigeria (Figure 2.1.) Both Braidwood and Willey, and also Wheatley, would argue that these are independent developments of urban civilisations, a scale of independence which discards most of the earlier notions of diffusion from single centres or from a very small number of centres. The concept of a single centre of diffusion in the Near East has always been difficult to maintain and, in particular, appearance of urbanisms in Central and South America has never successfully been accommodated. Most writers must accept that there were 'secondary' or 'derived' urban civilisations, as in Crete, south-east Asia and Etruria; there are well-documented examples of 'transplanted' cities which appear as part of a political process of imperial or colonial extensions. Towns in Roman Britain are of this type and McGee has attributed the earliest cities in south east Asia to a similar process. In summary, then, a number of independent centres of early urbanisation may be recognised in both the Old World and the New World. They certainly did not coincide in time and their features often differed; Meso-American cities, for example, were created without animal husbandry, the wheel or an extensive alluvial setting. Diffusion may have been less important in these very early periods than in late stages when imperialist and colonialist expansions used towns as instruments of control and administration. Both Childe and Sjoberg have stated that urbanis-

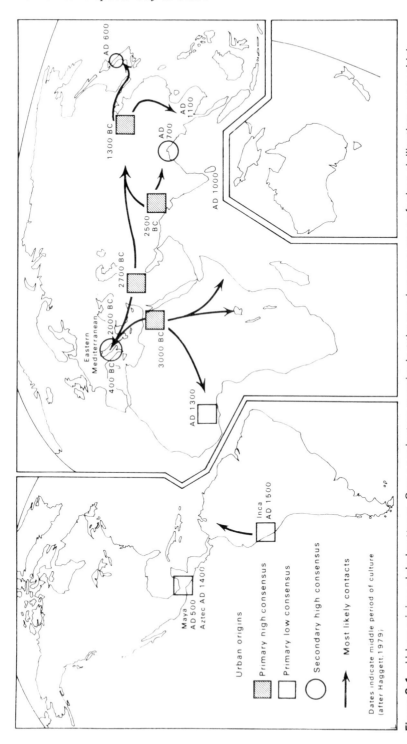

Figure 2.1 Urban origins: global patterns. Some conjecture remains but those *primary* sources of urban civilisation, upon which higher and lower levels of consensus have been reached, are shown together with most commonly agreed secondary sources and lines of contact (dates are extracted from Haggett (1979) Table 12.1)

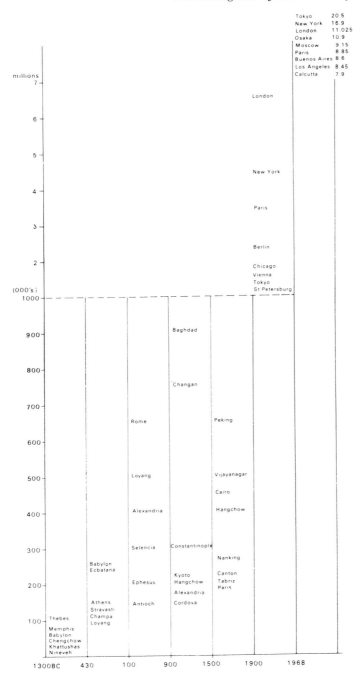

Figure 2.2   Cities over time. Data have been extracted from Chandler and Fox (1974) *3000 years of Economic Growth* and, although estimates, they give some indication of the rise and fall of urban civilisations

ation spread much more rapidly during the first five centuries of the Iron Age, with growth of empires, such as those of Persia, China, India, Greece and Rome, than during the preceding fifteen centuries of the Bronze Age.

The concept of surplus

To return to questions surrounding the origins of cities and the concept of surplus; Harvey (1973) has produced a succinct statement of the issue:

> There is general agreement that an agricultural surplus product was necessary for the emergence of city forms. Much controversy, however, surrounds the manner in which we should conceive of surplus and the way in which surpluses arise, are acquired and are put to use.

Part of the controversy refers to the concept of surplus and whether it is to be seen as an absolute or as a relative entity. It is clear that surplus can only be viewed in relative terms. A threshold of need, beyond which a surplus exists, may vary from one society to another and ultimately among individuals. As Wheatley (1971) has suggested:

> No primitive people have ever spent all their waking hours in eating, breeding and cultivating: even the most debilitated, by squandering some of their resources in non-utilitarian ways, have demonstrated the existence of a surplus.

Pearson has similarly argued that there are always potential surpluses available, and they must be measured not merely against biological needs, but also in relation to the social conditions in which they occur. Harvey warns against a 'formless relativism' in the context of surplus and argues the need for a general context from which to assess surplus, such as that offered by Marxism as a view of 'the universal human requirements of man's existence as a species' (Harvey, 1973).

A great deal of research attention has focused on the way in which surplus, when identified, becomes translated into the chain of events which leads to the emergence of cities (see Figure 2.2). Here the search is for those key individuals, institutions, or groups whose role is to initiate and perpetuate the processes of change once the conditions for it are sufficient. In this search, the likelihood of a multi-stranded rather than a single-stranded causation process is now broadly acknowledged. Several recent pronouncements reflect this view:

> It is doubtful if a single, autonomous, causative factor will ever be identified in the nexus of social, economic, and political transformation which resulted in the emergence of urban forms. (Wheatley, 1971)

> The catalyst was probably the intricately related role of temple, fortress and market place. (Carter, 1977)

A belief that there are important *economic* bases to urbanism has many adherents. Perhaps the best-known of these is Pirenne, who regarded trade and commerce as the creators of the medieval towns. The concept of the town as a point of exchange through the medium of the market-place has earlier applic-ability and is generally acknowledged as at least *one* relevant factor by most writers. Carter is sceptical of the extent to which this concept of city as market-place has general applicability and points out that many markets and fairs are itinerant and have not necessarily engendered permanent urban forms of settle-ment. Defensive functions are similarly regarded as having urban associations; most early cities were fortified in some manner, but are also likely to be ex-pressions of social and political organisations which led to cities rather than initiators in their own right. For Harvey, social institutions are secondary rather than primary effects and are underlain by fundamental changes in the economic bases of society. As economic change leads to a transition from reciprocal to re-distributive to market economies, the expropriated surplus is invested into permanent form as a city. These 'forms' are the monuments of urban culture, be they palaces, temples, market-places, guildhalls or city plans.

Cities in traditional societies

Although urban geography has focused its attention squarely upon modern cities and particularly upon those in Western societies, there is a relatively small but significant literature upon the nature of cities prior to this modern period. If the later eighteenth century with the Industrial Revolution and its enormous influence on people and settlements is taken as a divide, there is something of the order of 5000 years during which time cities existed in one or more parts of the world. Over this period urban civilisations grew and declined, periods of urban dominance were followed by times during which cities were abandoned or destroyed and rural forms of society gained ascendancy. These phases have been well documented and for some authors they suggest that a cyclic 'inevit-ability' may be associated with urban development. A time-period of these dimensions is clearly capable of detailed subdivision, but for our present purposes a simple two-fold division into cities in 'modern' and 'traditional' societies is sufficient; this section focuses on those cities of the pre-industrial period which emerged as parts of 'traditional' societies.

Compared with cities of the modern world, the pre-industrial cities were generally small in population size and relatively few in numbers. In 1300 BC, for example, Thebes was the largest city with a population of about 100,000 and there were only twenty cities with populations in excess of 20,000. By the fifth century BC Babylon was the largest city and may have approached 250,000 in size and in 100 AD Rome's population was put at 650,000. At this latter time it is estimated that there were about 60 cities with populations of more than 40,000. Primate cities, which were disproportionately larger than any others within their urban system, were thought to exist in these pre-industrial societies and Langton notes that in 1730 the vast majority of English towns had fewer than 5,000 inhabitants, with larger regional centres and ports of up to 25,000; but London was already over 500,000.

The concept of the pre-industrial city

Sjoberg's (1960) concept of the pre-industrial city is in many ways a pacesetter for theorising in this field. It has proved controversial and has certainly been vulnerable to detailed criticism, but in the debate many positive advances have been made (see Radford, 1979 for a recent view). Sjoberg, correctly, saw cities as products of their societies. He also, perhaps less correctly, saw technology as the central force for differentiation and change and his main distinction, between pre-industrial and industrial cities, rested upon the time divide of the Industrial Revolution and the ability to use inanimate sources of energy to power tools. In the long time-period prior to this 'divide', Sjoberg hypothesised that a single *broad type* of city was found. Society in this time-period was classified as feudal with a social stratification system which could be divided into a small elite and a much larger lower class. Radford argues that a vital component of Sjoberg's concept is control of the city by an elite whose dominance was derived from non-economic, extra-urban sources. In Charleston, South Carolina, for example, low-country planters built town-houses in which they spent only part of the year. Sjoberg contended that this two-part stratification of pre-industrial society had generality and could accommodate even apparently multi-stratified societies such as India with its caste system.

These cities were multi-functional and were not principally centres of economic activity. Religious, administrative, political, and cultural functions were dominant, and this was reflected in the power structure of the pre-industrial city, in its institutions, and in its built fabric and land-use. These economic activities which were contained within cities, such as trades and crafts, were of lesser status. Sjoberg also generalised upon the morphology of the pre-industrial city and upon the spatial arrangement of land-uses within it. Key morphological features of pre-industrial cities were the walls, which served as defences, as means of segmenting within the urban area, and as mechanisms for controlling the inflow of migrants and traders. Otherwise the internal morphology was typified by narrow streets, congested routeways, and an absence of order, 'houses, jumbled together, forming an irregular mass broken at intervals by open spaces in front of a temple or governmental building' (Sjoberg, 1960).

Sjoberg's statements on the internal arrangement of land-uses and on socio-spatial differentiation in the pre-industrial city have attracted the attention of urban geographers. Here, there are three broad generalisations. First, the elite groups of pre-industrial cities are typically located close to the central area in near proximity to prestigious buildings and sources of power. This residential location may have had the additional advantage of placing the rich well within the defensive walls and away from the more noxious elements of urban life. Their choice of a place to live was also affected, however, by the non-material factors which helped produce an exclusive, high-status core. As Langton (1975) has suggested:

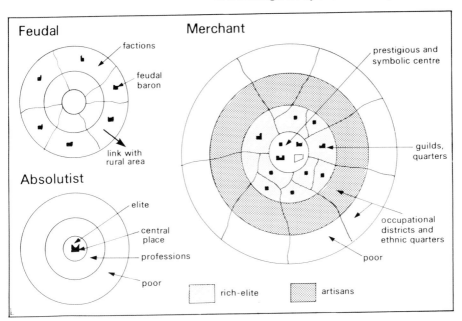

Some notes on types of pre-industrial city in Europe

Feudal city
1. The city was an adjunct to the countryside
2. Many of the wealthy were rural landlords
3. General population mix of rural workers and guild artisans
4. A city of factions with inter-group rivalry
5. Districts were mixed, each with central 'palace'
6. Each district faced its rural place of origin

Merchant city
1. The city rested on trade, craft and commerce
2. The guild was all-embracing – lowest apprentice to richest merchant
3. No necessary link with rural areas, power from urban activities
4. Most successful guilds dominated the city
5. City made up of occupational quarters, each guild had its area
6. Districts were mixed, each with central guildhall

Absolute city
1. The city was dominated by a single family
2. Political power, religious power, administration were keys
3. Greater control over form of city and its activities
4. Centre began to assume greater significance
5. Elite clustered around the central palace of the ruler

N.B. There was interplay and overlaps. Many European cities bear imprints of all three types. Florence, for example, was a hybrid with a feudal aristocracy and its wool guilds.

Figure 2.3 Pre-industrial cities. White (1984) suggested feudal, absolutist and merchant as three types of pre-industrial city evident in Western Europe. The last of these has been closely studied

Tight segregation was further encouraged by primitive transport technology, bad road surfaces, a street system designed more for house access than intra-city travel, the physical repulsiveness of the garbage-strewn, poorly built and crowded non-central area, and the tightly-knit structure of elite society, which was often re-inforced by bonds of kinship and inter-marriage.

As a first and dominant characteristic, therefore, the social geography of the pre-industrial city is typified by a prestigious central area occupied by the elite, and from centre to periphery in a general zonal form are found progressively less prestigious areas and less prosperous people (Figure 2.3).

As a second generalisation, Sjoberg recognised that outside the central core of the city there were other differences in residential pattern of a more detailed kind, but these were in his view of minor significance in the overall structure. There were ethnic, occupational and kinship bases to these finer levels of segre-gation; spatially they took the form of quarters or precincts within the urban area. Thirdly, Sjoberg argued that over much of the pre-industrial city there was a lack of functional differentiation of land-use patterns. Plots were put to multiple uses, the separation of workplace and residence was uncommon, and nothing which resembled compartmentalised land-use zones or sectors could be seen to exist in any detail or uniformity.

Sjoberg presents an attractively simple and graphic account of the nature and form of the pre-industrial city but there are questions on the accuracy of his intrepretation. Some are obvious and general. How acceptable, for example, is the idea that one basic type of city existed in different parts of the world for varying phases of time within a time-span of about 5000 years? As Sjoberg himself argues, cities are part of the societies within which they are contained and will therefore reflect contrasts among those societies. As Egyptian society in the Ancient World differed from medieval society in western Europe, so the cities of those societies will mirror these differences. Similar overgeneralisation, and some misuse of nomenclature, is revealed by Sjoberg's use of the term 'feudal' to describe all societies before the Industrial Revolution, when in the proper sense of the word some were clearly feudal and others were not. It is in his general use of historical data that Sjoberg has been most severely criticised. For Wheatley (1963) he had treated the evidence of the past in a 'cavalier' fashion and had grossly understated the significance of cultural and religious factors. Burke was of the view that Sjoberg had based his concept upon secondary sources of information from limited parts of the world and that the quality of these secondary sources was not high.

A further example of overgeneralisation is provided by Sjoberg's two-fold division of pre-industrial society into an elite and a lower class. As Jones and Eyles have pointed out, feudal stratification in medieval Europe had inter-mediate classes such as clergy and bourgeoisie and some societies were further complicated by intricate castes of priests, warriors, commoners and slaves; there were also other elements such as migrant and ethnic groups who played a large part in forming the residential mosaic. Langton, in his study of seven-teenth-century Newcastle-upon-Tyne, recognised a sharp stratification *within* the merchant community; again, below the merchants, the craft guilds were similarly differentiated in wealth and power.

Several authors have taken issue with Sjoberg over his depiction of the pre-industrial city as an essentially unplanned and disorganised collection of streets and dwellings. Wheatley argued that early Chinese cities had straight broad roads radiating from a nexus, along which lived the well-to-do with the poor in the interstices. Murphey described the remarkable uniformity of plan in Chinese cities with a square or rectangular form and walls surrounding a great cross with gates at the end of each of four arms. There are many other examples of planning in pre-industrial cities; Roman towns and, later, Renaissance or Baroque cities in Europe, had walls, processional ways and a grid-iron plan. Mabogunje, writing on the precolonial development of Yoruba towns, described the palace and market as forming a 'hub' from which roads radiated; these roads had importance as processional ways.

That part of Sjoberg's thesis which has had most corroboration is also the part which is of most direct interest to urban geographers. From many parts of the world and from many points in time there is evidence that cities in traditional societies possess a spatial arrangement of residential areas which can be generalised to the form of prestigious central areas and low-status urban peripheries separated by zones of decreasing status. De Planhof recorded Marco Polo's description of Lut, an Iranian city, as comprising a series of seven concentric walled circles, protecting various quarters, each of which was occupied by members of a single social class. The status of these classes increased towards the central citadel, progressing from peasants, through artisans, to tradesmen, warriors, and doctors of law. At a different place and time, Zweig described pre-industrial Vienna as a clearly ordered city. Nobility and their palaces occupied the heart of the city, diplomats the next districts followed successively by industry and merchants, petty bourgeoisie and workers. More recently, Langton has scrutinised studies of British cities in the seventeenth century and concluded that three of the five largest English cities, together with Dublin, exhibited spatial patterns of wealth distribution similar to those postulated by Sjoberg. Again, in a more general survey of seventeenth-century English towns, Langton states that information from hearth tax returns makes it clear that the rich lived near the centre and that wealth declined towards the periphery. Radford (1979) identifies in Charleston, South Carolina a social organisation of space with prestigious centre, gradient towards the periphery, and segmented slave quarters, broadly confirming the generalisations of Sjoberg's model. These examples could be replicated and the burden of evidence is such as to validate the Sjoberg hypothesis on the internal arrangement of land uses within the pre-industrial city. The key to its validity is of course the level of generalisation and the fact that it purports to be a model; in very general terms these arrangements of land-use can be discerned, and once details are scrutinised and the level of spatial generalisation is reduced, divergences and distortions become evident. White (1984), for example, shows in his analysis of Italian feudal cities that a centrally located elite was not the norm. This group was more widely scattered and did not cluster at the centre until a later stage when cities tended to be dominated by a single ruler (see also Figure 3.3). Two topics can be identified for further discussion. Firstly, the nature and symbolism of the functional centre of the pre-industrial city; secondly, the extent to which the 'finer details' of differentiation distort the broader zonal pattern.

Institutions and symbolism

Whilst the pre-eminence of the central areas of cities in traditional societies can reasonably be conceded, the institutions with which that pre-eminence was associated did vary. For the medieval Muslim, the key features of his city were the mosque, market and public baths; for the early dynastic Mesopotamian it was the temple; for the Carolingian, the keep, church and market; in Mauryan India, the palace and market, and so on. These institutions gave cities their definitive urban content and from them the strong symbolic value of the central area ensued. This symbolism came through most strongly in societies where religious institutions were paramount. McGee (1967) has described the south-east Asian city of Angkor Thom, built between 1181 and 1219 AD. At the centre of the city was the Bayon, the largest temple, a huge mountain of stone designed to symbolise the magical mountain which is the axis of the universe and abode of the gods.

> Surrounding the Bayon there was an enclosure in which the palace of the king was located and surrounding this were the walls and a wide moat, some eight miles in circumference, which represented the mountain, walls, and the sea of the cosmological universe.

Both McGee and Wheatley have stressed this *cosmological* significance of the centre and indeed of the whole plan and ethos of the city in traditional societies.

> No account of the spatial relations of pre-industrial cities in East and South Asia can afford to ignore the cosmogonic significance of the ritual orientation of urban space. (Wheatley, 1963).

Besides the prestige and wealth of the central areas, therefore, there was an additional and pre-eminent ritual or religious symbolism attached to such areas. Jones and Eyles suggested that the ceremonial cores of the Mayan cities with their grouped pyramids, courts and plazas had similar attributes.

Districts and sectors

Outside the central areas of pre-industrial cities, the evidence for simple patterns of zoning is by no means always present and unambiguous. In some societies, broader and vaguely sectoral divisions seem to exist. Tuan described the ninth-century city of Ch'ang-an as being divided into two parts by a long and very broad street. On one side of this street was the imperial court and its associated entourage; on the other were the merchants and other citizens. Jones and Eyles saw an analogy between this pattern and that which led to the development of the West End and East End of London. Regent Street acted as a boundary between what was later christened the West End, housing a complex of government and power around Westminster and St James, occupied by nobility and gentry, and the narrower streets and meaner houses of the later East End, occupied by mechanics and traders.

From many other parts of the world there is evidence that at a more detailed level, the structure of cities in traditional societies possessed a segmented or compartmentalised form. Mabogunje suggested that in Yoruba towns each street formed a quarter consisting of a number of compounds housing members of one or more extended families. The compounds were enclosed spaces with single entrances but many internal subdivisions; individual families occupied each subdivision but the compound as a whole was united on a kinship basis. These square or rectangular compounds were thus the most distinctive components of the residential area structure, but they varied in size and form in ways which reflected the status of their occupants. Whereas compounds of poor families would cover no more than one-fifth of a hectare, those of chiefs would have an area in excess of one hectare. Davis also identified compounds in the pre-industrial colonial cities of South America. Typically a 'monumental' centre, often fortified, was dominant but throughout the urban area native compounds occurred within which the Indian population was housed.

The merchant cities which emerged in the long period between the dark ages and the beginning of the Industrial Revolution marked an important phase of urban development. This was a time of transformation from a feudal to a capitalist society in which the growth of trade produced a mercantilist class, forming the 'third estate' after the aristocracy and the church. As trades and exchange-dealers they needed urban settings, and cities began to reveal their imprint. As early forms of craft and industry began to appear the medieval guilds accompanied them to regulate entry to professions and to control the supply of goods. With trade and industry came the need for a money economy and financing as a profession; the word 'bank' comes from the Italian *banco*, the table on which money-changers conducted their affairs (Short, 1984). The merchant cities of Europe became reflections of their age and new forms of society, new architectural expressions and new economic organisations typified them.

These merchant cities began to show typical forms and Vance (1971) has provided a closely argued thesis for the development of a segmented or compartmentalised city in medieval Europe during what he prefers to call the 'precapitalist' period. For Vance the critical stage in the transformation from pre-capitalist to capitalist city was that at which men began to own rather than merely to hold land. In the medieval city, Vance argues, land ownership was mainly functional in that it afforded a workman the place to practise his trade and shelter his family, apprentices and journeymen. The burgages which existed to provide for the land needs of city men were not intended to enhance personal wealth, but rather to provide an urban location suitable for their needs. Central to Vance's explanation for the emergence of a 'quartered' and many-centred medieval city was the role and status of the guild. Guild membership was the standard means of entry to established urban life, individual guildhalls were foci of interest and members tended to live within their precincts creating occupational districts. The guild offered a place of security, entertainment, social contact, surveillance of business and a religious orthodoxy – all effective bonds which cemented the territorial districts into cohesive communities. This 'factionalising' role of the guild had a strong effect upon the social geography of the medieval west European city; it was paralleled by other social divides. For example, early ghettos can be dated from the twelfth century when Jews began to be excluded from Christian quarters, and political rivalry within cities led to physically identifiable quarters such as the *societa della torri* in Florence. For Vance the medieval city in western Europe was segregated and multi-centred, and the guild system underlay most of this compartmentalisation:

> The supervision of the quality of products, the conditions of manufacture, the ways the goods were sold, became important offices of the gild, and roles that encouraged the clustering together, in gild districts within the city, of the individual practitioners of the various 'mysterious arts'.

Although portraying a segmented city with foci around many guilds, Vance also recognised some more general zonal order which served as an encompassing framework. 'Patrician' guilds, those which were pre-eminent in status, occupied the more central parts of the city. The notion of gradation from the centre is little developed by Vance and there is indeed scant reference to the place of the poor in urban society and city structure. Vance does, however, stress the vertical arrangement of land-uses and social classes which typified his pre-capitalist city. Ground floors of buildings may have been used to transact business, with the first floor as the family home and upper floors reserved for employees and others. Separation of workplace and home was not the rule.

Langton (1975) was critical of both Sjoberg and Vance and his detailed study of seventeenth-century Newcastle-upon-Tyne goes some way towards revealing the complexity of the city in traditional societies and the danger of overgeneralisation. From an analysis based upon the taxed population of 1665, Langton showed that occupational groups were, to a significant degree, segregated into distinctive concentrations in Newcastle. There were four groups of activities – mercantile, victualling, shipping, and manufacturing – which corresponded with a degree of clustering around strategic facilities. This segmented pattern was reminiscent of Vance's conception of the internal structure of the city, and there was also some evidence for spatial grouping of craft activities, though others were dispersed. This pattern in Newcastle was complicated by the fact that emergent 'class' zones could be identified within which were contained a heterogeneity of occupational groups who were united by comparable levels of wealth.

Newcastle was not a feudal pre-industrial city, nor was it a pre-capitalist or capitalist city. A merchant clique was pre-eminent in wealth and municipal power. Its social dominance was expressed geographically in the existence of a mercantile quarter in that part of the city where its economic purposes were best served and where the institutions through which it dominated the city were located. In addition, the city possessed other regularly patterned occupational districts which were in some areas re-inforced by 'class-zoning' and in others countervailed by it.

Summary

There is ample evidence for the belief that whilst models of the type proposed by Sjoberg have some very general validity, any more detailed and systematic study of the city in traditional societies will reveal divergences, contrasts and exceptional features. Whereas technology may well have been a relatively blunt instrument to monitor differentiation and change over the very long pre-industrial period, culture, tradition and social values were not and are much more telling sources of diversity. Factors of this type, as Wheatley (1963) so persuasively argues, underpin the nature of early cities. Vance (1977) identified strong contrasts within medieval Europe between merchant towns and Renaissance cities:

> No more revealing picture of the distinction between the city as the workshop of man and as the monument to enshrined and narrowly-held power could be furnished than by comparing Bristol in the West Country of England with the several dozen princely towns in Germany and Italy possessed of similar status.

Any view of the internal structure of the city in traditional societies may include broad generalisations, principally the existence of a prestigious central area with progressive zoning and a more detailed system of quarters, compounds and precincts, but it may also allow for diversity and indeed for change. Cities have rarely been static and the concept of urban change is as important as those of form, composition or ethos.

The city in transition:
nineteenth century change in Britain and America

For much of the nineteenth century the city in Western societies was in a stage of transition, the initiation and pace of which varied from one society to another and between larger and smaller urban areas. This transition had innumerable impacts upon the internal structure of the city, affecting its population size and density, its areal extent, morphology, economic functions, and a range of social and political characteristics, but it was underlain by far-reaching changes which were transforming the overall nature of societal organisation. Economic change prompted by the forces for industrialisation provided one dominant trend; a change from a traditional 'feudal' society to one dominated by the capitalist ethic was another. The changing social geography of the nineteenth century city must first be viewed against the contexts of these adjustments in the macro-structure of society. Beyond that it is essential to identify the 'enabling mechanisms' which allowed the adjustments to find spatial expressions. In some instances, the needs of the new economies and sets of relationships brought immediate and specific changes, more usually – and especially in terms of residential structure – the traditional forms of urban life responded more slowly to new circumstances. Whereas the wealthy could initiate change and provide the means to achieve it, the large mass of urban population was governed by constraints rather than by choices, and they could only respond to possible alternatives when presented.

Most writers would agree that the transition represented in the nineteenth century is one between the city in *traditional* societies to the city in *modern* societies. Many make use of ideas of stage models as represented by Schnore or Timms, which can usually be related to the transition from the type of spatial generalisation proposed by Sjoberg, in which high-status areas were located at the city centre and lowest-status areas on the periphery, to that associated with Burgess in which a reverse arrangement existed. At the broadest level of generalisation both these sets of ideas, of stages and of 'model' spatial generalisations, retain some usefulness; it is increasingly clear, however, that neither are adequate either to describe the complex processes of change or their expressions in urban form and sociospatial organisation. Whereas it is con-venient to work within a framework of stages and models, it is also necessary to demonstrate that the details of process and pattern are at least as significant as the generalisations.

For Vance (1971) the terminology of change from pre-industrial to industrial city is less appropriate than that of pre-capitalist to capitalist. It is this latter labelling which more adequately describes the changing relationship between employer and worker and the new interpretations which were put upon land and housing as they became 'commodities' in the new capitalist order. Industrialis-ation and the emergence of capitalism had many expressions in nineteenth-century society; for the study of emerging residential patterns the most sig-nificant were the increases in specialisation, differentiations, and stratifications which were eventually to form the bases of residential separation and segre-gation in the modern city. Allied to these, another key change involved the relationship between workplace and home. During the long age of the city in traditional societies, separation of workplace and home had been extremely limited; as increasing scale of enterprise prompted some levels of social stratification within the 'workshop' economy, it was contained within different floors of buildings rather than expressed in terms of different residences. As Vance suggests, floor-by-floor juxtaposition was very much the rule; the very poor occupied cellars or garrets and otherwise, apart from the fact that the ground floor was often used for business, the status of occupants declined with increasing altitude within the building.

Before the increasing social differentiation between employer and employees and among the labour force could become spatial segregation, there had to occur a much more general separation of workplace and home than hitherto existed. This did occur during the nineteenth century and is the central process in understanding the changing social geography during this transitional period. Essential adjuncts of this process were the development of an emerging housing market to supply accommodation and the evolution of a transport system which allowed this to be linked with workplace in a daily rhythm. The availability of these facilities was typically limited initially to those very small sections of society which controlled wealth and power; the long duration of the transitional 'stage' was related to the variable way in which these facilities became available to other sections of the population.

Much of the available geographical research on the nineteenth-century city has focused upon the task of providing snapshot pictures of residential structure at one or more precise points in time. This research is valuable and has been most successful in identifying patterns and their changes over time and in revealing the local processes of residential mobility which accompany those changes. It has been less successful to date, however, either in relating these patterns and processes to more general forces of societal transformation or in revealing the roles of the agencies which provide the conditions under which change can occur.

For Marxist geographers, the broad forces behind the city in transition can be squarely ascribed to the process of capital development which began, in the early nineteenth century, to force rapid urbanisation, new patterns of production and new divisions of social life; the choice of urban solution is sharply defined by the structural imperatives of the capitalist mode of production. Using a more broadly based perspective, Vance argues that the changes were engendered as the growth of the industrial city prescribed new forms of land use and made new demand upon labour. The capitalist ethic, given dramatic stimulus by the forces of economic change, transformed the nature of social relationships and established both land and housing as commodities to be owned rather than simply held. In the context of housing, in particular, a number of new characteristics had emerged. Whereas in the past the offer of employment had often carried the obligation to house, this became a decreasing feature; ability to pay rent became a criterion affecting both quality and location of residence. Significant changes in attitudes and impersonal relationships were occurring. Attitudes towards rent, property and profit, which would have been misplaced in medieval society, became acceptable.

Urban morphology began, slowly, to respond to these changing circumstances. If an individual had wished to enlarge his premises in the medieval city, he did so by building upwards, which created the tall house in northern Europe, and by extending backwards to infill the burgage plot. Such infilling was not normally for profit in a direct sense but to extend the family business unit or occupational group. Containment of the extended family under one roof was more typical of the better-off but under the workshop principle, master, workers and apprentices all lived under one roof (Figure 2.4). Under an

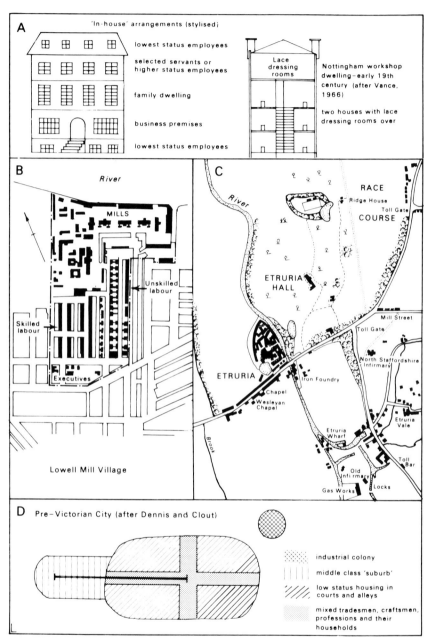

Figure 2.4   Work and residence in the city: the changing spatial relationship
(a) Work and residence within one building; social stratification by floors (derived
in part from Vance, 1966). (b) Lowell mill village with separation of works and
residence and 'social areas' (after Vance, 1966). (c) Etruria, Stoke-on-Trent.
Wedgwood's move from Burslem to Etruria Hall, separate works on the canal and
workers' cottages. (d) A schematic representation of the emerging early Victorian
city (after Dennis and Clout, 1980, *A Social Geography of England and Wales*;
reproduced by permission of Economic Geography)

emerging factory system, the processes which led to separation were initiated. Vance (1966) has traced the development of 'mill villages' in both Rhode Island (Figure 2.4) and Nottinghamshire as an early clear example of the new form of workplace/residence organisation. Under these first expressions of the factory system, the separate place of work became the focal point, and around this a landscape of small cellular units emerged involving short daily journeys by workmen. In these situations, the industrialist was still the provider of housing – which was an adjunct of productive activity – but an initial stage of separation had been achieved. For the labour force of these early factories, the employment link was short, direct, and highly specific.

As the workshop/domestic activity was replaced by the factory system, a demand for new labour was generated. These workers had to be accommodated in cottages and tenements which were constructed in the alleys and courts behind the main street facades. Infill now became a more direct source of profit, and as space was used congestion began to appear in the inner city (Figure 2.4). The merchants who occupied main-street housing now began to be faced with alternatives. Depending on the profitability of infill, the availability of new peripheral land and transport, there were possibilities of releasing ground-floor or first-floor space to business expansion, and managers rather than owners became the inner-city dwellers. As the attractiveness of the central city began to wane, higher-income groups began to accept short journeys to work in order to displace themselves from the workplace.

It would be wrong to locate the origins of these trends in the nineteenth-century city; in twelfth-century London there were high-status residences around the city periphery. These, however, the isolated mansions of the powerful, provide an early example of a continued preference for the rural retreat rather than any real beginnings of suburbanisation. Similarly, well before the nineteenth century, early 'industrialists' had left the towns in which they had established their production processes; Wedgwood, for example, had left the pottery town of Burslem to find a more rural setting for Etruria Hall (Figure 2.4). It was during the nineteenth century, however, that the trickle became a stream and newly emerging professional men and businessmen sought to emulate the new residential examples of the elite. For Vance (1971) the significant change was in the nature of housing; from being a specific contact between employer and employee, it became generalised and by 1850 a true urban proletariat had been formed. Housing supply had now to be extensive, so a housing market – distinct from any workplace contractual agreement – was necessary to administer it. This may have had deleterious effects: 'housing generalisation led to the creation of slums . . . it grew out of the abandonment of the self-correcting mechanism of enlightened self-interest that had existed in factory-tied housing'. (Vance, 1966, p. 324).

The acceptability of this last sentiment is questionable. That there were new attitudes to housing provision is clear; whether prior attitudes were necessarily good and subsequent ones bad is less obvious. More recently, the appropriateness of the appellation 'slum' has been questioned as a generalisation upon

Victorian low-cost housing. Whatever the quality of housing, however, a sequence of home/workplace relationships can be recognised from occupational district to mill village to proletarian residential quarter.

For the new professionals and businessmen, the separation of housing from area of economic effort brought new attitudes. High-income residential areas gave exclusion, a need to create symbols of affluence and power. The emerging high-income groups acted concertively to develop particular kinds of residential districts and imbued them with lifestyles and social flavours which set them apart. Several writers have argued that these changes affected family lifestyle as well. As employers loosened bonds with the workplace, they were able to choose where to live with the *nuclear* family; it was among the low-income areas that the *extended* family in close proximity was to be found by the end of the nineteenth century. As the higher-income and later the white-collar groups acted on a preference for 'rural' settings, an aversion to place of production and crowded living areas, and a desire to avoid the rising taxes of the central city, the advantages were clear to many others. For the working classes, the mid-nineteenth century was a time when it would have been desirable to secure less crowded and unhealthy quarters but their exodus had to await the development of trolleybuses in the late 1880s. The railroads had brought transport possibilities to the white-collar groups in the 1830s but, as Ward suggested, innovation and expansion of the streetcar system was achieved more rapidly in the United States than in Britain. Walker summarised the trends as they affected American cities: as a concentration of production and circulation in the central city, interwoven with workers' homes; and outward residential thrust of the bourgeoisie; and a dramatic increase in the economic and social differentiation of urban space. The essential mechanisms needed besides a transport system included a building and construction industry and a set of new agencies to administer the housing market. Whereas geographers have made limited contributions to the study of such agencies, social historians have, properly, ascribed to them a significant role.

> The character of the place and its different neighbourhoods, was determined by the builders themselves, or more strictly by the developers – those large builders . . . who took large leases of building land and organised its disposition, saw to the laying out of the lesser residential roads, the making of sewers and the provision of water supply, and who generally arranged sub-leases with smaller builders for individual houses or small groups of houses. (Thompson, 1977, quoted in Shaw, 1979)

Residential patterns in the nineteenth century

For a number of North American and British cities, detailed studies are now available which depict residential patterns at the mid-nineteenth century. For British studies the basic data sets are provided by census enumerators' returns which, after a lapse of a century, become available in their original detailed form. Within the *caveats* of the data a range of sound and detailed studies, mainly for the census dates of 1851 and 1871, have emerged.

Most empirical studies have the objectives of identifying the 'dimensions' or 'bases' of residential differentiation and the extent to which these find expression in spatial forms. Many have used factor analysis methods although there is no marked consistency in the particular technical procedures which have been adopted. Shaw (1977, 1979) studied Wolverhampton in 1851, when it had a population of 49,985 and in 1871 when it had reached 68,291. His interpretation was that by the earlier date it was well into the transition from pre-industrial to modern industrial city. A principal components analysis showed that, in 1851, social status was the main dimension though this was strongly linked with family status and with domestically organised trading. An ethnic dimension, specifically Irish, was evident. The social geographical divide was between areas of relatively high social status where servants were common, dealing was a principal occupation, and many household members were not related to the head, and the coalmining districts within the urban area in which social class was low, servants were rare and there were many children in employment. By 1871 some measure of change could be identified. The leading dimension was now more clearly related to family status with a range from low scores in the central district, business households were run by a manager and contained many single adults; the proprietor and his family had moved to the suburbs. A separate social status dimension had emerged which located the high-status groups in the western part of the town.

Lewis's study of Cardiff used three sources of data – rate-books, census records, and health reports – to identify residential patterns at 1851 and 1871. At the earlier date, vestiges of the pre-industrial city were discerned with high-status groups living mainly centrally in the main business streets and the rest of the population crowded into limited space between canal and railway. By the early 1870s, there were modifications to this pattern but the study concluded that modern conditions of segregation had not fully emerged.

The major British study concerned with the reconstruction of residential patterns in the nineteenth-century city has been based upon Liverpool. Here the transition towards the modern industrial city was found to be advanced at mid-century:

> . . . the rapidly growing city of the mid-Victorian period exhibited a high degree of residential differentiation: the main social dimensions of city structure had clear spatial expression and were reflected in distinctive social areas. (Pooley, 1977)

The bases of separation were demographic, economic and social – reminiscent of 'modern' patterns; the central area had long since ceased to be residential and trends towards suburbanisation were evident. These apparently clear trends away from pre-industrial patterns and the less convincing evidence of other studies, may well reflect the position of Lancashire as an early industrialising region and Liverpool as its most rapidly growing city.

Goheen provided one of the most detailed studies of a North American city with his analysis of evolving residential patterns in Toronto between 1850 and 1900. At the beginning of this period the wealthy were able to segregate in their quarters but remained at the centre where they could both take advantage of urban amenities and exercise influence on urban affairs. At the opposite social status extreme, the unskilled were segregated into pockets at the urban periphery with maximum disadvantage of environments and locations. Between these extremes, and accounting for a large part of the urban population, was considerable heterogeneity of functions, classes, and residences. By 1879, there has been significant change; economic status, family status and ethnic (Roman Catholic) segregation were distinctive and independent dimensions, even though they found only limited territorial expression. By the turn of the century, both the scale and texture of urban life had become transformed; the bases of social differentiation and the distribution of groups essentially corresponded with those of the modern city. Radford looked at the development of Charleston, South Carolina, as a 'slave city' in 1869 and 1880. Detailed patterns of segregation were emerging but a central feature was the pushing of the free blacks to the urban periphery, a pattern which persisted after the civil war. His detailed studies of Charleston in mid-nineteenth century have enabled him to recognise the main outlines of the pre-industrial spatial model although, as might be expected, there are deviations.

More generally Ward and others have argued that there was little residential segregation in the nineteenth-century American city; the destitute were clustered but larger areas contained admixtures of lesser professionals, craftsmen and labourers. There were still, however, cities in transition displaying processes of economic and social change.

The industrial city

Vance (1971) preferred the term pre-capitalist to describe European urbanisation in the merchant city period; he identified a key transformation as the process by which men began to own rather than to hold land within the city. This was, however, merely one aspect of the wider process of societal transformations which was to have profound effects on the city; this is best summarised as the growth of industrial capitalism. The change affected the nature of economic activity, the social organisation and the forms of urban settlement to a massive extent. These changes occurred at a pace which was unprecedented and were paralleled by major advances in areas such as medical science and technology which magnified their effects. Industrial capitalism was accompanied by demographic transition, a population explosion which was to find its main expression in the urban areas of the industrial era – this became truly the age of great cities.

Economic change proceeded through stages of employment at home, through a workshop system to the factory system and it was the last of these which underpinned the industrial city. The factory system brought specialisation of labour, workers undertook single tasks; continuous use of equipment, the 'conveyor-belt' syndrome; greater scales of production process with the accompanying economies of scale; and increased productivity per worker and overall level of output. The nature of the factory system was such that it needed a large pool of available workers, factories tended to cluster together in order to make optimum use of factors of location such as labour pools, markets, ancillary suppliers and services. The process of clustering led inevitably to urban forms and the Industrial city. Some of these were new cities at previously non-urban locations such as mining towns on coalfields, shipbuilding on tidal rivers, and transport towns at strategic points of conflux, but many became grafted on to pre-existing urban settlements; former market towns, rural service centres and merchant cities acquired the physical experiences of this new urbanising force. The 'great cities' became those in which the urban-industrial process was most successful and acquired its own momentum. Successful industries attracted new industries, the demand for services was multiplied, the availability of work drew in workers, the generated wealth began to find civic expression in the new 'monuments' of the industrial city with its civic buildings, cultural institutions and new infrastructures of roads, rail and services. As Robson has shown, the urban hierarchy, once established in nineteenth century Britain, became affected by the spread of innovations in an uneven way. Innovations first affected larger cities and so contributed to their growth and only later filtered down to lower reaches of the urban hierarchy.

Industrial capitalism therefore led to new forms of cities and different kinds of expression of an accelerated urbanisation process. It also led to re-alignments of social structures. Industrial capitalism created two main classes within society: the owners of capital who invest in labour to produce a profit or surplus and the labour force which sells its skills to the owners of capital in order to earn wages. This division between capital and labour was a keystone of Marxist theory and had profound implications for relationships within society and within the city. All power was now concentrated into the hands of the holders of capital, cities were formed to suit their needs and the industrial city was the physical manifestation of the imperatives of the capitalist system. These imperatives had expressions which subsumed the pre-industrial legacies of the merchant cities. In Europe (White, 1984) the development of industrial capitalism spread from Britain to Belgium, hence to Germany, France, the Netherlands, Scandinavia and the Alpine countries and later to Southern Europe.

The scale of this urbanisation was spectacular. Lawton estimates that almost all of the 27 million increase in British population from 1801 to 1911 was absorbed by urban areas. White commented on the growth of German cities and showed that the Ruhr had a population of 237,000 in 1843 but 1.5 million in 1895. The industrial city had its own new social classes, the 'bourgeoisie' of successful industrialists, businessmen and professionals, but more spectacularly the new working classes; proletarianisation was a general feature of nineteenth-century economic growth throughout Europe. Initially it was in the interests of capitalists to provide houses to rent for their workers, a labour-force close to the factory gates was a priority. In older and larger cities this was less the pattern and existing properties could be subdivided and the emergent speculative building industry could provide housing to rent. Much of this housing was of low quality and the pressure of population growth meant over-crowding and congestion. Again, White records that poverty and squalor generally characterised the conditions for the new proletariat and at Bochum, Germany in the 1870s, three quarters of the population was at subsistence levels.

The industrial city was of a radically different form to that of its predecessors. As Short (1984) notes, the infrastructures were stretched to impossible limits from the pressures of growth. Public sanitation and water supply services were overwhelmed, the lack of control meant high levels of pollution and low quality of housing and services. Engels wrote in 1892 of conditions in London where houses were occupied at high levels of overcrowding and had fallen into severe states of disrepair with narrow courts and alleys filled with filth and rubbish. Such conditions led inevitably to contagious disease and ill-health and to a breakdown in social order with high rates of crime and vice. Eventually society was to respond to these malaises with alternative communities such as garden cities and social reforms to impose control on standards of living.

Out of the industrial city there also emerged a new form in terms of the economic and social organisation of geographical space. Any kind of pre-industrial model could not survive the onset of industrial capitalism, the city centre became the commercial heart of the new society, the wealthy opted for space and more open surroundings on the edges of the industrial city, the notion of suburb was born. The poor were left at the heart of the city in their crowded tenements and high density terraces using space which others had discarded. Perhaps the best known British description was that provided by Engels (in 1844) for Manchester:

> Manchester contains, at its heart, a rather extended commercial district, perhaps half a mile long and about as broad, and consisting almost wholly of offices and warehouses...unmixed working people's quarters, stretching like a girdle (around this commercial district), averaging a mile and a half in breadth... Outside, beyond this girdle, lives the upper and middle bourgeoisie, the middle bourgeoisie in regularly laid out streets in the vicinity of working quarters...the upper bourgeoisie in remoter villas with gardens...in free wholesome country air, in fine comfortable houses.

In terms of a spatial model, Engels was of course recognising a general concentric zonal form which became more detailed over time as an improving transport system gave means of mobility to those sections able to move outwards towards the city's suburban periphery. As the pre-industrial city is one very general type and the industrial city is another, so the process of change from the one to the other is almost a category in its own right. The 'city in transition' is a phrase which fits older cities which became modified to the industrial city form. The rich gradually moved out from central locations, the city centres themselves became commercialised, the inner city gradually assumed its 'locus of poverty' character and the new suburbs grew. But those changes happened over decades and during this time hybrid cities occurred which were:

> . . . truly cities in transition. They contained vestiges of old patterns, portends of the new, always modified by local conditions. Virtually ubiquitous were the processes of change which were affecting all qualities of urban life. (Ward, 1975)

The post-industrial city

As with the terms pre-industrial and industrial, so 'post-industrial' is a generic term of convenience to cover the significant changes experienced by Western cities in the latter half of the twentieth century. As with industrialisation, 'post-industrialisation' implies a process of change which affects society as a whole and has an impact upon the city. Bell (1974) identified five primary characteristics of the post-industrial society:

(1) Changes in the economy which lead to a focus on services rather than manufacturing.
(2) Changes in social structure which give greater eminence to professional and technological classes.
(3) Changes from the practical to the theoretical as a source of ideas; and increased emphasis on research and development and its relation to policy.
(4) Changes in the control of technology, greater concern for the future impacts of technological change.
(5) A form of intellectual technology allied to advanced information systems.

Taking this view of societal change further, Johnston (1982b) identified five distinguishing features of late capitalism which would have an impact upon the urban system. **Concentration** described the process whereby a number of large and dominant companies emerged from the competitive market and many small firms either closed or were subsumed in the process; **centralisation** led to strong central control of finance and policies within these large and often multi-site enterprises. As manufacturing processes become automated and computerised they require fewer workers and more people are required for personalised services in tertiary (buying and selling) and quarternary (control functions of finance) sectors leading to rapid expansion of the **service sector**. In late capitalism, **material goods** with status connotations assume much greater significance and fuel the demand for production. **Government** has to assume significant roles as the regulator of the system, evening out wilder fluctuations and protecting the main institutions.

There is ample empirical evidence for these trends in post-industrial society. As Johnston shows, some 2000 American firms disappear each year through mergers and as an example, Sears-Roebuck controls 380,000 employees from its Chicago headquarters. Headquarters of these major, multi-site companies are almost invariably located in major cities. Greater automation led to considerable shedding of workers from manufacturing (though this was not the only factor). In the United Kingdom, steel tube manufacturers lost 28 per cent of their workforce 1976–1980, iron and steel 26 per cent and motor manufacture 16 per cent. This 'de-industrialisation' affected most Western countries in a dramatic way and led to a massive loss of manufacturing jobs. Economic upturn is not likely to produce significant change as the 'new' industries with automated, computerised and robotic processes require much less labour. Although the growth of services pre-dates de-industrialisation, it has assumed greater significance in the last half of the twentieth century. For Daniel Bell with his post-industrial society concept, a key point was that at which the non-manual, white collar work-force exceeded 50 per cent. By the 1980s in the USA, Britain and Australia this was around 60 per cent.

Societal changes of this kind have considerable implications for the form of the post-industrial city. A shift in the thrust of economic activities from manufacturing and heavy industry to high-technology, information processing and finance has major implications for locational needs of firms and their environmental impacts. There are several discernible trends.

- The larger urban centres may acquire greater significance as they are more fully equipped to act as world cities interacting on a global scale. Financial markets in particular operate in this kind of way and the importance of status addresses and face-to-face contact enhances such urban centres. Johnston argues that the general consequences of late capitalism have been to enhance the dominance of the largest centres. As headquarter locations they accrue multiplier effects and because of this central control, smaller urban places have relatively subservient roles.
- A second trend has some contradictory characteristics. The term 'counter-urbanisation' is used to describe a situation in which smaller towns and semi-rural areas beyond the traditional metropolitan rings begin to act as magnets for people and activities. Gordon identified the two processes at work in Britain as (a) an extension of the suburbanisation process, and (b) a form of product system dispersal in which small towns became new centres of activity.
- Changes in form of economic activity have had significant regional effects which influence urban change. In the United States much is written about the new Sun-Belt industries of South and West where new high technology industries, research and development and resource-led activities have had some re-distributive effects. In Britain, Hall identifies three Outer Metropolitan Area corridors outside London, based around the motorway system where there have been substantial increases in employment in the 1970s.
- A final comment on the form of the post-industrial city relates to the information base upon which it rests and the potential of inter-communicative systems. With the revolution in information transfers, the friction of space becomes less imperative and the ties which many activities have to specific locations are likely to diminish.

The most obvious manifestation of the post-industrial city is its dispersed form. The most obvious contrast is between the compact industrial city of the early twentieth century and the spread urban system of the 1980s. As always the urban form reflects the changing nature of its society but the massive redistribution, principally outwards, of people and activities can be related to specifics which include transport technology, communications, preferences, space and environmental quality.

Suburbanisation

The growth of suburbs has been the clearest expression of the expanding urban area. Enabled by improving transport systems and infrastructures, lower density residential areas on the edges of cities complemented the high density inner city, and the long process of selective out-immigration began. This kind of low-density peripheral growth was bound to add significantly to the land area of the built urban environment which doubled and trebled in size from the 1920s onwards. The scale of suburbanisation has accelerated and remains a key fact of urban growth. In North America in particular, public policy fuelled suburban growth. Between 1944 and 1961, the entire United States transport budget of $156 million was diverted to road construction; at its peak in the 1960s over one-third of all Federal grants were devoted to road programmes (Badcock, 1984). Modern suburbanisation is wedded to private transport so this commitment of public funds had powerful implications for peripheral growth. At the same time, in the United States and elsewhere, the funding of housing construction and purchase began to make home-ownership a highly desirable state and suburbs offered this opportunity. Mid-twentieth-century suburban development dwarfed nineteenth-century urban growth. As Badcock points out, this public support for suburban road programmes and funding for suburban homes was regressive. It meant less money for public transit systems, no compensation for inner city families displaced by road programmes and a starvation of housing finance for the inner city. In Britain the much stronger public sector intervention in housing meant more balance in new provision with local authority estates as well as private suburbs on the urban periphery.

There are different views on the imperatives behind suburban development:

(1) A conventional view is that the suburb arises from preferences within the private housing sector. Individual households composed of nuclear families with access to transport aspire to spacious and modern dwellings in relatively green-space settings. There may also have been push factors in the inner city with its congestion and social problems. Status is also a factor on both counts; an escape from the poor image of the inner city and a place in a higher status suburban community.

(2) A structuralist view regards suburbs as a means to stimulate consumption and a fresh demand for industrial goods in housing, domestic appliances and motor cars, a means of switching investment into the 'secondary

circuit' – the finance-capital market as part of a capitalist strategy for reproduction. In other words, suburbs grew as capital was diverted into the new
consumer industry for the production of material goods. This was not dis-
sociated from social engineering. Harvey argued that the promotion of
home ownership was a method of achieving social stability by giving a sense
of property to a much wider range of people. Suburbanisation was the
prime way of stimulating home ownership. For a capitalist class, suburbs
gave a way out of a situation of 'under consumption' whereby industrial
surpluses could not be absorbed.

(3) A less powerful but credible view of the suburb is one which views it as a
socio-economic-political process which creates municipalities independent
from the central city. Muller (1976) saw the suburbs as

> ... 'outer city' with high levels of autonomy and different life styles. Exclusionary
> political processes, such as zoning policies, are used to maintain the suburban
> landscape and the character of its community. Such suburban communities are
> sustained not merely by political and legal processes but also by localistic and
> humanistic concerns in which a suburban sense of place is grounded.

In the post-industrial city the suburb has a major role. There is now a hierarchy
of suburbs from inner rings to outer rings which reflect stages of urban growth;
there are status differences among suburbs which include the public
sector/private sector divide. Beyond the physical limits of the city, suburbanisation continues; and the growing small towns and villages of outer metropolitan
rings and in 'rural' areas to which the term counter-urbanisation applies may
well, at least in part, be suburbanisation writ large.

Whereas in Britain, North America and Australia the suburb has played a
major part in urban growth, it has much less significance in some West
European societies. As White (1984) shows this arises primarily from different
cultural contexts where access to urban facilities is rated more highly than
access to rural settings. Because land prices are high at the centre, only the rich
can afford to live there and it is the poor who are relegated to the urban peripheries. There are suburbs in European cities but they cannot be classified as
one type. *Industrial suburbs* did not rely on cheap transport but had industries
which acted as nuclei for a mixture of residential developments. New *working
class suburbs* in Europe are typically high-rise and large scale. Amsterdam's
Bijlmermeer complex houses over 100,000 people, the 'grand ensemble' of
Paris up to 80,000. To regard these as suburbs in a British or American sense is
misleading: they are more urban and quite different in character. *Middle class
suburbs* have appeared in European cities but are limited in scale for several
reasons:

● continued preference for city centre residence
● city centre apartment schemes
● inadequate financing arrangements
● significant numbers of second homes which allow an escape to rural areas.

Urbanisation as a process

Discussion so far has recognised the various processes involved in the emergence of the urban system but has been presented as a set of urban types from pre-industrial to post-industrial which are most appropriate to Western societies. Two further objectives can now be stated:

(1) To recognise key features of the urbanisation process itself.
(2) To recognise that different countries are at different points or stages along this process of urbanisation.

One example of an attempt to identify processes is provided by Reissman (1964) who listed four main components of the urban process: urban status, industrial status, prevalence of a middle class, and prevalence of nationalism. In order to derive measures which could be systematically applied to individual countries, Reissman selected a number of key single variables. Urban status was measured by the percentage of net domestic product contributed by manufacturing; prevalence of middle classes by *per capita* income; and prevalence of nationalism by rate of literacy. There is clearly a considerable gap between the conceptual objectives suggested by Reissman's components and the empirical variables which he uses to measure them. In combination, the indices add up to a general measure of economic development as most clearly indicated by the industrial status measure – as societies industrialise, then so also they urbanise. Reissman's typology of stages gives some indication of the positions of individual countries along this scale of urbanisation in the middle part of the twentieth century. According to this schema Zaire would have a small percentage of urban dwellers, little industrial development, low per capita income and low rates of literacy, whereas the United Kingdom would have opposite characteristics.

Another attempt to classify stages of urban development was provided by Jakobson and Prakash (1971) though their emphasis was upon a continuum rather than sharply demarcated stages. They make use of a three-sector theory of urban-economic development in which the sectors are labelled as those of *primary* or agriculturally based civilisation, *secondary* or industrially based civilisation, and *tertiary* or service-occupation based civilisation. Moreover, the secondary period is regarded primarily as transitory between primary and tertiary phases. Between the end of the traditional or primary civilisation and the beginning of the tertiary civilisation are three parts labelled as takeoff, expansion, and achievement. Jakobson and Prakash view the 'tertiary curve' as the S-curve of urbanisation as it progresses from 10 to 80 per cent urbanised levels of population. They also add distinguishing locational characteristics to each of the main periods. Whereas the primary period is location-bound by resource and the tertiary period by market, the transitory secondary period is less space- or location-bound. During the takeoff phase, Jakobson and Prakash associate urban growth with discrete nodes; during the expansion phase with metropolitanised (aggregative) areas; and during the achievement phase with megalopolitan (diffusive) spatial forms. Again, this theory is closely tied to economic and technological development but in their depiction of pre-industrial, industrial, and post-industrial society (Figure 2.5) Jakobson and Prakash itemise a large number of attributes which they associate with each period or stage.

	Pre-industrial	Industrial	Post-industrial
Population	Early demographic transition	Middle demographic transition	Advanced demographic transmission
Education	Low	Middle	High
Resources	Natural resource underdeveloped	Natural resources overdeveloped	Natural resources conserved
Economy	Dominantly agricultural employment	Mixed employment with strong manufacturing sector	Dominantly service employment
Politics	Colonialism to independence / Centrifugal tendencies	Empire to commonwealth / Integration-nationalism	Trans-national linkages / Less integration more trans-national
Linkages	Weak communication/transport network	Developing communication and transport	Highly developed communications and transport
Values	Localism	Nationalism-cosmopolitanism-activism	Trans-nationalism-megalopolitanism-Humanism
Power	Restricted elites	Multiple elites / National planning system	Dispersed elites / Trans-national planning systems

Figure 2.5   Attributes of the three-stage model: pre-industrial, industrial and post-industrial (Based upon information contained in Jakobson and Prakash, 1971)

Third world cities

This text has a primary focus upon the Western experience of urbanisation. At the risk of brevity and superficiality, however, this section draws out some of the main characteristics of urbanisation and cities in the Third World. Urbanisation is now a global characteristic and processes of change and interaction at this scale are intricately interwoven. Cities in various parts of the Third World have many distinctive features but the likelihood of no Western impact is remote.

Urbanisation as a global process

The industrial city, initially in western Europe and later in other parts of the Western world, was the product of the first major phase of modern urbanisation. Taken as the process of changeover from a predominantly rural-based to a predominantly urban-based population, this process gathered force in the United Kingdom from the late eighteenth century. The so-called 'logistic curve' can be used to demonstrate the process of change (Figure 2.6). From a low level of urbanisation, Western societies have moved, through a stage of rapid acceleration and a later stabilising stage, to a point at which around 80 per cent of their population could be classed as living in urban settlements. The United Kingdom was the initiator in this process but other Western countries have since moved in similar ways. This kind of urbanisation involved significant social change but its main underpinning forces were economic development and rural-to-urban

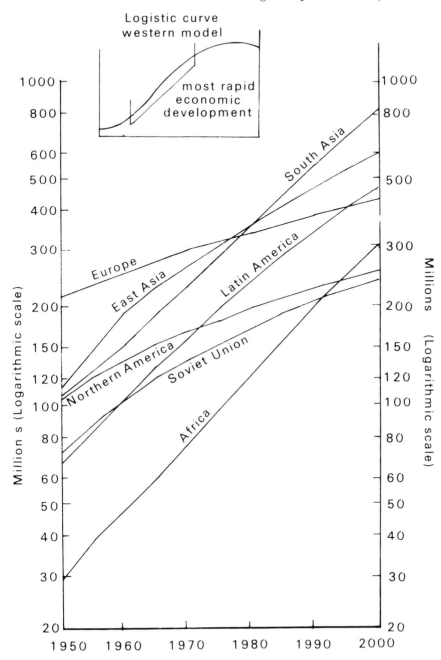

Figure 2.6   Urban population 1950–2000 in seven major areas. Inset shows the model 'logistic curve' as experienced in Western society. (Part of diagram from Abu-Lughod and Hay, 1979, Figure 2, p. 91)

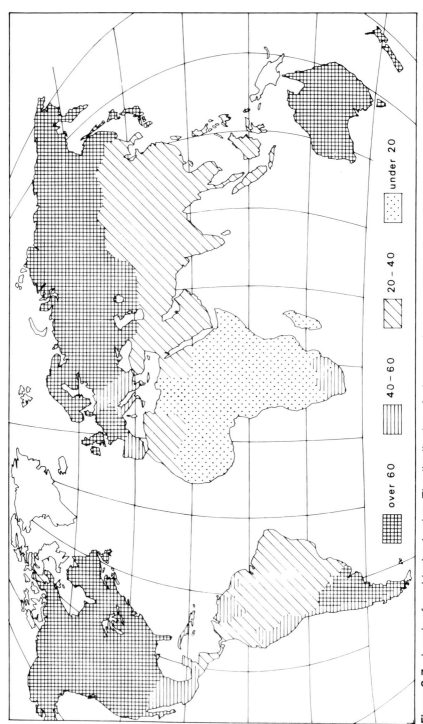

Figure 2.7   Levels of world urbanisation. The distribution of urban populations as proportions of total population is shown for major political units. (Data are for 1975 and have been extracted from Abu-Lughod and Hay, 1979, *Third World Urbanization* Table 1)

migration. As Western societies industrialised and experienced economic development, so the great cities emerged; as these cities and the smaller industrial towns came into existence, so rural areas began to export migrants and eventually to depopulate. This massive transfer of people was the major source of urban population growth. Western urbanisation coincided with the expansionary phase of the demographic transition process but it was some time before natural population growth became the dominant contributing factor in urban growth.

In Third World countries the 'modern' process of urbanisation is still unfolding. It has some characteristics which relate to the 'stage' already experienced by Western societies in the nineteenth century but is substantially modified by its own cultural contexts and by the fact that it is occurring in a radically different global framework. Figure 2.7 shows that many Third World countries remain relatively un-urbanised and that there are great differences among those countries.

The overall level of urbanisation in South-east Asia in 1981 was put at 24 per cent but the range was considerable from 64 per cent in Brunei (100 per cent in the 'city-state' of Singapore) to 14 per cent in Thailand. An average for Sub-Saharan Africa is 23 per cent, with a range from 50 per cent in South Africa and 38 per cent in Zambia to less than 10 per cent in Malawi and Mozambique. By contrast, Latin America is generally very urbanised with an average of 62 per cent. Argentina, Chile and Venezuela (all over 80 per cent) are fully urbanised, Bolivia (33 per cent) and Guatemala (39 per cent) are the only countries less than 40 per cent urbanised.

Whilst all countries show some trend towards increasing urbanisation, it is important to remember that the process has no global inevitability. A highly urbanised future world is a credible scenario but possibly a large number of Third World countries will never approach the high levels of urbanisation now evident in some Western societies and some may remain predominantly rural societies. Whatever the longer term outcomes, however, it is clear that major changes, expressed more dramatically in absolute urban growth rather than in relative urban/rural ratios, are affecting Third World countries in modern times (Figure 2.8, Table A) and all projections through to the end of this century suggests that this will continue. The 'great cities' of the Third World are likely to overshadow those of the Western World in their dimensions and absolute population size. Singh and Singh show that in India the numbers of urban places have increased only modestly between 1951 and 1981 (from 2867 to 3301) and the country remains less than 25 per cent urbanised (from 17.6 per cent to 23.7 per cent). But in that time the number of urban dwellers has grown by over 150 per cent from 62.1 million to 157.4 million.

Many attempts have been made to understand the nature of the urbanisation process as it affects Third World societies. Modernisation theory argues that the change from traditional agricultural to modern 'industrialising' societies occurs through the spread of Western technology, capital, institutions and sets of values. Modernisation focuses upon urban centres which diffuse its impacts to

A. Absolute population change in selected Third World cities

	1960 City	1960 Urbanised area	1977 City	1977 Urbanised area	2000* (m)
Bombay	4,941,000	—	5,970,575	—	17.1
Buenos Aires	2,966,816	7,000,000	2,982,000	9,749,000	12.1
Cairo	2,852,000	2,933,000	5,084,463	—	13.1
Calcutta	3,040,000	5,919,000	3,148,746	7,031,382	16.7
Karachi	1,912,598	2,060,000	3,498,634	—	11.8
Mexico City	2,832,133	4,666,000	8,988,230	13,993,866	31.0
Peking	4,010,000	—	7,570,000	—	19.9
Shanghai	6,900,000	—	10,820,000	—	22.7
São Paulo	3,164,804	—	7,198,608	—	25.8

Sources: *UN Democratic Yearbooks*, 1962 and 1978.
*UN estimates (1979) Patterns of urban and rural population growth 1950–2000, New York.

B. Migrants as a percentage of population growth

City	Period	Inc. (000s)	Migrants as % of total
Bombay	1951–61	1207	52
Caracas	1960–66	501	50
Djarkarta	1961–68	1528	59
Istanbul	1960–65	428	65
Lagos	1952–62	393	75
São Paulo	1960–67	2543	68

Source: Extracted from Berry (1973).
NB Qualitative evidence suggests that during the 1970s, higher proportions of total population growth in cities is accounted for by natural increase.

C. Squatter settlement in some Third World cities

City	Total population	Squatter
São Paulo (1980)	c 8,000,000	c 3,000,000
Hong Kong (1979)	5,010,000	500,000
Delphi (1983)	c 5,000,000	c 1,500,000
Rio de Janeiro (1979)	5,100,000	1,200,000
Manila (1973)	4,510,000	1,356,000
Mexico City (1977)	8,988,230	ca 4,000,000
Lusaka (1981)	540,000	250,000
Madras (1985)	3,700,000	1,100,000 (slum)

Figure 2.8   Some trends in Third World cities

surrounding rural areas. Observers look for something resembling the Western city as an indicator of the progress of urbanisation. Writers in this vogue often identify a state of over-urbanisation or pseudo-urbanisation in Third World societies whereby urban growth is not being matched by sufficient economic development, industrialisation and technological change to make it viable. The cities are structurally weak and because of their inadequate economic bases are merely 'formal' rather than 'functional' entities, even parasitic upon the rural societies within which they are placed. Whereas the great bulk of statistical evidence, demonstrating high unemployment and low economic growth on a variety of indices, supports this contention, some Third World writers have been less willing to accept the overurbanisation thesis. Bose argues that Third World countries in the later twentieth century are comparable to Western societies at similar stages of development and sees urbanisation as an essential element in the process of economic growth and social change in south and south-east Asia: a change which involves the transformation of traditional, rural, agricultural economies into modern, urban, industrial economies. The universality and indeed desirability of this scenario is open to debate.

Demographic change is the second variable which underlies urbanisation in the Third World and again there are important points of difference with Western experience. Firstly, it can be said that as urbanisation occurs many of these countries are experiencing unprecedented rates of general population expansion. Death rates have fallen, birth rates have remained high and, with a very few exceptions, have declined only slowly giving very fast rises in population. This 'explosion' has affected all kinds of areas, both urban and rural, and the continuing increase of rural populations has masked the relative impact of urban growth. Secondly, there are no sharp contrasts between natural rates of increase in urban and rural areas. In the United Kingdom case, for example, urban populations, because of demographic imbalance and bad living conditions, were not self-propagating for part of the nineteenth century and only the inflow of migrants caused growth. In Third World countries this situation does not exist and there is some evidence that cities, as places from which medical and other innovations are diffused, are healthier than rural areas. Thirdly, the role of rural-to-urban migration is different. In all Third World countries there are very large migrations from rural areas to cities (Figure 2.8, Table B) and these have very significant impact upon those cities in demographic and social terms. These migrant streams, however, are by no means the sole source of urban population growth, neither have they led to large-scale depopulation of rural areas. Urbanisation in the Third World needs to be viewed in the whole demographic context within which it occurs: the scale and nature of rural to urban migration, for example, means that the distinction between city and countryside is by no means as clear as is sometimes assumed in modernisation theory.

Dependency theory offers another approach to the understanding of urbanisation in the Third World. It implies broadly that less developed countries are 'used' by advanced countries over long periods of time from colonial to modern. Gilbert (1982) argues that in Latin America:

The social and economic structures that have emerged in the region represent the outcome of a historical process of interaction with Iberian, then British, and later North American expansion.

Dependency theory related the economic development of Third World countries to the demands of the world economic system into which they were inexorably drawn. International capitalism dictated the role of less developed countries and in so doing influenced the urban response. As external considerations were dominant, indigenous urban populations were marginalised and their consumption needs had low priorities. Again Gilbert offers a useful summary:

> Today the essential decisions about technology, employment, and economic growth are made in the metropolitan centres of Europe and the United States, and Third World urban functions and form have come to reflect their provincial status. The Third World city forms part of the world economy but its population does not share equal access to the world's resources.

Characteristics of Third World cities

Colonial cities provide a useful bridge with Western civilisation but by no means all Third World cities were colonial in origin. Urban forms in the Third World are a rich diversity inherited from different traditions and cultures and mediated by variable contemporary forces. Friedmann and Wulff (1976), in a summary which can usefully be followed, have classified knowledge of Third World cities under four headings of morphology, ecology, social organisation and economy.

Urban morphology
Land-use patterns in the Third World often reflect a dual city in which Western capitalism has been intruded into traditional culture and the two forms co-exist in a weakly integrated way. The *traditional*, precolonial city has a mixture of land uses and few clear functional areas. Open spaces only occur around institutions such as mosque or temple and many transactions occur in streets. Morphological elements of walls and narrow streets make for congestion and difficulty of movement; older prestige residences faced inwards towards interior courts in order to achieve a privacy denied by their densely built-up environs. The *modern* city, in sharp contrast, has more spacious layout and geometry and features reminiscent of the Western city. Where no urban nucleus predates the colonial city, as in Lagos, the dualism is not evident but in other situations, such as Delhi/New Delhi, where two urban forms have been grafted together, it is the dominant feature.

Social ecology
The relatively unambiguous bases of spatial segregation which can be identified for Western cities are less evident in the Third World. Ethnicity, caste, religion, language and similar cultural variables overlie the more basic variables of

economic and demographic nature to provide complex discrimination of socio-spatial structure. With the weight of rural-to-urban migration evident elsewhere and the accompanying struggle for an urban foothold, 'migrant status' is an important population variable in its own right. Districts in the city into which rural values have been imported and persist are distinguishable in many parts of the Third World. Mabogunje talks of the 'peasantisation' of African cities when peasant values and modes of production are imported into cities on a massive scale; the urban economy does not allow them to make the transition to urban dwellers.

In the evolving social geography of the city there are signs for both convergence and divergence when measured against Western experience. Whereas the elites aspire to Western modes of urbanism and are adjusting their styles of living in those directions, the differences inspired by sociocultural values and inertia are likely to remain. The aspirations of the elite:

> ... may simply come to nothing under the impact of accelerating migration and the growing inability of the urban economy to absorb the incoming workers in productive occupations. The Third World city under dependent capitalism is predominantly a poor city, and the poor are growing in both absolute and relative numbers. The resultant ecology of poverty may be a very different one from the essentially middle-class cities of North America and Western Europe. (Friedmann and Wulff, 1976)

Social organisation

Urbanites in the Third World can be placed both in a *horizontal* social dimension of kinship and informal social networks and in a *vertical* system of class structures. The persistent strength of kinship alliances has been reported from many parts of the Third World; they are critical amongst recent rural migrants and have strong locality-bases which rest on communal ties, shared services and mutual support. Whereas this 'haven' allows the migrant to find a place within the city and to fit into a familiar network, it also inhibits his eventual assimilation into urban living in a fuller, more innovative sense.

> Throughout the Third World, the proto-proletariat is encapsulated in a kind of ghetto, blocked from participation in wider social realms, only marginally absorbed by the urban economy, exploited by the elites, ignored by the middle strata and viewed with deep suspicion, if not hostility, by the blue-collar workers. (Friedmann and Wulff, 1976)

Class structures possess an inert inflexibility in the Third World with enormous gulfs between elite and poor. Some writers have identified voluntary associations which may serve to link classes and inject some fluidity into the social barriers. Awareness of the political overtones of poverty and the plight of the poor is a constant element of social organisation and control.

Urban economy

Many writers are unimpressed with the quality of research into the economy of Third World cities. Friedmann and Wulff (1976) suggest that economic models are either descriptive or 'structuralist' and used mainly for grand historical speculations about dependency, suffering and revolutionary potential. It is in relation to the impact of industrialisation and economic development that variations within the Third World become most striking. Parts of South-east Asia have moved dramatically into more advanced economies; in Singapore, manufacturing now forms 28 per cent of the gross domestic product compared with 12 per cent in 1960. It is now the third largest oil-refining centre in the world with a gross national product growth which has outpaced that of Japan and is on par with that of oil rich Middle-Eastern countries. McGee argues that there has been a substantial growth in the fluidity and availability of capital in the market economies of Asia aided by the growth of financial institutions. If these are indicators of successful economic growth, there are those of failure. Mabogunje states that urbanisation in many African countries is more a measure of despair than of hope; far from being a correlate of economic development, it is the very symbol of the failure of strategies aimed at achieving that goal.

Most societies have some level of industrialisation and a 'modern' sector of the economy which seems to point the way to progress. Such sectors are diverse in type, dimensions and potential and seem to have achieved limited success in stimulating economic growth. Whereas reliable statistics are rarely available, unemployment remains very high and only bureaucracy appears to proliferate. Recent research emphases have focused upon tertiary employment and in particular upon the 'informal sector' which by some estimates occupies 60 to 80 per cent of urban populations. McGee (1971) has suggested that the cities of south Asia can be divided into two economic sectors. A *modern* sector which is capital-intensive and a *bazaar* sector which is labour-intensive:

> The persistence of this dualistic structure, basically a symptom of economic under-development, is the most important variable affecting the function of contemporary Asian cities.

A central feature of the traditional bazaar economy is its capacity to absorb labour. This is drawn from both its intensive use of labour and its self-inflationary qualities – as more participants enter, more activities and transactions are generated. Kinship allegiances underpin the system and assist entry, it has strong links with the peasant economy. Roberts (1978), who studied Latin American cities, also detects a dualistic economic structure but not one which is directly analogous to McGee's south Asian case. Roberts identifies a large-scale sector on which modern economic growth is concentrated and a small-scale sector which operates on low wages and low profits, provides cheap services, and absorbs workers into a large reserve of unskilled and casual labour. Unlike the bazaar economy, however, the small-scale sector does not cater for a special segment of the population and has no 'neighbourhood' base. The integration of Latin American countries into world markets over a long time period, reinforced by foreign investment, has created patterns of consumer preference similar to those of advanced capitalist countries. The state, with its ever-increasing role in economic development enables the persistence of the small-scale sector but at the expense of investment in social infrastructure. In Africa, Mabogunje sees the informal sector as the continuation of a 'preferred peasant reactive strategy' to the development of cities in which they have no part. The informal sector grows by 'involution' whereby tasks and returns are continually subdivided to absorb more people. Okpara showed that migrants come to Nigerian cities to buy and sell in the bazaar tradition; they have no illusions of available job opportunities in the Western sense.

Housing and squatter settlements

As in most Western societies, the richer groups exercise considerable choice in terms of housing. Their traditional locations are generally adjacent to prestigious institutions in the central city with an emphasis on dwelling design to counteract the congested immediate environs. Whilst these locations may persist, there is also a good deal of evidence that the elite is abandoning the older core areas and moving to more peripheral locations. These trends vary cross-culturally and by size of city; pressures for change may be greater in large urban areas. There are also significant cross-cultural variations in the 'form' in which new prestige housing is being constructed; whilst preference for low-rise and space remains, much new construction in Third World cities is typically of high-rise apartments. Below the elite in the social stratification system, Johnston isolated two middle-class groups in Latin America which he labelled as 'upper-class mimickers' and 'satisfied suburbanites'. Whereas the former are upwardly mobile and seek to occupy housing adjacent to the upper class in a type of 'filtering' system, the latter are less status-conscious and their priority in housing is security of tenure which they normally find on the urban periphery.

Central questions on housing involve the conditions under which the poor live; several large-scale surveys have served to demonstrate their situations of extreme hardship. Abrams, in one of the best-known of these surveys, suggested in terms of housing three classes of poor urbanites could be discerned. First is the large class of homeless or the street sleepers who in some Third World cities can be numbered in hundreds of thousands. Often more recent migrants or refugees, or those who from some kind of disability have failed to assimilate, these people live in abject poverty. Second are the slum or tenement dwellers, especially in south Asia, who occupy densely built-up areas of the old cities. Their problems are of overcrowding in multi-occupied buildings with severe shortages of basic facilities; 'home' could be a small, windowless cubicle, shared by between 6 to 10 people, in the centre of a tenement building. Third, are the squatters or occupants of the shanty towns, ubiquitous throughout the Third World. Squatters are by definition illegal occupants of urban space though many, through length of tenure, have achieved a kind of *de facto* legality. Turner first focused attention on the squatter settlements as *acceptable* facets of urban growth with his argument that they should be encouraged to improve in quality. General opposition of city government to squatters had made for many sources of urban conflict over space in the cities.

Dwyer and others have documented the emergence of shantytowns, particularly since the 1940s. As Third World cities have increased rapidly in population, so the formal housing market has proved unable to cope and squatter settlements have provided the only form of shelter. Araud *et al.* estimated a deficiency of five million dwelling units in Mexico City by 1980; everywhere rates of house construction fail to approach the demand for shelter. This spontaneous housing is found throughout the Third World; in Latin America, Roberts (1978) suggests that between 10 and 20 per cent of all large city populations live in such squatter settlements, the figures for south Asia are more typically between 20 and 30 per cent.

The African situation may be worse and Mabogunje described the environmental conditions of many African cities as the most visible expression of what he termed 'backwash urbanisation' or the flood of rural peasants into urban areas. One half of Lusaka's population live in squatter housing, there are vast sprawls of urban slums or 'bidonvilles'.

As with other things, diversity is the key. Dwyer states that squatter areas are almost unknown in China; those most desperately in need of housing occupy overcrowded tenements in the inner city, these are often courtyards which lack basic facilities. Chinese rehousing centres on major, often high-rise schemes on the urban periphery of 12 to 15 storeys such as Beijing's Tuanjielu quarter which houses, 30,000, 70 per cent in two-roomed apartments. Singapore is another major departure in South-east Asia where all slums and squatter districts have been demolished in an urban renewal programme. Home ownership is encouraged in government-built housing and 90 per cent of the larger apartments are owner-occupied. Hong Kong retains its boat dwellers but Dwyer shows that over one million squatters have been rehoused in multi-storey resettlement schemes; the 'walled city' in Kowloon, one of the last tenement areas, was cleared in 1989/90.

The quality of shanty dwellings is normally rudimentary; initial squatter settlements in particular will use thatch, cardboard, wood, zinc sheets or any constructional material which happens to be locally available. In areas of general poverty or with a refugee problem, shanties persist in these forms; in other parts of the world where some foothold in employment or security of tenure is possible, space may be added, materials replaced, and there is improvement *in situ*. Severe absence of public services is often a problem. Unpaved roads, crude systems of sanitation, inadequate water supplies, educational and medical services, are all features. Such deficiencies have often led, particularly in Latin America, to shanties emerging literally overnight, clustered around high-status residential projects to which they are attracted by the possibilities of tapping supply lines for water or electricity.

Who occupies the shanties may seem an unnecessary question, and for the most part it is the urban poor. Laquian (1971) suggests that

> Almost all studies of slum and squatter areas in the cities of south and south-east Asia to date show that these settlements are peopled mainly by migrants from the countryside.

Several Latin American studies, however, have made it clear that not only the poor occupy shanties. Roberts (1978) argues that shanties cater for diverse needs. They attract families from inner-city tenements who have outgrown their cramped conditions, they suit specific groups – such as single women with children – and are not infrequently occupied by small businessmen or professional people who are trying to accumulate capital. Squatter settlements often have real attractions – a strong sense of community, a spirit of self-help and protection, and often some organised cooperative endeavours. Settlements with these qualities have the capacity to improve but many others have different qualities; Dwyer describes many squatter areas as static or consolidating but with no progressive upgrading.

It is in relation to the potential for improvement that Turner argues for more positive attitudes towards squatter settlements but attitudes of city government have varied considerably. Dwyer suggests that most official policies have the character of 'benign neglect', but incidents such as that in Manila where 3000 shanties were destroyed in three weeks are by no means untypical. Turner is critical of the instant, official development projects in comparison with self-built shanties. The latter offer much more space, scope for initiative, and the possibility of making an investment – the great need is for better services and security of tenure. Turner argues for improvement schemes to provide materials, legalise the position of squatter settlements, and erect an infrastructure to serve them. Not all would agree. At one extreme are those who view squatter settlements as 'infestations' which mar Third World cities; at another are those who see shanty improvements as a diversionary exercise. Roberts argues that although squatter settlements show what can be achieved by people with few resources and are not a social problem, neither should they be regarded as a solution to resource-scarcity. If token improvement schemes are introduced, squatter settlements may be used by governments as a means of patronising low-income population at little cost. Between these two extreme viewpoints, are involved the politics of the Third World.

> The activism of the poor, however, is a factor in urban politics since their behaviour constitutes an unknown element which is alternatively feared and sought after depending on the strength and political complexion of the government of the day. (Roberts, 1978)

The Socialist city

Many countries in the world, including the USSR, Eastern Europe and China, have state-planned or command economies and this form of central control is reflected in their cities. They arise from an organisation based upon Marxist and not upon capitalist premises, the state has the power to determine the pace and form of urban development. Cities within such societies are not uniform, there has been no monolithic response to socialist doctrine and variations occur for historical, social and even political reasons, but there are many common and distinctive features which give an 'urban type' in Socialist countries. Urbanisation has proceeded at differing rates in such societies in the present century. At the time of Russia's October Revolution of 1917, only 18 per cent of the population was urban despite the fact that the rural population of European Russia migrated in huge numbers to indiustrial towns in the later nineteenth century. In 1917, less than 20 per cent of Albania's population was urban but 44 per cent of Czechoslovakia and 67 per cent of East Germany. China had about 15 per cent of its population urban in 1917 but by 1979 this was little changed (13.2 per cent). By contrast the urban population of Russia had increased to over 60 per cent. Other current levels of urbanisation in Eastern Europe are East Germany 75 per cent, Poland 55 per cent, Czechoslovakia 65 per cent and Albania 40 per cent.

Socialist countries have also experienced the growth of large cities. In 1959 Russia had three cities with a population of one million or more, by 1976 it had 14. Moscow's population grew from 6.0 million in 1959 to 7.5 million in 1975, Warsaw's from 804,000 to 1,431,000 and Budapest from 1,590,000 to 2,083,000.

In Socialist societies there have been many new towns constructed and these have been planned in totality; there are some 1100 in the USSR. Many cities however pre-date the socialist revolutions and have carried forward their historical imprint, often with medieval street plans and historic monuments; Leningrad and Krakow, for example, are 'Socialised' cities rather than Socialist cities. St Petersburg (Leningrad) was the largest Russian city in 1914 with a population of just over two million; it was an orderly city with broad thoroughfares, common building lines and materials, its historic buildings remain within the framework of the modern city. Krakow in Poland offers the clearest example of the old, historic city juxtaposed with Nowa Huta the new planned industrial town. The Socialist city has also evolved over time with planning at first piecemeal and housing given a low priority in relation to economic imperatives. Thomas traces key features of the transformation of Moscow. In 1917, only about 5 per cent of working class people lived in the low density core bounded by Garden City Boulevard. This core was made up of many public buildings, commercial premises and large mansions set in spacious grounds. Immigration of rural peasants had been absorbed into northern, eastern and southern outskirts of the city. After 1917, the state expropriated the mansions and subdivided them into flats; many buildings, usually of wood, were constructed in the grounds and there were high levels of overcrowding. In the 1930s, public transport began to appear and five-storey buildings provided housing. By the 1960s 82,000 to 120,000 apartments were being built each year to house 390,000 to 530,000 people. High-rise blocks of 12 to 22 storeys became the norm. Overcrowding has always been a problem and by the early 1950s in Moscow a whole family occupying a single room was the norm. The new high-rise blocks provide families with no more than two or three rooms; in the 1980s alone in Moscow over 1.6 million people had moved to new, improved accommodation, mostly on the urban periphery.

Dwyer's study of Chengdu in China shows a similar form of modern urban growth in this city of 1.4 million people. A new physical plan involved the removal of the ancient city wall and its replacement by a ring road. The city is industrial with 40 per cent of the work-force in manufacturing employment. Before 1949, there were many single-storey wood and plaster houses in a dilapidated, overcrowded condition and lacking in services. Much of this has been demolished and there are many six- or seven-storey blocks with major construction on the periphery. New housing has a space allocation of six or seven square metres per person compared with the average of two and a half square metres so there is still much overcrowding in inner areas where some courtyards have 15 rooms shared by nine families.

Socialist cities have been developed against general plans though reality does not always match the strategic planning, and it has been estimated that only 20 per cent of such plans are actually realised. Hierarchical arrangements are common. The neighbourhoods (micro-rayon) have an ideal 10-12,000 population; the residential district (zhiloy-rayon or groups of neighbourhoods) has 30-50,000; the groups of residential districts (gorodskoy-rayon) have 100-300,000; and urban zones (gorodiskaya zona) 800-1,000,000. These cities have other common features:

(1) An adherence to the idea of optimum size designed to control growth.
(2) Equitable opportunities for access to housing and services and well-being.
(3) Minimal journey to work and an emphasis on public transport. There are qualifications here as homes are often too far from workplace and there is variable success in providing efficient transport.
(4) A rational, planned spatial ordering of functions with industry or residence separated by green belts.
(5) A rational distribution of services with 'neighbourhood' self-contained in terms of basic retail, health-care, education, recreation, etc. Again this ideal is by no means achieved.
(6) Central areas which may preserve some historic forms but are often dominated by heavy, grandiose 'Stalinesque' architecture such as Warsaw's Palace of Culture and broad roads with central squares.
(7) Blocks of flats, often prefabricated, as the standard housing response. Estates can house up to 120,000 people in uniform blocks with very little variety of style or quality.

All of this combines to give uniformity of time and place to the Socialist city; as French and Hamilton (1979) state:

> Indeed, if one were transported into any residential area built since the Second World War in the Socialist countries, it would be easier at first glance to say when it was constructed rather than to determine in which country it was.

The uniformity extends to street furniture, heroic statues, white on red slogans, central squares and kiosks.

The contrast with the Western city is clear. Basic differences emanate from the elimination of land speculation, central control of rent and massive public sector intervention in housing provision and all aspects of infrastructure. French argued that Soviet cities were only weakly differentiated by function, with far less concentration and segregation. The core of the city is still densely occupied with no true central business district. Overall there is a higher population density with no real gradient from centre to periphery. Spatial differentiation of social groups is limited though does appear in some Polish cities for example where there are the rudiments of a private sector in housing. Services are not of a high standard and employment is widely scattered with a higher reliance on public transport. Flows of workers between city and hinterland are increasing. Thomas estimated that in 1960 the inflow to central Moscow was 380,000 with an outflow of 90,000; by 1984 it was 600,000 inward and 140,000 outward.

Both from their distinctive components and their points of difference, Socialist cities warrant categorisation as a distinctive group. This distinctiveness flows most clearly however from fundamental differences in the forms of society – Marxist/Leninist as opposed to capitalist, planned as opposed to free market – from which these cities emerge. Differences are rarely clearcut and the convergence theory suggests that as Socialist cities relax their rigid precepts and as Western cities accept the need for some control, the gap will narrow. Events of 1989/90 in Eastern Europe which point to increasing democracy in government suggest that societal change will facilitate this process. However, as types of urban form, Socialist cities are likely to remain apart for some time; lack of private ownership of land and of inheritance, general austerity and central planning priorities are likely to ensure this continuing separate class of city.

CHAPTER 3

The Urban System

Chapter 2 considered the question of urban origins and traced the patterns and processes involved in the development of early cities. This perspective focused upon urban settlements as discrete elements in geographical and societal space. However, as individual cities became less localised in their impact and acquired functions of trade, commerce and industry, *urban interdependence* increased and networks of towns forming an urban *system* became functional realities. Throughout the nineteenth century, the urban system of Western societies became functionally and formally more complex; population in general, and urban population in particular, was increasing dramatically. Individual cities became functionally more integrated into the wider urban system and through increased physical extension created an integrated and larger economic and social system at the intra-urban scale; both 'systems of cities' and the 'city as a system' became accurate descriptions of urban development.

This process was evolutionary and Bourne (1975) has offered a schematic representation (Figure 3.1) which is still applicable to Western industrial countries:

(1) A *national system* dominated by metropolitan centres and characterised by a step-like 'size' hierarchy, with the number of centres in each level increasing with decreasing population size in a regular fashion.
(2) Nested within the national system are *regional sub-systems* of cities displaying a similar, but less clearly differentiated hierarchical arrangement, usually organised about a single metropolitan centre, and in which city sizes are smaller overall and drop off more quickly than in (1) above as one moves down the hierarchy.
(3) Contained within these are *local sub-systems* or *daily urban systems* representing the life space of urban residents which develop as the influence of each centre reaches out, absorbs and reorganises the adjacent territory. In small countries levels (2) and (3) may be difficult to differentiate, whereas in larger countries both of these levels may show further subdivision.

The notion of interrelated national, regional and local urban systems offers a broad introductory framework for the analysis of urban systems. The earlier literature of urban geography, however, has been dominated by more narrowly conceived approaches to classification of urban settlements which have focused

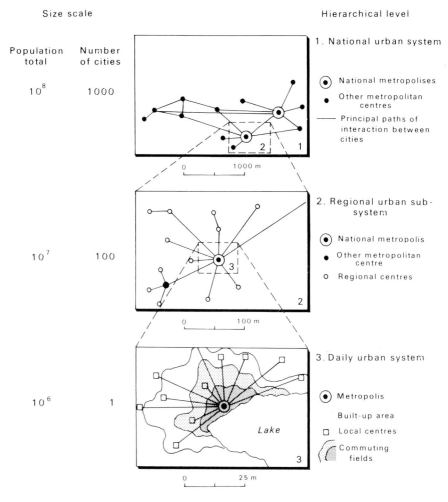

Figure 3.1 The urban system at the intra-urban, regional and national scales

(Source: Bourne, 1975; *Urban Systems: Strategies for Regulation* reproduced by permission of Oxford University Press)

on function and population sizes. A review of this work forms the basis of the next section.

Theories of the urban system

The law of the primate city

One of the earliest generalisations concerning the size and distribution of cities in a country was the 'law of the primate city' propounded in 1939 by Jefferson. This was based upon the observation that a country's leading city is usually disproportionately larger than any other in the system; London was seven times the size of Liverpool, Copenhagen nine times larger than Aarhus, and Mexico City five times the size of Guadalahara. Jefferson argued that in the early stages of a country's urban development the city which emerges as larger than the rest develops an impetus for self-sustaining growth. It becomes an expression of the national identity and for this reason tends to attract the political functions of a capital city. This results in the gravitation of all the 'superlatives' of a nation's life towards it, which ensures self-sustaining growth. While such a distribution persists, regional imbalances in economic opportunity can never be entirely redressed.

Jefferson, however, admits that extreme primacy is by no means universal. Some states incorporate more than one national identity, often coinciding with regional concentrations of identifiable ethnic minority groups. This may result in one or more cities of comparable size rather than a single primate city. In Spain, for example, Madrid is the centre of Castilian nationalism but Barcelona, central to the Catalan group, has comparable size and influence. On a smaller scale, Bilbao acts as the centre for the Basques. Similar patterns may also arise from the contemporary effects of size and distance. In the United States, for example, New York dominates the north-eastern seaboard, but there are several other regional clusters of settlement, each with their dominant urban centre. Both the USSR and China similarly demonstrate evidence for the emergence of more than one very large city as a result of both historical and modern forces.

Thus, the concept of the primate city has some limited significance if applied selectively to distinct regions defined in terms of cultural identity or geographical distinctiveness. With population growth and economic development, however, other cities emerge as alternative major growth points and erode the status of the primate city by creating a more complex city-size distribution. For this reason it has been suggested, notably by Berry and Linsky, that primacy is most relevant to countries which have a relatively simple economic and spatial structure, a small area and population, low incomes, economic dependence upon agriculture and a colonial history. In fact, a recent analysis by Paul of 28 Asian countries for the period 1960–80 noted that while 10 socialist countries demonstrated a degree of reduction in urban concentration, in the remainder policies to reduce primacy had achieved little effect. For the developed world, however, other more comprehensive concepts have been developed.

The rank-size rule

The rank-size rule (Stewart, 1947; Zipf, 1949), is the best known alternative proposition. Zipf suggests that the city-size distribution in integrated systems of cities in economically advanced countries is expressed by the simple formula:

$$Pr = \frac{Pi}{r}$$

where Pr is the population of a city ranked r, Pi is the population of the largest city, and r is the rank of city Pr.

Thus, the second ranking city of a country has one-half of the population of the largest city, the third ranking city one-third of the largest, and so on down the scale. The graphical plot of the rank-size distribution approximates to the lognormal statistical distribution. When represented on a double logarithmic graph this becomes transformed into a straight line (Figure 3.2). This is useful for comparative purposes since by plotting a country's city-size distribution on double logarithmic graph paper, the degree to which the distribution conforms to the rank-size rule is visually expressed by the degree to which it deviates from a straight line. In addition, if the city-size distribution of a country which has a strong degree of primacy is plotted on such a graph the resulting curve deviates considerably from the rank-size norm, indicating the domination of one very large city, the absence of cities of intermediate size and a relative profusion of small cities. This is graphically represented by an initial steep incline away from the rank-size norm.

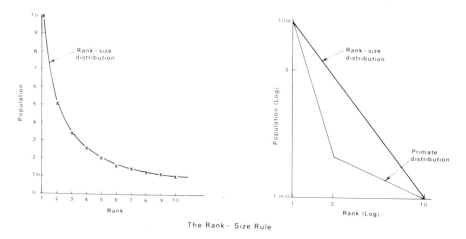

The Rank–Size Rule

Figure 3.2   The rank-size rule. Schematic representations of the rank-size rule by population sizes of cities on arithmetic and logarithmic scales

The association of primacy with the early stages of economic development and the rank-size with advanced, economically integrated countries, led to the hypothesis that a country's actual city-size distribution is a direct function of its level of economic development. Underdeveloped countries in the early stages of urbanisation are expected to demonstrate a near primate distribution, and highly urbanised, economically advanced countries a rank-size distribution.

This contention was refuted in Berry's 1961 analysis of the city-size distribution of 38 countries at varying levels of development. Rank-size distributions were found in advanced industrial countries; but were also evident in Third

World countries with a long history or urban development such as India and China; and in large developing nations such as Brazil which have a proliferation of large resource-based cities. On the other hand, primacy is expected to be associated with a few simple strong forces. This may typify the urban system of newly developing countries where the primate city may be associated with an emerging capital; but such a condition can also be found in small countries such as Denmark where the forces of economic centralisation create a tendency towards primacy; or in countries which have been developed under colonial influences and which have a relatively short urban history such as Australia and New Zealand. Thus, the progression from a primate to a rank-size distribution can be used as a framework within which generalisations relating to the urban system of a country may be made, not simply in relation to levels of economic development and urbanisation, but by consideration of the length and degree of complexity of the urban development forces which has considerable empirical validity as well as intuitive appeal. This basic conclusion remains valid and the progression from primacy to the rank-size distribution provides a neat framework within which to view variations in the city-size distribution of countries albeit of descriptive rather than explanatory or predictive value.

Central place theory

Spatial analysis *per se* has been of only secondary interest in the studies of city-size distributions and of functional classification. Central place theory, however, introduced an explicitly spatial dimension into the study of settlement systems. Much of this work has been based upon the seminal study of Walter Christaller *Central Places in Southern Germany* (1933, translated 1966) and focuses on the attempt to develop a deductive theory to explain the distribution and sizes of towns in terms of the services they performed for surrounding hinterlands, in other words, their *centrality*. Thus, the theory is most applicable to an understanding of urban systems which have developed principally as centres of *tertiary* activity, although it should be noted at the outset that the current relevance of the theory is not restricted to such systems. Most towns, even if based initially upon specialised primary, secondary or quaternary functions tend to accumulate a tertiary function, and the concepts and methodologies developed within the context of central place theory can be used to provide insights into the nature of urban systems in general.

Christaller's central place theory

Christaller observed an element of order in the spacing and sizes of service centres in southern Germany. Few large centres, spaced relatively far apart, provided specialised goods and services to large complementary regions (hinterlands). These were termed *high-order* central places. Conversely, more numerous smaller centres were found at a number of different levels. These were located close together, provided less specialised goods and services to geographically more localised populations, and were termed *low-order* central places. Christaller's theory sought to explain the principles which determined the nature of such a system.

At the outset it should be noted that the theory was based upon an *idealised* landscape. The characteristics of this landscape were such that each point had an equal chance of receiving a central place, and the relative accessibility of one point to any other was a direct function of distance, irrespective of direction – in other words there was a uniform transportation surface. This degree of abstraction is not, however, as comprehensive as that included in the concept of the *isotropic* surface which many subsequent commentaries have assumed to be associated with Christaller's theory. Isotropism assumes the existence of a homogeneous plane surface and an even distribution of population and consumer purchasing power. Beavon (1977) suggested that Christaller's scheme does not depend upon the latter elements of isotropism; variations in these factors in space would merely result in minor variations in the deductively derived idealised settlement system. This consideration will be examined further following the discussion of the derivation of Christaller's theory.

At the next stage of theory derivation, Christaller considered that every good or service provided from a central place has a range with an upper and a lower limit. The upper limit of the range is the maximum distance a consumer will travel to a centre to obtain the goods, beyond which he is more likley to travel to an alternative nearer centre or, if there is no nearer centre, will go without the good altogether. This notion can be measured in terms of the distance (r) over which the good with the strongest degree of attraction (highest-order good) provided in a centre can be provided from that centre. Consequently, the maximum area to be served from a centre will be a circular complementary region around the centre of radius (r), given the uniform transportation surface of the idealised landscape. The lower limit of the range (r') is the minimum distance necessary to circumscribe a service area with sufficient population to generate enough consumer demand to make the offering of the good just economically viable from a centre. The relationship between the upper and lower limit of the range of a good is significant to the later stages of the analysis. If the lower limit of the range (r') is greater than the upper limit (r), then clearly such a good cannot be economically provided at a fixed location in the area. This provides the rationale for the emergence of *periodic markets* whereby traders will move from place to place, outside their immediate hinterlands to accumulate sufficient revenue to be economically viable (see later section). If the upper limit (r) of the good is equal to the lower limit (r'), then that good can just be provided profitably. In addition, if the upper limit range (r) is greater than the lower limit (r'), then the good can be provided and the trader can potentially earn excess profits by serving the population in the area between the two circles.

The goods and services required by the population of the idealised landscape will comprise an array from high order to low order. High-order goods were considered to be those, such as large items of furniture or fashion clothing, which are relatively costly and tend to be required at infrequent intervals. Thus, consumers are usually willing to travel relatively long distance to high-order centres, which are likely to offer the greatest range of choice, to obtain them. Clearly, the upper and lower limits of the range of such goods are likely to be relatively distant. Conversely, low-order goods are those such as groceries which may be perishable or required in relatively large amounts at frequent intervals. Thus, consumers will tend to be unwilling to travel far to obtain them and a wide range of product choice will not normally be demanded. The ranges of such goods are consequently likely to be small. An array of goods and services with consumer characteristics intermediate to these two extremes can also be envisaged.

From these initial observations Christaller deduced a model of settlement distribution for the idealised landscape. However, since he was initially concerned to develop a theory to explain the characteristics of a settlement system which was based upon the evolution of rural-market service centres over a long period of time, he suggested two organising constraints on his system which comprised the *marketing principle*. These were that (1) there should be a minimum number of points of supply of all sizes so that trader profits could be maximised; and (2) the whole population of the area should be supplied with each good and service. The relevance of these constraints will become clear in the ensuing discussion.

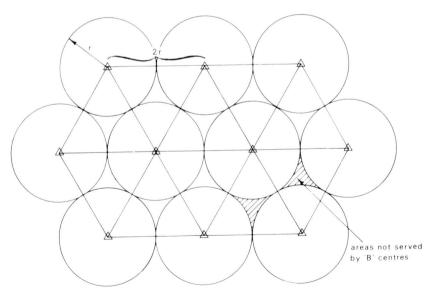

△ 'B' centres (First Order)

Figure 3.3 Relationships among B-centres in central place theory; the derivation of regular equilateral triangular lattices of centres

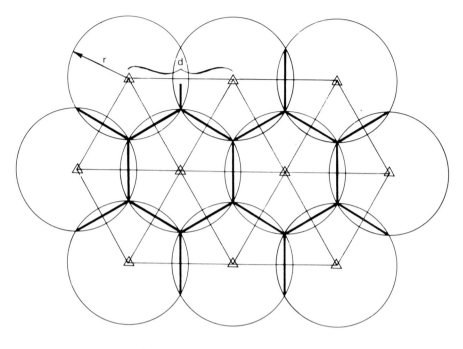

△   'B' centres (First Order)

Figure 3.4   Relationships between ideal circular hinterlands of centres in central place theory and their generalisation into hexagons

To satisfy the first constraint, the most important element in the generation of the settlement model is the upper limit of the range of a good supplied from a centre. This is necessary if the number of centres of any size is to be minimised. Accordingly, as a first step, Christaller assumed the existence of a series of settlements ranked 'B'. The upper limit of the range of the highest order good provided in such a centre is designated (r) and, notionally, the area can be covered with B-centres spaced at distances of 2r and arranged on a regular equilateral triangle lattice (Figure 3.3). However, such a system does not satisfy the second constraint, since there are limited areas between any three circular hinterlands which cannot be served with the highest-order good offered at the B-centres. Thus, a slightly modified structure of overlapping circles becomes necessary to conform to the marketing principle, although the fundamental spatial geometry of the system is largely maintained (Figure 3.4). The B-centres are still arranged according to a regular equilateral triangular lattice spaced slightly more closely together at distance (d), which is a direct function of the upper range of the B-centres. In addition, the hinterlands of the B centres can be generalised to give exclusive regular hexagonal areas rather than the overlapping circles, the rationale for which is that consumers will tend to use the nearest centre to them if each offers the same goods and services.

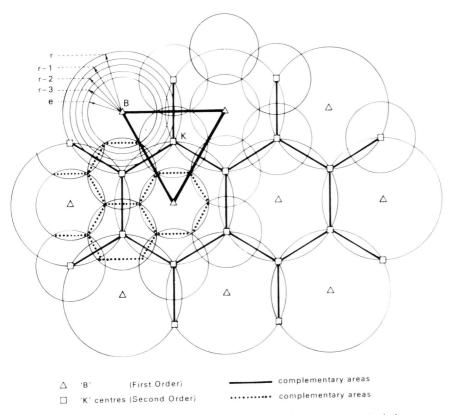

△ 'B' (First Order) ───── complementary areas

□ 'K' centres (Second Order) ·········· complementary areas

Figure 3.5 The derivation of a second lower order of centres in central place theory

Since, by definition, sufficient consumers can be attracted to each B-centre to make its highest-order function economically viable – in other words, the lower limit of the range of that function has been superseded – it follows that all goods and services with less extensive lower limits to their ranges can also be provided at B-centres, since sufficient people visit them to make such functions economically viable.

Proceeding to the next stage, the outer limits of the ranges of successively lower-order functions can be diagrammatically represented as having radii of r–1, r–2, r–3, etc. (Figure 3.5). Any function supplied from a B-place which has an outer range of less than (r) cannot be supplied to all parts of its complementary area without some consumers undertaking excessively long journeys, or by obtaining the lower order functions while visiting the B-place for its highest order functions. This consideration provides the logical basis for the formation of a lower grade of central places, designated 'K' by Christaller, which will be located at some distance from the B-centres, in the centre of the peripheral parts of their complementary areas. To be most competitive with the B-grade centres, and at the same time central to the peripheral areas, the K-centres will be located in the centre of the equilateral triangles subtended by three B-grade centres. This coincides with the point at which the hexagons defining the hinterlands of the B-centres intersect. The highest order function which can be provided by the K-centres is geometrically determined by radius (e) which defines the outer limit of its range. Consumers requiring functions which have outer limits to their ranges of greater than radius (e) but less than radius (r) will, therefore, have to obtain them when travelling to the B-centres for their highest-order functions.

For the same reasons as noted for B-centres, the K-centres can provide all the functions with less extensive lower limits to their ranges than the outer range of the highest-order function provided in the K-centres. In addition, in a similar manner to that described in the previous paragraphs, successively lower order centres can be generated. The resulting system of central places derived by

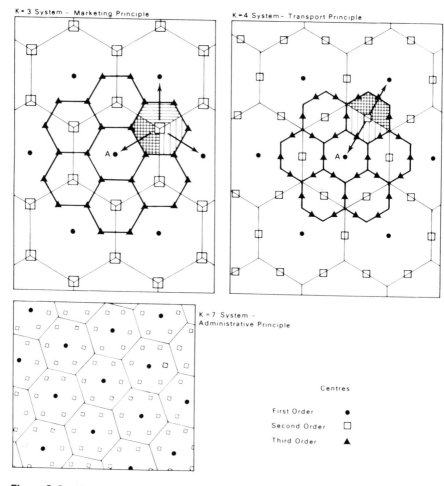

Figure 3.6   K = 3, K = 4, and K = 7; the marketing, transport, and administrative principles

Christaller according to the marketing principle is represented in hexagonal form in Figure 3.6.

The settlement system derived in this manner according to the marketing principle by Christaller was termed the K = 3 framework. This expresses the number of hexagonal trade areas of one order which are contained within a hexagon of the next highest order (Figure 3.6). In this illustration the centrally located first-order centre marked 'A' is taken to transact the whole of the first-order trade for the second-order hexagonal trade area immediately adjacent to it, as well as a third of the first-order trade of the six second-order hexagons surrounding it. In addition, there will be three times as many centres at each successively lower order. Note also that according to the system the first-order centre 'A' will also transact the second-order trade for the second-order hexagonal area adjacent to it.

However, Christaller recognised the fact that systems of settlements did not all necessarily develop based upon the evolution of rural market centres over a long period of time. Two major variants were noted: the *transportation* principle and the *administrative* principle. These represent inductive modifications to the original theory. In the first case, he considered that many settlements systems do not develop in areas which have a uniform transportation surface. Historically, early established routeways are very persistent in their effect upon the development of settlement nodes, while the relatively rapid colonisation of new territory in the nineteenth and twentieth centuries has been markedly influenced by the development of railways and roads. In these circumstances the development of B-grade centres will develop in an area in much the same manner as that already described, although the centres will be orientated along lines of transportation rather than placed initially at random in a more idealised landscape. In addition, the development of a next lower order of centres is not expected to gravitate to a median position between three higher-order centres to maximise competitive impact as is expected to occur in the K = 3 system. Such a location would clearly be off the main transportation links between the higher-order centres and, for this reason, would not have the competitive advantages of accessibility associated with a routeway location. Thus, the K-grade centres would be expected to develop on the routeway, at a midpoint between any two B-centres, and successively lower-order centres would be expected to develop in a similar manner. This results in the development of the K = 4 framework illustrated in Figure 3.6. In this case the hexagonal trade area of any one order contains within it the equivalent of four trade areas of the next lower-order centre. Also, the relationship between the number of centres of successively lower orders tends to be represented by a factor of four.

The deviation of the framework associated with the administrative principle tends even more strongly towards empiricism. Again in this instance the development of the B-centres is expected in the manner already described. However, the settlement pattern of the area is now assumed to have been developed primarily within the context of stronger administrative or political control. Thus, the complementary regions of the successively lower-order centres have to be completely contained within the boundaries of a higher-order centre in order to eradicate the administrative ambiguity which might be associated with the 'border' locations of centres of successively lower order in the $K = 3$ and $K = 4$ arrangements. The resulting system is termed the $K = 7$ framework since the complementary region of any one order of centres contains within it the equivalent of seven regions of the next lower order, although for geometrical reasons these cannot now be regular hexagonal arrangements. This underlines Christaller's attempt to move away from the initial deductive theory towards real-world settlement systems (Figure 3.6). It also is interesting to note that the number of centres of successively lower orders tends towards the much higher factor of seven, while the much smaller complementary regions of successively lower orders suggests that the actual size of the settlements declines precipitously. The resulting arrangement of few high-order centres exerting an element of control over relatively numerous small low-order centres suggests that this system incorporates a much stronger element of primacy than that associated with the alternative frameworks. Thus, it is anticipated that this system is most likely to be found in the very early stages of development or in areas which have been developed based upon a strong element of administrative or political control.

A further important consideration should also be introduced at this point. The most important element in the derivation of the settlement systems of Christaller was the upper limit of the range of the highest-order good supplied from a centre. It follows from this that the central place system which develops in an area tends to be in a state of adjustment (equilibrium) with the societal characteristics which existed during its initial development:

(1) Of particular note in this respect is the density distribution of the population. Clearly, the denser the distribution of the population, the greater the potential consumer expenditure contained within an area of unit distance from any location. Hence, the greater the potential number of levels in the hierarchy and the greater the degree of functional specialisation of the highest-order centre.

(2) Of similar note is the effect of variations in the amount of consumer expenditure available, usually in association with variations in the degree of sophistication of consumer demand. In a peasant society, barely above subsistence level, expenditure will be low and demand will only exist for very basic requirements. Thus, a hierarchy of few levels with a low level of specialisation of functions available in even the highest level is likely. In contrast, the opposite hierarchical characteristics are likely to typify a prosperous society with highly sophisticated consumer demands.

(3) The transportation technology available to the society will also be of considerable importance. Slow or high-cost transport facilities will increase the friction of distance and promote a large number of levels in the hierarchy because of the importance attached to the demand for local offerings of goods and services. Conversely, convenient rapid low-cost forms of transport reduce the importance of local low-order centres relative to the enhanced significance of relatively more distance, highly specialised centres.

Since all three factors vary considerably in societies over time and space, it should be expected that the detailed characteristics of central place systems will vary from place to place, although the basic elements should remain whatever the area.

The resulting systems are organised functionally and spatially into *hierarchies* with recurring structural and behavioural characteristics:

- There are a relatively small number of the highest-order centres serving the widest hinterlands with the highest order goods and services. They will also serve their own local hinterlands with all the lower-order functions.

- There are larger numbers of smaller centres at successfully lower order. These orders will be distinguished from each other by marked discontinuities in the population size and range of functions offered.

- Successively lower order centres will provide a smaller range of goods and services to increasingly localised trade areas. The population living in or near such centres will, conversely, depend upon the higher order centres for more specialised goods and services (a 'nesting' relationship).

- It is assumed that consumers will use the nearest centre offering the goods and services they require (nearest centre assumption).

- The entry of suppliers of goods and services into the system occurs so that the number of establishments and centres is minimised (profit maximisation assumption). This assumes that the system develops in conditions of perfect competition.

Lösch's central place theory

An additional major contribution to central place theory is that of August Lösch, originally published in German in 1940 but translated as *The Economics of Location* in 1954. Like Christaller, Lösch developed a deductive system to explain the size and spacing of settlements in a region, although it differed from that of Christaller in a number of fundamental ways. It was derived for a hypothetical area with the degree of homogeneity associated with the isotropic surface rather than Christaller's less regular idealised landscape. Lösch assumed a vast flat plain with an equal distribution of raw materials, an equality of transportation costs and a regular and continuous distribution of population and associated consumer demand. Also, unlike Christaller, he did not initially assume a hierarchy of centres and develop a theory to explain its spatial organisation, proceeding from the location of the highest order to the lowest-order centres. Instead, he deduced an optimal pattern of centres of *production* and their associated hinterlands for each of the commodities required by the population of the plain, proceeding from a consideration of the lowest-order commodity to the highest. The last sentence also indicates another difference between the theories of Christaller and Lsch. Lösch initially developed his theory with respect to centres of *production* and their associated hinterlands.

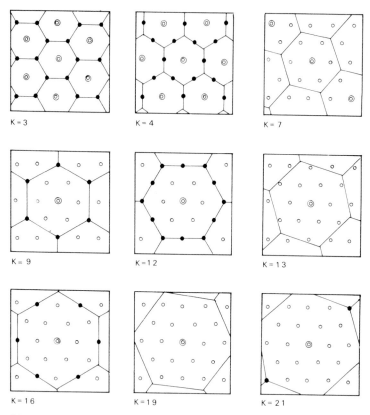

K = 3

K = 4

K = 7

K = 9

K = 12

K = 13

K = 16

K = 19

K = 21

Nine smallest hexagonal lattices of Lösch

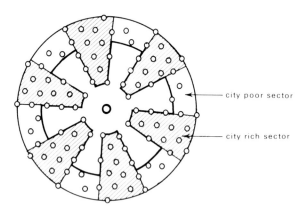

Lösch's Economic Landscape (after Lösch, 1954)

Figure 3.7   The nine smallest hexagonal lattices of Lösch and the Löschian economic landscape

(Source: Lösch, 1954; reproduced by permission of Gustav Fischer Verlag)

Thus, interest focused on the market-orientated manufacture, or the secondary sector of the economy, rather than the tertiary service function. However, this difference has not subsequently been considered since many authors agree (for example, Beavon, 1977) that Lösch's theory is as appropriate to tertiary activity as it is to secondary activity. This stand-point has been adopted here.

The derivation of Lösch's economic landscape

The derivation of Lösch's central place system is based initially upon the *threshold* requirement of the *lowest-order* function which it is possible to supply to the population of the plain. (This contrasts markedly with Christaller's theory which was based upon the *range* of the *highest-order* function required by the population). Given a uniform transportation surface and a uniform distribution of population, this threshold value can be translated into a radius necessary to circumscribe sufficient consumer demand to allow the function to be offered from any point on the plain. This can be elaborated in a manner analogous to the K = 3 framework of Christaller to create a hypothetical set of centres arranged on an equilateral triangular framework with regular hexagonal hinterlands (Figure 3.7). This defines the basic lattice upon which Lösch's theory is based. The whole of the population of the area can be supplied with the lowest-order function from this arrangement of centres, and because it is based upon the threshold, each supplier is only just economically viable. In other words, there are no excess profits in the system, or the *minimisation of excess profits* is a basic organising principle.

However, so far, an ideal pattern of centres and their associated hinterlands for the provision of only *one* function has been considered. Hypothetically, as many similar networks can be constructed as there are functions required by the population of the plain, the details of each being directly related to its threshold requirement. In fact, an infinite number of such networks could be envisaged. However, Lösch constrained his consideration of such networks to those which are derivative of the basic K = 3 lattice. The constraint *implied* by Lösch, but made explicit by Beavon and Mabin, is that the centre of each hexagon in a network of hexagons must be located at a point on the basic lattice. Thus, lattices of successively larger size have K values of 3, 4, 7, 9, 12, 13, 16, 19, 21, 25, 27 ... etc. The nine smallest lattices are illustrated in Figure 3.7.

Lösch further hypothesises that these networks can be laid over the plain at random. Despite the resulting disorder and multiplicity of centres, every person on the plain would have access to every product and, since each network is based upon the threshold of each function of successively higher order, excess profits will not be obtained by suppliers. However, this arrangement will be uneconomic due to the multiplicity of points of supply, many of which will be relatively close to one another and yet supply only one function. Thus, Lösch proposes a more economic arrangement of the networks. Each can be laid out in such a way that all have one point in common, the pivotal point. By definition, at this point all the functions required by the population of the plain can be provided so that here would develop the highest-order centre, the metropolis. Lösch further suggests that the nets can be rotated about the pivot point in order to produce six 'city-rich' and six 'city-poor' sectors in which the greatest number of points coincide. It is interesting to note that Beavon (1977) demonstrates that the production of city-rich and city-poor sectors is the result of a geometrical *constraint* on the rotation process rather than a *consequence* of it, as seems to have been implied in Lösch's original work.

This process results in the 'economic landscape', which Lösch considers provides the most economically efficient system of centres of supply of goods and services. It consists of a central metropolis which is the highest-order centre providing the full range of goods and services required by the population of the plain; six city-rich sectors which have relatively numerous, higher-order centres; six city-poor sectors which have fewer centres of generally lower order (Figure 3.7). Because of the complexity of the rotation process a complex combination of functions will coincide at particular points so that each larger centre will not necessarily offer all the functions of a lower-order centre. This is an important deviation from the theories developed by Christaller. For the same reason the size-distribution of centres is likely to be a continuum rather than a distinctly stepped hierarchy, while the K value for the whole landscape is likely to vary from area to area depending upon the variety and threshold requirements of the functions demanded, rather than approximate to a 3, 4 or 7 relationship.

In the current context, interest in this system lies in the provision of a theoretical rationale for the continuum of centre-sizes so commonly found by empirical investigations of city systems. Similarly, it suggests an expectation of a degree of variability of function between centres of similar size, a feature which is not allowed for in the alternative schemes. Perhaps its greatest value, therefore, lies in the suggestion that, in contrast with hierarchical systems, a greater degree of flexibility might be expected in the size and spacing of settlements in a region.

Whether Lösch's model, in fact, provides a more comprehensive explanation is far more problematic. The principles upon which the model is based have even less behavioural validation than that of Christaller's. Lösch's scheme is strongly related to the principle of the minimisation of excess profits. It may well be that this is an important generative principle governing the development of a system of service centres in competitive market economies, but until this is specifically examined within the context of central place theory it remains unproved. Even more important, the derivation of the economic landscape is based upon the geometry of regular hexagonal trade areas, the constraints associated with their successive relationship to each other, and the geometric constraints imposed upon the rotation process necessary to create the six city-rich and six city-poor sectors. The justification for the procedures seems to be that they minimise the total number of central places in the system and this might be considered a natural extension of the need to minimise excess profits.

If these procedures are behaviourally valid, they clearly form a significant element in the derivation of a deductive theory designed to provide an idealised explanation for the development of a central place system. However, the degree of homogeneity assumed to be necessary for the development of the economic landscape has not been found in reality. Thus, it seems highly unlikely that Lösch's economic landscape will ever be validated with reference to a real-world situation. As a result, while central place theory in general might be considered to provide an approximate explanation for the development and change of systems of service centres in specific geographical contexts, it is not yet possible to distinguish whether they are most closely associated with the theoretical details proposed by Christaller or Lösch.

Berry and Garrison's reinterpretation of central place theory: the theory of tertiary activity

Much of the work stimulated by central place theory did not derive directly from the preceding theoretical postulates but from Berry and Garrison's reinterpretation in the form of the theory of tertiary activity. This is related to the fact that the English translation of Christaller's work did not become easily available until 1966. Unfortunately, recent re-evaluations of the theory of tertiary activity, notably by Saey and Beavon suggest that Berry and Garrison misinterpreted some of Christaller's ideas and that these misinterpretations have become irretrievably entrenched in the literature. Since this creates confusion in the minds of students introduced to the notions of central place theory, a number of points of clarification are perhaps necessary at this stage of the discussion.

In the first instance, Berry and Garrison assumed that Christaller's theory depended upon a homogeneous distribution of consumer expenditure in the area. This implied a degree of isotropism which Christaller did not envisage for the idealised landscape. Thus, the theory was not dependent upon this assumption. In addition, Berry and Garrison considered that the idealised spatial frameworks were derived from the lower limit of the range of a centre (redesignated the 'threshold') rather than the upper limit (redesignated the 'range'). This was also considered to provide a strong reason why most suppliers of goods and services could earn excess profits in the system, a consideration which was assumed (erroneously) to be excluded from Christaller's version. It is assumed that the population of an area has to be supplied with n central functions and that these can be ranked from 1 to n in ascending order of threshold expenditure requirements. The highest-order centres in an area offering function n will be spaced in much the same manner as that described for the B-grade centres in Christaller's scheme, but in this instance with reference to the threshold of the highest-order function rather than its range. Functions with lower threshold requirement such as n–1, n–2, etc., will now earn excess profits since their effective ranges will extend beyond their particular threshold distances. Again, as in the case of the Christaller scheme, a second order of centres can be envisaged developing in the centre of equilateral triangles subtended by three first-order centres. The highest-order function to be supplied from these centres can be designated n-i, the threshold of which is defined by the geometry of equal hexagonal trade areas centred on a first-order centre and on the six nearest second-order centres. By definition function n-i will not be able to earn excess profits since its hexagonal trade areas only circumscribe a bare threshold population. Functions n and n-i were termed hierarchically marginal functions since they introduce new levels into the hierarchy where only normal profits are possible. In the same manner, lower-order centres with thresholds n-j, n-k, etc., can be postulated. Again, by definition functions n-j and n-k can only earn normal profits but it clear that suppliers of all other functions can obtain excess profits.

This interpretation of central place theory is geometrically valid, but it does not provide any clear reason why the economically precise threshold rather than the more nebulous range of central functions should be the 'preferred' generative force. The use of the threshold implies that excess profits in the resulting system are minimised. It may well be that this is considered the normal tendency in a competitive free market economy as more and more suppliers freely enter the market. However, the spatial and hierarchical characteristics of the central place systems derived from Christaller or Berry and Garrison have strong similarities despite their detailed theoretical differences.

The conceptual value of central place theory

The early empirical tests of the theories in the 1950s and 1960s were unable to determine whether settlement systems conformed more closely to the stepped *hierarchy* of Christaller or to the *continuum* postulated by Lösch. This is not too surprising since Christaller had anticipated a number of factors which would create deviations from a stepped hierarchical structure. Possible spatial variations in population density or purchasing power and the tendency for consumers to maximise their total travel effort by combining trips for high and low-order goods were both considered likely to transform an idealised stepped hierarchy into a continuum. Physiographic variations and deviations from a uniform transportation surface typical of real-world situations were similarly likely to result in deviations from the expected norm. Consequently, interest in the detailed differences between the central place theoretical formulations has declined in recent years.

Nevertheless, an extensive body of literature generated by central place theory has provided many methodologies and concepts which have been used widely in the study of urban systems, irrespective of whether they clarify aspects of the original theoretical formulations. The search for hierarchical and spatial order in systems of cities has, for example, resulted in the derivation of a large number of *indices of centrality* of varying degrees of statistical sophistication,

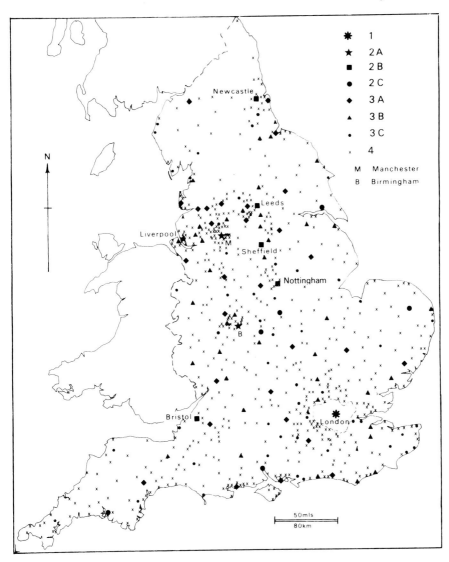

✳	1
★	2 A
■	2 B
●	2 C
◆	3 A
▲	3 B
•	3 C
×	4
M	Manchester
B	Birmingham

Figure 3.8 The urban hierarchy of England, 1965

(Source: Smith, 1968)

designed to describe the relative status of centres in a region. Christaller devised a measure of centrality based upon the relative concentration of the telephones of a region in particular central places:

$$\text{Centrality} = Tz - Ez . \frac{Tg}{Eg}$$

where TZ is the number of telephones in a particular centre, Ez is the population of the centre, Tg is the number of telephones in the region, and Eg is the population of the region.

Others have been based upon the number and degree of specialisation of retail facilities and other services provided in a centre (*key criteria*). Smith, for example, derived an eleven level hierarchy of central places in England using 35 retail and service criteria (Figure 3.8). *The functional index* derived by Davies (1967) is a more quantitatively refined measure of centrality. This was based upon the location coefficient of a single establishment of each defined functional type in a specified area:

$$c = \frac{t}{T} \times 100$$

where c was the location coefficient of function t, t was one outlet of function t, and T was the total number of outlets of t in the whole system.

The multiplication of the location coefficient of a particular function by the number of establishments of that function in a centre gave the centrality value of that function for the centre. The addition of the centrality values of each function used in the study then gave the functional index of the centre. A comparison of the functional indices of different centres was considered to provide a measure of their relative service status.

Despite the difficulties involved in obtaining data sufficiently refined to be indicative of the urban status of a centre, measures of centrality are widely used in contemporary urban geography. They are used to describe the relative status of centres at national, regional or intra-urban scales of analysis, and might be considered an essential prerequisite for a more detailed analysis of some specific aspect of the urban system.

Analyses of the behavioural aspects of central place theory have similarly resulted in a fuller understanding of the determinants of *consumer behaviour* and the complex nature of the functional interrelationships between urban centres. Consumer behaviour in classical central place theory is considered to be determined by the *nearest centre assumption*, by which the time-cost budget of journeys for particular goods and services are minimised. An early consumer behavioural study by Berry, Barnum and Tennant in south-western Iowa demonstrated the expected relatively localised hinterlands of centres for the provision of low-order functions such as food, shopping, banking and dry cleaning (Figure 3.9). By contrast, shopping for higher-order goods such as clothing and furniture was much more highly concentrated on the higher-order centres, as anticipated by central place theory. However, the study provided only approximate support for the existence of an idealised central place hierarchy. The hinterlands of the centres for the different functions overlapped to a significant degree since consumer behaviour patterns only roughly approximated the nearest centre assumption. Similar doubts as to the simplicity of the expected patterns of behaviour have been a recurring theme in investigations of consumer behaviour. In fact, consumer behaviour has been shown to be related

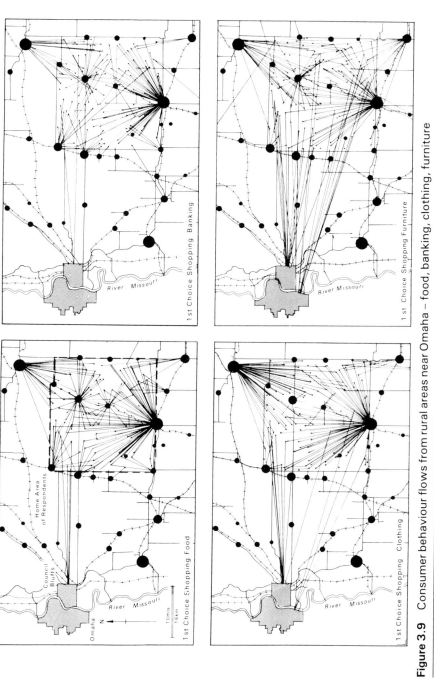

Figure 3.9 Consumer behaviour flows from rural areas near Omaha – food, banking, clothing, furniture

(Source: Berry, Barnum and Tennant, 1962, *Papers and proceedings of the Regional Science Association, 9*; reproduced by permission of the Chairman, Regional Science Association)

to a complex, and as yet not entirely explained, trade-offs between the attractions of increasing centre size and the disincentive associated with longer journeys. Nevertheless, a rich methodological heritage has been added to urban geographical analysis. Questionnaire survey techniques have been enhanced, techniques such as graph theory and spatial interaction theory have been developed to investigate the functional relationships between centres, all of which have had significant practical application for planning by both public agencies and commercial organisations (see Chapter 10).

It was also a basic assumption of central place theory that the hierarchical and spatial characteristics of systems of cities tend to be in a state of equilibrium with the density distribution of population, the amount of consumer expenditure, and the level of transport technology. This has been taken to offer *dynamic-predictive* possibilities for the theory. Traditionally, this has not been the case since many writers have formerly considered central place theory to provide only a static model of settlement systems. However, whatever the basic characteristics of a system which develops in an area these will change over time in a reasonably predictable manner. For example, changes in the density of population, change in relative levels of affluence and associated consumer demand, as well as changes in the personal mobility of the population are all likely to precipitate change in various levels of the central place hierarchy. The problem of prediction is, of course, that all three factors may be changing at the same time and may be interrelated. Nevertheless, the theory has predictive value, even if only at a conceptual level, and has been used in this manner in recent years.

Hodge's study of Saskatchewan for the period 1941–61 was one of the first to use central place theory in this way. Fundamental changes had occurred for all three factors mentioned above. Increases in the mechanisation of agriculture and the associated amalgamation of farms into fewer, larger units resulted in a decline in the rural population, but for the remaining farmers, a concomitant increase in their income occurred. This created a decline in demand for low-order convenience goods, but an increase in demand for the more specialised, expensive goods and services normally found in higher-order service centres. At the same time, the growth in car ownership resulted in a greater personal mobility which made the rural population less dependent upon their local low-order service centres for the provision of goods and services. The combined influences of these changes pointed in the same direction: towards the decline of the lower-order service centres and the increased status of the larger centres.

This was reflected in changes in the number and status of service centres. The lowest three of seven orders of centres had been subject to a drastic decline in status. In addition, smaller centres located within 16 km of a higher order centre were particularly susceptible to decline and the four higher order centres demonstrated a significant enhancement in status. The likely implications of the continuation of these trends were then used to formulate a settlement planning strategy, incorporating the stimulation of growth nodes at locations likely to suffer unacceptable declines in the availability of local services such as schools, health care, local government and public transport. The conceptual use of central place theory in this manner continues to be widely used in urban geography and regional planning.

The incorporation of a time element and the notion of change over time in central place systems has also been an important element in the context of modern research into *periodic markets*. In many Third World countries where low levels of consumer demand and mobility generate insufficient expenditure to support fixed service centres, periodic markets continue to be a major component of the retailing and wholesaling system. Such markets because of their periodicity and the fact that they only occur on specific days of the week in a given location means that traders will migrate in well-defined ways from one market to another. Analysis must thus be undertaken in a temporal as well as a spatial setting. Such markets continue to exist in the developed world; between one and two per cent of British retailing and between 20 and 50 per cent of its wholesaling, for example, is still transacted through periodic markets. In less developed countries, such as Mexico, depending upon the commodity, between 20 and 80 per cent of trade is conducted in this type of institution. In terms of the settlement hierarchy within less-developed countries, periodic markets are most dominant in rural areas and small towns but are still found in large cities, though it is there that they are most subject to pressure of modernisation.

In a typical market situation, a basic daily market will function on the site each day of the week but will be augmented considerably on one or two days of the week. Evidence suggests that as a city develops or 'modernises', the differences between the peaks and lows of activity will gradually diminish as the transformation towards a permanently established market takes place. The length of weeks is a critical feature in the periodicity of markets and will vary with cultural norms from one society to another. Whereas the most common Christian and Muslim week is of a seven-day duration, in China it is ten or twelve days, in Java five, and in various parts of West Africa ranges from two to eight days. The length of a week will determine the *cycle* as the market, or more accurately the market traders, move around. In a study of rural China, Skinner identified a ten-day cycle which was subdivided into three units of three days each, with no business on the tenth day. There are three levels of markets from the central or highest order to intermediate to standard or lowest order. An individual trader may spend days one, four and seven in the central market and follow regular routes among *various* lower order markets on the intervening days. Figure 3.10(a) idealises the distribution of market locations and the main days of activity; in this system central goods can be circulated around several markets on a regular schedule and traders can accumulate enough trade to remain profitable. There is a time-space system of rotating rather than fixed central place functions.

Skinner's study and others have been interpreted in terms of traditional central theory, as suggested by Figure 3.10(a), in which periodicity is incorporated with spatial location to suggest a hierarchy and an ordered distribution of centres. Bromley, Symanski and Good argue for a more complex system influ-

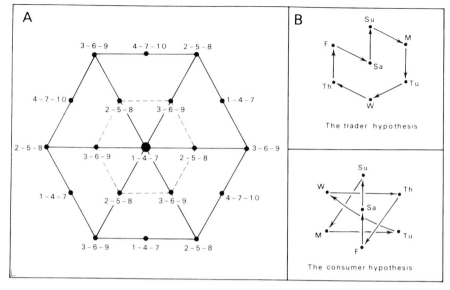

Figure 3.10   Periodic markets: consumer and trader hypotheses

enced by the lack of divorce between producing and selling and an inertia factor which relates to non-economic considerations. The market in the Third World is normally much more than a commercial activity; it has religious connotations and provides the opportunities for recreation, social and business contacts.

Some of the attempts to measure amounts of spatio-temporal integration in systems of periodic markets have used Smith's trader and consumer hypotheses (see Figure 3.10(b)). Whereas the *trader hypothesis* suggests that markets are synchronised to enable traders to follow routes which minimise their weekly travel costs, the *consumer hypothesis* suggests that the synchronisation is designed to enable dispersed rural populations to have easy access to markets through the week. Neither of these has been shown to have general validity and the *commodity hypothesis* which suggests that market schedules will be attuned so that adjacent market-places that supply different types of goods would meet on different days and that these will normally be at different levels of the market-place hierarchy, may well provide a more appropriate concept.

Such theoretical concepts have been reviewed extensively elsewhere and cannot be adequately discussed here. It is clear that periodic markets raise time-space relationships into central focus in the study of central place systems, it is also clear that such markets are still of considerable economic and social significance in many parts of the world despite the evidence that 'modernisation' is diminishing their roles.

Urban systems in the modern world

The various theories of the urban system offer insights into the relationship between the city size-distribution and the process of development, as well as into the dynamic spatial interrelationships between themselves and their hinterlands. For many types of analyses, however, the city has also to be viewed in the context of the more localised 'urbanised region' of which it is part. This section is concerned with attempts to characterise and classify urbanised regions. Initially, these will be placed in an evolutionary context since their development is intimately related to the historical process of urbanisation (see Chapter 2). The simplest evolutionary framework is that of the three stage 'industrial' model, each stage of which has a typical population size, spatial form, and level of inter-connectedness. While the universality of these stages remains questionable, in advanced societies they, at least, tend to reflect particular levels of technological development in transport and communication. The three-stage model used as a framework is briefly summarised and attention is focused primarily on its implications for city-hinterland relationships.

Stages of urban systems development

1. The pre-industrial stage: an urban nucleus
The great majority of pre-industrial cities were small. Most had population of less than 50,000 and a rudimentary form of economic, social and political

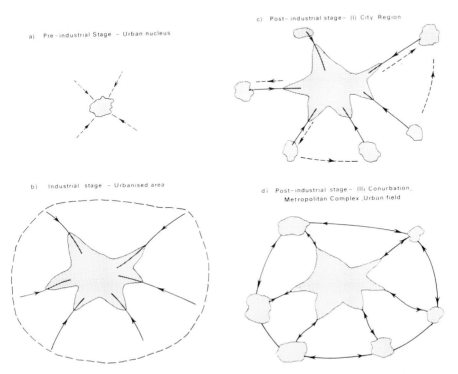

a) Pre-industrial Stage – Urban nucleus

b) Industrial stage – Urbanised area

c) Post-industrial stage– (I) City Region

d) Post-industrial stage– (II) Conurbation, Metropolitan Complex ,Urban field

Figure 3.11 Types of urban regions with stylised functional inter-relationships

organisation which was reasonably typical of the period prior to large-scale industrialisation. Only in primate cities, usually capitals of more powerful states, did populations exceed 100,000. The transport technology associated with the development of these cities was equally rudimentary. Communications depended upon the pedestrian or on draught animals. Thus, the urban fabric tended to be arranged so that journeys within the city could be kept relatively short. Consequently, despite the continuing debate relating to the variety of reasons for the development of pre-industrial cities and their internal patterns of sociospatial differentiation, most authorities are agreed upon their character-istically compact form (Langton, 1975; Sjoberg, 1960; Vance, 1971). Similarly, because of the limitations of transport facilities, the spheres of influence of such cities were either: restricted to the provision of urban services for a relatively localised population living within the area of a day's 'round trip'; or if the city only provided commercial, religious, social or political functions for a wider hinterland, then the frequency of visits by long-distance travellers and the associated functional interrelationships between the city and the outer limits of its hinterland tended to be relatively low. In either case, the city tended to be a distant urban nucleus loosely related to a wider rural area and to other cities (Figure 3.11(a)).

2. The industrial stage: urbanised area

In the early stages of industrialisation, town growth was usually associated with the localisation of particular resources, and many towns increased considerably in size in relation to the natural advantages which they possessed. Canals and railways provided more efficient means of intercity transport, principally for the conveyance of industrial materials and finished products, and this increased the economic interlinkages between towns with complementary industrial structures and also between industrial towns and major market areas. However, since a town's prosperity tended to be related to the processing of raw materials, the early relationship between neighbours was as often competitive as it was complementary and economic linkages were frequently stronger between relatively distant markets than between near neighbours. In effect, despite the steady increase in economic linkages over space, individual towns still tended to retain a distinct and separate functional identity to a significant degree. Nevertheless, towns became much larger than their pre-industrial counterparts, although they retained their relatively compact form. Intra-city mobility for the most part depended upon public transport. However, the relatively long hours and low wages of the industrial workers necessitated the avoidance of the time and cost associated with a significant journey to work and this gradually became linked with increasing residential differentiation on social class lines. Thus, low-status housing gravitated markedly to areas of industrial employment, while new industrial areas and higher status residential suburbs tended to develop along the public transport routes of the major arterial roads radiating outward from the city centres, creating a distinctly tentacular urban form. This process of development resulted in the 'urbanised area' of the industrial period, characterised by larger, but still relatively compact, cities than those of the pre-industrial period and increasing, but still relatively weak, functional linkages extending beyond the city boundaries (Figure 3.11(b)).

3. The post-industrial stage

The post-industrial period is characterised by a considerable increase in the speed and efficiency of communications. Of particular note was the development in the late nineteenth century of the telephone which initiated the growth of improved forms of electronic communication. Similarly, the rapid growth in importance of motor vehicles from the early years of the twentieth century, and particularly in the period since 1945, has changed the emphasis of interurban transport from canal and rail to road, while intercity personal mobility has shifted from public transport to the private car. These changes have reduced the constraint of distance on the development of economic and social linkages both between and within cities. Thus, spatial dispersal has become an increasingly important element of the urban system. The distinction between urban and rural, and the functional separateness of individual cities has been reduced drastically as communicative efficiency has increased. Also, ease of communications has allowed amenity considerations to influence the locational characteristics of urban systems. A significant section of the more mobile labour force have gravitated to attractive areas for their homes in wider areas. This has resulted in the suburbanisation of vast tracts of land around most major cities. Similarly, industries which have high inputs of skill and labour relative to raw materials have been able to gravitate to formerly smaller urban concentrations in the more attractive regions of a country. (See also decentralisation, counter-urbanisation, de-urbanisation, Chapter 4). In effect, more dispersed forms of the 'urbanised region' have emerged as the central features of the urban system (Figure 3.11(c) and (d)).

A typology of 'urbanised regions'

A typology of 'urbanised regions' can now be suggested. While the types discussed can be taken broadly to represent evolutionary stages, they are not necessarily mutually exclusive and there is a transition from one stage to the next rather than sharp discontinuities. Furthermore, irrespective of the sophistication of communications technology, the more extensive types of urbanised region tend to be confined to the larger, more populous areas.

The city region

The term 'city region' has generally been applied to an area including the major employment centre of a region and the surrounding areas for which it acts as a strong focus for employment and the provision of major services. Its develop-

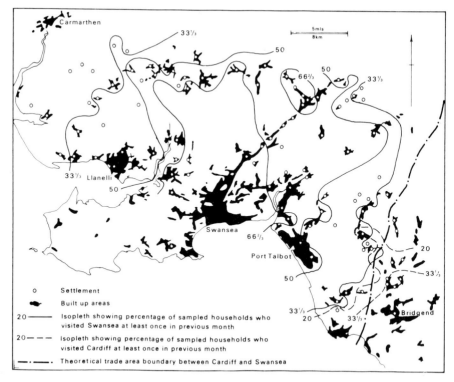

Figure 3.12   An example of a city-region: Greater Swansea – showing generalised consumer behaviour and trade area boundary

(Source: Davies, 1971, in *Regional Studies*, 6; reproduced by permission of W. K. D. Davies and Regional Studies)

ment represents the first stage in the functional integration of urbanised regions. Mackinder, in *Britain and the British Seas* (1902), was one of the first writers to use the term in this manner to convey the view that the city region of London already encompassed the greater part of the whole of south-eastern England. The essential functional relationship between city and region is considered to be one of dependence and for this reason functional relationships are nodal, focusing on the major city (Figure 3.11(c)). The delimitation of the city and its complementary region has subsequently been an important theme in urban geographical investigation. It was an important element of Christaller's work, which stimulated the development of a number of methods designed to define the spheres of influence of cities. More recently, Davies used the concept to define the city region of Greater Swansea based upon an investigation of high-order shopping trips. It was suggested that the 33 per cent line provided a reasonable indication of the limits of the city region and encompassed an area just in excess of 500,000 population (Figure 3.12).

Evidence of this kind suggests that the city region remains an appropriate concept to describe unicentred urban regions of less than 500,000 population found in the less populous parts of even the most highly urbanised countries. In fact it is interesting to note that investigations of the structure of large urban concentrations frequently use variants of the city-region concept based upon employment nodes and associated commuter fields as the basic statistical building block for the purposes of comparative analysis. For example, in the United States the Standard Metropolitan Statistical Area and the Daily Urban System have been used. Similarly, in Europe the extensive surveys of Cheshire and Hay (1989) relate their comparative investigations to nodal regions comprising an urban centre or core and contiguous areas comprising a bounded hinterland or ring. These were termed *Functional Urban Regions*.

Conurbation, metropolitan complex or urban field

In the more populous, rapidly growing parts of a country, urban development rarely produces a single urban centre. Instead, from the fortuitous circumstances which promote growth, a number of important cities may develop in relatively close proximity. Such a situation developed in Britain during the industrialisation of the nineteenth century. Largely based upon the location of coal reserves and associated port facilities, a multicentred form of development emerged which initiated the development of large urban agglomerations centred on Birmingham and the Black Country, Liverpool and Manchester, Clydeside, Tyneside and the West Riding of Yorkshire. The growth of these initially separate, but close-packed, centres resulted in the physical coalescence of the urban units of these areas, although each major centre tended to retain a partially separate identity despite the strong functional linkages which often developed. The resulting urban form was described by Geddes in 1915 as a *conurbation*, a term which stressed the characteristic feature of physical agglomeration. Subsequently, with the improvement of communication and transport the functional influence of the conurbations has spread throughout a wider surrounding hinterland, well beyond the limits of their built-up areas, so that the term is now widely used in the British literature to describe not merely physical spread but also multinodal *functional* units. Usually the most advantageously located centre in the conurbation grows larger than its neighbours and exerts a degree of economic, social and cultural dominance over the whole unit. However, the functional relationships *within* the conurbation have some special features and are essentially different from those of the city region. There is, for example, an element of dominance by the largest unit, but the other relatively large specialised cities have many functional linkages; there is no exclusive focus on the major city.

Elsewhere, in areas of population growth which have developed in relation to the locational advantages of centrality rather than the localisation of natural resources, a similar type of urban form has tended to develop. Maximum initial growth tends to take place in the most advantageous location so that, initially, the urban form is similar to the city region. However, as the forces promoting growth gather momentum, increased land costs, congestion and the associated deterioration of the urban environment stimulate an element of decentralisation of development to the surrounding region. Many of the small towns in such areas accumulate increased economic significance and develop into moderately sized cities which usually have close functional linkages with the major centre but again develop significant degrees of economic independence. Thus, while the central city tends to retain an element of dominance in the urbanised region, the functional complexity typical of the conurbation is greater than that of the city region. In Britain, the increasing functional linkages of London with towns throughout the south-east of England, as far afield as Southend-on-Sea, Luton, Reading, Southampton, Portsmouth and Brighton, have stimulated a number of regional planning proposals. The strategy of the early 1960s considered the south-east of England, with a population of upwards of 17 million, as a conurbation or metropolitan complex for practical planning purposes. Similar units termed 'mega-cities', with populations in excess of 10 million, have been discussed in the context of New York, Los Angeles and Tokyo, as well as for Mexico City and Shanghai in the developing world.

Metropolitan growth in the economic centre of the Netherlands has resulted in an interesting variant of the conurbation form, termed Randstad Holland (Hall, 1984). This has a population of approximately 4.5 million and differs significantly from the other metropolitan complexes discussed above in that it incorporates a much stronger element of polycentrism. It comprises the three major cities of Amsterdam, Rotterdam and the Hague with populations of between 500,000 and 1 million, Utrecht of approximately 250,000 and Haarlem and Leiden, both larger than 100,000 population. In addition, a number of smaller towns and suburban developments are so located as to create a significant element of urban continuity among the larger cities. The conurbation has a pseudo-circular shape of approximately 176 km (110 miles) in length, open towards the south-east with a relatively undeveloped centre – hence the term Randstad (ring city) or the alternative 'greenheart metropolis'.

This particular urban form is the result of a combination of physical geographical, historical and economic factors, all of which have tended to promote urban dispersal. Of particular note in this respect were the early land-drainage problems associated with the central delta region. Similarly, in the latter half of the nineteenth century the developmental pressures associated with the growth of governmental administrative functions encouraged decentralisation from the traditional commercial and cultural centre of Amsterdam to the Hague, while the attraction of port installations to the increasingly economically significant mouth of the Rhine established the basis of the tripartite urban form which exhibits a stronger degree of functional decentralisation and specialisation than is typical of most other conurbations. In fact, it might be suggested that an approximation to the *dispersed city* concept exists in Randstad Holland, albeit on a much larger scale than that originally envisaged by Burton in 1963.

In the Unites States a unit similar to the conurbation has been described as the *urban field*, considered to be the basic urban territorial unit of post-industrial society in the United States (Friedman, 1978):

> The urban field may be described as a vast multi-centred region having relatively low density, whose form evolves from a finely articulated network of social and economic linkages. Its many centres are set in large areas of green space of which much is given over to agricultural and recreational use. The core city from which the urban field evolved is beginning to lose its traditional dominance: it is becoming merely one of many specialised centres in a region.

Friedman does not define urban fields with any precision, but they are regarded as core areas and hinterlands of at least 300,000 population, with an outer limit of two hours' driving time, which relates to an assumed limit of periodic recreational trips. The urban fields defined in this manner range in population size from half a million to as many as 20 million and cover that third of the areas of the United States in which 90 per cent of the population live (Figure 3.13). Urban fields are more spatially extensive than the European conurbations and metropolitan complexes since they are related to higher levels of personal mobility. Thus, urban fields tend to include more extensive areas of low popu-

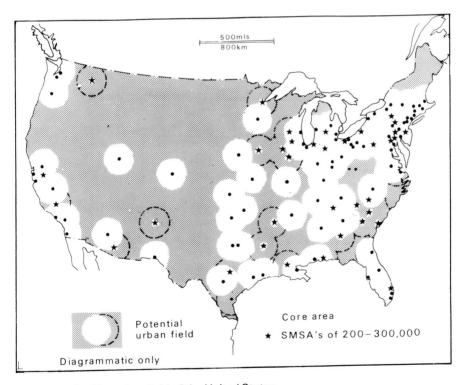

Figure 3.13 The urban field of the United States

(Source: Friedmann, 1978)

lation density. Nevertheless, the concept of the urban field may well become increasingly relevant to an understanding of the functional realities of urbanised regions outside the United States as improvements in communications and transport of a similar kind occur elsewhere.

Megalopolis

As the outer limits of the urban fields of the United States coalesce the emergence of higher order but more loosely articulated urbanised regions has been suggested. Gottmann first introduced the term 'megalopolis' in 1961 to describe the major urbanised areas of the north-eastern seaboard of the USA extending from southern New Hampshire, 800 km south to northern Virginia; and from the Atlantic an average of 240 km inland to the foothills of the Appalachians. The population of this area was 38 million, orientated around the major urban centres of Boston, New York, Philadelphia, Baltimore and Washington. Based upon this initial analysis, Gottmann (1976) subsequently suggested the characteristic features of megalopolitan urban systems. He considered that the term should be reserved for very large urban units with a suggested minimum population of 25 million. Usually it was anticipated that the emergence of such a unit would be significantly related to its potential for performing an important international exchange function for trade, technology, population and culture for the state in which it was located. Consequently, transactional activities would be a significant element of economic structure, and they would also tend to be located at major international transportation breakpoints. In addition, because of the scale of their growth they would typically have a distinctly polynuclear form, but with sufficient internal physical continuity and functional interrelationships for each to be considered a system in itself, which was distinctly separated from other units by less urbanised areas. Complete physical continuity was *not* considered a necessary feature of the megalopolitan system. In fact, in the archetypical area of the north-eastern seaboard of the United States a population density of only 250 persons per square kilometre was used to define its outer edge, while as much as 48 per cent of the urbanised region comprised commercial forest. Instead, the cohesiveness of the system was considered to depend upon, and to be best indicated by, the relative incidence of communication facilities such as highways, railways, waterways, pipelines and telephone lines, combined with transaction flows of commodities, traffic, people and messages. Also, due to the importance of communications in the efficient functioning of such units, it was anticipated that they would usually develop along major transport axes. The high levels of economic, political and social interaction typical of such areas was also considered likely to result in a strong element of self-sustaining growth with some adverse effects. The urban and social environmental problems associated with overcongestion at the centres of the major urban concentrations in developing megalopolitan systems create severe management problems for urban planning.

Defined in this manner the megalopolitan form is significantly different in both scale and function from the conurbation. It was considered by Gottmann to be restricted to six cases: comprising the type-area of the north-eastern seaboard of the United States; the Great Lakes area first described by Doxiadis as extending from Chicago to Detroit and the southern shores of Lake Erie; the Tokaido area of Japan centred on Tokyo/Yokohama; the English megalopolis, centred on the south east and extending north-westwards to include the West Midlands, Manchester, Merseyside and the West Riding of Yorkshire; the megalopolis of north-western Europe considered to be emerging in the area of Amsterdam, Paris and the Ruhr; and a sixth case centred on Shanghai.

In addition, Gottman considered that three other areas are growing fast enough to be considered as emergent megalopolitan systems. In South America rapid economic development is resulting in a corridor of development between Rio de Janeiro and São Paulo. In Europe, megalopolitan-type development centred on Milan, Turin and Genoa, extending southward to Pisa and Florence and westward to Marseilles and Avignon, is suggested; while a third case is considered likely to result from developmental pressures to link the San Francisco Bay Area with the Los Angeles/San Diego complex. A possible additional case has been suggested by Yeates (1975). This comprises 'Main Street' Canada, a corridor of development extending along Lakes Erie and Ontario and the St Lawrence Valley, reaching from Windsor in the south 1100 km north-eastward to Quebec City and centred on the urban regions of Toronto, Ottawa and Montreal. This forms the economic and political centre of Canada in which approximately half of the population live, and three-quarters of manufacturing and three-fifths of Canada's total income is produced. With a population of just over 10 million in 1971, distributed over a wider area than that of the north-eastern seaboard of the United States, this area does not strictly conform to the definition of a megalopolis. Nevertheless, its degree of primacy in the Canadian context, its international functional significance and its internal functional cohesion and polynuclear urban form, combined with its physical contiguity and interrelationships with the Great Lakes megalopolis, suggest that it has megalopolitan features despite its relatively small population.

Megalopolis has been designed to provide a description of the macro-scale urbanised region, but it has only weak functional and physical connotations. Nevertheless, it provides a broad context for the study of emerging urban systems at a scale which is becoming increasingly common.

Ecumenopolis

A yet more futuristic urban form, 'ecumenopolis', has been suggested by Doxiadis (1968). This is based upon speculative forecasts of world population trends which assume that a level of population, approximately ten times the current figure, will be reached towards the end of the twenty-first century. In these circumstances it is envisaged that a massive increase in functional linkages will occur among separate urbanised regions and there will be a related increase in the physical continuity of urban settlement. This continuous urban system which could emerge in the inhabitable world has been termed the 'universal city' or 'ecumenopolis'. Its spatial limits will be determined by the existence of reasonable flat land and climatic conditions suitable to support human settlement in the future.

Obviously, long-term forecasts of this kind involve numerous imponderables so that the population levels upon which such a structure is based must be considered highly speculative. Nevertheless, the concept of the ecumenopolis is not without value. The 'population explosion' is currently the most important facet of the demography of all Third World countries, while steady population growth – though at much lower rates – is also a characteristic feature of the great majority of developed industrial countries. Thus the increased significance of megalopolitan structures and a tendency towards the development of something resembling ecumenopolis might be anticipated. Since such eventualities are considered likely to be accompanied by an accentuation of the urban and social environmental problems associated with overcongestion, the concept of the ecumenopolis serves to underline the potential dangers of unconstrained urban growth. In fact, in North America the physical and functional divisions between the urbanised regions of the north-eastern seaboard, the Great Lakes and 'Main Street' Canada are already becoming blurred. Indeed, should the

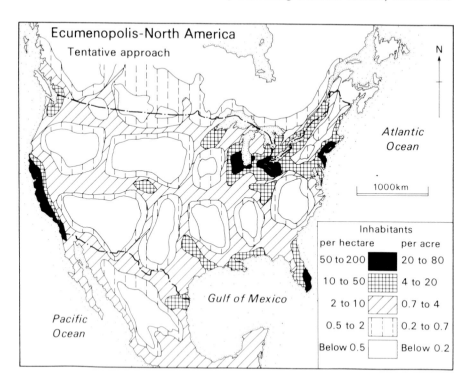

Figure 3.14   The American ecumenopolis (After Doxiadis, 1968, in *Ekistics*, 22)

Figure 3.15   European 'megalopolitan' growth zones 1950–70

		Population 1950	Population 1970	Per cent change	National rates of change 1950–70
1	Madrid	1,984,033	3,950,686	99.13	21.58
2	Basque Coast (Spain)	1,133,238	1,992,833	75.85	21.58
3	Turin	1,228,320	2,037,738	65.90	13.94
4	Lorraine	708,886	1,160,381	63.69	22.80
5	Milan	2,896,628	4,558,966	57.39	13.94
6	Rome	2,532,233	3,970,345	56.79	13.94
7	Barcelona	2,510,382	3,827,988	52.49	21.58
8	Provence-Cote d'Azur	2,788,690	4,242,828	52.14	22.80 (France) 13.94 (Italy)
9	North London fringe	3,054,552	4,578,760	49.90	10.58
10	Lyon-Grenoble	1,767,740	2,548,729	44.18	22.80
11	East Randstad-North Rhine	8,690,394	12,312,128	41.66	
	(German component)	3,792,987	5,383,917	41.94	19.38
	(Dutch component)	4,532,534	6,383,590	40.84	30.60
	(Belgian component)	364,873	544,621	49.26	14.26
12	Geneva-Lausanne-Annecy	1,031,072	1,499,659	40.59	32.35 (Switzerland) 22.80 (France)
13	Paris	7,230,690	10,068,911	39.25	22.80
14	Upper Rhine (East Bank)	9,975,364	13,855,652	38.90	
	Central Switzerland (German component)	7,684,137	10,729,651	39.63	19.38
	(Swiss component)	2,291,227	3,126,001	36.43	32.35
15	Munich	1,814,585	2,508,972	38.27	19.38
16	Stockholm	1,354,434	1,828,893	35.03	14.58
17	Valencia	1,952,185	2,585,482	32.39	21.58
	Total	52,653,426	77,475,951	47.14	16.82 (Europe)

Source: Hall, P. and Hay, D., 1980, *Growth Centres in the European Urban System*

degree of functional coalescence of the urban fields of the United States illustrated by Friedmann (1978) be followed by an increased element of physical integration, the North American element of the ecumenopolis might soon be considered more than a futuristic notion (Figure 3.14). Similarly, in western Europe with the development of the European Economic Community, international developmental pressures have increased in the area encompassed by the major urban concentrations centred on London, Paris, Brussels, Randstad and the Ruhr. In an extensive survey of European growth centres for the period 1950-70, Hall and Hay recognised seventeen 'megalopolitan' growth zones with a combined population of 77 million (Figure 3.15). These were categorised into two types: the axial developments such as those along the Rhine and its tributaries, the Rhone/Saone corridor, and the Cote d'Azur; and the more nodal growth associated with the largest cities of southern Europe such as Rome, Turin, Milan and Madrid (Figure 3.16). Fourteen of these were considered to lie within an extensive 'golden triangle' bounded by North Holland, Madrid and Rome, while the remaining three centres of Stockholm, Valencia and London

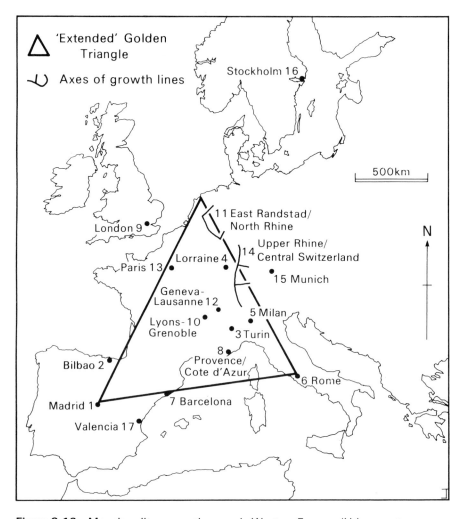

Figure 3.16   Megalopolitan growth zones in Western Europe. (Urban centres are those suggested by Hall and Hay, 1980, *Growth Centres in the European Urban System*)

are located in only marginally peripheral situations. It seems likely that with new transportation developments such as the Channel Tunnel, more motorways and advanced forms of high speed railways, the physical articulation of these units will be substantially increased.

Summary

The literature generated under the heading of the theories of the urban system has provided much of conceptual and methodological value to assist in the investigation of the characteristics of urban systems in general. Of particular note are the methods developed which are capable of providing useful hierarchical descriptions of systems of cities. Similarly, techniques have been developed by which it is possible to illustrate the functional interrelationships of centres, while concepts have also been introduced which are capable of providing additional insights into the process of development of urban systems. More particularly, central place theory has provided one of the main platforms from which the 'spatial analysis' paradigm in human geography, which has been so influential throughout the 1960s and early 1970s in particular, has developed.

The more specifically physical and functional characteristics of modern urban systems directly reflect temporal change and the impact upon urban form of a changing technology of transport and communications. The compact industrial city has given way to the modern metropolis as deconcentration and decentralisation have come to increasingly dominate urban life in the Western city. The typology of 'urbanised regions' used here accurately reflects the scale of these new 'cities' and suggests the need to view the city in a broad regional/national context. It follows that increasing attention needs to be paid to the regional/economic dimension or urban development and the problems will benefit from being viewed initially in the context of regional and national urban planning policies. The importance of economic issues for an understanding of the contemporary urban system and the significance of a regional perspective will be developed in Chapter 4.

The Urban Economy

From previous chapters it is evident at a general level that the nature of urbanisation and its associated urban forms in a country are related to the characteristics and level of economic development. This chapter seeks to examine the relationship between economic change and urban development more closely, and in the process aims to illustrate its spatial expression and associated problems at a variety of geographic scales. The historic and contemporary place of a country in the international economic system is obviously likely to influence its economic development and urban system. Countries with strong economies, at the forefront of economic advance, are likely to have urban systems and problems dominated by the need to accommodate growth, while attempting to maintain the quality of the urban environment at an acceptable level. Alternatively, areas with a heritage of outmoded forms of production face problems of economic restructuring and environmental regeneration, while those in the early stages of economic development need to develop a physical and social infrastructure capable of generating self-sustaining growth. Such features are also likely to vary regionally within countries, and between and within urban areas, in relation to the nature and relative health of the local economy. Thus, an explicitly economic perspective is considered fundamental to an appreciation of the functional characteristics of urban areas at spatial scales ranging from the global to the intra-urban.

The traditional pattern of regional economic imbalance

Until as recently as the late 1960s, the situation of a country in relation to the international economic system was perceived in terms of centre-periphery relationships. A country either formed part of the industrialised *centre* of the world economy, characterised by the countries of North America and Western Europe, or, alternatively, it was part of the underdeveloped (Third World) *periphery*, relying upon the export of natural resources to the centre and exhibiting the characteristics of a dependent economy. Consequently, the nature of the national urban systems in the countries of the centre exhibited to varying degrees strongly articulated hierarchical structures, while the countries of the periphery demonstrated stronger elements of externally-orientated primacy.

98

Within this broad framework, the great majority of the more detailed analyses of the economic context of urban development were undertaken largely from the perspective of individual countries. Attention has focused on explanations for regional inequalities in levels of economic development and their findings provide some understanding of spatial variations of the incidence of the variety of urbanised regions discussed in Chapter 3. Again, however, the importance of centre-periphery emerged as the principal analytical perspective.

Prior to the late 1950s inter-regional variations in levels of economic development were generally considered to be the result of temporary maladjustments in the economic system. The assumption was that if labour and capital were relatively mobile and reasonable information existed on the availability of economic opportunities, then eventually movement of the factors of production would bring about a *regional equalisation* of economic development. However, the development of such a state of *spatial equilibrium* clearly did not accord with the pervasiveness of regional economic inequalities in most parts of the world.

The inability of the mechanisms promoting spatial equilibrium to account for the persistence of regional inequalities resulted in the formulation of new conceptual models. The most important of these is that of Myrdal (1957), initially developed in the context of underdeveloped countries. The model was based upon the process of 'cumulative causation'. During the earliest stage of economic development it was assumed that the greatest amount of economic development would occur in that region which has some initial advantage, while the remaining regions of the country would lag behind. With subsequent

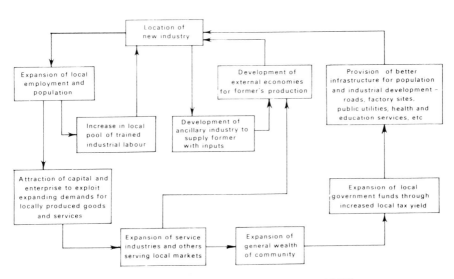

Figure 4.1 The cumulative causation model (after Myrdal, 1957)

(Source: Keeble, 1967, in Chorley and Hagget *Models in Geography*; reproduced by permission of Associated Book Publishers Ltd.)

economic development, rather than an emergence of counter-balancing forces promoting spatial equilibrium, the initial economic advantages of the 'core' region were considered more likely to result in the accumulation of 'derived advantages' which would maintain its pre-eminent economic position. These advantages include: a concentration of skilled labour; the availability of capital and enterprise; a good economic and social infrastructure resulting from past development; access to government agencies; and the opportunity to develop ancillary and service industries. These advantages were considered by Myrdal to be interactively related in such a way (Figure 4.1) as to create *cumulative* economic growth in the core region of a country.

Myrdal's model, however, incorporated additional elements. Once economic growth has been initiated in a core region, it attracts both capital investment and the in-migration of skilled labour from the peripheral regions of a country. The concentration of the provision of goods and services in the core is also likely to stunt the development of similar economic activities in the periphery. In addition, the relative poverty of the periphery might well result in the provision of a less adequate level of public services than is offered in the core region and this would further deflate the attractions of the periphery. This combination of features, termed by Myrdal the 'backwash effect', was considered likely to accentuate significantly the economic concentration associated with the cumulative causation mechanism.

The opposite, 'spread effect', by which growth in the core area might ultimately result in the stimulation of development in the peripheral regions, was also postulated by Myrdal. The core area was considered likely to stimulate demand at the periphery for such things as agricultural produce and raw materials. If the effects of this were sufficiently great, it was considered possible that this could initiate the mechanism of cumulative causation in the periphery with sufficient impetus to promote self-sustaining economic growth. However, it was considered that such a 'spread effect' was only likely to occur in the most highly developed economies, usually with the assistance of positive government policies, and even then the level of economic development was unlikely to rival that of the core.

Empirical evidence tends to support the Myrdal model. The fundamental importance of the cumulative causation mechanism, and the backwash or polarisation effects, have been widely accepted as an explanation for economic and urban concentration in the earlier stages of economic development. However, it is worthy of note that evidence for the spontaneous operation of the spread or trickling-down effects to create a measure of regional equalisation in the long term is sparse. It may well be that forces of concentration are much stronger than was initially thought by Myrdal, and this tends to support the greater importance attached to the need for directive government influence to promote a degree of regional equalisation as proposed in Hirschman's model. Nevertheless, it can be concluded that Myrdal's model provides a strong conceptual rationale for the emergence and persistence of inter-regional inequality in levels of economic development and associated urban concentration.

Building upon this base, Friedmann combined the ideas concerning the chronological stages of economic development with those relating to the development of regional inequalities to develop the more spatially explicit *centre-periphery model* as a guideline for regional development policy. The model also contributes to an understanding of the distribution of urban regions. Regional inequalities were characterised as arising from the spatial transformations associated with the cycle of economic growth. Four distinct stages are recognised (see also Chapter 2) defined according to the percentage which industry contributes to the Gross National Product of a country:

(1) Pre-industrial, 0–10 per cent
(2) Transitional, 10–25 per cent
(3) Industrial, 25–50 per cent
(4) Post-industrial, declining.

In *pre-industrial* societies regional inequalities were considered unlikely to be marked. The urban system consists of small independent centres serving restricted local areas, the size of each reflecting the agricultural wealth of the local hinterland. The development of urban hierarchies is also limited, although it is possible that the capital city or a centre with some distinct locational advantage could demonstrate a degree of primacy. During the *transitional* stage, centre-periphery contrasts begin to emerge as those places with locational advantages show the highest rates of growth. A fear of the politically disintegrative repercussions of regional contrasts may lead to policies designed to ameliorate or redress the imbalance. A mature *industrial* stage will be reached if such policies are successful and an integrated system is maintained, though forces of centralisation are likely to ensure that centre-periphery differences will remain. Again, depressed regions may occur if changing demand or technology adversely affect a particular area. Lower levels of dependence on industrial activity and more dependence on services presages the *post-industrial stage*, envisaged as being accompanied by the culmination of policies aimed at greater integration and equalisation and a shift towards urban and environmental planning. The development of regional equalisation during the post-industrial phase is, however, questionable. Friedmann regarded the USA as the best example of a post-industrial economy, yet many peripheral regions in America continue to be disadvantaged and are in receipt of aid. In fact, the national economic and spatial implications of the nature of the modern international capitalist system are far more complex than envisaged in the post-industrial stage of the early centre-periphery model. This has been fully recognised by Friedmann and Wolff (1982) and this issue will be developed in a later section. Despite this reservation the centre-periphery model continues to provide a useful introductory framework in which to view the emergence of regional inequalities in the nation state. This is summarised for the British experience in Figure 4.2.

Figure 4.2   Stages in the development of the British urban system

Urban pattern	Population	Economic development
Pre-industrial stage before 1750		
Small towns serving local rural hinterlands. *Exception*: London as a primate city; smaller port cities, such as Bristol, Liverpool	Low and fluctuating, slow growth, mostly rural	Reflects the relative prosperity of local agriculture: commercial development in London and ports
Transitional stage 1750–1850		
New urban concentrations, principally in the coalfields. London continues its growth by the 'cumulative causation' mechanism – already a million city by 1801. A centre-periphery structure more evident *within* the separate regions than at a national scale	Acceleration of growth; rural-to-urban migration. In England and Wales population increased from 8.8 million in 1801 to 17.9 million in 1851 – urban population from 33.8 per cent in 1801 to 54 per cent in 1851	Early industrial development based upon coal and steam: iron, steel, textiles and shipbuilding become the basic industries
Industrial stage 1850–1950		
London added 5.5 million to its population 1801–1911; Birmingham, Liverpool and Manchester grew by only *ca.* 1 million each in the same period. Cities of the peripheral regions grew even more slowly. The north and west began to display downward transitional characteristics and a *national* centre-periphery structure emerged	Population growth (England and Wales) 17.9 million in 1851 to 36.0 million in 1911; 78.9 per cent of the population lived in cities by 1911. Slower growth in the interwar depression years; larger cities grew more slowly as innovations ceased to enter the urban system	Emergence of international competition, basic industries face international competition. Increasing importance of secondary manufacturing; development of cheap efficient transport; economic advantages of a centralised market location for light industrial development are emphasised. Conversely industrial decline in the north and western peripheral regions
Post-industrial stage 1950–1980		
As economic forces and environmental planning policies spread London's urban development, the 'Centre' gradually expands to include the South-East, the Midlands and south-east Lancashire. Amelioration of urban decline in the periphery by decentralisation policies, but regional disparities persist.	Stabilisation of the population, with a tendency to grow slowly except in times of economic growth. Birthrates fluctuate at a low level.	Emergence of service employment as the growth sector of the economy. The attraction of a centralised urban location re-emphasised for such development. New economic element added with exploitation of oil and natural gas in the North Sea in the 1960s and 1970s. Marginal regions and inner cities remain problem areas.

The changing form of the urban economy

The international dimension

Centre-periphery relationships continue to be broadly applicable to an understanding of the regional space economy of individual nation states. However, fundamental changes in the nature of the international capitalist system developing since 1945 have initiated substantial changes in Western industrial economies. These have since the early 1970s precipitated significant spatial shifts in regional economic growth and decline which have had marked effects upon the process of urban change in Western countries. Of primary significance has been the steady increasing *globalisation* of manufacturing and markets associated with the growth of *multinational corporations*. Such economic institutions can organise the acquisition of raw materials, the manufacturing processes and the provision of services in ways which are increasingly independent of state boundaries and the associated national political and policy controls. In fact, the turnover of some of the largest multinational corporations rival the Gross National Products of all but the largest national economies. Friedmann and Wolff (1982), for example, note that in 1978 Exxon and General Motors ranked between the GNP of Czechoslovakia and Austria, or 23rd and 24th in the world. The internationalisation of economic activity has been assisted by falling relative costs of bulk, long distance transport, while the relative ease of mobility of capital combined with the lack of international mobility of labour has had a similar effect (Cheshire and Hay, 1989).

Together, these changes have produced an uneven international restructuring of economic activity based upon spatial variation in the potential profitability of capitalist production. The low unit labour costs available in the *newly industrialised (developing) countries* have attracted increasingly mechanised manufacturing processes. Industrial expansion in Hong Kong, Singapore, South Korea, Taiwan and Brazil are indicative of this effect, while equivalent development has occurred in Portugal, Greece and Ireland in the European economic periphery. The competitive impact of this trend has resulted in the steady *de-industrialisation* of the older developed industrial countries, particularly in the regions dominated by concentrations of extractive industry and traditional and heavy manufacturing activities. This has been most marked since the worldwide economic recession from the early 1970s, particularly in the countries and regions exhibiting high costs of production and outmoded working practices.

By contrast, the *post-industrial* characteristics of the economies of the developed world have become accentuated. In part, this reflects the declining significance of the traditional manufacturing sector, combined with a possibly defensive reaction to the competitive aspects of de-industrialisation. However, the opportunities for specialisation in a wide range of service activities and high technology industry afforded by the heritage of skills and knowledge associated with the earlier phases of industrial development, have resulted in a steady 'tertiarisation' of their economies. In such situations, service employment has been the main source of job creation since the early 1970s, although net job loss continues to be the general result. Government administrative services, consumer-oriented services such as retailing, and the distributive services of warehousing and transportation have maintained a steady growth. Of particular significance, however, has been the rapid growth of the *producer services*, with an attendant shift from the manufacture and processing of goods to the processing of information. Producer services comprise a wide array of private commercial activities designed to offer expertise to all sections of the economy. Foremost amongst these are finance and banking, insurance, legal advice, communications, research and development, market research and advertising. Such services along with the accumulated experience of the earlier era have a positive attraction for the development of high technology industries, particularly those associated with advances in micro-electronics and computing.

Friedmann and Wolff suggest that the emerging world economic system has introduced a strong global dimension into the urban hierarchy. The internationalisation of production and markets is viewed as articulated spatially through a network of 'world cities' located in the principal urban regions in which most of the world's active capital is concentrated. These are seen as a small number of 'control centres' in which corporate decision-making and finance are concentrated, and they provide the function of integrating national economies with the world system. Their economies are strongly orientated towards post-industrial transactional activities and they tend to contain population concentrations of 5–15 million, foremost amongst which are New York, Los Angeles, San Francisco, Chicago, Miami, Tokyo, London, Paris, Randstad, Frankfurt, Zurich, Hong Kong, Singapore, Bangkok, Cairo, Mexico City and São Paulo. Hall subscribes to the same argument, but in countries large enough to generate important regional sub-centres of economic control a 'quasi-world city' status is considered a more accurate description of their subordinate position. Chicago, San Francisco, Los Angeles and Atlanta, for example, are placed in this category. In either event, the emerging world cities are perceived as the spatial expression of the world capitalist economy.

The global changes have important implications for the processes of urban development at a number of overlapping spatial scales. These will be examined in greater detail in the succeeding sections.

Inter-regional variation

The *de-industrialisation* of the economic peripheries has been a marked feature of most Western industrialised countries over the last twenty years. This reflects a combination of the international competition of the newly industrialising countries in manufacturing and the worldwide economic recession. This has resulted in job losses resulting from a reduction in demand along with the need for greater productivity in the remaining plants. In the British context Massey and Meegan highlight the explanatory significance of the interrelated processes of *intensification* of labour productivity, *investment and technical change* designed to reduce labour inputs, and the *rationalisation* of production by dis-investment in plant. This has resulted in the gradual collapse of the economies of the older industrial conurbations of the North-East, North-West, Scotland and Wales, while major problems have also been felt in the formerly prosperous region of the West Midlands. In total, 2.8 million jobs or 36 per cent of manu-facturing employment was lost between 1971 and 1988. As a result, the economic health of Britain has increasingly been characterised as exhibiting a north-south divide, with all but the south and eastern regions suffering the negative effects of stagnation and economic restructuring. The 'north' conse-quently has all the problems associated with a decaying urban infrastructure and has been able for the most part to attract only weak forms of economic development largely confined to routinised *branch plants*, usually externally controlled by multinational corporations. The only exceptions occurred in restricted areas which offer attractions such as good access, skilled or cheap labour and environmental amenities capable of appealing to service activities or new forms of high technology industry. To date the only notable cases have been Edinburgh and Cardiff as a consequence of their enhanced government functions since the early 1970s, and 'Silicon Glen' in Strathclyde. Elsewhere, the attractions of the industrial periphery of Britain have been insufficient to redress the problems associated with de-industrialisation. In fact, Gripaios *et al.* recently noted in the case of Plymouth that the problem of peripherality continues to act as an obstacle to the development of a substantial interlinked high technology sector, despite the locational advantages of an attractive environment and relatively cheap labour. In effect, it is widely considered that the free market economic ethos espoused by the Conservative Government has accentuated the traditional centre-periphery divisions and socio-economic inequalities, and has accumulated a heightened political division between an increasingly Conservative south and a Labour north. This is likely to be exacer-bated further by the developmental pressures in the South-East contingent upon the completion of the Channel Tunnel.

The same trend has also emerged throughout Western Europe. The decline of the traditional manufacturing areas combined with the weak development of the tertiary sector has resulted in the familiar pattern of population loss, in association with economic, social and urban environmental problems. This is most evident in north west Italy centred on Turin and Genoa, in eastern and northern France (Valenciennes), the Saarland and Ruhr (Duisberg and Essen) of West Germany and throughout southern Belgium (Charleroi) (Cheshire and Hay, 1989). The ports within the economic peripheries were considered particu-larly vulnerable since the development of containerisation and roll-on/roll-off facilities has resulted in the loss of trans-shipment functions and processing associated with former breaks-of-bulk.

A similar feature is exhibited in the older manufacturing areas of the 'Frostbelt' (Snowbelt) of the north east and mid west of the USA (Figure 4.3).

Figure 4.3 Changes in employment in selected cities in the USA, 1972–82

City	Manufacturing N	%	Wholesale N	%	Retail N	%	Services N	%	Total N	%
Baltimore	− 32	− 35	− 6	− 25	− 11	− 20	2	6	− 47	− 19
Boston	− 12	− 20	− 7	− 28	− 5	− 9	32	57	7	4
Chicago	− 203	− 47	− 30	− 29	− 53	− 26	58	37	− 228	− 25
Cleveland	− 39	− 29	− 4	− 15	− 13	− 29	1	2	− 55	− 22
Detroit	− 75	− 41	− 16	− 45	− 29	− 41	− 10	− 18	− 129	− 38
Milwaukee	− 28	− 27	− 1	− 4	8	21	8	29	− 13	− 7
Minneapolis/ St. Paul	− 29	− 27	− 2	− 5	− 5	− 9	19	42	− 17	− 7
Newark	− 13	− 28	− 4	− 35	− 10	− 49	*1	1	− 27	− 28
New York	− 228	− 30	− 39	− 15	− 75	− 18	113	26	− 229	− 12
Philadelphia	− 78	− 38	− 14	− 28	− 21	− 20	9	12	− 104	− 24
Pittsburgh	− 10	− 16	− 2	− 11	1	3	10	33	− 1	− 1
St. Louis	− 29	− 29	− 7	− 26	− 7	− 19	− 5	− 14	− 48	− 24

N.B. *indicates a figure 'less than'.
Source: Kasarda in Dogan, M. and Kasarda, J. D. (eds), 1988, *A World of Giant Cities. The Metropolis Era*

Over the period 1972–82 all the larger cities lost substantial proportions of their employment in manufacturing, wholesaling and retailing, while the growth of service employment did not compensate for the losses. The situation was particularly problematic in Detroit and St Louis where significant losses were also recorded in the service sector. Employment decline was, however, the general pattern, with substantial net losses evident in Chicago, Newark, Philadelphia, Cleveland and Baltimore.

Europe demonstrates an additional dimension of urban deterioration, paradoxically associated with population growth, and still within a general context of economic peripherality. Agricultural restructuring in the poorer rural areas of southern Italy, central Spain, Portugal and Greece has stimulated a rural-urban migration without the development of an equivalent urban employment base. This has created overcrowding and the proliferation of unplanned and underserviced housing around the edges of cities such as Lisbon, Athens, Salonika, Cagliari, Naples and Palermo, reminiscent of a Third World situation (Cheshire and Hay, 1989).

By contrast, the effects of *post-industrial* change have created positive pressures for urban growth, and this has been most marked in the regions offering the strongest attractions. Hall notes that tertiarisation is most advanced in the USA. In the period 1963–83 industrial employment fell from 35–28 per cent of the total, while services expanded from 58–68 per cent. By 1983, 40 per cent of Americans were employed in information processing activities, while closely similar trends were portrayed in the UK, West Germany and Japan. In Britain services now contribute 50 per cent to the Gross Domestic Product of every region and account for two thirds of employment, but the equivalent figures for the South-East are 70 per cent and three quarters. Consequently, the industrial job losses associated with de-industrialisation were partly redressed by a gain of 1.5 million service jobs in the period 1973–83, largely concentrated in the information processing sector in the South-East. With the internationalisation of the capitalist economies corporate head-quarters and producer services have been attracted particularly to the trad-itional centres of finance, business and government. These are the areas which offer the contacts with financial institutions and government, and the markets, specialised labour and communications most conducive to economic success in the new circumstances. Such facilities are also attractive to high technology and related defence-orientated growth industries. It is likely that the interactive relationships which emerge between producer services and high technology industry contribute a multiplier effect which accentuates the developmental attractions of the economic core areas. Concentrations of both forms of activities also generate high incomes which support the additional attractions of high order specialised retail, leisure and entertainment facilities. Marshall suggests that the combined influence of this array of factors lends continued support to the strong regional centralisation tendencies associated with the cumulative causation process.

In contrast, the less attractive economic and physical environment associated with the de-industrialisation of the older centres of manufacture have little to offer in the new conditions. In the absence of strong government intervention to redistribute growth impulses, a spiral economic decline is maintained and service employment growth is largely confined to the public and consumer service sectors. This process has led to the accentuation of the 'dual space' economy of the UK, epitomised in the concept of the north-south divide.

On a continental scale, however, there are usually a number of economic regions centred on 'world cities' capable of sustaining concentrations of post-industrial development. In Western Europe, Cheshire amd Hay (1989) draw attention to the contemporary experiences of Paris, Frankfurt, Brussels, Amsterdam and Copenhagen. In the USA the situation is even more complex. The size and historical evolution of the country predisposed it towards an economic multipolarity, epitomised by the status of New York, Chicago and Los Angeles. Recent economic changes have added substantially to the com-plexity of the situation. The de-industrialisation of the Frostbelt stands in stark contrast to the attraction of new industry to the 'Sunbelt' of the south and west. In part this reflects the exploitation of large oil and gas resources and is illus-trated by the elevation of Houston from 20th to 13th place in the urban hierarchy between 1950 and 1975. However, the attractions of the Sunbelt also reflect a heritage of low wages, non-unionised labour, low taxation and less government control, combined with climatic and associated recreational con-siderations. Thus, while the older industrial cities of the north east and mid west have steadily lost their manufacturing bases at rates of 20–40 per cent over this period 1970–84, many cities of the Sunbelt have demonstrated significant growth in the traditional industrial sector. Houston, for example, exhibited an 81 per cent growth rate, while San Francisco and Denver respectively added 21 per cent and 19 per cent to their traditional manufacturing bases. At the same time, consistent with Friedmann and Wolff's (1982) world cities concept, the major regional centres in both the north and south attracted substantial numbers of jobs in producer services. Thus, while not redressing the industrial losses in the north, the south added a particularly buoyant new sector to the economy. Growth rates were typically greater than 40 per cent in the fourteen-year period and reached a high of 144 per cent for Houston. Thus, cities such as Los Angeles, Houston, Miami, Dallas and Atlanta have accumulated a significant producer service dimension which has resulted in a less concentrated pattern of national corporate control than existed formerly.

The differential economic growth rates between Frostbelt and Sunbelt have been heightened by the distribution of investment in high technology defence and space orientated industries. A significant proportion goes to the Pacific states for historical-strategic reasons but the great majority of the remainder has been distributed throughout the southern belt. This reflects the need for large testing sites and good weather. In Castells' view, however, this accords with the anti-big-city aura of the military establishment for political and amenity reasons. Thus, the contemporary shift from Welfare State expenditure to 'Warfare State' expenditure has served to accentuate the underlying economic trend. Castells further characterises the process of regional urban restructuring as an abandonment of the oldest, a maintenance of the largest and the appearance of the new. Drawing on the earlier work of Mollenkopf a typology of cities in the three different situations is suggested:

(1) Cities based on older manufacturing activities, e.g. Cleveland, Detroit, Buffalo. Decline of traditional manufacturing, little growth of new sectors – urban economic decline.
(2) Cities with a mixture of old manufacturing and new activities, e.g. New York, Boston – simultaneous growth and decline.
(3) Cities based upon the new economic sector, e.g. Houston, Dallas, Miami – rapid growth.

The regional economic restructuring associated with contemporary world economic changes are clearly capable of generating complex spatial results.

Intra-regional change

Economic changes at the regional scale, however, also find differential expression within regions, particularly in the context of pressures for growth. Despite advances in telecommunications technology, general opinion supports the view that the advantages of spatial agglomeration in large city centres continue to attract the more specialised transactional functions performed by the headquarters for a wide range of business activities. The advantages of ease of interaction between business associates, with government decision-makers, providers of specialist services, higher educational establishments, and ease of access to major airports, combine with the complementary attractions of concentrations of hotels and leisure and entertainment facilities to promote the continued centralisation of specialised business activities. This is reflected in the continued demand for offices for space intensive functions in most of the World Cities, and particularly in the largest financial centres such as London, New York and Tokyo. Greater London alone accounts for 20 per cent of all service jobs in Britain and it is the base for more than 32 per cent of the producer-service employment in banking and finance, with much of the latter concentrated in the central area. The emergence of large *transnational* corporations in Japan in recent years has created comparable pressures for reconcentration in the Tokyo metropolitan region despite attempts to spread the pressure for urban growth. In fact, it has been estimated that by the year 2000 a quarter of the population of Japan comprising more than 32 million people will live within a 50 km radius of central Tokyo.

At the same time, the diseconomies of urban concentration associated with rising land prices, the costs of transport and traffic congestion, competition for labour and the reduction of environmental amenity have for many years asserted the advantages of *decentralisation*. The site constraints and transportation considerations have been important to extensive manufacturing space users since the inter-war period, while in more recent years the labour availability and amenity factors have proved appealing to routine office functions and high technology industry. The initial response was a *suburbanisation* of industrial employment to free-standing sites or industrial estates on the fringes of most cities, while office employment gravitated initially to suburban shopping centres and, more latterly, to office parks. The pressures for decentralisation have, however, been so great that these intra-urban responses have been succeeded by more marked intra-regional expressions of decentralisation termed *counter-urbanisation* and *de-urbanisation*.

The emergence of counter-urbanisation as initially defined by Berry stressed the importance of individual preferences for the environmental attractions of a semi-rural (*ex-urban*) lifestyle and the avoidance of the problems and stresses associated with life in big cities. Subsequently, counter-urbanisation has been equated more closely with the more pervasive forces of *de-urbanisation* or *deconcentration*. This is considered to reflect the influence of a number of factors. In Britain, Fothergill and Gudgin suggested the importance of a 'constrained location theory' resulting from a lack of suitable space for the expansion and development of the new forms of post-industrial employment in the older cities. Fielding stresses the influence of the search for labour reserves conducive to the new forms of work practice, while Keeble, Owens and Thompson highlight the significance of attempts to reduce production costs associated with lower rents, rates and wage levels offered by rural areas. Apparently, the balance of advantages for employers operates strongly in favour of counter-urbanisation and the key influence in the process are considered to be the decisions made by firms and government departments.

Within regions of economic growth this results in the faster growth of the smaller towns and sub-regional centres in the vicinity of the large conurbations and often involves migration flows from the central cities or from the de-industrialising peripheries. Expressed in this way, counter-urbanisation can be considered an intra-regional variant of the emergence of the Sunbelt of the USA. Ironically, the migration dimension tends to be socially selective and primarily involves intermediate white-collar and technical operatives, not the semi-skilled and unskilled manual workers displaced from the declining industrial sectors. The latter theme will be examined further in the next section.

Characteristically, the largest cities demonstrate net population losses, while gains are highest in the medium and small-sized settlements in the growth regions. The process is now a well-established feature of urbanisation in the USA. During the period 1970–80 Castells indicates that the proportion of the population living in urban areas of greater than 2,500 remained static at 73 per cent. At the same time the rural population grew by 12 per cent, equivalent to the rate of growth of the metropolitan areas. This he attributed to a process of *ruralisation* associated with the counter-urbanisation of employment to rural areas. A similar decentralisation of service employment and high technology industry has been identified widely throughout Western Europe.

In Britain in the last two decades new high technology and defence related industries have also gravitated largely to the small and medium-sized towns of the South-East, South-West, the East Midlands and East Anglia. The particular attractions of the South-East for the development of producer services has already been noted. It is consequently in these areas that the effects of counter-urbanisation have been most marked and dispersed-city forms have become increasingly evident. Attention has been drawn to the emergence of a high-tech 'Western Crescent' extending from Hampshire, through Surrey and Berkshire,

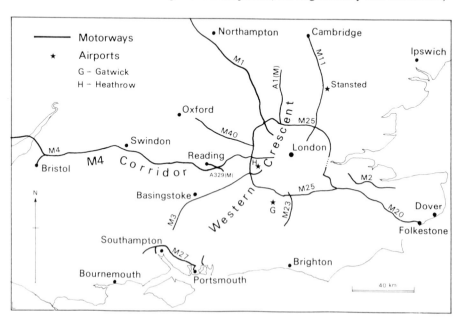

Figure 4.4   Britain's Sunrise Strip and the M4 Corridor: Britain's Sunbelt

north-westward to Hertfordshire, taking in parts of the 'M4 Corridor' (Figure 4.4). Similar developments have occurred around Cambridge ('Silicon Fen'), while the effects of functional decentralisation are evident in places as far afield as Southampton, Portsmouth, Northampton and Norwich. In fact, the greater part of the south and east of England has been described as Britain's Sunbelt. Within this area the concentration of the electronics industry, aerospace, defence and producer services along the M4 Corridor has resulted in its lyrical description as Britain's 'Sunrise Strip', with close parallels drawn with California's 'Silicon Valley'.

The intra-urban dimension

The recent economic changes are also reflected in land use patterns and the social geography of the city. Concentrations of employment are an important element of the urban fabric which has been subject to substantial physical and functional change. The traditional pattern of manufacturing activities reflected the importance of historical influences (Figure 4.5). Early industrialisation, based upon bulky raw materials and fuels, asserted the locational advantages of sites suitable for river transport, canals and railways, outside the already congested pre-industrial city. In such locations relatively large amounts of cheap land were usually available which offered advantages for ease of assembly of raw materials and the distribution of manufactured products, as well as access to water for use in the production processes and for waste disposal. Inner city industrial concentrations such as these were a well marked feature of most major British cities, and were characterised for Manchester by Lloyd and Mason, for Clydesdale by Bull and for the Lower Swansea Valley by Humphrys and Bromley (A). At the same time, the expanding central business districts attracted a variety of associated functions such as wholesaling, warehousing and business machine maintenance, while the early concentration of newspaper offices often attracted printing and publishing to city centre sites (B). The availability of cheap immigrant or itinerant labour in the low status 'transition zones' which developed around the expanding city centres also encouraged the development of small-scale manufacturing. The garment trade of New York, London and Paris are well known examples of this phenomenon.

Subsequently, with the growth in scale of heavy industry towards the end of the nineteenth century the need emerged for large railway-based sites on the peripheries of cities (C1), while the use of larger ocean-going vessels necessitated the migration of port-based industries from early waterfront sites to large estuarine or reclaimed coastal locations (C2). In Britain the decline of the London docks and the development of the Thames estuary was indicative of this trend, as was the concentration of heavy engineering and chemicals on Teesside; while the postwar development of Europoort, Rotterdam is a spectacular example of the same process.

More recently, however, with the expansion of road transport and electrical

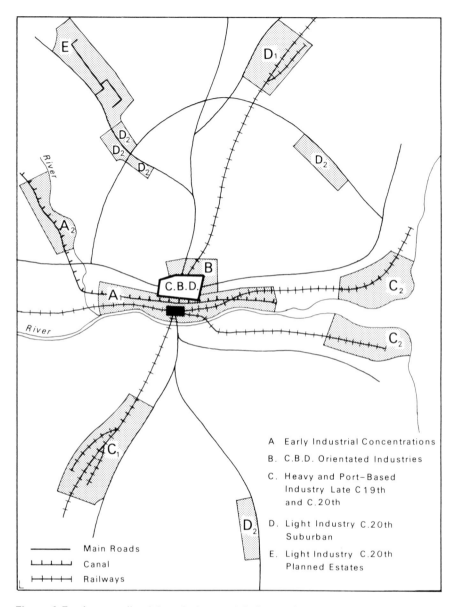

Figure 4.5   A generalised descriptive model of manufacturing areas in cities

power in the twentieth century, the newly developing light industries gravitated to the less congested and environmentally more attractive suburban peripheries (D). Nevertheless, the process of dispersal was not entirely unconstrained since the need for communications and public utilities promoted a degree of centralisation within the suburbs. Later, to offset the environmental dis-advantages of uncoordinated dispersal, the planning of industrial estates by public authorities in Britain and the zoning of land for industrial parks in the USA has had a similar effect (E). To this pattern has been added the development of office employment. The initial concentration of offices in the central business districts has been followed by a decentralisation of many routine operations to the vicinity of the major suburban shopping centres of the largest cities and, ultimately, to the development of office parks (see Chaper 8).

This general pattern of employment opportunities has been modified substantially by the economic changes of the last two decades. The post-industrial shift towards a service-dominated economy has generated a considerable demand for office space for corporate headquarters, related producer services and government administration in all the major world cities. This has created a buoyant demand for office space in the traditional concentrations in the central business districts, with an associated displacement of some of their traditional functions. In London, the decentralisation of newspaper printing and publishing from the Fleet Street area and of fruit and vegetable wholesaling from Covent Garden has been accompanied by an increased concentration of finance and business services in these areas. Kasarda notes a similar trend in most of the major cities of the USA. This was exemplified for Pittsburg and St Louis, both of which were suffering from severe industrial, commercial and residential decline in their central areas until as recently as 1975. By 1985, however, both had experienced significant commercial revival, St Louis having attracted over a billion dollars worth of investment in a combination of office, business convention, tourism, business services and medical activities (Cheshire and Hay, 1989). Similarly, in Greater Copenhagen the compensation for a loss of 78,000 jobs in manufacturing between 1970–83 by a growth of 173,500 jobs in services is indicative of a comparable situation. At the same time, office expansion has been a continuing feature in the established suburban nodes of the largest cities and in the wider regional context of counter-urbanisation noted earlier.

At the intra-urban scale, however, the adverse effects of *de-industrialisation* have also been widespread. Employment in manufacturing has been lost on a prodigious scale in most major industrial cities, and particularly in the principal conurbations. This has been exacerbated in port cities by the loss of goods-handling activities associated with technological changes and rationalisation in bulk goods-handling. These changes have not been confined to the peripheral regions of countries. Inner London lost 45 per cent of its manufacturing employment in the period 1971–81, while Birmingham, Liverpool and Glasgow exhibited similar situations. In the USA the situation was substantially the same. St Louis, for example, suffered a prolonged period of urban decline and a central city population loss of 47 per cent between 1950 and 1980 (Cheshire and Hay, 1989). This has resulted in the widespread abandonment of the large former industrial sites in inner cities and in the obsolete docklands. In most cases this has resulted in the creation of industrial dereliction over extensive parts of most inner cities. The poor urban environment and high rates of unemployment amongst the relatively immobile semi-skilled and unskilled former industrial workers have combined to create disadvantageous economic and social conditions which have been associated with social problems such as delinquency, criminality, alcoholism and drug abuse; in short, the *inner city problem*. In the USA and the UK this has been accentuated by the ethnic minority dimension. The low levels of social and physical mobility, particularly of the black and Hispanic groups, associated with discriminatory practices in employment and house sales, have served to heighten the negative conditions of such areas.

In recent years, however, in the older industrial cities which have benefited from the pressures of post-industrial economic growth many of the formerly derelict sites have been subject to *regeneration* resulting in a positive transformation of the urban environment. The Quincy Market redevelopment of central Boston is a small scale example of this effect, similar to Covent Garden in London and the Les Halles redevelopment into the Forum and Pompidou Centre in Paris. On a larger scale the Harbour place redevelopment of the Baltimore waterfront has created a shopping and hotel 'festival market place' which is estimated to attract over 20 million visitors per year. This has its counterpart in the Harbourside scheme in Sydney which is liable to be extended into the Darling Harbour shopping, convention and exhibition centre complex, projected to cost £760 million and including a monorail rapid transit link to the central business district. The redevelopment of the London docklands is an even more extensive example of the same effect. Pressures for central area development have been channelled eastward from the traditional commercial core of the 'City' to the adjacent 40 square kilometres of former dockland. The redevelopment of such an extensive area required coordination so the Conservative Government established an Enterprize Zone incentive scheme in 1980 to stimulate development in the Isle of Dogs, while the commercially orientated

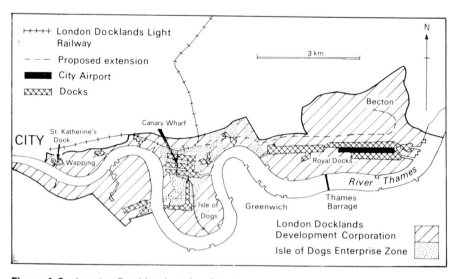

Figure 4.6   London Docklands redevelopment

London Docklands Development Corporation was appointed for the remaining area in 1981 (Figure 4.6). This has resulted in a redevelopment programme which includes extensive areas of housing, the relocation of most of the national newspapers from Fleet Street, the development of office complexes and a small airport. A major office complex of around 0.8 million square metres, designed to employ in excess of 60,000 people is currently under construction at Canary Wharf, and it has already been suggested that the London Dockland Light Railway which provides easy access to the eastern edge of the City may well need to be supplemented by a higher capacity new underground extension. The effects of urban decay and an obsolete dock system are being transformed into a prestigious commercial, residential and recreational environment which is seen potentially as a valuable tourism resource. Physically and socially 'secure' residential development predominates, characterised by 'post-modernist bunker architecture'; the natural habitat of the 'yuppies' (young upwardly-mobile professionals). (Short, 1989)

The regeneration of extensive derelict sites has not, however, solved the social problems of the inner city; quite the contrary. The majority of the new job opportunities are in white-collar occupations, while most of the new residential development is orientated towards the middle to upper status market, as is the *gentrification* of the old. The redevelopment of the London docklands illustrates these trends. The immobile, unemployed, semi and unskilled population in the inner city are largely unable to benefit from the process of change ('yuffies' – young urban failures). Apart from a minority of inner city residents involved in the more menial domestic and cleaning occupations associated with the growth in hotels, restaurants and high status housing, the economic opportunities available to the resident population are not significantly improved. This constitutes a 'mismatch' between job types and employee types in the context of an increasingly service orientated economy since the resident population is isolated from suitable job opportunities. Thus, social polarisation is increased in the inner city, particularly if the resident population is predominantly composed of the ethnic minority groups. In the USA, Castells considers that this results in the emergence of *'urban reservations'* for destitute workers and minorities. Friedmann and Wolff (1982) characterise the disadvantaged groups as an *'underclass'* marooned in the inner city and condemned to a life of economic and social disadvantage and draw the distinction between the 'citadel' and the 'ghetto'. In these circumstances, it is not surprising that alienation and demoralisation are features of inner city life and civil disorder has been an intermittent feature of the American city since the late 1960s. In Britain, the emergence of similar situations in Toxteth, Birmingham, Bristol, Hackney and Brixton in the 1980s is based upon broadly comparable conditions.

In the peripheral areas which have not benefited from economic growth, the adverse environmental impact of urban dereliction also continues to be problematic. This is particularly evident in Britain where little redevelopment has occurred without government policy initiatives. In this context the Glasgow

East End Area Renewal programme (GEAR) is considered to be the most successful. This was initiated in 1976 by central and local government under the leadership of the Scottish Development Agency and was designed to improve the residential environment and generate new employment opportunities. Improvements to the urban environment and to the social conditions have resulted, although the employment benefits are considered to have been achieved at the expense of nearby areas rather than to be indicative of fundamental economic improvement. The relative success of the Glasgow experiment has resulted in a number of additional area-based initiatives designed to solve the problems of the inner-city:

(1) *Inner city partnerships* of local authorities and government departments were established under the 1978 Inner Urban Areas Act, for Liverpool, Manchester/Salford, Birmingham, Newcastle/Gateshead, Hackney /Islington and Lambeth, but finance has been limited.
(2) *Urban development corporations* were created in 1980 for the London and Merseyside docklands and have been extended subsequently to include schemes in all the major conurbations. These have adopted a commercial orientation and aim to work closely with the private sector.
(3) *Enterprise zones* were also established in 1980 in derelict inner city sites throughout the country, offering a relaxed planning regime and financial incentives designed to attract new employment. In the peripheral regions, like the GEAR Scheme, they appear to have mainly redistributed development rather than attracted significant new investment, while, in the absence of investment in manufacturing, retail development has usually been encouraged.

These measures have been supplemented by the redevelopment of relatively restricted sites which are sufficiently advantageously located to attract private investment for residential, leisure or commercial users. Usually, such schemes are orientated towards a niche in the local market rather than reflecting regional economic regeneration. The transformation of part of the former Swansea docklands into the residential Marina Quarter and the redevelopment of Salford Quays are typical examples.

Despite this array of activity and the associated environmental improvement of some inner city locations, the adverse economic and social consequences of de-industrialisation in the cities of the north and west have not been substantially redressed by these essentially urban initiatives. In the absence of a comprehensive public sector intervention to redistribute the economic growth impulses to the downward transitional regions it seems unlikely that the existing policy instruments can have more than a local 'cosmetic' effect on the inner city problem.

Planning policies for national urban systems

The implication of the previous sections is that if regional inequalities are to be reduced, strong government intervention is necessary. Such policies are increasingly evident and are usually implemented through the urban system. However, regional decentralisation policies vary enormously among countries and a considerable literature relating to this subject now exists. The major themes emerging from this work will be introduced here to provide additional insights into the nature of national urban systems and the ways in which they are subject to change. A four-fold classification suggested by Berry (1978) provides a useful framework within which to identify some of the current trends in urbanisation and the kinds of policy-responses which are emerging. Berry's four types of society are:

(1) Free-enterprise, decentralised, market-directed societies
(2) Welfare states of western Europe
(3) Socialist states
(4) Third World states.

Free-enterprise, decentralised, market directed societies

In societies in this group, of which the United States, Canada and Australia are considered prime examples, decisions relating to the location of economic activity are made by individuals or small groups and are regulated in the market place through the free interplay of the forces of supply and demand. This creates a tradition of free-enterprise, with government intervention restricted to the maintenance of the market institution and the alleviation of crises. Such a system encourages the centralisation of economic activity in the initially advantageous locations at the expense of others, a situation which has been exacerbated by the growth of corporate and oligarchic decision-making organisations in the twentieth century. Although a limited amount of government intervention has appeared in such societies, the forces of centralisation continue to dominate the location of economic activity and urban growth. Such regional decentralisation policies as exist tend to be piecemeal and crisis-orientated, so that redistribution of a sufficient magnitude to solve the problems of regional inequalities does not result. Major regional shifts in urbanisation tend to reflect the emergence of new localisation factors such as 'counter-urbanisation' or the development of the 'Sunbelt' of the USA.

Welfare states

In Western Europe more radical attempts have been made by governments to modify the spatial form of economic development. This has usually involved a variety of fiscal, legal and urban policies designed to reduce area inequalities in levels of living by stimulating growth in peripheral regions and curtailing development at the centre. In most cases these measures have been combined with policies designed to maintain at a minimum the diseconomies of overcongestion and urban environmental deterioration in the principal centres of economic activity.

The general principles upon which economic decentralisation policies have been based are contained in the early work of Friedmann. The principle of 'comparative advantage' suggests that development should be concentrated in those locations and on those resources which are most likely to attract new development rather than be dispersed in order to alleviate local pockets of economic depression. In the short term the latter policy appeals to governments on social grounds, but it should not be the central objective since in the long term it is unlikely that such locations will develop strong economies and prove sufficiently attractive to promote self-sustaining growth. A sequel is that investment should aim at the improvement of the basic infrastructure of the areas designed for development. Particular attention should be paid to the improvement of transport and communications, the housing stock, educational, cultural and recreational facilities. Additions to the urban system could take the form of new towns or satellite communities in particularly attractive locations. Friedmann stresses the importance of the quality of the socio-political leadership in the peripheral regions. If such leadership is lacking as a result of a prolonged period of selective out-migration, then it should be provided through government agencies or attracted by financial incentives. Clearly, this might involve the decentralisation of government decision-making powers to some new forms of political or administrative institutions. Finally, if the rural economy of the peripheral region is also in a state of decline, this should be regenerated.

Principles of this kind have been translated into practice in a variety of ways. In *Britain*, for example, policy has had a distinctly economic rather than urban orientation and has focused on the two issues of inducement and control. Industrial development subsidies in the form of building grants and tax allowances to reduce new construction costs, loans and grants for the acquisition of industrial sites, the construction of advance factories by the government, and the payment of regional employment premiums to private firms have all been used to encourage industrialists to locate in the relatively depressed northern and western regions of the country. These policies were initiated with the Special Areas Act of 1934 and have been varied in relative importance in a complex but well-documented manner in the subsequent period. However, since the advent of the Conservative Government in 1979 the traditional policies have been progressively 'dismantled' in favour of a more definitive market-orientated approach which in a period of recession has done little to redress the regional disparities. In fact, it might be argued that Britain now approximates more to a free-enterprise situation than to the Welfare State model of regional development.

By contrast, *French* regional planning has forged much stronger links between national economic policies and the urban hierarchy. The principal problem has been to redress the regional imbalances associated with the domination by Paris of French political, economic and social life. In fact, in the early

1960s the population of Paris was 8.5 million, comprising nearly 20 per cent of the total while the next tier of Marseille and Lyon was 750,000 and the remaining major cities less than 200,000. Nevertheless, prior to 1945 there was little support for decentralisation since Paris was regarded as the centre of 'high culture' in contrast to the backwardness and parochialism of the provincial regions. However, increasing dissatisfaction with this pattern of development in the postwar period, epitomised in Gravier's (1947) work *Paris et le Désert Français*, has resulted in a number of innovations in regional planning policy. These sought to alleviate existing and potential problems of urban congestion in Paris and to promote overall economic development by making more effective use of peripheral resources – aims which are conceptually similar to those in Britain.

Initially, detailed strategies also paralleled those of Britain. Throughout the 1950s and early 1960s attempts were made to control the location of manufacturing and office employment, combined with incentives to stimulate

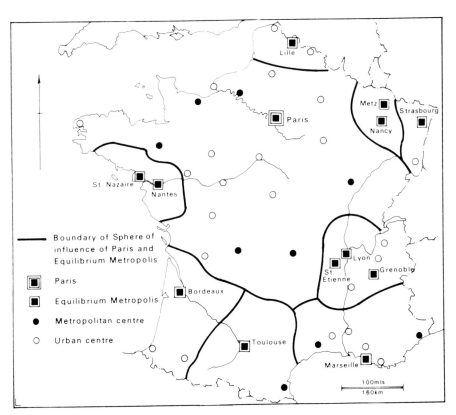

Figure 4.7 Equilibrium metropoles and metropolitan centres in France. The planning hierarchy emphasises the supremacy of Paris and the more localised regional importance of other equilibrium metropoles (After Rodwin, 1970. Reproduced by permission of Houghton Mifflin & Co.)

decentralisation. These were largely ineffective, partly because national political and economic reconstruction were more important issues at the time, and partly because the mechanisms of control were considered insufficiently strong to solve the problems at hand.

Consequently, a fundamental change of policy was introduced in the Fifth Economic Plan for 1966–69. This made the concept of the *growth centre* the basis of regional decentralisation policy. This strategy was most strongly advocated by Boudeville (1966) who adapted the theoretical economic notion of the *growth pole* to the more empirical geographical concept of the growth centre. The growth centre strategy was based on the assumption that to stimulate growth in a peripheral region potentially propulsive investment should be directed to specific, more advantageous urban concentrations. It was anticipated that subsequently economic and social development would spread to adjacent areas and produce a more equitable distribution of development among regions on a national scale.

This ideal was translated into the strategy of the *metropoles d'équilibre*. Eight existing urban concentrations were designed as growth centres and it was considered that each of these could achieve a minimum population of 1 million (Figure 4.7). They already possessed a basic urban infrastructure capable of assisting further development, yet were located sufficiently distant from Paris to enable regional decentralisation. The aim was to develop a central place structure for France which would maximise intra-regional interdependency within the eight growth regions and also promote the inter-regional interdependency of Paris and its peripheral metropolitan regions (Hall, 1984). Clearly, the policy incorporates a stronger link between national and regional economic policy and the urban hierarchy than the British case.

The French policy has achieved a reasonable measure of success. Significant growth has taken place in the *metropoles d'équilibre* and the dominance of Paris has been contained. In fact, Cheshire and Hay (1989) note that Bordeaux, Nice, Toulouse, Montpellier, Rennes, Strasbourg and Lyon are amongst the most rapidly improving 'functional urban regions' in the European Community. The adverse impact of de-industrialisation, however, continues to be exhibited in the older industrial concentrations centred in Lille and St Etienne. At the same time Paris continues to grow and to attract investment, and a population of 12 million is anticipated by the year 2000 (Hall, 1984).

A closely parallel policy was initiated in Japan in 1980 with the aim of dispersing new high-technology industries to science-orientated growth centres, termed *technopolises* (Fujita, 1988). Nineteen sites were designated, ideally with a base population of around 200,000, to act as counter-magnets to development, particularly in the Tokyo-Osaka axis. To date the policy has achieved a reasonable measure of success, although progressive urban concentration continues to characterise the Tokyo metropolitan region, and Glasmeier suggests that the success of the programme would be enhanced if it was extended to incorporate existing industry as well as high-technology.

A final observation on the policies of the welfare states is worthy of note. A recurring theme is the dilemma in these countries between two apparently conflicting aims. On the one hand there is a desire to redress regional imbalances by promoting the periphery and controlling the largest metropolitan concentrations. On the other, governments are drawn towards a *laissez-faire* attitude on the assumption that this will maintain the steady growth of the whole economy. The latter proposition is particularly attractive during times of economic recession. Generally, governments tend to strike a balance and rarely follow decentralisation policies to their limits. Physical planning to improve environmental quality and innovations to improve efficiency are frequently incorporated into policies principally designed to contain the growth of metropolitan concentrations. Usually this has the effect of enhancing the attractions of such areas with the result that regional imbalances tend to persist despite official commitment to the contrary.

Socialist states

The control of economic development has been taken a stage further in the socialist states with a fundamental commitment to greater uniformity in the pattern of economic development and urban concentration. This aim, which can be traced back to the ideals of Marx and Engels (Berry, 1978), is epitomised in the concept of a 'unified settlement system' which determines the growth of the urban system in the USSR:

> The essence of the concept is that in the longterm, through the regional distribution of the forces of production of separate regions, the historically formed settlement pattern (both its concentrated and dispersed forms) will be transformed into integrated regional systems of settlement units which are socially and economically interlinked; their size will depend on local conditions. These units will together form the unified (economic) system of settlement. (Khodzhaev and Khorev, 1973)

Complete uniformity is not the aim but there is a far stronger commitment to spread the forces of urbanisation over wider areas so that the distinctions between town and country will be blurred. Similarly, there is a firm intention to preclude the development of a significant dependence relationship between centre and periphery at a regional or national scale. Central political control of the economic system provides a stronger mechanism to achieve these aims with their outcomes of comparable work conditions and lifestyles for all parts of the national system.

As a result, the relative importance of the largest cities of the USSR has declined significantly. In 1926, for example, the seven cities with populations of greater than 1 million - Moscow, Leningrad, Kiev, Tashkent, Baku, Kharkov, and Gorki - contained 60 per cent of the population of large towns, but this had declined to just over 23 per cent by 1970. Also, the network of large towns has been extended in the postwar period by the stimulation of industrial development in provincial centres (Khodzhaev and Khorev, 1973). In fact, there are now 273 cities with populations of greater than 100,000 and 51 of these have been designated as major regional centres designed to spread the effects of urbanisation and industrial development throughout the country. Although the largest centres are still growing at disproportionate rates, this is seen as a short-term problem which will gradually diminish.

Third World states

Regional equalisation policies in the Third World are generally the least well developed and most variable of the four groups, and this reflects the early stages of economic and political development of these countries. Many of their economies remain dependent upon the exploitation of natural resources or the agricultural sector, while those with longer or closer contacts with the developed world might have attracted labour-intensive manufacturing due to the availability of cheap labour. In either event there tends to be a substantial dependence upon foreign export markets which in turn usually promotes a significant degree of urban primacy in and around the capital city or principal port. Third World governments find such concentrations difficult to control since there is usually only a small public sector over which they have direct influence; promotion of development is the priority rather than its spatial distribution. Problems of physical fragmentation associated with physiographical barriers also occur frequently and these are often compounded by ethnic diversity or a growing distinction between modern urban society and traditional rural culture. The political integration of the various parts of these societies has rarely been achieved; one-party governments or military dictatorships create an additional element of potential political instability (Berry, 1978). In these circumstances, government policies are concerned more with economic expansion and political integration than with the solution of problems associated with emerging regional disparities. Nevertheless, most Third World countries aim to reduce their degree of urban primacy in order to promote a more widespread national economic development in conjunction with a secure political future. The economic growth of the primate cities is balanced by the counterproductive problems associated with contingent pressures of rural-urban migration and the accentuation of regional disparities incorporating a potentially politically disintegrative dimension. There is, however, no shortage of policies designed to achieve economic development combined with urban and regional decentralisation. A wide range of 'National Urban Development Strategies' has been reviewed by Richardson including variants of the growth centre concept, counter-magnets and development axes; usually associated with administrative reform, fiscal incentives and migration controls. In most instances, however, a strong commitment to the development of small and intermediate urban centres has emerged.

In detail, regional urbanisation policies vary considerably with individual circumstances. Berry (1978) argues that in most instances this results in attempts to replicate the experiences of either the welfare states or of the socialist economies of the USSR and eastern Europe, while at the same time attempting to preserve elements of their distinctive cultures. However, such policies rarely reach a successful conclusion due to a poor appreciation of the functional characteristics of the necessary policies, a lack of administrative ability, or a loss of resolve related to a concern for wider economic and political issues.

This assessment might be considered unduly negative in some cases. Instances occur of the development of far more coherent urbanisation policies designed to minimise spatial imbalances in levels of economic and social development. For example, in Venezuela, American expertise has been used to promote the development of an integrated system of growth centres to extend modernisation to significantly wider parts of the country than might otherwise have been the case. Similarly, in China, which exhibits both the characteristics of a socialist and Third World state, both Berry and Kim note the anti-urban bias of government policy which consistently seeks to channel new industrial investment into relatively small cities in previously remote rural communes. The ultimate aim is to spread the benefits of industrialisation and modernisation uniformly to all areas in order to avoid the potentially destructive, de-humanising and corrupting influences assumed to be associated with the urban concentrations of industrial capitalism. The origins of this policy are clearly related to the rural basis of the Chinese Communist Revolution. In more recent years such policies have promoted a greater dispersal of economic growth and development to interior urban centres and their associated rural hinterlands. This strategy has at least contained the progress of centralisation and diverted the migration of part of the 'surplus' rural population away from the largest cities.

However, recent evidence for 28 Asian countries for the period 1960–80 indicated that urban concentration had not declined substantially. The average percentage of the population living in the capital cities only declined from 33 per cent to 31 per cent. It is, nevertheless, interesting to note that deconcentration tended to be greatest for the socialist states.

Summary

The central theme of the preceding discussion has been the effect of economic changes on the patterns and problems of urban development at a variety of spatial scales. It was particularly apparent that international economic considerations have become increasingly important over the last two decades, to a degree that without an appreciation of economic internationalisation it is not possible to understand the nature of urban change in particular countries, or indeed in particular cities. In this respect the steady tertiarisation of the economies of the Western developed countries and their increasingly competitive relationship with the newly industrialising countries is paramount. Within the Western countries there has been a consequent heightening of the importance of centre-periphery economic, social and political distributions, particularly in the context of centralised and increasingly free-market situations as exemplified by the UK. Tendencies towards a more even spread of economic development are, however, evident in the larger countries capable of supporting more than one focus of economic growth, while there is evidence to support the contention that devolved political systems with strong regional or provincial authorities and administrations tend in the same direction. Bannon, for example, contrasts the situations in the centralised systems of the UK and Ireland with the more diffuse patterns of economic growth exhibited in the USA and West Germany. In fact, the majority of commentators on the strikingly uneven pattern of development in the UK consider that the related problems of regional imbalance and inner city decline are unlikely to be substantially redressed in the absence of strong government intervention aimed at instigating a regional equalisation of economic growth. The immediate prospects of this are, however, slight since the current Conservative Government has no great enthusiasm for a regional economic policy. On the contrary, the last decade has witnessed a steady reduction in aid to the depressed regions and a partial 'dismantling' of the organisational apparatus of regional planning.

CHAPTER 5

Theories of the City

A second set of theories is concerned with the internal structure of urban places, with city as area. This dichotomy of cities in space and city as place is well established in all texts that claim to be comprehensive urban geographies. Within this set of theories, or perspectives, which may be a better term, there are well defined approaches; some are 'indigenous' to geography, others are derived from elsewhere in the social sciences. Urban morphology, perhaps the only truly indigenous line of evolution within urban geography, has its origins in site-situation studies and developed as an analysis of the built fabric of the city and the way in which it had evolved over time. It is the best example of continuity within urban geography.

Urban morphology

More traditional studies of the sites and situations or urban settlements were also typically concerned with the historical growth phases and ways in which these could be related to urban form and morphology. Regular street lines of early Roman settlement, for example, could sometimes be discerned as nuclei to which less well-ordered medieval quarters were subsequently added. During the late 1940s and 1950s some British geographers moulded this type of perspective into what can be termed the urban morphological approach. Their first task during this period was to introduce a more specifically geographical methodology into a type of study which had been dominated by essentially historical approaches. In *The Geography of Towns* (1955), Smailes developed the concept of 'townscape' which in its simplest terms is the urban equivalent of landscape and comprises those visible forms of environment which may be recorded and classified. The three main components of townscape are street-plan or layout, architectural style of buildings and their design, and land-use; of these, plan and land-use have been the most generally studied by geographers, and the relationship between town plan and building design on the one hand and land-use on the other – the form-function relationship – has produced useful research. Many cities display considerable internal variety of building-types, often dating from specific historical periods, and it is this diversity of townscapes within individual cities which formed the focus of most morphological analyses. There are cities, however, which, because their urban development was contained within or dominated by a particular time-period, have an overall plan or grand design. The planned towns of early medieval Europe, the *bastides* with their regular grid form, offer one example of these, the more ornate and aesthetically designed Baroque towns of the later Renaissance period form another. There are more recent examples of uniform city plans affecting wide areas. Stanislawski traces the origin and spread of the grid-iron town in the United States with its regular rectangular form and right-angled intersections. Modern 'new towns' in various part of the world are not unified by a single design but are all products of preconceived blueprints which specify the locations in space of various land-uses and the design forms which they assume. All these examples of an overall plan involve a high level of central control and an 'authority' able to specify design characteristics to a high level of detail. Planning of this kind has often affected quarters within cities, such as the colonial districts of some Indian cities and the Baroque areas of larger European capitals. In other instances, uniform historical imprints upon townscape emerge less from the imposition of some overall plan than from less organised common practices and shared values of like individuals. The Georgian squares of London and Dublin and their equivalents elsewhere are of this type of genesis.

During the most active period of urban morphology, much of the emphasis was upon the classification of sub-regions within individual cities and the relating of urban growth phases to these. Most of the townscape studies took this form and Carter provided a large number of case studies as part of his more general survey of Welsh towns. Smailes was particularly interested in identifying broad classes of morphological divisions which could have more general application to British cities, and did in fact suggest a model. His categories of morphology, however, such as 'terrace-ribbing' and 'villa-studding' were broad and imprecise and had no more than a general descriptive value. Conzen developed the technique of town-plan analysis which involved a much higher order of detail and greater focus upon the need to relate form to process and to seek generalisations.

Conzen argued that of the three components of townscape – plan, architectural style, and land use – the former is the most resistant to change whereas the latter is the most dynamic. Discord between form and function will occur as changing land-uses produce the need for functions to adapt to built-forms which were originally designed for different purposes. In the original case study of Alnwick, a central thrust of town-plan analysis was that of matching plan-elements, with their associated architectural features, to specific time-periods or urban growth. Town plan analysis included concepts which were explicitly process rather than pattern-oriented and which provided bases for generalisation. The burgage cycle concept had reference to a specific form of land-holding system and traced the development of a parcel of land through institutive, repletive, climax and recessive stages. Each stage described the extent to which urban building occupance affected the parcel of land. The fixation line concept recognises the limits to the urban built-up area which can be identified during a still-stand period in the urban growth process. Fringe-belts are zones of land, beyond fixation lines, which become locations for those urban functions which require large amounts of space and peripherality rather than centrality. Typical fringe-belt functions in the modern city are cemeteries, golf-courses and public utilities, but each historical growth-phase tends to be marked by its own fringe-belt with a typical cluster of functional uses. As urban growth proceeds, following a period of still-stand, former fringe-belts are engulfed within the larger city and remain as recognisable, though fossilised, components of urban land-use. Conzen's work undoubtedly added an extra dimension to urban morphological analysis by the early 1960s which was characterised both by its depth of detail and its search for recurrent phenomena. Along with the rest of urban morphology, town-plan analysis became subject to severe criticism and disregard by the 'new' geographers of the 1960s who were more interested in functional classifications and the economic bases of urban systems. In the best-known critique of this time, Garrison characterised urban morphology as mainly descriptive, lacking in good measurement techniques and failing to develop a general theory. It was a critique which contemporaneously at least did not produce convincing counter-arguments

Since the early 1960s there has been continued interest in urban morphology along a limited number of fronts. The more significant developments have been those which reduce the 'isolation' of the urban morphological approach and seek to integrate its concepts with other dimensions of the urban system. White-hand (1967) has continued to develop some of Conzen's ideas and focuses on the nature of urban fringe-belts. He has investigated the competition for fringe-belt sites and the way in which the outcomes of this competition have to be seen in the context of building cycles and the activities of house-builders. Institutional land-uses are likely to be most successful in obtaining sites during times of housing slump, and a cycle of booms and slumps in house-building will be reflected by zones of varying admixtures of residential and institutional land-use. Davies has developed analysis of the form-function relationship in which he shows that morphological adaptations can be used as indicators of functional changes in commercial streets. Watson's study of Halifax, Nova Scotia provides a clearly argued example of the influence of relict morphologies and their associated land-uses, upon the subsequent development of an urban area.

House-type studies in the older morphological tradition were often guilty of adopting gross classifications and paying too little regard to architectural detail. Some later studies moved some way towards correcting these deficiencies. Forster (1968) used thirteen measures of house-style, including information of building material, roof material, windows and entrance styles to characterise house-types constructed in Hull between 1854 and 1914. The cul-de-sac court was identified as a dominant and recurrent type of architecture in the city during this period. This approach has been little developed and has value in identifying key features of buildings or house-types which are indicative of a particular region or time-period.

Whitehand (1987) has been the most consistent proponent of urban morphological research in what might be termed the Conzenian tradition. Whitehand identifies central Europe, Britain and the United States as the source areas for research and also acknowledges the debt to urban historians. This research revolves around themes such as fringe belts, building cycles, urban rent theory, city centre change and historico-geographic theories of urban form. Whitehand seeks to move forward the theoretical base upon which urban morphology rests and his directions are usefully summarised in the phrase:

> Urban landscape is a cumulative, albeit incomplete record of a succession of booms, slumps and innovative adaptations within a particular locale. (Whitehand, 1987)

The theory focuses on building cycles, economic fluctuations waves of innovations and land values and the relationships which these hold with urban use and form. Whitehand comes to a number of useful conclusions:

(1) Different elements of the urban landscape change at different speeds.
(2) There are persistent elements in urban landscape, notably main street lines.
(3) Whereas survival of morphological elements is the most obvious legacy, imprints and influences can remain long after the physical form has gone.
(4) Development of urban landscapes is uneven: both the extent of change and the form it takes are subject to cycles.

Most recent research on morphology focuses on *agents* of change and finds, for example, that external agents, architects or developers, are more likely to introduce innovative change to a locality. Once a new style is established, local agents are often quick to adopt, adapt and diffuse it. Residential change is typically augmentative, creates new space by subdividing plots, commercial development is adaptive as it it more constrained by existing morphology.

Urban morphology has had an important role in the development of urban geography, especially in Britain, and provided an impetus for the identification of a separate branch of geography during the immediate postwar period. Morphological research usefully continues and there is a more general awareness, expressed through concepts such as the fabric effect, of need to consider the involvement of morphology in more general urban processes. Criticism of urban morphology during the early 1960s in part explain its partial demise but more telling may have been the fact that urban geographers found more interesting themes to attract their research activities. Urban morphology, an indigenous geographical perspective, focused on the observable and the inanimate. Other derivative perspectives demonstrated that this was merely the framework and that the people who occupied urban space provided it with its dynamism.

Derivative sources: land economics

Ideas from land economics strongly influenced urban geographers during the

1960s, though there were often considerable time-lags between the original exposition of these ideas and their general adoption in urban geographical study. Among the more influential sets of ideas were early theories on city location, such as those of Cooley in 1894 and Weber in 1899, who attached central importance for urban development to the nature of routeways and nodal points in the transportation system. Again, the work on urban land-values, rents and costs within cities focused on accessibility and became very influential. Haig saw rent as a charge for accessibility or a saving in transport costs which involved a bidding process to determine the occupancy and use of land. Ratcliff (1949) developed the argument, and the eventual model involved the concept of bid-rent curves and their influence upon land-use patterns within the city. Under model conditions, the assumption is that the central point within the city has greatest accessibility and that from this location centrality-value will decrease in a regular manner towards the urban peripheries. An efficient land-use pattern emerges within the city as various activities compete for locations by 'bidding' at various rent levels; their bids are calculated by weighing their need for centrality against their ability to pay higher rents and the fact that increased transport costs may be incurred with distance removed from the central city.

> The use that can extract the greatest return from a given site will be the successful bidder . . . from this emerges an orderly pattern of land-use spatially organised to perform most efficiently the economic functions that characterise urban life. (Ratcliff, 1949)

Figure 5.1 illustrates the bid-rent model and the way in which it can be translated into broad concentric bands of land-use within the city. Those retailing functions which have the greatest need for accessibility in order to maximise profits pay the highest rents for the most central locations. Land in such locations is normally intensively used and involves vertical building development. Outside the retailing zone is a broader industrial/commercial zone containing functions which need centrality but cannot match the higher levels of rents and are content to settle for lower accessibility in slightly less central locations. Many activities in this zone, such as warehouses and offices, may in fact need less public accessibility and for them an optimum location has been achieved. Residential land-use occupies a large amount of urban space and involves a number of trade-offs between land-costs, transport-costs and density. Closer to the centre, higher valued land will be occupied at high densities by groups who incur low transport costs. On the urban periphery where land is cheaper, large amounts of space may be involved per dwelling, giving lower densities, but high transport costs will be incurred. This type of trade-off model does make a number of assumptions which depart from reality, and recent empirical research has modified its interpretation in significant ways. Knos showed that the actual land-value surface of a city is more variegated than the model suggests with lesser peaks outside the central city. The model is necessarily simplistic but can be modified to increase its relevance to the complex modern city and has continuing value to urban geographical studies.

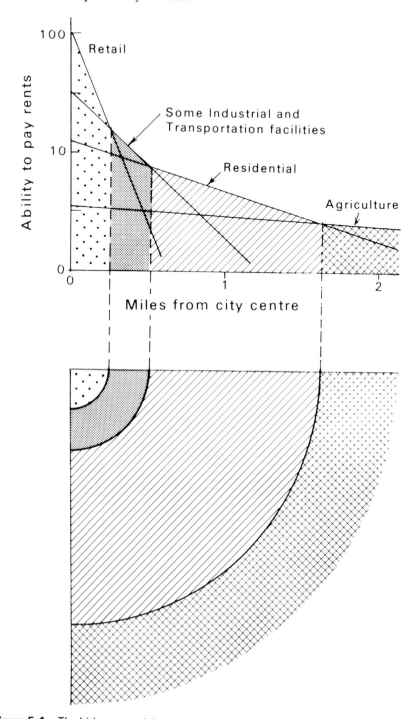

Figure 5.1   The bid-rent model and urban land-use zones

Derivative sources: urban ecology

The Chicago school of social ecology, most closely associated with Robert Park, provided a second derivative source of concepts and ideas for urban geography. The book by Park, Burgess and McKenzie (1925) collected some of the early work of the Chicago ecologists and had a profound and lasting influence on contemporary social sciences, though again the full impact upon urban geography was delayed significantly.

A great quality of Park and his contemporary ecologists was their first-hand knowledge about the city of Chicago. This intimate knowledge of the city and its people, based upon intensive field-work and involvement, was reflected in their many papers on the subject. Park has been described as an undisciplined empiricist, excited by the patterns and apparent explanations which he saw in city life, but his adoption of a general framework within which to study his patterns led him into a methodology which was committed to theory-building. This framework Park derived from an analogy with the biological world, and the belief that the patterns and relationships evident there could be paralleled by land-use and people within cities. This enthusiasm for a biological analogy can only really be understood in the context of the early part of this century when the appeal of Social Darwinism in particular, and the guidelines of classical economics, prompted lines of thought which found expression in many disciplines. A major attraction of the biological analogy was its totality: if offered a *gestalt* model which was simple and logical, the similarities to the biological world could everywhere be observed, measured and recorded, and each segment could be seen in its relevant place within the overall broad framework and explained by the same guiding principles.

Beyond the overall framework, biology also provided a source of other concepts and a terminology for the urban ecologists. *Symbiosis* described the most basic set of relationships and the mutual interdependence of the elements of the city. Park showed how symbiosis operated in the biological world, his best-known example being that of the humble bee and its place in the 'web of life'. McKenzie sought direct analogies within the city: 'In the struggle for existence in human groups, social organisation accommodates itself to the spatial and sustenance relationships existing among the occupants of any geographical area'. Closely allied to symbiosis was the concept of *competition*, translated into economic terms, whereby space would be allocated among alternative uses on a competitive basis. The essence of this kind of competition was that it operated at an impersonal level in a way reminiscent of the biological world. The concept of *community* borrowed directly from biology, was applied to the city as a population group inhabiting a distinguishable geographical space and coexisting through a set of symbiotic relationships. Such a population group within the city was territorially organised and interdependent in the 'natural order' of the community. Within such a community, further symbiotic relationships and ecological processes could be identified. The *dominance* of one particular group within a community could be ascribed to its superior competitive power. *Segregation* of distinctive groups would occur within communities: 'Every area of segregation is the result of the operation of a combination of the forces of selection'. Other crucial ecological processes were those of *invasion* and *succession* which described the gradual incursion of one group into the territory of another and the eventual displacement as succession took place. Invasion and succession could be viewed as elements of a cycle which proceeded through a number of stages with, ideally, a complete change in land-use or in population type between first and last stages.

The analogy provided the framework and most of its conceptual ingredients, but there is ample evidence in the literature or urban ecology that differences between biological and human society were appreciated. It was never denied that human society had an extra dimension of cultural and traditional values not apparent in the biological world. Robert Park suggested that social organis-ation could be studied at two levels, the *biotic* in which competition was the guiding process, and the *cultural* in which consensus and communication among members of society were the main factors. Park's notion here was that the biotic level could be studied separately as an analysis of aggregate behaviour and structure, ignoring the myriad of cultural or non-rational values which might be measureable on an individual basis. Despite this acknowledgement of non-biotic factors, however, the paucity of their treatment was to prove one of the major points of criticism of urban ecology. It is clear that Park, Burgess and the others consistently understated and often omitted to include the distinct-ively human qualities of the city in their conceptual framework which was essentially mechanistic and generalised.

The critics of urban ecology seized on this neglect of human and cultural factors as a basic deficiency and questioned the validity of using analogies. Perhaps the best-known example of this line of criticism is the work of Walter Firey (1947) in his study *Land Use in Central Boston*. Firey found ecological laws were not satisfactory explanations of the patterns which he observed. Cultural factors, which he described variously as non-rational values, sentiment and symbolism, were the dominant influences in some parts of the city: thus the motivations of the families who acted to preserve Beacon Hill, an old and prestigious residential district, against the encroachment of commercial functions and lower-status groups, were not economic. Others have found similar evidence, for example, Emrys Jones's study of the social geography of Belfast. Milla Alihan rejected the biological analogy on the same grounds but had wider-ranging criticism of the urban ecologists. She suggested that the Chicago monographs, although of lasting value as studies of urban-social structure, had not followed ecological rules, and used terminology incon-sistently thus affecting the interpretation of key concepts such as community and society. This obsession with words was later to evoke cynical rejoinders: 'Human ecology has already inspired a generation of critics too easily irritated by figures of speech'; but contemporaneously the defences were few. McKenzie died in 1940 and Park acquired a reputation as an undisciplined empiricist. Louis Wirth, always a less committed ecologist, attempted to redefine a position for urban ecology as a perspective which focused attention upon localised or territorially defined social structures and phenomena. With this focus, he suggested, community has a central position in the conceptual framework but the term is inevitably ambiguous because all communities are also societies and all societies bear some characteristics of communities. Ecology provides a perspective but behaviour in the human world can only be understood in the light of habit, custom, institutions, morals, ethics and laws. Wirth's statement was a careful reappraisal of ecology in which the biological analogy had no necessary part.

Recent assessments of human ecology have helped to place it in perspective. Saunders (1981) sees basic tensions in Park's work arising from:

● use of the term 'community' to refer to both a physical entity and to a process;

● use of 'community' to imply biotic forces involved in human competition for space, and 'society' as an expression of consensus in which cultural values prevail.

Saunders classified some of the criticisms of human ecology as misguided:

(1) Firey's argument on the invalidity of ecological laws was misguided because he and Park asked different questions. Firey was interested why Beacon Hill survived, Park in why the rich lived there in the first place.

(2) Alihan argued that the Chicago monographs failed to distinguish between biotic and cultural forces but they never intended to. Biotic factors had created natural areas by ecological theory, the monographs sought to examine them as cultural forms.

(3) Robinson's ecological fallacy argument, individual versus aggregate values, was invalid, as Park always emphasised the irreducibility of community as area.

Finally, Hawley and Duncan resurrected human ecology only by jettisoning its specific relevance to the city and placing it as a subset within functionalism.

Urban geographers did not take a serious interest in the urban ecology approach until the 1960s, by which time its misconceptions were well understood. At this time it held several attractions. Firstly, although the biological analogy basis of its approach had been largely discredited, there were still reviewers such as Reissman (1964) prepared to describe ecology as the closest we have come to a systematic theory of the city. Secondly, urban ecology had a strong empirical and field-work content which had direct appeal to geographical method. It had a clear interest in land-use and space and the monographs could be viewed as rich, ethnographic studies of urban communities. Park was not consistent in his use of the term 'community' but he did regard it as:

> A visible object. One can point it out, define its territorial limits and plot its constituent elements, its population and its institutions on maps. (Park *et al.*, 1925)

Many of the concepts of human ecology such as invasion, succession and segregation had empirical reality and could be examined as processes within the city without resort to biotic forces. Thirdly, there were important land-use models and territorial concepts which had developed as part of the work of urban ecologists and these had very direct appeal.

Of the so-called 'classical' models of urban land-use, that proposed by Burgess, Park's principal collaborator, is undoubtedly the best known. The concentric-zonal model (Figure 5.2(a)) offers a descriptive framework in which to view both the spatial organisation of land use in the city and its change over time. Burgess was aware of the work on urban land values and bid-rents and his model was partly founded upon the kind of economic base which this proposed. Differences in land values were regarded as the mechanisms by which different functional groups were distributed in space in an orderly, efficient yet un-planned way.

The model made a number of assumptions which included a uniform land

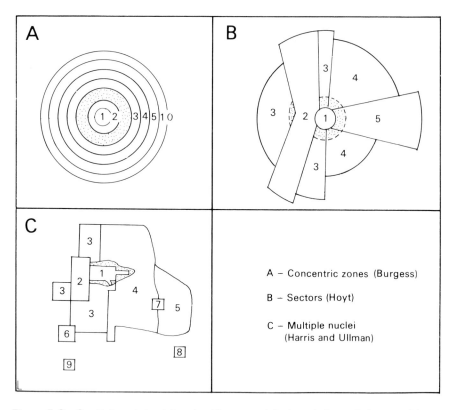

Figure 5.2   Spatial models of the city. These models, largely intended to provide descriptive generalisations of residential structure, are often described as the classical models. 1. CBD; 2. wholesale, light industry; 3. low status residential; 4. medium-status residential; 5. high-status residential; 6. heavy industry; 7. outlying business; 8. residential, suburb; 9. industrial suburb; 10. commuters' zone. Dot-shading marks the zone-in-transition

surface, universal accessibility to a single centred city and free competition for space. These assumptions were a mixture of those usually made for a pure model, such as an isotropic surface, and those typical of contemporary American society. In line with the latter, for example, assumptions included a heterogeneous population, a mixed industrial-commercial base, cheap transit and a capitalist system. Under conditions of this kind, Burgess suggested that the zonal arrangement of land-uses from centre to periphery would be:

(1) Central business district;
(2) Transition zone;
(3) Zone of workingmen's homes;
(4) Zone of better residences;
(5) Commuters' zone.

Whilst clearly acknowledging that this model would not hold for each and every city, Burgess nevertheless thought that it might have some generality within North America, and its outlines could be recognised in Chicago and some other cities in the United States. The Burgess model was a description of urban structure but was also intended to serve as a mechanistic framework for urban growth and change. The main ecological processes involved in the dynamic aspects of the model were those of invasion and succession by which population groups gradually filtered outwards from the centre as their status and level of assimilation improved. The constant process of change was most pronounced in the transition zone where an expanding CBD forced land-use change and increased land values. As inhabitants abandoned the inner city, migrants replaced them giving high rates of population turnover. This mobility was seen as the main cause of social disorganisation in the transition zone and the social problems which typified this area. Social disorganisation, defined as decrease of influence of existing social rules of behaviour upon individuals, was used frequently in Chicago ecology.

Later empirical tests of the zonal model offered a variety of criticisms. Some of these questioned the generality of the model, but as already suggested it was based upon existing conditions in interwar United States and was never intended to have universality. Empirically, researchers have argued that gradients are more easily demonstrated than zones and that related concepts such as 'natural areas' tend to emphasise the heterogeneity that can exist within zones. Much of the criticism arises from expectations of the zonal model which were never part of its original formulation. It is a *model* and its persistence can in many ways be attributed to its simplicity and breadth of generalisation. The real world is more complicated and the search for concentric zones in many empirical studies was one of the less enlightened practices of the 1960s.

The sector model of urban land use formulated by Hoyt (Figure 5.2(b)) is normally regarded as the second of the classic models of urban spatial form. The Hoyt formulation was constrained by its narrow focus on housing and rent. He obtained rental and other data which he mapped by blocks for 142 American cities and from this empirical research suggested his sector model. The model took the form of a central business district with a series of sectors emanating from it. The high-grade residential areas pre-empted the most desirable space and were powerful forces in the pattern of urban growth. Other grades of residential area were aligned around the high-grade areas, with the lowest-grade areas occupying the least desirable land, often adjacent to manufacturing districts. The various residential areas took the spatial form of sectors, extending from the central city towards the periphery, and were thus in apparent contrast with the concentric zones suggested by Burgess. The common elements were the focal nature of the central business district and the presence of a transition-zone which was clearly identifiable in American cities. The sector model was also a growth framework and Hoyt's formulations on neighbourhood change were mainly aimed at describing the dynamic characteristics of the high-grade residential areas which he regarded as key elements. The high-grade areas would move, he suggested, towards amenity land, along transport routes, and towards the homes of leaders of the community; production of new housing on the urban periphery could therefore act as a catalyst for change.

The third classic model was that by Harris and Ullman (1945) which they termed the multiple nuclei model (Figure 5.2(c)). Its main distinctive quality was its abandonment of the central business district as a sole focal point, replacing it by a number of discrete nuclei around which individual land-uses were geared. As the conditions for the location of these nuclei may vary, there was no one generalised spatial form which could be suggested.

The merits of the spatial models of the city, in particular concentric zones and sectors, have been extensively discussed but some summary points can be made.

(1) Whereas these models are often labelled as land-use models, and do in fact refer to commercial and industrial activities, they are essentially concerned with residential structure and change.

(2) Burgess used the ecological processes of invasion and succession in his explanation, describing these as processes of distribution which sift and sort and relocate individuals and groups by residence and occupation.

(3) Hoyt focused on a 'filtering' process whereby housing stock was passed down the income hierarchy as the wealthy moved to new homes.

(4) Burgess explained residential change on the 'demand-side' as new arrivals competed for space in the inner city and caused ripples to spread outwards: Hoyt saw stimulus on the 'supply-side' as new housing on the periphery prompted filtering downwards of older housing (Badcock, 1984).

(5) Hoyt had less reliance on accessibility to a centre and introduced the *preferences* of social groups for locations and contiguities; Burgess had more mechanistic assumptions and was closer to the rationale of the bid-rent model.

(6) Empirical research has tended to support Hoyt rather than Burgess: though the 'model' status is not best assessed by a search for spatial forms. Davie was critical of Burgess from his New Haven Study, Schnore found that not all US cities showed increased residential status towards the edge of the city, Robson talked of the game of 'hunt the Chicago

model', and Saunders (1981) argues tests of the models inevitably led up a cul-de-sac.

(7) Although the models take different spatial forms, they should be assessed for the insights into the processes of residential differentiation.

(8) Spatial forms are however useful summaries of urban structure under certain assumptions of underlying conditions. The different forms of zones and sectors are not necessarily contradictory; they may measure different aspects of urban structure and have a complementarity which subsequent research into social areas (see Chapter 9) has revealed.

(9) As a 'geometry of space', the zonal form has considerable generality and has been used to compare pre-industrial and industrial cities (change over time) as well as modern regional variations (see Figure 5.2).

(10) The spatial models, especially of zones and sectors, continue to have useful roles in the teaching of urban geography as a means of organising study of the city, testing more general theories and introducing the theme of functional differentiation in space.

Subjective approaches and the focus on place

Urban morphology, land economics and human ecology can all, for the most part, be described as examples of positive science. There are qualifications to this statement. Urban morphology, for example, was initially criticised for its exceptionalism and its tendency to focus on the unique qualities of towns and cities though more recent studies have sought to build models and to generalise. Again, though much of human ecology could be classed as positive science it did contain the ethnographic tradition with its central interest in the subjective dimensions of social structures and processes within the city. Ley would place some of the early work of Robert Park himself, who said that the land-use unit becomes a neighbourhood when it is stained by the particular *sentiments* of its population, in a similar category.

Subjective approaches are now contained in the humanism perspective within urban geography. Humanism has many strands but is united by an interest in man's subjective experience:

> Every image and idea about the world is compounded of personal experience, learning, imagination and memory. (Lowenthal, 1961)

Subjective approaches have a long heritage in the literature of human geography, though less so in urban geography. Vidal de la Blache contributed a balanced humanism with all the virtues of subjective interpretation to French regional geography though this was to be submerged in the more formal approaches of Brunhes and Demangeon.

In general terms the 'subjective' approach can initially at least be more clearly stated as a critique rather than as a precise methodology with a cohesive structure. There are signs, particularly with attempts to provide a philosophical underpinning or 'cement' to the diverse contents of the critique, that this situation may change but the attainment of that goal is not yet apparent. As a critique, subjective perspectives have in common a reaction against the mechanistic, aggregative and 'dehumanising' qualities of spatial analysis. As Ley (1977) argues, spatial analysts in their zest to construct models fail to separate fact from value and reduce place and space to abstract geometries in which man is a 'pallid entrepreneurial figure'. Because of its continuous thrust to generalise and to abstract from reality, spatial analysis forms only a superficial view of human behaviour with no real attempt to understand internal motives and the real nature of processes which are at work. Ley (1977) states:

> the emergence of behavioural geography witnessed the explicit commitment to delve beneath the distribution maps and spatial facts to an examination of social and cognitive processes in their everyday context.

As the spatial analysts threatened to transform geography into a geometry of space and to characterise place as an isotropic surface, subjectivists sought to reassert the role of human values in the way in which space is regarded and to study the meanings which underlay a sense of place. Location theory is not to be regarded as a series of equations which weigh cost and distance but as a complex and subtle process of decision-making in which the 'black box' itself – why and how a decision is made – is a central focus for research. Subjectivism has led to a number of important strands of study in urban geography. These will be summarised here and developed in their appropriate context in later chapters.

Firstly, there is a general emphasis or re-emphasis on the subjective meanings of place and space. More particularly in urban geography, writers such as Buttimer and Ley have been sensitive to the needs of making subjective values central to the comprehension of urban environments and sociospatial behaviour. As in Firey's essay on the sentiments and symbolisms attached to a Boston neighbourhood and Emrys Jones's persistent emphasis of the social values attached to place, so Buttimer's emphasis upon the 'anchoring points' in urban space which are 'stamped by human intention, value and memory' retains and reinforces the need to understand the subjective qualities of the urban life-world. Ley has been particularly forceful in advocating the role of the 'social dynamic' with which place is endowed, as exemplified by his study of the Black inner city and of graffiti. For the growing band of humanistic geographers, land-value gradients and morphological unities are of less significance than the sociocultural values with which place and space are invested. Relph expressed this well in his study of Place and Placelessness:

> Places are fusions of human and natural orders and are significant centres for our immediate experiences of the world. They are defined less by unique locations, landscapes and communities than by the focussing of experiences and intentions onto particular settings. (Relph, 1976)

and similarly,

> For most aspects of daily living, individuals do not experience the world as an object but are rather fused to the world through a web of feelings. (Seamon, 1979)

These definitions of place have their problems. If there is no single objective but a plurality of subjective places, where is the common ground? At what point does inter-subjectivity lead to shared meanings? Can place be viewed as a product of common meanings and constructed around a *group* and its concerns?

A second expression of the influence of subjectivism in urban geography can be found in studies of behaviour and decision-making. In this context there are contrasted perspectives to be disentangled. The strand of behaviourism *per se* has strong links with the biological sciences and with work in environmental psychology; it rests substantially upon the notions of stimulus and response developed by psychologists in intensive experimental research, often under laboratory conditions. This type of behaviourist approach is quantifiable, has the goal of generalisation, and belongs squarely in the tradition of positivist science. Applications of behaviouralism in urban geography have borne traces of this type of systematic study and range from Stea's qualified but very explicit use of the behaviourist analogy to other less explicit but still essentially 'scientific' analyses of human behaviour.

If experimental psychology provided an example of the study of behaviour in the tradition of positivist science, another psychologist introduced concepts which led to an emphasis upon the subjective limitations which are imposed upon social activity. H. A. Simon argued that two concepts were needed to qualify the assumption of *economic man*, a 'being' endowed with perfect knowledge – the wish to optimise, and the ability to calculate which course of action would achieve the desired optimum – which had formed the reference point for positive science and, in urban geography, for the models of spatial analysis. The concept of bounded rationality suggests that although man may strive to be rational, he is hampered by an incomplete knowledge and limited ability to calculate. That of 'satisficing' suggests that man may work towards a level of attainment which is satisfactory even though it may well fall far short of optimal. These are generalised concepts but they have led urban geographers into closer studies of individual behaviour and decision-making which are far removed from the abstractions of spatial analysis. 'Satisficer' man is a figure much closer to reality than economic man; behavioural studies maintain some modes of analysis which are in the positivist tradition but have added to these in the ways in which they collect their data, and research in this field has developed towards the subjective position.

Geographers working within the behaviouralist perspective have become progressively less interested in the stimulus-response heritage of scientific behaviourism and more interested in qualitative studies of decision-making at an individual rather than at an aggregate level. Pred was concerned with goals and information levels of decision-makers considering alternative locations; Wolpert introduced concepts such as place utility to the study of migration and pointed to the uncertainty with which men encounter the real world and to the importance of individual goals, levels of knowledge, and personal preferences. Such studies took urban geographers away from depiction of spatial patterns in the city and a mechanistic view of macro-processes to detailed studies of the individual decision-makers and the micro-processes which produced these patterns. This new emphasis with its early assumption of choice in movement had its own *caveats*, but the immediate benefits were the concerns with process and the decreasing dependence on aggregate statistics and models.

A further development within urban geography of the move towards subjectivism was the interest in spatial imagery and cognitive mapping. Boulding's (1956) work on the image was a key reference and his concept became central to much geographical work concerned with behaviour. In its simplest terms, Boulding's concept of image was the picture of the world carried around in the mind of the 'actor' which became the reference point for his behaviour. The form which the image takes is moulded by external conditions of socialisation, experience and context and also by internal factors such as values and prejuduces. For many urban geographers, image formed the link between phenomenal and behavioural environments but there is no consensus on the nature of this link. The two key questions are:

● Does an image underlie human behaviour?
● Can we use known behaviour to understand preferences?

Jackson and Smith (1984) conclude that cognitive images are only hypothetical constructs whose relation to actual behaviour is far from clear. This bears directly on the studies of mental maps and images of the city with which urban geographers have been associated. A variety of techniques to tease out and represent mental maps now exists but doubts are expressed on the significance as well as the accuracy of cognitive mapping. Downs suggested a three-fold typology of cognitive studies in urban geography; structural, which measures awareness of place; evaluative, which recognises the qualities of place; and preference which expresses levels of desirability. This kind of research has used measurement techniques and has sought to generalise but it is still a long way removed from the mechanistic procedures of positive science and has much to offer subjective approaches.

It can still be argued that subjective approaches are deficient in method and coherent theory and are best viewed as a critique of scientific geography. Even by this reckoning they fulfil critical roles in introducing humanistic concerns. Further than this, there is growing clarity and cohesion in a strategy for a geography of a life-world and Ley's (1977) plea for the use of humanism to modify scientific postures.

Ley's objectives are description which recognises the pervasive presence of the subjective as well as the objective in all areas of behaviour, adoption of a philosophical base which embraces both fact and value, recognition of the 'intersubjectivity' of the life-world, and a view of place as an amalgam of fact and value. These objectives are not dismissive of normal science, nor are they an advocacy of the primacy of the individual. They go some way towards meeting the plea for a hermeneutic approach to help specify consensus and clarify the conditions under which understanding can take place. Entrikin

(1977) may be right and humanism is best seen as a form of criticism, but the criticism is considerable and the modifications of a spatial analysis perspective which humanism requires are pervasive and far-reaching. The subjective approach constitutes an additional perspective in urban geography.

Structuralism and the urban question

Structuralism in itself does not present a coherent strategy but rather a diffuse tendency. For the purposes of this limited discussion, the focus is on structualism as a holistic scheme which views patterns and processes as outcomes of structural imperatives, the clues to urban issues lie not in urban environments *per se* but in the encompassing social system of which the city is but one outcome. Urban geographers have contributed to the development and application of structuralist theories, none more so than David Harvey whose ideas have developed from *Social Justice and the City* (1973) to the *Urbanization of Capital* and *Consciousness and the Urban Experience* (1985). It is as well to acknowledge the contributions of sociologists and political scientists to this theory, structuralism has become very much a social science driven set of ideas. The 'urban question' is whether the city can be theorised as a discrete objective and Saunders argued that:

> Weber, Durkheim, Marx and Engels all came to very similar conclusions ... all agreed that the city played an historically specific role in the development of Western capitalism, but they also argued that, once capitalism had become established, the city ceased to be a theoretically significant category of analysis ... The city in other words was not seen as a significant object of study in its own right. (Saunders, 1981)

Even though these giants of the literature appeared to come to a shared conclusion, the 'urban question' was not concluded and the demise of the Chicago school left a vacuum in urban theory which others sought to fill. One significant research direction was concerned with allocation of resources:

> ... the outcome of resource allocation is etched or registered in urban space ... an inquisitiveness about spatial organization must assuredly lead to a questioning of the mechanisms and processes that produce spatial inequalities and uneven urban outcomes. (Badcock, 1984)

Rex and Moore saw the housing market as the point at which social organisation and spatial structure intersected. Urban dwellers aspired to better housing but it is not available for all and this leads to housing as a scarce resource over which there is conflict. This notion of scarce housing and conflict is not specifically urban, but there are important processes within the city which can be identified and studied in their own right. Rex and Moore used Weber's concept of class and class conflict to produce 'housing classes' in conflict over housing as a resource. Weber did use class in the Marxian sense of 'classes' working together, he focused on individual so 'ideal types' were needed to provide collectivities or groups. Rex and Moore (1967) initially postulated five housing classes – outright owner occupiers, council tenants, private tenants, lodging house proprietors and lodging house tenants – but the list was added to over time. Saunders (1981) pointed out that in Weberian terms these were housing status groups not classes as Weber defined *class* as life chances in the market and *status* as endowment with goods. Saunders could visualise three housing *classes*:

- those who live off economic returns from housing (landlords, developers);
- those who use housing purely for consumption (tenants);
- those who consume housing but still enjoy an investment return (owner occupiers).

Pahl has also argued that allocation of resources within the city offers a fruitful avenue for the pursuit of an urban theory. The argument takes the form that whatever kind of society exists, resources will always be scarce and procedures to allocate lie in the hands of specific agents. This 'managerialist' thesis will be developed in relation to housing market studies but it does offer a further application of Weberian concepts to urban analysis.

Marxist theory proved the driving force for a revival of interest in a political economy approach to the study of the city despite the fact that Marx said little explicitly about urban space (see Badcock, 1984). A number of scholars such as Castells (1977) and Harvey have developed theories of the city from a Marxist base. Castells wished to apply a theory of the total system to the urban system and used the term spatial structure or urban system to describe the particular way in which the basic elements of the social structure are spatially articulated (see Saunders, 1981). For Castells the way in which space was organised in the capitalist city was underpinned by the process of collective consumption which enables the reproduction of labour power. Castells sees consumption as important because:

- it prompts industry to maintain high levels of production;
- the level of state involvement is high;
- class conflict over consumption has become more marked (see Badcock, 1981).

For Castells, therefore, the city is theoretically significant as the physical context within which the process of reproduction of labour is situated. Harvey on the other hand views the city as significant as a spatial configuration which facilitates and expresses the process of capital accumulation, he begins with the question of capitalism and seeks to apply this to the city. Harvey, for example, argued that the creation of social areas in cities:

> is produced in its broad lineaments at least by forces emanating from the capitalist production process and is not to be construed as the product of the autonomously and spontaneously arising preferences of people. (Harvey, 1975)

In a similar vein, Walker showed that although preference may have influenced suburbanisation, home-seekers were severely restricted in their residential investment and location decisions by a range of structural effects which left them with few real alternatives (see Badcock, 1984). This kind of perspective is well summarised:

> If the city is considered to start with as a market where labour, power, capital and products are exchanged, it must be equally accepted that the geographical configuration of this market is not the result of change; it is governed by the laws of capital circulation. (Lamarche, 1976)

The key argument is therefore that a capitalist society – as any other – provides its imperatives. The city is the expression of those imperatives and the processes which we can seek at work within urban environments and the tangible forms which those environments take cannot be divorced from this wider societal context in which they are placed. The relevant urban question is one of how we interpret the city *within* society; the other question of whether we can distinguish the city *from* society is interesting but is not of great significance. The city is the most spectacular outcome of social, political and economic processes, it is a microcosm we can study. As Bourne (1982) argues:

> Urban structure is firstly a spatial mirror of society and its historical and organizational principles. That is, it reflects the previous and currently prevailing operating rules – of culture, technology, economy, and social behaviour – of the society within which the city has developed.

Summary

This chapter has discussed the main theories which relate to the city as area. Although they represent different perspectives they have given the means to develop urban geography in significant ways, most of which will be exemplified in the chapters which follow.

CHAPTER 6

The System of Control: Local Government and the Local State

In the previous chapter it was demonstrated that the intra-urban spatial structure of cities reflects a combination of the specifics of their historical origins and evolution, along with the level of economic development and political ethos of the surrounding society. In all societies, however, the process of urban growth has necessitated a degree of coordinated control to minimise the potentially adverse impacts of conflicting land uses, and to ensure the efficient functioning of the economic and social life of the city. Historically, the maintenance of the health of the city by the abolition of infectious diseases has often precipitated the development of legislative controls and the provision of public utility services such as pure water suppliers and efficient sewage disposal systems. The steadily increasing spatial concentration and spread of cities has served to confirm the need for the control and organisation of an ever-widening range of services designed to preserve the efficiency and quality of urban life. In most countries, however, the size of the State and its associated bureaucracy is too large for the control of urban areas and the representation of local issues to be undertaken by a central organisation. Central governments are concerned primarily with national and international issues and are usually too remote from local issues to be sufficiently responsive to local needs. This provides the basic reason for the development of local government or the local state. Since such organisations have increasingly influenced the details of the processes and patterns of urban growth throughout the twentieth century a consideration of their impact is opportune at this point.

The functions of local government and the local state

There are alternative views on the functions of the local state. The *pragmatic* basis of local government has been explored by Sharpe (1976) who identified its three major functions as promoting liberty, participation and efficient service provision. Local forms of organisation provide *liberty* by acting as a counter to the lack of local responsiveness usually associated with over-centralisation. *Participation* in the process of government was also considered likely to be enhanced by some form of local electoral accountability and control. Similarly, local organisations were considered most likely to maximise the *efficiency of service provision* since they were well placed close to the point of service delivery to assess local needs. This rationale of local government represents a *consensus* perspective emanating from a liberal-democratic tradition. Emphasis is placed on the maintenance of the status quo by making central government responsive to local problems by a system of local organisations operating in a *functionalist* manner through a series of balances and checks.

More recently, however, an alternative *conflict* or *dissensus* view of local government has gained considerable support. This has its origins in the Marxist interpretation of the capitalist state and has now evolved to offer a *materialist-structuralist* dimension to the nature and functioning of local government and the local state. The local state is seen as a natural but dependent extension of the central state, and is developed to further the aims of the State. In the capitalist state Saunders (1980) identifies three principal functions of the local state. It assists the promotion of *private production and capital accumulation* by providing the infrastructure of transport, land-use planning, and the wide array of public utility services necessary to sustain the local economy. It provides for the *reproduction of labour* by providing services designed, for example, to educate and train the labour force; to house in public sector accommodation those who cannot afford a home of their own; and to provide for the cultural and recreational needs commensurate with the maintenance of a 'contented' (compliant) workforce. At the same time, the local state is responsible for the *maintenance of social order* by providing policing and social welfare functions. Thus, the essence of the argument is that the local state is supportive of the capitalist state by promoting economic efficiency and ensuring that potential conflicts between capital and labour are minimised.

Johnston (1982a) subscribes to this view of the local state and offers additional supportive speculations. It is, for example, *convenient* for infrastructural facilities to be provided in accordance with local needs. This has the additional advantage of *deflecting complaints* or *diffusing conflict* away from the central state, while the involvement of local decision-making adds to the *legitimation* of the central state. Moreover, the establishment of a competitive relationship between spatially fragmented local states, for example, for the attraction of employment opportunities by offering infrastructural inducements, diverts additional finance towards capital accumulation, while automatically reducing expenditure on social forms of 'non-productive' collective consumption. Consistent views of the local state have also been expressed by Dear, Taylor, and Cox and Johnston (1982).

In most Western countries it is not possible to distinguish clearly whether the consensus or conflict interpretation of the local state is more appropriate to an understanding of the manner in which it functions. Does local government serve a purely pragmatic function designed to enhance the overall quality of life by providing services and reconciling conflicting local aims; or is it an agent operating primarily to promote the aims of capitalist accumulation? These questions cannot be answered with any degree of precision since they require an intimate knowledge of the motives of, and pressures upon, central governments. Furthermore, the relative significance of the two interpretations is likely to vary significantly over time and between countries. Nevertheless, it is likely that under most forms of modern capitalism each has some relevance. Thus, the alternative perspectives on the functions of the local state provide a useful contextual framework offering insights into the potential effects of local government agencies on the nature of urban life.

The spatial structure of local government

Whatever the broad societal functions of the local state, the influence of local government on the geography of the city reflects a combination of its degree of executive independence, its spatial structure and the specific activities which it can perform. Local government is most usually characterised by a hierarchical form of organisation as the central government operates in a 'diffusive' way downwards through a number of increasingly localised levels. Within this general framework, however, there is scope for considerable variation. The levels can vary with respect to their degree of financial and political autonomy. The elected state legislatures of the USA, for example, have considerable independence from Federal government control for the provision of a wide range of services such as highways and social security. This far exceeds the powers of the second tier of County Councils in the UK. Similarly, despite tendencies towards tiered hierarchical structures comprising regional, metropolitan and community levels, the precise number of levels as well as their relative spatial extents and population sizes can be subject to marked variations, even within a single country. Likewise, substantial variations exist between countries in the range of functions performed by broadly comparable units; while the situation can be complicated further, as in the USA, by the creation of special district jurisdictions frequently performing single functions. Such variations tend to reflect the political-historical development of a country in combination with the range of local services to be provided and the nature of the problems to be resolved. Thus, in Western cities, despite a degree of underlying communality of issues and problems, the nature of the local government administrative system and the manner in which it affects the geography of the city can vary widely. The USA and the UK, for example, exhibit markedly contrasting systems of local government which have affected the processes of urban growth in different ways.

The local government system of the USA: spatial fragmentation

From its earliest political origins the development of the local government system of the USA has maintained a premium on the importance of local democracy. This has been manifest in a strong tradition supporting the decentralisation of political authority which was accentuated by a history of gradual colonisation. Thus, local autonomy, the associated importance of property ownership interests, and a political ethos which has incorporated only a weak element of directive-compulsion from government at all levels, are basic to an understanding of the nature of the local government system and the manner in which it has influenced urban development. The local government system reflects directly these considerations. The individual **States** are, for example, of considerable importance to the political life of the country. They are more important spenders on service provision than the Federal government and retain control over transport, housing, health, safety and welfare. The Federal government has only an indirect control over these functions by offering grants or inducements to act in accordance with wider Federal policies. Below this level the **County** was initially the basic unit of political devolution for the rural areas, with the range of services provided related to their populations (Johnston, 1982b). In counties without substantial clusters of settlements the legal

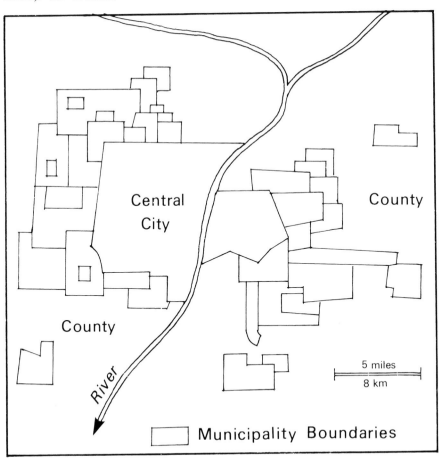

Figure 6.1   The local government structure of the USA

minimum of services provided are policing, road maintenance and public welfare, but more populous units offer a broader base of public utilities such as sewage disposal and refuse collection.

In the nineteenth century, however, the growth of large cities necessitated the *incorporation* of urban **Municipalities** for the control of service provision independent of the counties. This accentuated the spatial fragmentation of the local government system since relatively small suburban concentrations often comprising as few as 500 residents were able to petition for incorporation as separate municipalities. This also resulted in a functional fragmentation because the range of powers devolved from the counties varied relative to the population of the new units. Initially, the problem of coordinating service provision between municipalities in the growing metropolitan areas was resolved by state support for the *annexation* of the smaller units by the larger central cities.

By 1900, however, States had become nervous of the growth of the potential political influence of the largest cities. This combined with suburban preferences to avoid the financial burdens associated with the management of the inner areas of modern industrial metropoli, which was exacerbated in the postwar period by the increasing ghettoisation of the inner city. Together, these forces ensured widespread State support for the preservation of the autonomy of the suburban interests. Thus, annexation has virtually ceased for much of the twentieth century and the fragmented administrative structure illustrated by Figure 6.1 and characterised by Johnston (1982b) as 'municipal balkanisation' is the usual result.

The problems of coordinating service provision resulting from this process introduced further complexity with the incorporation of ad hoc **Special Districts**. These were designed to offer a single service such as policing, fire services or transportation planning to a specified area by overriding municipal boundaries. The majority, however, are the School Districts, established usually to include areas of relatively homogeneous social character in order to retain a degree of social and ethnic exclusivity. The potential complexity of a bewildering array of local administrations, each with the power to raise and spend money, is illustrated graphically by the 1467 units operating in the New York Metropolitan Region (Hall, 1984). This has resulted in a fundamental political dualism between central cities and suburbs, and divisions between one suburb and another, which is basic to an understanding of many of the urban conflicts within the American city in the twentieth century.

Administrative fragmentation has had major implications for the spatial structure of cities and for the degree of social segregation of residential areas. Most municipalities have zoning powers to control land use. In practice *exclusionary zoning* has been the typical response, designed to retain the residential status and environmental quality of an area. This has been accomplished by discouraging high density developments likely to attract low income groups and ethnic minorities. Noxious and costly-to-service industrial development has similarly been excluded, while revenue generating light industry or shopping malls have sometimes been encouraged by financial inducements to locate in non-intrusive locations to enhance the local tax base. In effect, policies have aimed consistently to minimise 'negative externalities' and maximise 'positive externalities' offered by the opportunities provided by the 'jurisdictional partitioning'.

The application of such policies across metropolitan regions has produced recurring geographical results. The larger and older central cities tend to retain only the least attractive industrial development. Here also will be concentrated the lowest status white and ethnic minority groups whose unemployment levels will be accentuated by the migration of the newer opportunities to suburban locations beyond their travel limits. Both the industrial and social areas of such central cities are costly to service, particularly since they are located at the hub of the intra-city transportation network. This necessitates high rates of property taxation on a usually declining tax base. By contrast, the administrative fragmentation combined with the greater mobility of the middle classes and the attractions of suburban life have encouraged suburbanisation by allowing them to 'vote with their feet'. The higher status suburbs are also less costly to service and can consequently offer the additional incentive of low levels of property taxation. The resulting *fiscal dislocation* between central city and suburbs acts to the continued disadvantage of the centre and has precipitated a spiral decline in the quality of the environment and its efficient functioning. This is summed up in the notion of the *urban crisis*. In extreme situations some central city administrations have become virtually bankrupt, the most spectacular example of which was the case of New York in October 1975 (Johnston, 1982a). Paradoxically, however, many suburban residents continue to work in the concentrations of business activities in the CBD and use the associated historical concentrations of cultural, entertainment and recreational facilities. This suggested to Neenan the existence of an exploitative relationship between suburbs and central cities, and the characterisation of the suburban residents as 'free-riders'.

The intermittent financial crises suffered by central city administrations have, however, not resulted in radical 'structural changes' to the local government system. Instead, financial aid has been obtained from lending institutions or from State and Federal agencies, all of whom have tended to impose budgetary restraint to 'solve' the problem rather than substantially improving the situation of the inner cities. This represents a veiled movement in the direction of increased political centralisation. This reflects the unwillingness of the suburban communities to voluntarily relinquish their entrenched financial, social and racial advantages, while State governments have been loth to alienate their political strength. In practice, the ideal of local democratic control has been synonomous with the particular interests of suburban America. Thus, for the most part, change has been gradual, involving 'procedural adjustments' rather than radical reform. Exclusionary zoning, for example, has been attacked in State legislatures by resorting to the fourteenth Amendment of the US Constitution whereby 'No State shall make or enforce any law which shall abridge the privileges or immunities of citizens of the United States'. Zoning ordinances might be seen as restrictive, but legal battles have been long and complex and little success has been achieved. Similarly, the desegregation of schools by amalgamating school boards and instituting busing to ensure racial integration has found support in State and Federal courts, but not without considerable opposition and real progress has been slow. In recent years the situation has been complicated further by opposition to reform from central cities such as Detroit, Los Angeles and Washington DC where the black population are a majority and have obtained effective political control (Johnston, 1982b).

Elsewhere, 'voluntary cooperations' and 'service agreements' have been established between closely related municipalities to assist the coordination of services such as policing, sewage disposal, water provision and landuse planning for economically viable units. Such devices have the appeal of resolving the immediate problems of service provision without relinquishing local control. As such, they constitute defence mechanisms against reorganisation. This frequently has the effect of increasing social polarisation in a metropolitan region since socially similar units are those most likely to be involved.

Of wider significance are the Metropolitan Councils initiated with the aid of State and Federal support grants in Detroit in 1954, and later developed for New York, Philadelphia and San Francisco. These are multi-purpose advisory bodies designed to enhance cooperation and the coordination of service provision, ideally at a city regional scale. However, efforts to give these bodies directive powers have been resisted strongly by the constituent municipalities.

Examples of radical structural changes designed to achieve economies of scale and efficiency of service provision, while aiming to reduce the worst effects of socio-spatial segregation do, nevertheless, exist in the USA, particularly if overall white political control is likely to be maintained. Integration occurred in Nashville, Tennessee in 1965, while Dade County, Florida encompassing the Miami Metropolitan Area followed in 1971. Indianapolis and Jacksonville are more recent examples of the same trend. Similarly, some States have instituted legislation to curtail the balkanisation process and encourage metropolitan forms of government. Texas and Missouri have positively encouraged annexation in the vicinity of large cities, while Ohio, Georgia, Arizona and North Carolina do not allow the incorporation of new municipalities within specified distances of existing large towns. For the most part, however, the essence of a spatially fragmented local government system remains throughout the USA.

The fragmentation of local government has clearly served to emphasise social and spatial segregative tendencies and to accentuate the central city-suburban dichotomy (Johnston, 1982b). In effect, Soja's (1971) notion that:

> ...there is no doubt that the maze of counties, cities, townships and special districts, many tending to pursue narrow local interests at the expense of the larger functional community, both directly and indirectly exacerbate some of the major problems facing predominantly urban America...

continues to be relevant.

The local government system of the UK: hierarchical structures

The local government system of the UK is fundamentally different from that of the USA. Its early development reflected the practical need for forms of local control rather than being related to ideals of local democracy, and major changes in its subsequent development have been largely imposed by central government rather than reflecting local pressures. Central control has consequently been stronger throughout its evolution and a neater hierarchical ordering has resulted.

Prior to 1974 the system was dominated by the structure established in the late nineteenth century. The 1888 Local Government Act established the County Councils and County Boroughs as a top tier, while the 1894 Local Government Act established a lower, second tier for the County Council areas comprising Municipal Boroughs, Urban Districts and Rural Districts (Figure 6.2). This was a radical reorganisation necessitated by the rapid urban expansion in Britain following the Industrial Revolution. The earlier system, comprising a multitude of local health boards and sanitary authorities conceptually similar to the fragmented structure emerging in the USA, often pursued independent and conflicting policies, occasionally with dire results for the health of the urban and rural areas alike. In effect, the county boroughs were created as unitary authorities for the largest towns to replace a confused structure based upon the Medieval Charter Boroughs and their subsequent appendages. The county councils were to control the areas remaining outside the major towns, while a degree of local autonomy was to be given to the smaller urban units (the municipal boroughs and urban districts), and to the rural districts. The structure gave belated recognition to the functional interrelationships of the Victorian era rather than being appropriate for urban expansion in the twentieth century. The division between the county boroughs and county councils gave credence to the persistence of a functional distinction between town and country, while the lower tier authorities paradoxically recognised the spread of urban influences into the country margins.

In the twentieth century this structure became increasingly irrelevant to the efficient operation of the rapidly developing range of local government activities. The process of suburbanisation overrode administrative boundaries and established strong functional linkages between separate administrative units. The county borough/county council division became particularly unreal, while in the larger conurbations a number of county boroughs had physically merged (Figure 6.2). Problems were most apparent for landuse planning. The great majority of county boroughs had restricted administrative boundaries throughout the period of rapid urban growth. At the same time, they had to provide substantial numbers of public sector council houses for the needs of the lower status groups and for slum clearance schemes. Large scale boundary extensions to undertake imaginative urban planning were the exception and usually involved protracted legal disputes due to the conflicting interests of the

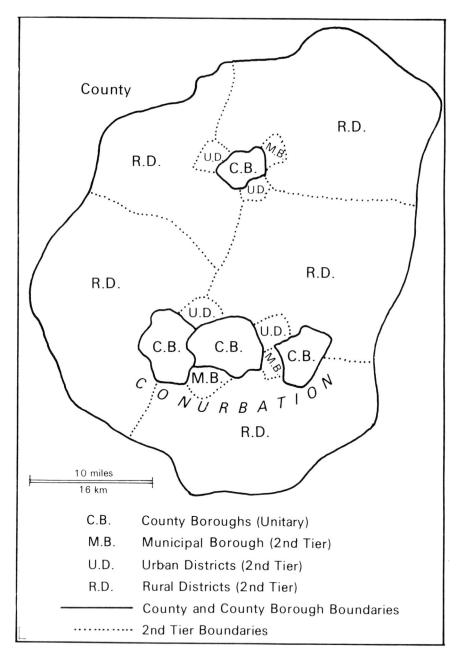

Figure 6.2   The local government structure of England and Wales, 1894–1974

urban-oriented County Boroughs and the rurally-oriented County Councils. Thus, in most of the larger cities urban planning schemes were constrained by restrictive boundaries and dominated by local authority housing estates. This had the additional effect of accentuating social polarisation between the lower status inner cities and the higher status suburban margins.

In fact, by the late 1950s there was widespread agreement at central and local government levels that radical structural reform was long overdue. Reform focused on the need to promote the dual aims of 'administrative efficiency', while preserving 'local democracy' in a period of rapid change. Fewer, but larger, units were envisaged to achieve economies of scale. These were to reflect the functional realities of a 'city regional' ideal to facilitate coordinated strategic planning, and to enhance a sense of social identity in order to promote 'participation' in local government affairs.

In Britain, however, central government is the dominating influence over local government change. The nature of the subsequent reform consequently owed much to national political considerations as it did to the needs of the principles of reform. The Labour Government of 1966 set up a Royal Commission under the chairmanship of Lord Redcliffe-Maud with wide terms of reference to report on the future functions and areas for local government in England. This initiated a protracted period of investigation and debate which culminated in the publication of the proposals in 1969. England was to be divided into 58 'unitary' city regions with populations ranging from 250,000 to 1 million. However, for the larger urban concentrations a two-tier structure of Metropolitan Areas and Metropolitan Districts, based upon the model of the Greater London Council initiated in 1964, were to control the three large conurbations centred on Birmingham, Liverpool and Manchester. This structure constituted a radical reform, but according to Derek Senior, a member of the Royal Commission, the boundaries paid too great accord to the previous limits to reflect functional realities, while being both too small to promote administrative efficiency and too large for local democracy. Consequently, an alternative two-tier structure of larger City Regional Authorities (35) and smaller Districts (148) were proposed in a memorandum of Dissent.

The actual process of change, however, reflected political rather than administrative considerations. The decision to adopt the Redcliffe-Maud proposals met with the major obstacle of a change of government in June 1970. The incoming Conservative government disagreed with the idea that large unitary authorities for most of the country would provide administrative efficiency and local democracy. Instead, a system comprising a top tier of 38 County Councils and 6 Metropolitan Counties, complemented by a lower level of around 370 District Councils, was proposed in 1971 and became operative in April 1974. The counties were to be responsible for broad 'strategic' functions such as structure planning, transport and education, while the district authorities retained substantial powers such as the formulation of local plans and the provision of public sector housing.

The precedence given to the pre-existing counties was considered to reflect

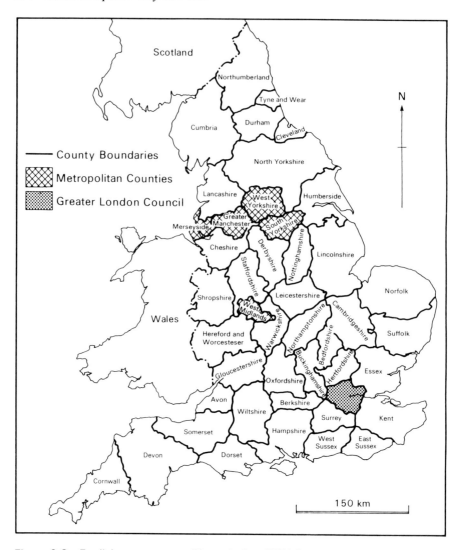

Figure 6.3   English county council boundaries: 1974 Conservative Government reform

traditional Conservative support, while the restricted boundaries for the large conurbations have been seen as a mechanism designed to contain the areas of traditional Labour control. Paradoxically, however, the city regional concept was promoted with the creation of the new counties of Avon, Cleveland and Humberside (Figure 6.3).

While the 1974 reforms constitute a significant rationalisation of the earlier structure, in subsequent years problems inherent in the new system have become increasingly evident. The metropolitan counties, for example, were seen as too spatially restricted for strategic planning purposes and characterised as major urban units 'embedded' in wider economic regions. Similarly, the widespread adherence to pre-existing county boundaries is inconsistent with emerging functional entities, particularly in the south east of England. The two-tier structure has also proved problematic. The ideal of the lower tier operating policies consistent with the broader strategic aims of the counties had been largely illusory. Instead, the strength of the districts has frequently allowed local interests to confound wider strategic aims. This has generated costly conflicts between the levels which has a detrimental effect on the image of both local government and central government to the public. In fact, Self suggested that by the early 1970s the inherent weakness of the two-tier system in Greater London was weakening the strategic planning potential of the Greater London Council, while Hall (1989) ascribes its limited subsequent success to a lack of sufficient independent power.

The dependence of the local state upon central government in Britain is further demonstrated by recent events. The Conservative government has since 1979 pursued an anti-inflationary, monetarist policy designed to resolve the economic crises of late capitalism. The reduction of public expenditure is a central issue and has involved curtailing local government spending by exerting firmer central control. This coincided with a deterioration of the quality of life in the early 1980s in the inner cities most adversely affected by economic recession, and brought the usually Labour controlled county and district councils into direct conflict with central government over levels of expenditure. This culminated in the 'rate-capping' legislation of 1984 designed to curb the activities of high spending local authorities. Ostensibly to cut the cost of local government bureaucracy the Government subsequently abolished the Greater London Council in 1986 and the remaining six metropolitan counties in 1987. The trend is clear. The last ten years has witnessed a significant shift in political control towards increased centralisation combined with a devolution of financial responsibility to the most local level. Whether this will be reflected in a more cost-effective and efficient provision of local services, while ensuring the coordination of planning and transportation strategies is, however, highly debatable. The scale and spread of the functional interrelationships associated with modern urban development suggests the need for at least a city-regional form of strategic control rather than a polarisation between central government and highly localised units. In fact, Hall (1989) notes that in Western Europe Britain is alone in moving towards the abolition of a strong middle tier of local government.

Summary

Despite fundamental differences between the local government systems of the USA and the UK, both have had a significant effect on the process of urban growth. In the USA the tradition of local democratic control has allowed both socially and spatially defined interest groups to accentuate segregation in the city and has presented major obstacles to the development of reforms necessary to institute effective metropolitan planning. In Britain, integrated urban development policies have also been restrained for much of the twentieth century due to the entrenched heritage of the Victorian local government reforms. Positive planning has been restricted by the location of administrative boundaries, although adverse social segregative tendencies equivalent to those in American cities did not reflect the local government structure. The potential for radical restructuring has been much greater in Britain, yet the key position of central government in the process of administrative change has, in part, compromised the needs of urban planning. In recent years, however, it is notable that in both cases fiscal issues have instituted a shift towards a greater degree of centralisation and reduced the immediate prospects for the emergence of city-regional forms of government.

CHAPTER 7

Transport Issues in the City

In all cities there is a close interactive relationship between the transportation network, the urban morphology and the spatial patterns of urban functions. Behaviour in the city, such as journeys-to-work, shopping trips, visits to health centres and to leisure facilities are also closely related to the system of urban transport. In fact, the efficient functioning of the city is directly dependent upon the efficiency of the components of the urban transportation system. During the process of economic development the evolving system both *connects* the various functional elements of the urban fabric and *directs* the pattern of urban growth. A generalised evolutionary sequence is portrayed for the Western city (Figure 7.1), and this is closely associated with innovations in transport technology (Figure 7.2).

This evolutionary sequence is most relevant to medium-sized cities in which development was initiated in the nineteenth century and has resulted in strongly centralised urban systems. However, variations in the scale of cities and the societal context of the urban development process are responsible for significant deviations from the general model. A number of examples will serve to illustrate the potential variability.

Urban transport systems

Western cities: centralised systems

The most marked deviations occurred in cities experiencing high and rapid rates of urban development in the nineteenth century. London, for example, reached a population of 6 million by 1900, and to, a lesser extent, a similar situation occurred in the smaller British conurbations. In these circumstances, the pressure for urban growth could not be accommodated by the relatively inefficient, road-based public transport system, and railways, which had been introduced initially for the inter-city transportation, became a much more active agent of urban growth. Thus, from 1860 to 1914 the London Underground system and suburban railway lines were basic formative influences; they allowed extensive suburbanisation and the development of commuter settlements well beyond the city centre. Access to stations was critical

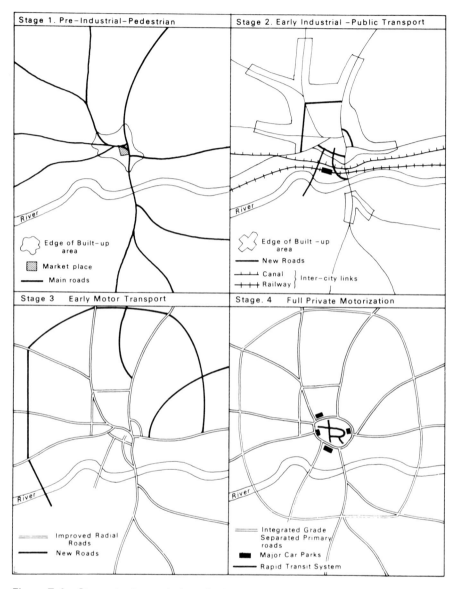

Figure 7.1   Stages in the evolution of urban transport systems

as the railway became a much more important element in the intra-urban transportation network. The process had social consequences since the higher status groups were those financially most able to benefit from the pleasant environment of the suburbs and social polarisation between the inner city and the outer suburbs was initiated during this period.

Paris exhibits a different variant. Residential densities in the inner city were

Figure 7.2 Evolution of the transport system of Western cities

	Urban functions	Transport technology	Transportation system	Urban form
Stage 1 Pre-industrial	defence, marketing, political-symbolic, craft industry	pedestrian, draught-animal	route convergence, radial	compact
Stage 2 Early industrial	basic industries, secondary manufacturing	electric tram, streetcar, public transport	radial improvements, incremental additions	high density suburbanisation, stellate form
Stage 3 Industrial	broadening industry, tertiary service expansion	motor bus, public transport, early cars	additional radials, initiation of 'ring' roads (incomplete)	lower density suburbanisation, industrial decentralisation
Stage 4 Post-industrial	addition of quaternary activities	towards universal car ownership	integrated radial and circumferential road network	low density suburbanisation, widespread functional decentralisation

nearly three times those of London, due to the constraining influence of successive historical fortifications, a feature which Paris has in common with many European cities. The high density allowed urban growth to occur without the necessity for an intra-urban railway system, although the resulting traffic congestion provided the impetus for the urgent construction of the Metro after 1900. Thus, the Paris Metro did not direct suburban growth but was designed to integrate the existing parts of the inner city and remains confined largely to that area to the present day. As such, it has the form of a 'modern' inner city rapid transit system and the subsequent process of suburbanisation in Paris had a simpler form, related to the early radial road system.

With the growth of the Paris agglomeration to 8.5 million by the early 1960s and the expectation of continued development, a drastic re-evaluation of the transport network was made. In 1961 the Government approved a new regional metro system to provide a rapid suburban rail service for the whole agglomeration (R.E.R. – *Réseau Express Régional*). This was designed to complement, and was integrated with, the inner city Metro by the mid 1980s. The subsequent urban planning strategies dating from the *Schema Directeur d'Amènagement et d'Urbanisme de la Région de Paris* of 1965, initiated the improvement of the radial road system, the development of circumferential routes starting with the inner ring *Boulevard Périphérique* along the line of the outermost fortification, and the development of east-west routes both north and south of the Seine along the lines of the preferred axes of urban development (Figure 7.3). Thus, despite the initial deviation of the Parisian transport network, recent modifications have brought it closer to the suggested Western model.

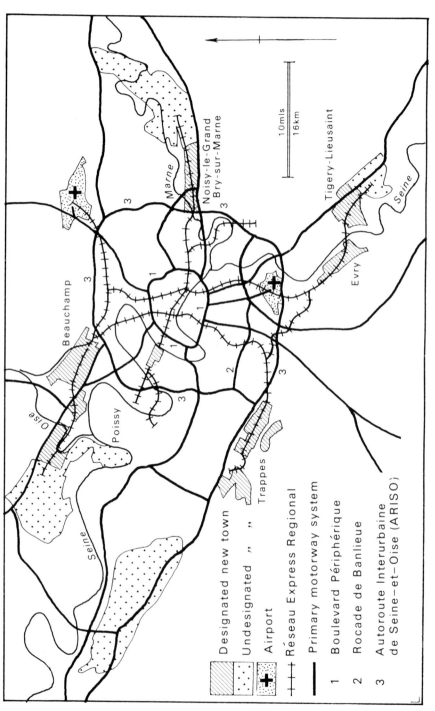

Figure 7.3   Transport systems and new town developments in Paris

Developing world cities: centralised systems

Other variations characterise the rapidly growing metropolitan centres of the Third World. Here, urban growth is more closely related to the 'population explosion', and to the strong rural-urban migration flows. By the early 1980s Mexico City had reached a population of 14 million, Calcutta 9.5 million, while Lagos is currently estimated at 5 million. In fact, Brunn and Williams suggest that all the cities of the world growing at a rate of greater than 50 per cent over the period 1975–85 were located in the Third World.

In most of these cities, where poverty is endemic, there is a lack of finance to develop adequate public controls over the structure and quality of the urban environment. High density and low quality residential developments predominate and are served by rudimentary improvements and extensions to the early radial road networks. Public transport normally consists of an inadequate bus or tram system, largely confined to the radial routes which are frequently the only roads sufficiently wide for this purpose; traffic congestion of pedestrians and vehicles is usually considerable. The resulting urban structure tends to be highly centralised and inefficient, while the possibility of developing a more sophisticated transport system based on radically improved roads and railways is usually far too costly to be contemplated in anything other than a partial and piecemeal manner (Figure 7.4(a)). A dependence upon a bus-based public transport system supplemented by the emergence of an electric commuter rail service and a city centre underground system conforms to this model.

Western cities: decentralised systems

A radically different transport network evolves in situations typified by the development of high levels of private car ownership. This has been particularly widespread in more recently urbanised parts of the USA, Canada and Australia, and is epitomised by the case of Los Angeles where a metropolis of 10 million people had developed by 1970, almost entirely within the era of mass car ownerships. The combined influence of high levels of personal mobility, affluence, and the absence of significant space constraints on urban growth, encouraged low density suburbanisation. This in turn had a fundamental influence upon the functional structure of the urban system and the closely associated transport network. The dispersed population and high levels of personal mobility have positively encouraged the decentralisation of employment and service activities throughout the urban system on a scale much larger than that experienced in cities more reliant upon public transportation. At the same time, the cost of providing unrestricted car access to the traditional central business districts has acted as a significant constraint upon the development of a strongly centralised urban structure. In fact, it has been suggested that whatever the scale of a metropolitan area the largest central

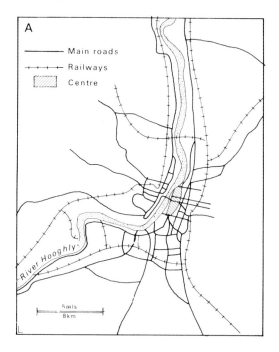

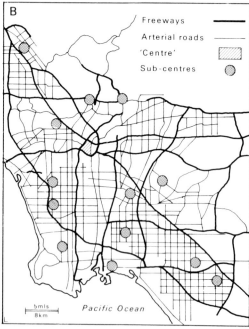

Figure 7.4   Two cities contrasted: (a) Calcutta's centralised transport system; (b) the decentralised system of Los Angeles

business district can provide for a maximum of only 150,000–180,000 car commuters, and even then significant peak hour traffic congestion is likely to result (Thomson, 1977).

Thus, the initial centre of Los Angeles has not dominated the intra-urban system of central places and a number of alternative functional nodes have emerged. This is reflected in a transport network in which the radial component of the road system centred on Los Angeles is only very weakly developed (Figure 7.4(b)). Instead, by the early 1940s the demands of a highly motorised society had necessitated the extensive development of urban motorways or freeways with their characteristic grade-separated intersections at potential points of congestion (cloverleaves). These were supplemented by the construction of a rectilinear grid system of secondary arterial roads designed to incorporate the expanding suburbs into the loosely-knit urban structure. In such a system, the influence of public transport has been minimal with buses accounting for only two per cent of all motorised trips and 23 per cent of those to the Los Angeles downtown area.

Thus, urban development in the motor age is characterised by the archetypical 'suburban city' of Los Angeles. Whereas these features are particularly well marked in cities of the western USA developed in the post-war period, such as Denver and Salt Lake City, they have increasingly been superimposed upon the urban fabric of cities originally developed in earlier technological conditions.

The urban transportation problem

Transportation problems are virtually universal facets of urban growth whatever the detailed characteristics of the transport system in specific areas. They take the form of peak-hour congestion of public and private transport particularly in city centres and at other nodal points on the transport network; parking difficulties; noise and atmospheric pollution; and pedestrian and vehicular accidents. This reflects the fact that the growth of traffic demand, whether for public or private transport in a developed or developing world context tends to be faster than the development of either public controls or of the finance necessary to provide an efficiently functioning system.

More specifically, the number of vehicles, both public transport and private cars, can respond rapidly to the growth in demand in the absence of public controls on levels of vehicle ownership typical of most countries and this process has been aided by the vigorous development of a car-manufacturing industry. By contrast, the provision of a system capable of accommodating the increasing traffic levels requires, in the long term, comprehensive planning and control and high levels of investment in transport infrastructure. Thomson (1977) has stressed the economic basis of the problem and the central importance of '*pricing deficiencies*'. The greater part of the cost of supplying transport facilities is seen, with the partial exception of public transport, not to

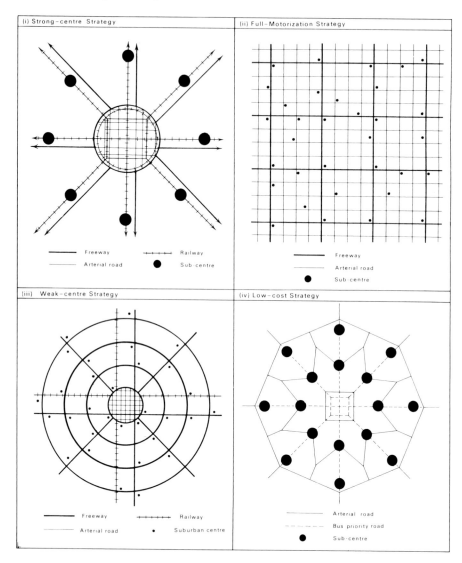

Figure 7.5   Urban transport planning strategies: (i) strong centre, (ii) full motorisation, (iii) weak centre, (iv) low cost

(After Thomspon, 1977. Reproduced by permission of J. M. Thompson)

be borne directly by the user. The provision of adequate roads, parking, and the minimisation of environmental problems have been perceived traditionally as publicly provided activities, serving the community at large rather than specific groups of transport users. Thus, the system has been funded from the general pool of central and local government expenditure, in which transport has to compete with the financing of the whole range of additional public service facilities, usually from an inadequate overall budget. As a result, insufficient investment in the transport infrastructure of cities tends to occur due to the failure to apply strict economic principles to the development and rearrangement of urban transport over a long period of time. At a broad conceptual level Thomson (1977) identifies four main strategies designed to improve a particular type of transport network (Figure 7.5). These were proposed as 'ideal types' rather than offering specific solutions to urban transport problems, and as such are of continuing interest.

Private transport versus public transport

Whatever the transport planning strategy adopted in a city, the steadily continuing growth in levels of private car ownership in most societies in relation to alternative modes of public transport has tended to confound solutions to the urban transportation problem. This reflects a combination of the economic problems of public transport and the behavioural attractions of the private car. Public transport systems are usually designed to cope with peak-hour journeys to and from workplaces. In the interim periods considerable investment in capital equipment and labour is underutilised and involves costs which have to be covered by a combination of relatively high fares and cuts in off-peak services. Usually, these measures have a detrimental effect on demand, which further compounds the financial problem and frequently leads to a decline in the quality and financial viability of the services offered. By contrast, apart from peak-hour journeys to city centres in the larger highly centralised cities, the private car is usually a more flexible and convenient means of travel. Also, it is perceived as less costly since the marginal cost of a specific journey is usually compared with the public transport fare. Thus, increasing road traffic has created pressures for more highways and this has tended to increase costs and exacerbate environmental problems.

Usually, the initial planning responses have aimed at a combination of *car accommodation* and *environmental preservation*. Typically, this involves a comprehensively upgraded road network comprising the main radial routes, an inner ring road surrounding the CBD and one or more suburban ring roads (Figure 7.1, stage 4). Ideally, major intersections are 'grade-separated' with flyovers, while the segregation of pedestrian-precincts and other traffic and vehicular traffic with the creation of pedestrian free 'environmental areas' has been given some priority. The provision of car-parking facilities and their integration with major trip destination points is also of central importance. For the central business districts various traffic limitation and management schemes in association with public transport strategies have been the usual response. Such strategies are epitomised by the 1964 Buchanan Report for British cities.

However, since the early 1970s a wider official realisation of the economic and environmental impact of the unrestricted use of the car in cities has been linked with the *'suppressed demand'* argument. In Britian, this argument was

Figure 7.6   Urban transport planning strategies

(i)	**Strong-centre strategy: centralised cities**
Aim	To maintain economic advantages of centralisation and minimise central city congestion.
Policy	1. Efficient public transport, suburbs to centre and within the city centre.
	2. Decentralisation of functions to nodal points to spread traffic loads.
Problems	Tends to peak-hour congestion
(ii)	**Full-motorisation strategy: decentralised cities**
Aim	To retain high levels of car accessibility throughout the system.
Policy	Decentralised functional structure based upon the extension of urban freeways.
Problems	Land and construction costs, long distances travelled, energy costs, environmental impacts, lack of social identity, possible nodal congestion.
(iii)	**Weak-centre strategy: inner centralised and outer decentralised cities**
Aim	To retain commercial and social advantages of a city centre and ease of mobility throughout the suburbs.
Policy	1. Integrated system of radial and circumferential roads.
	2. Supplementary commuter rail services to the centre.
Problems	Tends towards decentralisation in the absence of sufficient investment in public transport and central redevelopment.
(iv)	**Low-cost strategy: Third World cities**
Aim	To alleviate congestion and assist economic development.
Policy	1. Improvements on the radial roads and public transport system.
	2. Controls on central development and the encouragement of decentralisation to peripheral nodes.
Problems	City growth tends to be faster than levels of investment in transport infrastructure.

(After Thompson, 1977. Reproduced by permission of J. M. Thompson)

promoted initially in the Buchanan Report and has been reintroduced regularly in the urban transport debate (e.g. Thomson, 1977), most notably by Mogridge (1987). In situations of steadily increasing car ownership it is suggested that there is an enormous suppressed demand for car journeys. Thus, any new roads built quickly attract more traffic until a new equilibrium of congestion is reached (around 19 km per hour in central London). In fact, it is considered '. . . impossible to improve traffic speed where demand is in excess of any possible supply of road space . . . ' (Mogridge, 1987). The near capacity traffic levels and frequent congestion experienced on the M25 London orbital motorway only completed in 1987 is a classic example of this effect. It follows that journey times can be improved only by improving the quality and speed of public transport systems since they dictate the levels of car use. This constitutes a strong argument for near universal moves towards both *traffic limitation* strategies and the positive promotion of *public transport* in Western cities. In centralised systems this involves the decentralisation of activities to nodal locations in the suburbs, while in decentralised systems a greater degree of concentration of functions in the central city and a limited number of suburban locations is considered appropriate. In either situation, the siting of urban activities is undertaken with a view to encouraging the use of public transport, and at the same time cars are actively discouraged from situations which would give rise to heavy social costs.

Public transport: public service or commercial service?

The urban transportation literature suggests that in most countries public transport is not commercially viable for the reasons outlined earlier. Thomson (1977) demonstrates its almost universal inability to meet costs so that the quality and efficiency of public transport facilities in cities reflects their degree of subsidisation; a point reiterated recently by Palin. Thus, for the purposes of transport planning it has been argued that it is better to regard public transport as a publicly provided rather than a commercial service.

The adherence of governments to this view, however, varies significantly. This is epitomised by the increasing politisation of the transport issue in the UK over the last fifteen years. In the mid 1970s, for example, the Labour Government made a firm commitment to the promotion of public transport in British cities. Finance was to be directed more strongly to the public sector and coordination of the different modes of transport was a primary aim. A Transport Policy and Programme was to be formulated via the strategic planning function of each county and subject to an annual review by the Department of the Environment. The official view was that:

> If nothing is done, then rising car usage and the worsening financial situation of public transport operators will inevitably lower the quality of urban transport and even of urban living. (Daniels and Warnes, 1980)

This resulted in a number of fare-cutting experiments in the early 1980s based upon local rate subsidies designed to increase the attractions of public transport. Notable examples occurred in South Yorkshire and the 'Fares Fair' policy of the Greater London Council, along with an integrated fare structure covering bus, tube and rail.

Such initiatives, however, were contrary to the commercial orientation of the Conservative Government elected in 1979 and committed to a reduction in the public service expenditure. Rate-capping subsequently abolished local government subsidies to public transport while the 1985 Transport Act instituted the 'deregulation' of public transport, aiming to promote competition and innovation. The full effects of the change in orientation are not yet apparent but the early evidence is not encouraging. Higher fares and lower levels of use characterise bus services in Sheffield with the exception of the profitable routes, while a National Consumer Council survey reports a general reduction in the quality and reliability of services, along with a widespread loss of confidence. Serious doubts are also being expressed that private finance will be attracted to invest in public transport on a scale necessary to instigate radical improvements.

The promotion of public transport

Irrespective of political philosophy, policies designed to increase the importance of public transport in cities incorporate a number of common elements. To be most effective, strategies must both *enhance the attractions* of public transport, while at the same time *restrict the use* of private cars. Also, such policies need to be related to journeys *between* suburbs and destinations, and *within* major destinations such as city centres or concentrations of employment. A wide range of devices exists.

(i) Enhancing the attraction of public transport

For public transport to appeal to the public at large a number of general issues are of fundamental importance. Ease of access at both origins and destinations is critical and a five-minute or 450 m trip is accepted widely as an outer limit. Similarly, a cost or time advantage is important, especially if assisted by a frequent, reliable service offered over a dense route coverage.

A number of methods have been adopted to achieve these aims, most notably in the context of bus travel. Since the early 1970s restricted *bus lanes* have been introduced widely in Britain for both central city and selected suburban routes, while *express bus services* to city centres from collecting points in the outer suburbs are common. Conceptually similar *park and ride* schemes have been adopted with varying degrees of enthusiasm, some such as the Oxford example with a significant measure of success (Figure 7.7). Demand responsive *dial-a-ride* minibus services have also been tried. For the most part, however, these devices have been introduced in a piecemeal fashion as 'curative' rather than 'preventative' action so that their full potential has been difficult to assess. The exceptions, however, are the new town experiments such as the *bus priority Superbus* system in Stevenage and the largely segregated *Busways* as the basis of the urban fabric of Runcorn (figure 7.7). The relative success of these schemes is encouraging but the opportunity to introduce similarly comprehensive systems into large towns with established routeways and travel patterns is both economically and behaviourally problematic.

A piecemeal approach has also characterised the use of high capacity *rail systems* to solve the transport problems presented by specific routes in major cities (50,000–60,000 passengers per hour compared with 10,000 for buses). Frequently, these are based upon new technology such as the *monorail* service between Tokyo International Airport and the city centre, although the extension of conventional systems such as the London Underground to Heathrow Airport are not uncommon. Rail has also been used to stimulate economic development in particular parts of cities. A *Light Rapid Rail Transit* route (LRRT) forming a 10 km corridor from the city centre of Buffalo through the declining inner suburbs was constructed to revitalise retailing and employment in the city centre and adjacent suburbs. In London the Docklands Light Railway from the eastern edge of the City to the Isle of Dogs has stimulated redevelopment, most notably in the major office concentration emerging at Canary Wharf (Figure 7.7). Half of the capital cost was financed by

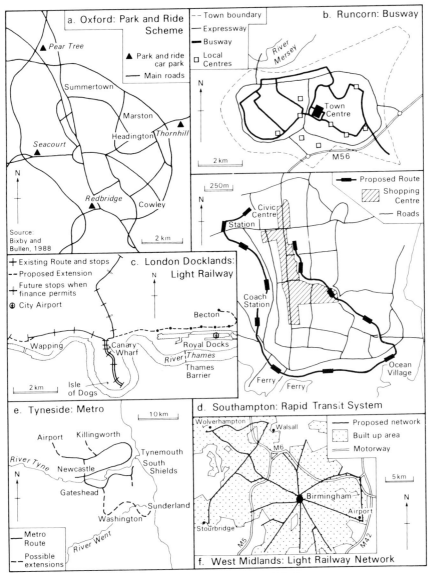

Figure 7.7 Enhanced public transport schemes in Britain

the development company and its extension to the Royal Docks and Becton is already at an advanced stage of planning with the anticipation of similar results.

Rapid transit rail systems have also been used to maintain accessibility between the component parts of the largest city centres. The underground systems of London, Paris and New York are obvious early examples. However, as the scale of business activities and the traffic demands upon the central areas have continued to increase, incremental improvements have had to be made. In

London the Victoria Line (1972) and the Jubilee Line (1979) are indicative of the pressures, while in Paris the construction of the Metro link between the Gare du Nord and the Gare de Lyon is the result of similar pressures. Elsewhere, in many Western cities of greater than a million population, the development of inner city rapid transit systems to facilitate internal integration has been a frequent response as exemplified by Toronto, Montreal and Glasgow. On a smaller scale, the Loop-and-Link underground railway system designed to join the mainline rail termini in the centre of Liverpool with the suburban systems of Merseyside and the Wirral has a counterpart in the recently completed Windsor Link in Manchester. In fact, in many smaller provincial cities the need to maintain an attractive city centre environment and to link the increasingly dispersed central functional nodes is, in the face of the competitive forces of decentralisation, resulting in moves in a similar direction. Cardiff, for example, has experimented with a 'Flydacraft' driverless vehicle capable of carrying 5,000 passengers per hour on an elevated track 3 m high and 2 m wide, while Southampton is currently developing an inner city rapid transit system linking a number of destinations around the city centre on a 7 m high elevated rail system (Figure 7.7).

In recent years, however, attempts to enhance the attractions of public transport have recognised the need to develop comprehensive systems integrating inner city rapid transit with suburban services. The Bay Area Rapid Transit System (BART) completed in the early 1970s in San Francisco incorporated these principles and aimed to avoid the financial and environmental costs of urban motorways, while at the same time maintaining the advantages of a recognisable 'metropolitan centre' in a rapidly decentralising urban structure. The system has not been without difficulties. These reflect a combination of problems with the high degree of new technology used in and underestimating the difficulty of effecting behavioural shifts from the car to public transport. Such problems, however, are not inevitable and the Metropolitan Atlanta Rapid Transit Authority (MARTA) has been operating a more conventional system since the late 1970s with a greater measure of success. In fact, Hall (1989) has recently suggested that the integrated strategy outlined earlier for Paris would have considerable advantages for London, while the potential advantages of rail based rapid transit systems has been demonstrated by a comparative analysis of British and West German cities.

In Britain the most recent comprehensive public transport system is the Tyneside Metro. Learning form American and European experience the network was based upon proven technology and, apart from the underground section between Newcastle and Gateshead, the majority of the 55 km, 47-station system uses upgraded British Rail tracks (Figure 7.7). Nevertheless, the £70 million cost projected in 1974 escalated to £300 million by its opening in 1981, and the system has been heavily subsidised ever since. The system is now integrated with bus services, and park and ride facilities at a number of stations. The Passenger Transport Executive claims that the Metro has proven a cost-effective means of improving mobility and supporting economic regeneration, and hopes to extend it to the whole of the urban agglomeration of

Tyne and Wear. It is unlikely, however, that a similar network will be developed elsewhere in Britain in the foreseeable future due to the change in Government attitude in the 1980s to the subsidisation of public transport. The advantages of comprehensive integrated public transport have, nevertheless, been accepted and a number of major cities are now planning conceptually similar systems; albeit with the intention of using electric trams along existing roads to limit costs and by attempting to attract a substantial proportion of private investment. These have been modelled on modern European systems exemplified by such cities as Grenoble and Hanover. The 95 km Metrolink network for Manchester is already under construction, while a substantially more extensive system of 200 km has been proposed for the Birmingham conurbation (Figure 7.7). The potential for such developments, however, is heavily dependent upon the availability of sufficient finance if they are to have a significant impact upon the urban transportation problem.

(ii) Restricting the use of private cars

To promote public transport effectively, it is not enough to increase its attractions. Such policies have to be complemented by restraints on the use of private cars. Again a wide range of devices has been used to achieve this end and these have been aimed principally at the areas of greatest congestion in city centres. Policies generally involve the motorist paying for access in order for public authorities to recover at least part of the costs imposed by the high levels of traffic. In most Western countries, however, the restriction of the private motorist is a politically sensitive issue so that a gradual introduction of increasingly Draconian measures, as the scale of the problem increases, is the usual progression.

The initial response is the introduction of *traffic management* schemes comprising a combination of parking restrictions, car parking charges, one-way systems and exclusive bus lanes. Apart from the smallest towns, such policies usually do no more than partially contain a deteriorating situation and often exacerbate conflicts between pedestrians and vehicular traffic. This necessitates the introduction of more comprehensive policies based upon directive forms of *parking control* in combination with the progressive *pedestrianisation* of commercially or environmentally sensitive areas. Leeds introduced a particularly innovative example of such policies in the early 1970s. Long stay low-cost parking, designed to attract commuters, was concentrated around the periphery of the central area. This was complemented by the provision of short-stay high-cost parking within the centre for shoppers and business visitors, while bus termini were given priority at the principal destinations.

Beyond this stage, stronger measures involving road pricing and traffic restraint are achieving wider acceptance. As yet, *road pricing* has been introduced only in Singapore on a significant scale, in conjunction with parking controls, public transport provision and infrastructural improvements. Since 1975, motorists without a full complement of passengers must buy an entry licence before making a peak-period journey to the city centre. This had the effect of reducing the number of cars entering the centre during the morning peak period by a third. The more technically sophisticated Hong Kong experiment involving electronic meters attached to cars which were activated by sensors in the roads has now been discontinued. While such devices have until recently been considered exotic or fanciful, it is notable that the general idea of road pricing, the use of entry permits for central London and a wider use of toll roads are becoming increasingly common elements in the debate on urban transport in Britain (Hall, 1989).

In practice, *traffic restraint* has been used more widely. This has been particularly evident in western Europe and the experiences of cities such as Bonn, Stuttgart, Vienna, Bologna and Copenhagen have demonstrated that traffic restraint in the city centres combined with improved public transport and extensive pedestrianisation have distinct commercial and environmental advantages. In Florence, this has involved comprehensive restrictions on motor vehicles within the area of the former city walls, and residents' passes restricted to one per family. Parking has been concentrated on the periphery and the centre is served by shuttle bus services.

On a note of caution, however, it is evident that policies of traffic restraint in city centres must be considered in the context of broader land use planning and public transport strategies in the city region. Pressures for suburbanisation and functional decentralisation are fundamental tendencies associated with rising levels of private car ownership in the post-industrial city. Consequently, undue restrictions imposed on city centres are likely to channel developmental pressures to more accessible suburban nodes. This can be used to advantage to spread traffic loads but care has to be taken if the demise of the traditional city centre is not to result.

Summary

Clearly, there is no shortage of possible solutions to the urban transportation problem. A number of important issues, however, remain to be resolved and are likely to be central to the continuing debate. Of primary significance is the Governmental attitude to public transport. Its potential is likely to be closely related to the degree to which it is considered a publicly subsidised or commercially viable service. In either event, radical improvements will incorporate substantial financial implications. In practice, it is also apparent that policies designed to enhance the attractions of public transport have to be integrated with both restraints on private vehicle usage and wider issues of land use planning. Similarly, to be most effective the various modes of public and private transport need to be coordinated with one another. Finally, it is evident that the 'choice' of transport mode used is as much a behavioural as an economically-based decision. The existing literature pays scant regard to the detailed determinants of modal choice. Thus, to maximise the effectiveness of the wide array of urban transport strategies, additional insights into this issue are necessary.

Chapter 8

Urban Services

The city as a supplier of services

The physical expansion and increasing functional complexity of urban life in Western cities in the twentieth century has resulted in a proliferation of the quantity and variety of services needed by the urban population. The resulting range of services is provided by a variety of commercial and governmental agencies so that their spatial distributions, associated functional characteristics and patterns of usage also vary significantly. Nevertheless, five centrally distinct but overlapping categories can be suggested for preliminary analysis.

Shopping
The most widely evident are the services normally associated with shopping. These comprise retail outlets; personal services such as hairdressers, dry cleaners and photographers; professional services such as banks, building societies, solicitors and estate agents; and a range of catering and entertainment facilities. Their unity derives from the fact that they are provided usually for individual customers drawn from relatively local urban hinterlands. Also, their traditional locational patterns have in the past resulted from the competitive decisions taken by a large number of small suppliers aiming to maximise the commercial advantages of accessibility to the perceived distribution of consumer demand. However, in recent years the emergence of large supply organisations, comprehensive commercial property development companies and the influence of physical planning controls have tended to complicate the latter situation significantly.

Wholesaling and warehousing
The wholesaling function and associated warehousing activities comprise a second category which traditionally has had close functional and geographical associations with shopping. In its simplest form the wholesaling activity sets out to serve such functions as retailing, consumer services, office activities, public utilities and industry by providing them with goods which are subsequently sold to the public, consumed by the recipient organisation or used to produce a profit. The emphasis is, therefore, on the distribution function. The service is performed mainly for users who are companies and institutions of varying sizes

rather than individuals. Also in many cases the customer does not visit the point of sale. For these reasons the wholesaling function tends to be found in a greater variety of locations than are shopping centres.

Offices

Offices concerned with transactional and administrative activities associated with the collection, processing and exchange of information comprise a third category of service. Notable amongst these are the international, national and regional headquarters of organisations involved in finance, insurance, commerce, industry and government. The 'consumers' of the services in this instance are the business organisations and administrative institutions involved in all sections of economic, social and political life rather than individual customers. Thus, the locational patterns of offices tend to demonstrate a greater degree of concentration in larger centres at both the national and intra-urban scale than in the case of shopping centres. Traditionally, this has been considered to reflect the stronger forces of centralisation associated with the need to maintain close communication linkages between the different office functions and maximum access to a highly diversified labour market.

Medical services

A fourth category of medical services comprising hospitals, general practitioners, dental surgeries can be suggested. These services are closely connected functionally and are significantly different from the previous groups since in most countries they are subject to a stronger degree of public control. The locational decisions of, for example, general practitioners and dentists are restricted usually by a combination of professional or governmental licensing controls. In the case of hospitals, the individual units tend to be larger relative to the scale of the system as a whole and, therefore, less responsive to changes in the nature and location of user demand, while their location policies are usually subject to a greater degree of public control than shopping facilities.

Public utilities

The fifth category comprises public utilities such as schools, public libraries, museums, leisure centres, local government administration offices and police and fire services. Their location policies are subject to public control in most countries and have little dependence upon a competitive market mechanism.

In summary, it is clear that while the five categories of activities outlined above have been introduced under the general heading of 'urban services', this title subsumes considerable variability. Thus, it must be stressed at the outset that due to the differences in the nature of, and controls over, the specific categories of services, both the locational decisions – which determine their spatial patterns – and the associated user decisions – which relate to their use-exhibit considerable variation in detail both between and within the categories suggested.

The city centre

In the early stages of city development rudimentary versions of the urban services noted above emerged near to the city centre in order to serve the relatively compact urban area. With continued growth there was an associated growth in the scale, degree of specialisation and range of services provided. In the context of the growing city the particular locational requirements of the various services tended to result in the emergence of a spatial segregation by function, initially in relation to an expanded central area, and subsequently to serve an extended urban area following the process of suburban expansion. Most central areas, however, continue to contain concentrations of urban service activities, partly because the accessibility of the central area allows it to provide services performing a city-wide or wider regional function, and partly because the forces of inertia have maintained elements of the original pattern. Frequently, the historic environment of the city centre also contributes to its commercial attraction. Thus, the city centre remains as a primary focus of many urban service facilities, around which the subsequently developed intra-urban service systems are arranged. For this reason it will be instructive to consider the distribution of urban services in the city centre as a first stage in the development of an understanding of the spatial patterns of service facilities in the city.

The central business district

Much of the early urban geographical interest in the city centre focused on the central business district (CBD), particularly through the pioneering work of Murphy, Vance and Epstein. The CBD was characterised as the functional core of the city towards which their economic urban activities which required an accessible location for the economic viability or functional efficiency tended to gravitate. Typically, it comprised concentrations of retailing and associated consumer services, commercial and public office activities, wholesaling and warehousing and an array of entertainment such as theatres, hotels and cultural activities.

To facilitate comparative analysis Murphy and Vance developed a method of *CBD delimitation* for medium-sized cities based on detailed land use surveys. Certain activities were considered definitive of CBD status. These comprised retail and consumer services, including restaurants, entertainment facilities and hotels; and commercial office activities. Other land uses were designated non-central business since their central location was not considered to be related to the commercial advantages of centrality. Wholesaling, railyards, industry, residences, parks, schools, churches and government administration were excluded on these grounds, although it was recognised that some individual establishments in these categories gained an economic advantage from a central location. From this data a central Business Height Index (CBHI) and a Central

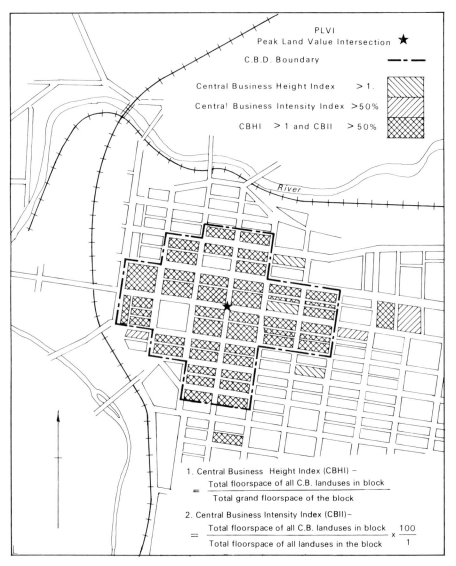

Figure 8.1   Delimiting the CBD – a conceptual representation

(Based on Murphy and Vance, 1954, in *Economic Geography* **30**)

Business Intensity Index (CBII) were derived, and where a block exceeded both values of 1 and 50 per cent respectively, it was included in the CBD. The technique is schematically illustrated by Figure 8.1.

The technique has a number of limitations which were recognised by the original investigators. The most important concern the arbitrary decisions taken at a number of stages in the regionalisation procedure, while Herbert and

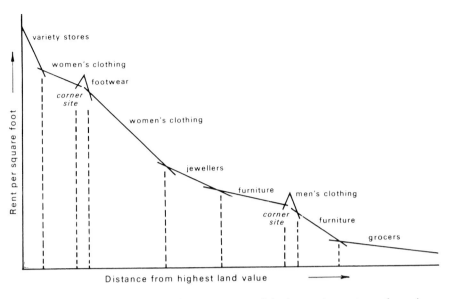

Figure 8.2   Hypothetical spatial arrangement of the internal structure of a major unplanned CBD shopping centre based upon the bid-rent curve

(Source: Scott, 1970; reproduced by permission of P. Scott)

Carter have argued that the technique requires too much effort to define a boundary which, at best, can be only an approximation. Nevertheless, the methodology stimulated interest in the need to define and investigate the variety of urban functions found in city centres and simpler variants of the technique have been used widely in the initial stage of a range of subsequent analyses of the CBD.

Considerable effort has been directed towards achieving an understanding of the *internal spatial structure* of the CBD. Murphy, Vance and Epstein (1955) considered that the spatial differentiation of business activities was directly related to the relative value per unit area of sites, itself an indicator of accessibility. Thus, the extent to which an activity can profit from exploiting the commercial advantages of accessibility will determine the price it is willing to pay, and this will be reflected in the spatial arrangement of business activities. This contention was combined with the concept of the bid rent curve by Scott (1970) to suggest a broad concentricity of like retail types reflecting their hierarchical status (Figure 8.2). However, this relationship only holds true at a highly generalised level. Relative accessibility within the city centre is rarely a function merely of distance from the peak land value intersection (PLVI). The morphological complexity associated with physical site constraints such as rivers, coasts and hills act as substantially modifying influences, while the development of canals, railways and public open spaces in the early stages of urban growth are of similar significance. The influence of physical and hist-

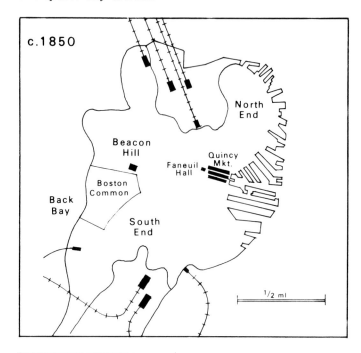

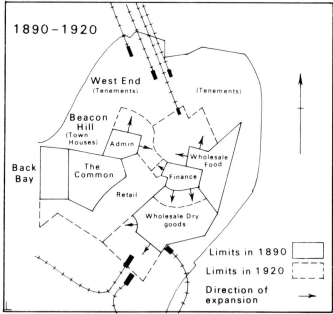

Figure 8.3   The historical development of Boston's CBD, 1850–1920.

(After Ward, 1966; reproduced by permission of *Economic Geography*)

orical factors has been demonstrated for Boston and for Cardiff to have had a marked formative effect on the internal spatial structure of their CBDs which persists to the present day (Figure 8.3). Particular functions were shown to gravitate to locations which offered some functional or commercial advantage and this superimposed a strong segregative effect upon any tendency towards concentric zonation. This effect was noted in the case of the American cities studied by Murphy, Vance and Epstein (1955) and for the six Australian state capitals and was expressed in a tendency for the retailing zones to be elongated along the main traffic axes and for the office activities to be segregated in the section of the CBD in which they first emerged.

There are also spatial regularities within the CBD at the microspatial scale of analysis. The detailed decisions of both businesses and individuals tend to result in a degree of spatial ordering amongst retailers. The advantages obtained from a location adjacent to other retailers were identified in the early work of Nelson. He developed the *theory of cumulative attraction* based on the premise that a number of stores dealing in similar or complementary types of goods will attract more business if they are clustered. This results in an increase in shared business because shoppers can compare quality and prices or because customer interchange is encouraged between stores offering complementary goods and services. Together, these principles constitute the *rule of retail compatibility*. Conversely, stores selling standardised convenience products may well be mutually repelled to *minimise competitive hazard*. These ideas initiated an interest in the recognition of regularities in the distribution of shop types rather than of functional associations suggested by Nelson. According to Kivell and Shaw the bulk of the available evidence suggests that high-order or quality comparison goods retailers tend to cluster into particular sections of a centre, while low-order goods outlets are significantly more dispersed often at the margins of a centre. A recent study of Belfast confirms the continued significance of these tendencies, and the inference is made that the patterns still reflect the principles suggested by Nelson. Another study reveals that food retailers dislike neighbours in the same line of business. Wallpaper, paint and electrical goods stores show similar, although not as pronounced attitudes to locations near competitors. By contrast, retailers of quality comparison goods such as furniture and carpets favour agglomeration. The behaviour of shoppers demonstrates consistent findings. The importance of strong comparison shopping linkages between large magnet stores in the centre of Newcastle Upon Tyne is demonstrated by Bennison and Davies. There is also limited evidence to suggest that a functional complementarity between clothing and footwear stores, and furniture and furnishings has a comparable effect.

Despite the complexity of the resulting structure, Davies has proposed a structural model for central area retailing functions (Figure 8.4). The location decisions of retailers are considered to reflect three separate accessibility dimensions. The traditional city centre shopping activities tend to locate in accordance with *general accessibility* to the distribution of consumers. These tend to be distributed in a concentric zonal pattern, reflecting their hierarchical

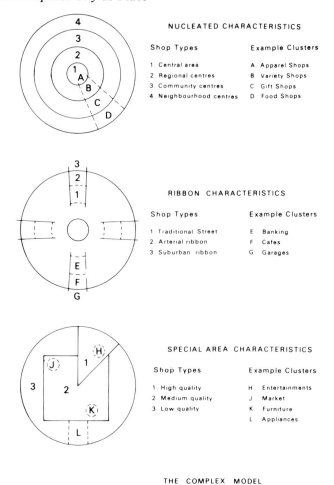

NUCLEATED CHARACTERISTICS

Shop Types	Example Clusters
1. Central area	A. Apparel Shops
2. Regional centres	B. Variety Shops
3. Community centres	C. Gift Shops
4. Neighbourhood centres	D. Food Shops

RIBBON CHARACTERISTICS

Shop Types	Example Clusters
1. Traditional Street	E. Banking
2. Arterial ribbon	F. Cafes
3. Suburban ribbon	G. Garages

SPECIAL AREA CHARACTERISTICS

Shop Types	Example Clusters
1. High quality	H. Entertainments
2. Medium quality	J. Market
3. Low quality	K. Furniture
	L. Appliances

THE COMPLEX MODEL

Figure 8.4   A structural model of central area core retailing facilities

(Source: Davies, 1972, in *Transactions*; reproduced by permission of the Institute of British Geographers)

status. Other functions such as garages and restaurants were considered more likely to take advantage of the linear accessibility associated with the major traffic arteries entering the city centre – *arterial accessibility*. Finally, the location of some specialised functions, such as entertainment facilities, furniture showrooms or produce markets was considered likely to reflect the *special accessibility* attached to sites, relating to particular historical or marketing environmental circumstances.

The resulting 'complex model' was found to provide a reasonable approximation of the retail structure of central Coventry and has recently been demonstrated to have retained its broad applicability for Belfast.

The issue of *dynamic change* in the CBD has also been addressed by a number of workers. Murphy, Vance and Epstein (1955) noted that the CBD was advancing in the direction of the *zone of assimilation*. This was typically located in the direction of the higher status residential parts of the city and characterised by new speciality shops, office headquarters and new hotels. Conversely, the *zone of discard* was usually located adjacent to industrial and wholesaling activities, near the railroads and lower status residential districts and became typified by concentrations of pawn shops cheap clothing stores, low grade restaurants and transport termini; an area later characterised by Griffin and Preston as the *transition zone* around the CBD.

A subsequent historical study of San Francisco for the period 1850–1931 provides additional insight into the process of change. Functions needing ease of access to a market were found most likely to shift their location in the direction of their clientele. For example, clothing retailers tended to shift towards the growing higher status parts of the city and hotels towards centres of entertainment and focal points in the transport network. Conversely, the financial district did not move significantly since its orientation to direct consumer access was slight. Rapid and sustained phases of urban growth were shown to result in a distinct segregation of CBD activities into locations particularly suited to their functional characteristics. In the largest 'world cities' such as London, New York and Paris it was considered that this process imitated a characteristically fragmented spatial structure (Figure 8.5). Some similarities are evident in these cities but detailed differences in spatial structure reflect the local physiographic and historical constraints, and the socio-economic variations in which such cities need to be viewed.

The CBD: contemporary issues

Since the mid 1950s the character, internal structure and problems of city centres in Western Europe and North America have been transformed by a number of major modifying influences. In the USA the Urban Renewal Programmes introduced by the 1949 Housing Act have improved the environmental character of the zone in transition, reducing its functional complexity, and distinguishing it from the CBD; the West End redevelopment project and the construction of the Government Centre in Boston are cases in point.

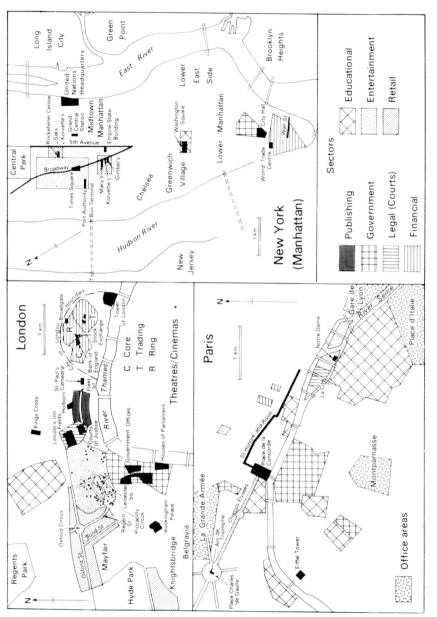

Figure 8.5   The CBD of world cities: spatial fragmentation of functions in London, Paris and New York

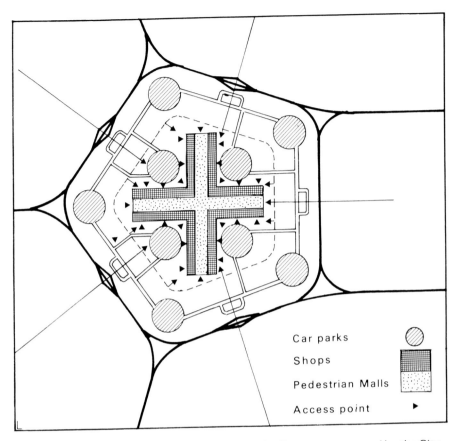

Car parks

Shops

Pedestrian Malls

Access point

Figure 8.6 An idealised central area structure for Coventry, proposed by the City Planning Department

(Source: Davies, 1976; reproduced by permission of R. L. Davies)

In Britain a sequence of planning ideas have had even greater effect. The central area redevelopment introduced in the early 1950s for the bomb-damaged centre of Coventry (Figure 8.6) demonstrates the principles involved. Similar ideas were developed further by Sir Colin Buchanan and were officially endorsed by the Ministry of Transport. Thus, a number of recurrent elements have come to increasingly characterise the spatial structure of the central areas of British cities. Inner ring roads with associated car parking facilities usually surround the CBD; pedestrianised retail concentrations, separate office districts, civic centres and possibly entertainment districts are more easily distinguishable within the CBD, while conservation areas to preserve historic city centres are frequent. In short, town planning has emphasised the separateness of functional elements in the central area and has produced a move towards less complexity and greater structural uniformity.

Of greater consequence, however, has been the adverse commercial impact of urban decentralisation, characterised by Berry *et al.* (1963) as 'commercial blight'. This has been most marked in the USA where a rapid increase in car ownership and associated improvements of urban highways has considerably improved intra-city mobility. This initiated a decentralisation of employment opportunities from the restrictions of a city centre location, while at the same time an increased desire for spacious living encouraged residential suburbanisation which resulted in the reduction of residential densities by a factor of between 4 and 8. These trends favoured the development of planned car-orientated shopping facilities in the outer suburbs. Pressures to this end were accentuated by the lack of effective planning controls and the availability of suitably large, relatively cheap suburban sites with the result that the postwar period has seen the proliferation of planned suburban shopping malls, mostly at nodal locations on rapid transit routes. By contrast, the ease of access to the city centres has been reduced, while the replacement of the middle class white population of the inner suburbs by low status groups (usually Blacks) has undermined the spending power of the inner city market. Inevitably, the combination of the attractions of the new suburban centres along with the deterioration of the commercial environment of the city centre, exacerbated by social and racial problems, resulted in the widespread decline of the CBD in North American cities throughout the 1950s and 1960s. More recently, studies by Robertson and Lord record the continued decline of retailing in a wide range of American city centres.

In fact, Lord suggests that the traditional city centre in the USA has become less of a retail-commercial district and more of an office-commercial and cultural-entertainment complex. Its weakness as a retail centre results from its increasing dependence on 'internal markets' comprising CBD employees, tourists and city centre residents, rather than its traditional orientation towards the metropolitan area shoppers now intercepted by the profusion of suburban shopping opportunities.

However, these adverse circumstances have not led to the inexorable decline of the CBD everywhere, since many city centres have retained significant advantages for the provision of specialist shopping activities. Potentially, they are still at the point of maximum accessibility to the whole city region in comparison with the sectoral accessibility of the suburban regional centres. Again, due to historical inertia, the CBD retains concentrations of office employment, governmental activities, entertainment, medical and cultural facilities which bring significant numbers of people regularly to the city centre. Many city centres have also developed an important and expanding tourist function. In addition, a significant demand by selective groups – the unmarried, childless, mobile sections of the higher-income categories – for middle and high-cost apartments in central locations has resulted in the residential regeneration of formerly socially declining districts in some of the environmentally more attractive city centres. This process of gentrification has the effect of enhancing the potential retail expenditure of the inner city population.

During the 1970s and 1980s the declining centres of a significant number of North American cities have witnessed a partial revitalisation. Speciality, theme, or festival centres have been developed in a number of city centres. Faneuil Hall and Quincy Market in Central Boston, the Ghiardelli Centre on the San Francisco waterfront, Harbour Place in Baltimore and the Trumps Centre in New York are notable examples. Similarly, a number of mixed, office, hotel, convention centres and shopping complexes exemplified by the Prudential Centre in Boston and the Renaissance Centre in Detroit have added distinct but separate commercial precincts to traditional city areas; a smaller number of large shopping malls have been added to link older department stores in Grand Avenue, Milwaukee and in St Louis. Lord, however, considers that, apart from the limited number of central shopping malls, these developments have not significantly offset the competitive impact of the suburban facilities since their retail activities are of limited size and are strongly orientated to the tourist market.

However, in Canada, while subject to similar competitive pressures, the situation of the city centres is apparently, as yet, less problematic; probably due to sustained population growth combined with the absence of a substantial inner city racial problem. In Vancouver, for example, the Pacific Centre has been constructed virtually at the centre of the CBD, while the Eaton Centre has consolidated shopping in central Toronto.

Similarly, in Western Europe the impact of retail decentralisation has been less marked, due principally to more restrictive planning controls. This has been particularly evident in Britain where prior to the 1980s central and local government strongly subscribed to the potential efficiency of the traditional hierarchy of shopping centres for urban areas. This found strongest expression in a widespread commitment to the maintenance of the city centre as the commercial and social hub of urban life. Thus, large scale retail redevelopments were initiated in the 1950s with the development of open-air pedestrian precincts similar in design to the reconstruction of central Coventry. This phase was followed by the construction of covered malls from the mid 1960s and Gibbs reports that in the period 1965–81, 88 per cent of towns of over 100,000 population had undertaken town centre shopping developments of greater than 4644 square metres. These reached a peak in 1976 but continued to be developed as a competitive reaction to out-of-town retailing. In most cases these largely 'planned' developments have had the effect of increasing the centralisation of shopping facilities into a particular section of the CBD, usually close to the existing major shopping zone. For example, Davies and Bennison show how the Eldon Square shopping development in Newcastle consolidated the principal focus of shopping activities into a significantly smaller area. Such developments inevitably have repercussions elsewhere in the CBD. A shift in the focus of shopping trips in the direction of the new development often precipitated the decline and blighting of a significant number of small shops in the streets marginal to the CBD. This type of impact was noted in Newcastle and also in Utrecht (Netherlands), as a result of the opening of the large Hoog Catherigne Centre.

Also, new precincts tend to increase the significance of the larger multiple goods shops at the expense of small independent businesses in city centres, since the former are more financially capable of renting the large units usually favoured by the letting companies.

Even in Britain, however, the effects of gradual retail decentralisation since the mid 1960s has been accelerated in the 1980s by the relaxation of restrictions associated with an increasing government adherence to a market philosophy. Consequently, widespread concern is now being expressed on the future of the city centre, and the notional ideal of a complementarity between city centre and suburban shopping is giving way to a recognition of the growing competitive impact of unrestrained decentralisation. Davies graphically illustrates the decline of secondary shopping streets in British cities, combined with a general environmental deterioration, and exacerbated by problems of access and parking for car-borne shoppers. A wide array of improvements are now being investigated. These range from the development of the covered malls noted earlier, more imaginative pedestrianisation schemes, improved car parking facilities and general environmental refurbishments. A number of studies also stress the need for stronger partnerships between the public and private sector for the provision of finance, and good design and management, while the active management and promotion of the city centre has recently been pioneered in Manchester.

Similar circumstances have been recognised in Europe. Following the less restrictive attitudes to retail decentralisation of the 1960s and early 1970s, both France and West Germany, for example, introduced regulation in the mid 1970s to reduce the adverse competitive impact of retail decentralisation on historic city centres (Davies, 1984). In both cases, however, more imaginative car parking and pedestrianisation schemes are generally considered to have maintained better access along with a more amenable shopping environment than characterised the British situation. Hass-Klau, for example, illustrates the effectiveness of comprehensive pedestrianisation programmes instituted under the 'Verkehrberuhigung' concept (traffic calming) for many West German cities. Likewise in central Copenhagen the problems of commercial decline associated with retail decentralisation resulted in the formulation of 'Ideplan 77', comprising a wide range of environmental improvements focusing on enhanced pedestrianisation, improved car parking, and the functional segregation of a variety of speciality retail and leisure precincts.

In all cases, however, it seems that the critical issue for the continued strength of retailing in city centres is the vexed question of access. The location of city centres at the hub of the urban transport network has obvious advantages for attracting a significant proportion of the users of public transport. The ease of access for car-borne shoppers offered by most suburban shopping centres is still, however, nowhere nearly matched by city centres. In an increasingly motorised society, whatever the improvements undertaken in the traditional city centres, the continued commitment of the large magnet stores and investment in new retail facilities is still critically dependent upon car-borne shoppers being able to park with ease; in close proximity to the major retail concentrations; at minimal cost; and in amenable surroundings. The failure to grasp this particular nettle is likely, in the absence of severe restraints on continued decentralisation, to result in the progressive decline of city centre retailing in European cities.

The experience of the largest international centres such as London and Paris are an exception to this generalisation. Despite the scale of traffic congestion in both cases the strength of the 'internal market' support provided by the international office and governmental functions, the associated residential gentrification, as well as thriving tourist industries has avoided widespread commercial blight. In London, the buoyancy of retailing in the Knightsbridge area and the development of speciality retailing exemplified by the redevelopment of the Covent Garden wholesale market and the Trocadero centre in Piccadilly are indicative of this situation. In Paris, the maintained exclusivity of the Rue Faubourg St Honoré and the redevelopment of the three-level Forum shopping centre (40,000 m^2) at Les Halles are of equivalent significance. Even so, the tendency towards commercial decline intermittently noted in Oxford Street, London is symptomatic of the loss of the metropolitan area trade and the environmental deterioration associated with traffic congestion.

The suburbs: decentralisation of services

The suburbanisation of shopping facilities

With the physical expansion of urban areas well beyond the original city centres a point is soon reached when significant numbers of people are located too far away from the CBD to be supplied conveniently with the most frequently required goods and services. New suppliers of the most frequently required, lowest order functions respond to this situation by establishing premises in locations accessible to the increasingly dispersed population. If dispersion of demand continues, it becomes for feasible increasingly more specialised functions to decentralise. Usually, these additional functions will gravitate to the most accessible of the original non-central locations and, in the process, create a series of second-order service centres. This process is schematically illustrated in Figure 8.7. These centres will not normally achieve the degree of specialisation found in the CBD because they will be less accessible to the city-wide population necessary to support the highest-order functions. The remainder of the original non-central service locations will continue to provide lower-order functions in positions interstitial to the higher-order centres. These form a series of low-order centres. This process ideally leads to a nested hierarchical spatial pattern of service centres in cities, similar to the central place system conceptualised by Christaller.

The application of these concepts to the study of the intra-urban service centres was first developed in the North American literature. Berry, *et al.* (1963)

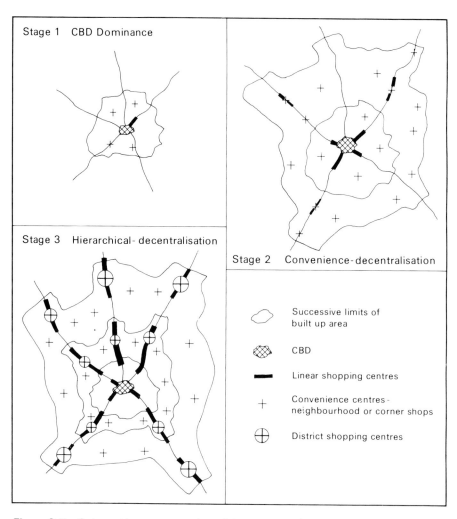

Figure 8.7   Schematic representation of the process of retail decentralisation

indicated that Chicago demonstrated a central commercial dominance until 1910, but by 1935 75 per cent of business establishments were located beyond the CBD. Commercial land use extended in ribbons along most grid and arterial routeways and at the busiest intersections outlying business centres developed which could be differentiated into neighbourhood, community and regional hierarchical orders, relative to their size and degree of centrality to the surrounding population. The essentially linear pattern was related to the dependence of the population on public transport routes in the densely populated inner suburbs.

Since 1950 the strong forces promoting retail decentralisation noted in the previous section have resulted in the transformation of the intra-urban system

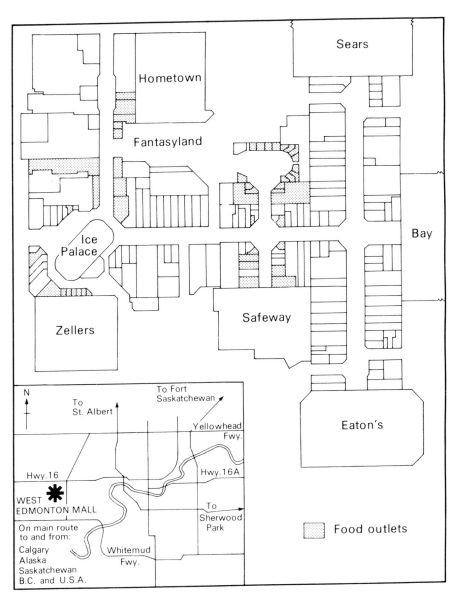

Figure 8.8 The West Edmonton Mall, Canada: a super-regional shopping centre

of shopping centres in American cities. Planned car-oriented shopping centres have been developed at a profusion of accessible locations on the intra-urban highway network. Lord records that between 1950 and 1980 the number of such centres increased from 100 to 22,000 by a process characterised as the 'malling of the American landscape'. The newly developed centres have tended to increase in size from neighbourhood to regional status as personal mobility has increased. In the process the enhanced sophistication of design and the degree of specialisation of the centres has developed from parades of small shops with fore-court parking facilities providing essentially convenience items, through larger parades including superstores and junior department stores, to the enclosed regional shopping malls including superstores and department stores set in vast car parks. Lord (1988) records that in the Baltimore metropolitan area alone (population 2.2 million) there were 10 regional shopping centres of greater than 46,500 m^2, two of which exceeded 92,900 m^2; while even larger examples such as the City Post Oak area in suburban Houston (185,750 m^2) are not uncommon. Currently, however, the most spectacular example is the West Edmonton Mall in Canada. This comprises a comprehensive shopping and leisure centre of 375,000 m^2, including the 46,500 m^2 Fantasyland indoor amusement park. Five major department stores are represented in the two level centre, along with an ice skating rink, indoor lake and over 400 shops, effectively forming an alternative city centre (Figure 8.8). Dawson's (1983) almost poetic portrayal of the transition of the regional shopping centre from a 'great cash register in verdant suburbia' to a 'space station with a full life-support system acting as a refuge for travellers through urban space' is clearly not far wide of the mark.

In the USA Lord (1988) notes that by 1982 there were already 14 metropolitan areas in which a total 25 major suburban retail concentrations exceeded the retail sales levels of the CBD, the trend being particularly marked in Atlanta (3) and Indianapolis (6). Thus, the American city was characterised as moving from the traditional monocentric form orientated around the CBD to a distinctly polycentric structure. In many instances, however, the more rudimentary early centres of all sizes are now suffering from the competition of the larger, more attractive recent developments and many require extensive refurbishment.

The system of shopping facilities in North American cities has also demonstrated increased spatial fragmentation since improved personal mobility has allowed the locational specialisation of retail conformations to take place. Specialisation has occurred by product, particularly for infrequently purchased goods such as automobiles and furniture, and also by social class, leading to both high status fashion centres and low-status discount-stores. In addition, highway-orientated functions such as service stations, restaurants, drive-ins and motels have accentuated the linear pattern of commercial land use. In addition, the commercial blight evident in the CBD has also afflicted the inner suburbs. Decline has been substantial and prolonged. Retailers of the higher order goods traders have gone out of business. Vacancy rates of a third to a half are not uncommon as the residential areas have declined in status.

The outcome of this overall process of change, unmitigated by planning intervention, is what Berry *et al.* (1963) have termed 'spatial anarchy'. In situations of this kind, while accepting that some systems of order can still be recognised based upon a hierarchical arrangement of shopping centres, the recognition of ribbon developments of various kinds and the emergence of specialised functional areas; the appropriateness of the concepts derived from central place theory as a basis for the analysis of the system of shopping centres in American cities has become increasingly questionable.

The pressures for change noted for the North American situation have emerged in most other Western countries. However, the growth in personal mobility and affluence, and the associated decentralisation and suburbanisation, have not proceeded as rapidly elsewhere, while urban planning controls have exerted a variable influence. This is reflected in international variations in the process of adjustment.

In the Australian and European intra-urban systems the process of change is well advanced. As early as the mid 1960s Johnston and Rimmer indicated the existence of six large planned centres in suburban Melbourne, one of which was of regional significance. In addition, the initiation of a process of commercial blight was demonstrated for the inner suburbs in which recent Southern European immigrants were concentrated. Alexander and Dawson also demonstrated the familiar North American pattern of central area decline for the six Australian state capitals. Similar tendencies have emerged throughout Western Europe, initially involving the widespread development of superstores and hypermarkets (ranging from 2325–$23,250 \, m^2$). Davies (1984) notes 433 in France in 1981 accounting for nearly 20 per cent of food sales and 10 per cent of non-food products. Subsequently, the development of planned suburban shopping centres of all sizes is of equivalent significance. In West Germany there were 500 new centres by 1977, 57 of which achieved regional status; while in Paris alone 15 new regional shopping centres were designated in conjunction with a strategy for planned suburban growth which included five new towns. The recognition of the competitive impact of retail decentralisation, however, has led to moves towards stricter controls throughout Europe since the mid 1970s. This was initiated with the French 'Loi Royer' in 1973 and has been replicated in Belgium in 1975 and the Netherlands in 1976. West Germany has also used existing planning legislation to similar effect (Davies, 1984).

A more cautious attitude to retail decentralisation, supported by restrictive planning controls, serves to distinguish the British experience. Throughout the period 1960–80 central and local government was committed to the retention of the traditional shopping hierarchy focused on the city centre and complemented by a range of district centres, neighbourhood parades and a range of more localised facilities. This has involved the encouragement of investment in CBD redevelopment, along with the improvement of the shopping, traffic and parking environment of the smaller unplanned centres. A limited number of planned district centres, such as Seacroft in Leeds and Cowley in Oxford, were envisaged to ensure equality of access to services throughout a city region. Below this level a series of neighbourhood or corner store facilities were considered necessary to provide convenience goods for the less mobile sections of the community, while also serving a supplementary convenience function for the population at large.

Despite the constraints or decentralisation imposed by most structure plans, steady commercial pressure has ensured that change has been a continuous and marked feature of the geography of retailing in British cities over the last twenty-five years. Suburban decentralisation, central area redevelopment, the commercial blight of the older inner city facilities and small shops, and the recent regeneration of the convenience store have all characterised the process of change. The changes have substantially modified the traditional hierarchy, to a degree that Dawson (1983) suggests that they constitute a 'retail revolution'.

Retail decentralisation has been the most graphic expression of change. This was initiated by the establishment of superstores and hypermarkets in the mid 1960s and has been termed the 'first wave' of retail decentralisation. This was followed in the mid 1970s by a 'second wave' characterised by retail warehouses, initially selling DIY products and bulky durable goods such as furniture, carpets and electricals. More recently, the range of goods offered in retail warehouses has expanded to include clothing, footwear and toys.

The locational requirements of most superstores, hypermarkets and retail warehouses have similarly stressed the need for ease of access and parking, along with the financial advantages of low site costs. Consequently, large accessible sites adjacent to major intersections, central to newly developing residential areas, on the edges of cities, or on the fringes of industrial estates have been favoured. Also, as a result of ad hoc planning decisions, individual stores have often been developed in isolated free-standing locations. Initially, these developments added a distinct element of spatial fragmentation to the system of shopping centres in many towns.

Since the early 1980s the increasingly 'free-market' orientation of central government has resulted in the relaxation of restrictions on such developments. This has operated primarily through the appeals procedure rather than by the formulation of a comprehensive new strategy. The situation was exacerbated by the Enterprise Zone Policy announced in 1980 which has encouraged retail developments in the many enterprise zones where investment in new manufacturing was considered unlikely. With the increasing scale of retail decentralisation planning authorities have directed development to industrial estate or enterprise zone sites. This has resulted in the emergence of loose agglomerations, or occasionally planned concentrations of retail warehouses, in industrial estate locations or articulated along main arterial roads. Such developments have been termed 'retail warehouse parks'. Where such developments incorporate superstores, a more balanced shopping environment results, with a potentially greater impact on the local or even regional shopping facilities. These have been termed 'retail parks.' The retail park has become a distinctive new element in the retail structure of most British cities, the largest of which are to be found in enterprise zones. The unplanned Swansea enterprise zone retail park, for example, included two superstores and 24 retail warehouses by 1988. These total 39,000 m², a scale fast approaching the threshold for a small regional centre (46,500 m²).

The forces generating retail decentralisation have gathered even greater momentum in recent years. In fact, Schiller has identified a 'third wave' dating from the proposal by Marks and Spencer in May 1984 to open out-of-town

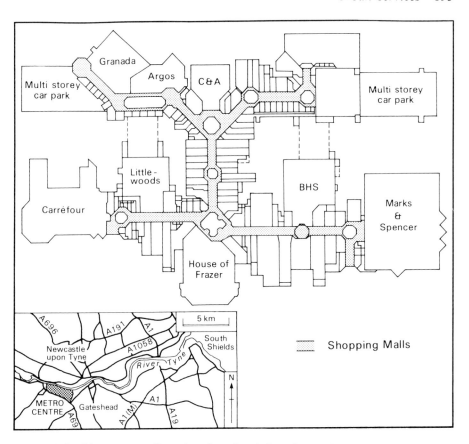

Figure 8.9   Metrocentre, Gateshead: regional shopping centre

stores. The third wave is, thus, characterised by the decentralisation of a wide range of quality comparison goods shopping and supporting services, exemplified by the intentions of firms such as Habitat, Laura Ashley and World of Leather. The spatial form of the new wave and its status in the retail system is of critical significance to the process of retail change. The logical conclusion of the decentralisation of quality comparison goods retailing is the development of regional out-of-town shopping centres. The opening of the Metro Centre in the Gateshead Enterprise Zone in 1986, planned as an integrated regional shopping and leisure complex, is the first major example of the new phase (Figure 8.9). This has been followed by a plethora of similar applications and reflects the recognition of the potential commercial importance of the third wave.

Schiller, however, considers that the development of new regional centres is likely to be limited in number and largely confined to the edges of the major conurbations due to site constraints. There are few locations with sufficiently good road access to serve catchment populations in excess of 250,000; which would not generate unacceptably high levels of local traffic on or near to major

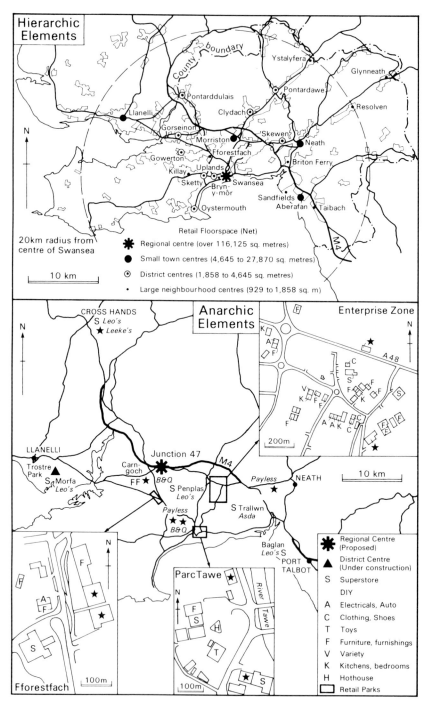

Figure 8.10   Retail change in the UK: hierarchic and anarchic elements in Greater Swansea

inter-regional traffic arteries; and which at the same time would be large enough to accommodate such developments. These considerations are reflected in the re-emergence of official caution on the issue of new regional shopping centres. Instead, Schiller considers that the more likely effect of the third wave will be the addition of quality comparison goods retailing to existing retail parks. This will result in the creation of hybrid centres, which if developed in excess of 46,500 m² will form unplanned or de facto regional centres. In fact, developments under construction in the Dudley enterprise zone will far exceed this threshold.

Retail change in Britian has been subject to two powerful and conflicting sets of forces. On the one hand, the commitment of local government planners to the assumption of the social and commercial efficiency of a traditional hierarchical system of urban shopping centres has tended to retain a strong element of centralisation and inertia in the system. By contrast, the commercial pressures, for large decentralised facilities, increasingly supported by central government, reflects the combined influence of deep-seated forces affecting both social life-styles and the economic organisation of retailing. The relationship between these two sets of forces has not at any stage been accommodated by a comprehensive retail planning strategy. Consequently, the cities of Britain demonstrate a combination of evolutionary and revolutionary features, epitomised by 'hierarchic' and 'anarchic' retail forms. This is illustrated for Greater Swansea (Figure 8.10). Clearly, the spatially anarchic retail system which developed in the cities of the USA in the postwar period has not emerged in Britain. In fact, the evidence still offers support for the contentions of Bennison and Davies (1980) that Britain ' . . . has avoided the worst excesses of decentralisation found in most other countries' and that ' . . . we may well see the British restrictive stance being vindicated in the future'. The recent re-assertion of central government caution on the issue of retail decentralisation following the profusion of applications for regional centres has provided a temporary respite. This offers the opportunity for formulating a retail planning strategy capable of accommodating both commercial and planning considerations to their mutual benefit.

Wholesaling and warehousing

The essence of the wholesaling and warehousing functions is that they provide a distribution and supply service for other business and industrial functions and thus gravitate towards these 'primary' activities. With the increasing demand for larger modern premises on extensive sites, the improvement in the intra-urban communications networks and the decentralisation of the activities which wholesaling and warehousing serve since 1945, pressures for decentralisation have also affected these functions.

There has, however, been little geographical analyses of wholesaling and warehousing. Early work by Vance (1970) proposed a 'Wholesaling Taxonomy' for the city centres of North America. A variety of *traditional wholesaling* districts were sited on the edges of city centres to supply the business community of the surrounding hinterland, along with *produce* districts serving small scale customers such as hotels, restaurants and produce retailers; while *stockholders* of speciality office equipment gravitated to similar sites to service the business community of the CBD.

Changes in transport technology, particularly associated with the increased importance of road haulage, have prompted general wholesaling functions to migrate to a variety of peripheral urban locations which offer convenient road access. Again, the general increase in city centre traffic congestion and site costs, with associated growth in both the scale of operations and the service areas has produced major difficulties in central city sites. Consequently, planners have encouraged suburban relocations such as the Covent Garden market from central London to Nine Elms and the Les Halles produce market to Rungis in suburban Paris.

More recently, however, the emergence of large organisations in all facets of economic life has resulted in both producers and retailers becoming more directly involved in distribution to improve all aspects of operational efficiency. This has resulted in a shift in emphasis away from traditional wholesaling transactions towards larger bulk transference and warehousing operations; either by manufacturers, retailers or specialist transport hauliers (Davies, 1984). The close relationship between concentrations of the wholesaling and warehousing function and the urban hierarchy has therefore declined. Instead, large modern distribution centres near to accessible motorway interchanges are becoming a marked new feature of the distribution in accessible locations along the main motorway corridors, particularly near the major conurbations. For food products the pattern is more regionally dispersed, reflecting the wider spatial dispersion of outlets offering convenience goods.

Offices in the suburbs

Offices are concerned primarily with transactional and administrative activities serving business organisations and administrative institutions involved in all sections of the life of a country or region. Consequently, office location patterns reflect the need for access to, and intercommunications between the broad economic, social and political forces central to the life of the country. This expresses itself in a greater degree of concentrations of office activities into a relatively small number of the largest cities in the centrally significant or rapidly growing regions of developed countries than occurs for the services previously considered. In the UK, London dominates the distribution of the headquarters of the top industrial companies, while Paris with 90 per cent of the headquarters of major national companies and nearly half of the civil service jobs dominates the French pattern. The only exception is the USA where the scale of the space economy combined with the location of areas of rapid growth have resulted in the emergence of secondary nodes in Chicago, the industrial cities of the Mid West, Los Angeles and San Francisco, although none rivals the concentration in New York and the associated cities of the North East Seaboard.

Similarly, at the intra-urban scale there has until relatively recently been a characteristic dominance of clusters in the CBD and its periphery. This reflects the pervasive influence of the centralisation forces associated with the need for access, for direct contact between decision-makers, to the investment and money markets, to government agencies and to expert consultation in the professions and higher educational establishments – the so-called external economies of a city centre location.

The combined influence of these forces is directly reflected in the postwar office building booms in the centres of the largest Western cities. Manners notes that between 1960 and 1972 the gross office floorspace in Manhattan increased from 9.7 million m^2 to 22.7 million m^2, while the second largest concentration in Chicago expanded by 50 per cent to 6.8 million m^2. Similarly, in central London the 7.2 million m^2 of 1945 has expanded to approximately 16.7 million m^2, employing 750,000 people by the early 1970s.

However, the scale of centralisation has contributed to locational diseconomies in city centres associated with the familiar problems of traffic congestion and rising site costs. This has resulted in a re-appraisal of city centre locations as advances in telecommunications technology have reduced some of the advantages of centralisation, particularly for routine operations. At the same time, suburban locations usually offer lower site costs, the opportunity to provide more car-parking and the flexibility to allow incremental increases in floorspace. Also suburban locations might offer shorter journeys to work and an attractive suburban working environment. The factors promoting office decentralisation have, however, not proved as strong as those operating in the retail system, and Alexander notes important counter-pressures associated with inertia and risk minimisation.

Nevertheless, clustering does occur in North American cities in the inner suburban service centres of the larger metropolitan areas, at nodal points on the interstate highway network, near to airports, and, more recently, in the vicinity of regional shopping centres. Lord (1988) notes that the latter locations, now termed suburban business centres, have been particularly favoured and the City Post Oak regional shopping centre in suburban Houston has attracted a concentration of 1.9 million m^2 of office development.

In the Western European cities office decentralisation has been weaker and more fundamentally affected by central and local government controls. In Britain by the mid 1960s London was the only city where a limited dispersal had occurred spontaneously. This initially took the form of an uncoordinated speculative scatter, with more organised exceptions in Croydon, Ealing and Wembley. The Greater London Development Plan of 1969 attempted to assert a greater degree of order by directing development to the largest twenty-eight shopping centres to minimise potential problems of traffic congestion and service coordination, while maximising external economies of concentration and public transport provision. The policy achieved a measure of success and large urban office concentrations such as Croydon emerged, although the relative autonomy of the London Boroughs resulted in local deviations from the overall strategy.

The relaxation of Government control in the 1980s, however, combined with advances in telecommunications and a buoyant demand for office accommodation is introducing significant spatial changes. Redevelopment proposals for the formerly blighted sites near the main railway stations involve integrated office, shopping and residential complexes. Notable examples in London include the Broadgate development near Liverpool Street Station, the Holborn Viaduct Site and the King's Cross redevelopment scheme. At the same time, Government encouragement of the commercial redevelopment of the London Docklands will result in large new office complexes at Canary Wharf on the Isle of Dogs and ultimately also at the Royal Docks. Altogether, current proposals involve an estimated 2.8 million m² of floorspace in the City and 2.6 million m² in the Docklands. The functional fragmentation of the largest cities noted in an earlier section is poised to increase in London (Figure 8.5).

Elsewhere in Western Europe there are similar trends and policies. In Paris development pressures in the 1970 resulted in new office concentrations in the inner city at the Avenue de la Grande Armée in the west, Montparnasse in the south, the Gare du Lyon in the east, and the Place d'Italie in the south east. Office development has also been directed increasingly to nodal suburban sites, and to the system of regional shopping centres and new towns. Of these the most spectacular development has emerged at La Défense in the inner suburbs only two miles north west of the Arc de Triomphe. The site of 300 ha. offers excellent access with its own railway station, bus terminus, extensive car parking, and direct links to central Paris via the new express underground (RER) and the urban motorway network. It comprises 10 per cent of the office floorspace of central Paris and provides for 100,000 jobs in an integrated retail, leisure and residential complex (Figure 8.5). The City Nord office park located 6 km north of the city centre of Hamburg was developed for similar reasons (Husain, 1980). The scheme was used to divert development pressures away from the city centre and now provides for 30,000 jobs in an accessible and attractive suburban location.

The suburban decentralisation of offices is now a well-established feature of most Western cities and in most cases urban planners are attempting to control the process of relocation. The most favoured solution has been to concentrate the dispersal at a limited number of nodal locations on the urban transport system, while integrating office employment with the suburban provision of shopping facilities, leisure activities and housing. The rationale behind this policy has been the need to avoid the diseconomies of central area congestion, while at the same time maximising the attractions of the external economies of concentration in non-central locations.

The medical services system

Like shopping centres, the medical services system has been viewed by geographers broadly within the conceptual framework of central place theory. The upper hierarchical levels are characterised by large specialised medical centres and teaching hospitals, while at the lowest levels a more ubiquitous distribution of partnerships of general practitioners, individual physicians or para-medical personnel located in health centres or home based situations provides a less specialised entry to the system. Similarly, the number of levels in the hierarchy are considered to reflect a combination of the density of population, levels of personal mobility, the varying degree of specialisation and frequency of treatment required, and the finance available to provide the service.

However, the 'commercial' analogy cannot be taken too far. General practitioners are not market orientated to the same degree as retailers, but are usually restricted by professional codes – which, for example, discourage

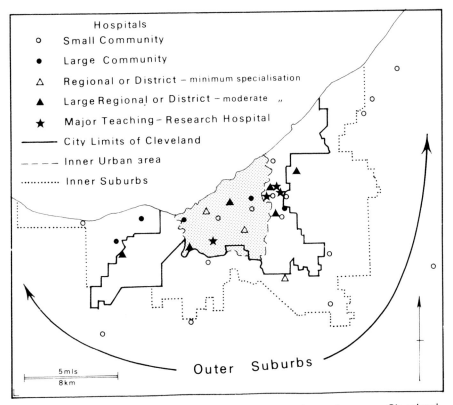

Figure 8.11 The hierarchy of hospitals within an American urban area: Cleveland, Ohio

(Based upon Shannon *et al.*, 1975, in *Professional Geographer*, **27** by permission of the Association of American Geographers)

advertising – or government licensing controls – which aim at a socially equitable spatial distribution of surgeries. Similarly, for hospitals the individual units tend to be larger relative to the scale of the system as a whole compared with an individual retail outlet and, therefore, are less responsive to changes in the nature and location of demand, while in many countries hospital location policies are becoming subject to direct governmental control.

Nevertheless, in the USA the fee-for-service basis of the health care delivery system is sufficiently strong for central place theory and the methodology of retail studies to have been used initially as an analytical framework. Market considerations of profitability and the ability of the patient to pay have strongly influenced the spatial structure of the system, and are reflected in the locational behaviour of physicians. Most are located in commercial centres and their levels of specialisation are related to the hierarchical status of the centres. Similarly, changes in the locations of physicians over time closely follow the changing pattern of demand of their middle and high status patients in a process closely analogous to that of commercial blight. De Vise illustrates the catastrophic decline in the number of physicians in the inner suburbs of Chicago 1950–70 from 475 to 76 associated with a transition from middle class white to low status negro communities.

The locational determinants of hospitals are even more complex. Hospitals vary with respect to the type of care and the degree of specialisation offered. There may also be variations in hospital type according to their religious affiliation and to the degree to which they will accept negro and charity patients and this is paralleled by variations in demand for their services. The relationship between the supply and demand criteria results in a hierarchy of hospitals, conceptually similar to the hierarchy of shopping centres (Figure 8.11). In general, the largest, most specialised hospitals are found in the central city, while the lower order district and community hospitals are more frequently located in suburban and urban peripheral sites. Locational inertia is, however, characteristic of the specialised hospitals located in city centres. Imbalances in the location of supply and demand are overcome in the short term by suburban patients undertaking relatively long journeys, but this situation need not necessarily operate in favour of the inner city concentrations of low status communities. Their access to hospitals is still via a physician, frequently in a suburban practice, and in any event is restricted to the relatively small number of hospitals admitting charity patients wherever they are located.

More recently, Rosenberg questioned the free-market analogy of the American medical system. Instead, he argues that medics should not be regarded as individual entrepreneurs but as oligopolists who maintain a high status professional ethos and control the supply of personnel and charges for services. Their concerns are characterised as primarily commercial and this is reflected in a strong orientation of service provision towards the financially stable sections of the community. The corollary is that the system is more socially and spatially regressive than simple market considerations would justify. The poor, the elderly and ethnic minorities, and particularly those living in deteriorating inner cities or remote rural areas, are typically most adversely affected. The ameliorative policies associated with the Federal *Medicare* and *Medicaid* programmes, designed to assist the aged and the poor respectively, have since 1966 attempted to redress these imbalances. This has had the effect of increasing the Government contribution to health expenditure from around 25 per cent in the early 1970s to a current level of 40 per cent, despite an unenthusiastic commitment to 'socialised' medicine.

Mayer (1986) considers that the commercial orientation of the system has precipitated an enduring financial crisis which threatens to precipitate fundamental changes. The fact that finance 'drives' the system may well promote more capital intensive medical tests and procedures than are perhaps clinically necessary; a tendency which is accentuated by the 'defensive' stance adopted by fears of litigation. At the same time, the high costs of continuing care associated with an ageing population, along with the high cost of administration related to the organisational complexity of the system, have similar inflationary effects. As a consequence, Mayer suggests the emergence of a new disadvantaged group estimated at 12 per cent of the population: those with insufficient incomes to provide for themselves and yet earn too much to qualify for Federal assistance. Thus, in 1984 medical services cost $1500 per head, compared with $800 for France and only $400 in the UK. The central policy issue, therefore, is how cost-cutting is to be achieved without reducing the quality of service to the fee-payers, while at the same time reducing the imbalances in the system.

In the public sector economies have involved the introduction of maximum payments based on ailment diagnosis rather than the cost of care (Diagnosis Related Groups: DRGs). This has the potential for increasing the division between public and private medical care. The private sector has, by contrast, witnessed the emergence of Health Maintenance Organisations which contract with employers or individuals to provide fixed-fee medical services in order to contain escalating costs. The Government is supportive of such 'preferred provider organisations' with their focus on financial viability at minimum cost, a trend which is leading to the 'corporatisation of American health care' (Mayer, 1986). It is anticipated that the competition offered by these organisations will have general deflationary effect on the cost of health care. The social and spatial inequalities of access inherent in the system, however, appear likely to persist into the foreseeable future.

The medical service systems of the UK and USA can be placed virtually at opposite extremes of the continuum between public and private organisational control. The British National Health Service introduced in 1948 is largely financed and controlled by the government, and traditionally services have been provided with minimal direct charge. The NHS replaced a variety of private and voluntary general hospitals and private medical practitioners, reminiscent of the system in the USA, by a less complex organisational structure based upon a hierarchical ordering of services. This has been subject to intermittent change but the principles of coordinating control and planning at the upper levels of the hierarchy, along with the devolution of service provision to the local level to

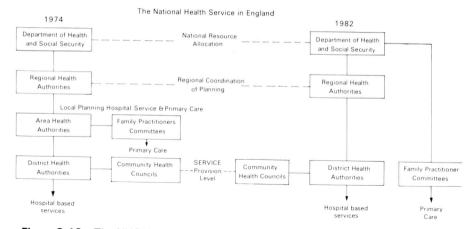

Figure 8.12   The NHS Health Care Delivery System in the UK

maximise responsiveness, was maintained in the last major restructuring of 1974.

The Department of Health and Social Security is responsible for overall resource allocation (Figure 8.12). In England the coordination of planning is administered via fourteen Regional Health Authorities and, initially, local operational planning was devolved to the ninety Area Health Authorities. The latter were the key units in the structure since they employed the majority of the NHS staff. Spatially, they coincided with the Metropolitan Districts and County units of local government in order to coordinate medical services with the social welfare, school health and environmental health services of the local authorities. Below this level a system of District Health Authorities were responsible for the delivery of hospital, general practitioner and community health services for populations of approximately 250,000.

In terms of service provision, since 1962 increasing centralisation has characterised the system. For hospital services, a General Hospital of 1500–2000 beds with associated ancillary convalescent and special care units for the integration of facilities in each Health District of 200,000–300,000 population has been the administrative and medical ideal. Below this level, primary care has been provided by general practitioners, each serving approximately 2000–2500 persons, although significant and persistent imbalances have been apparent in the peripheral regions of the country and in the less attractive parts of the major cities. General practitioners have, however, also been encouraged to centralise into large group practices to serve 10,000–15,000 people. Ideally, these were to operate from health centres, providing a wider range of more specialised diagnostic and therapeutic out-patient facilities than the smaller practices, and were designed to allow hospitals to concentrate on more serious ailments. This is reflected in the rapid increase in the number of group practices, irrespective of whether they operate from fully-fledged health centres. In 1961, only 17 per cent of general practitioners functioned in group practices of four or more, but this had increased to 52 per cent by 1986, comprising a total 12,734 practices in England alone (Figure 8.13) (Department of Health and Social Security, 1988).

Figure 8.13 General medical practitioners in England

Types of practitioner (unrestricted principals)	1961	Per cent	1981	Per cent	1986	Per cent
One doctor	5337	28.3	2990	13.4	2925	12.0
Two doctors	6384	33.8	4004	18.0	3824	15.6
Three doctors	4008	21.2	5132	23.0	4976	20.3
Four doctors	1984	10.5	4255	19.1	4390	18.0
Five doctors	715	3.8	2940	13.2	3805	15.6
Six or more doctors	450	2.4	2983	13.4	4539	18.6
Total	18878	100.0	22304	100.0	24460	100.0

Source: DHSS *Heath and Personal Social Services. Statistics for England* (1980; 1988)

The publicly funded NHS, organised via a neat administrative structure and incorporating service provision ideals appears more likely to offer administrative efficiency, combined with a social and spatial equality of access to health care than the American system. Nevertheless, a wide array of problems have emerged and remain to be resolved. By the late 1970s, for example, the administrative structure was viewed by both medics and politicians as being too cumbersome. Too many resources were considered to be spent on administration rather than treatment, and the system was adversely characterised by Drury as a 'mechanistic and technocratic bureaucracy'. Thus, in 1982 the Area Health Authorities were abolished and their functions devolved to the District level to reduce costs and enhance responsiveness to public needs (Figure 8.12). In the rapidly changing economic climate of the 1980s it is virtually impossible to assess the effectiveness of the change, but it is indicative of the increasing Government commitment to the application of principles of economic management to the delivery of health care.

Throughout its history the NHS has also been considered to reflect the managerial and bureaucratic viewpoints. The needs of the patient or consumer of the service (consumer sovereignty) have always occupied a secondary role. Until 1974, the consumer was represented by the lay appointees to the various administrative committees, and their loyalties were usually divided ambiguously between managerial responsibility and community representation. The major decisions to develop District General Hospitals, and to amalgamate general practitioners into health centres and group practices did not necessarily represent the best interests of the consumer. Both decisions reduced the accessibility of medical services to the patient, with scant attention given to the social implications of these actions. Obviously, professional medical considerations, managerial decisions and financial limitations have to be accommodated; but a socially optimal spatial allocation of medical services must take account of the needs of both the supply system and the users.

To redress this imbalance, in 1974 the control of service provision was devolved to the most local level. In addition, Community Health Councils were created to represent public opinion, but these are still largely composed of representatives nominated by local authorities, health group interests and medics and, as currently constituted, have very limited representative power. CHCs thus tend to adopt one of two roles, depending upon a combination of the nature of local issues and the personalities of their members. Either there is a general *compliance* with official NHS proposals, or a *conflict* on issues involving controversial change. In either event, the status of the CHCs is not conducive to a constructive dialogue between service providers and the public. The situation was exacerbated further by the changes of 1982 (Figure 8.12). Since that date the eminently local Family Practitioner Committees responsible for the organisation of general practitioner services, dentists, opticians and pharmacies, become responsible directly to the DHSS rather than to the District Health Authorities. This also had the effect of reducing the formal links between CHCs and the FPCs along with the consumer viewpoint.

Also, despite the existence of the NHS for 40 years with its accredited aims of reducing social and spatial inequalities of access to health care facilities, significant imbalances remain. The typically high geographical concentrations of ill-health and premature death characteristic of the lower status groups in the declining industrial regions, the deteriorating inner cities and the poorer suburbs have been demonstrated to persist in a wide range of recent studies. In part, this is considered still to reflect the 'inverse care law' by which the availability of good medical care varies inversely with the needs of those served, although the influence of past working conditions and contemporary lifestyles are also contributory factors. Policies initiated in the mid 1970s to redress these imbalances, such as the regional redistribution of finance via the Resource Allocation Working Party (RAWP), or the provision of financial incentives to attract general practitioners to under-provided areas, are indicative of an official recognition of the geographical dimension of the problem.

Finally, over the last ten years the political ideals of the Conservative Government have begun fundamentally to alter the nature of health care delivery in Britain. The need to introduce economies associated with the recession of the early 1980s has been succeeded by a financial philosophy designed to contain expenditure on public services like the NHS. Eyles and Woods' (1983) structuralist interpretation of this trend stressed a Government commitment to '. . . reduce unproductive social expenditure' and a shift in 'systemic imperatives' from social issues to economic considerations. This trend has been given formal expression in the recent Government White Paper *Working for Patients*. The aim is to create a more cost-effective and consumer responsive system by introducing stronger elements of financial accountability and competition between providers, along with a growing private sector. The effects of the potential changes are not possible to predict. Early evidence, however, on the effects of hospital privatisation in England suggest that an American-style system is unlikely to resolve the problem of social and spatial inequalities.

Whatever the detailed nature of the health care delivery system, there are a number of lines of investigation to which urban geographical research can be directed. Of particular interest is the spatial structure of the *systems of supply* of hospital facilities, primary medical care and associated pharmaceutical services. Investigation is needed of the spatial imbalances of accessibility to the various services enjoyed by the different communities of an urban region, a notable example of which is provided by Jones and Kirby. Alternatively, the *demand* side of the system can be investigated in a manner analogous to the consumer behaviour studies of retail geography. A considerable amount of research has in fact already been undertaken under the general heading of *health care utilisation behaviour* and is comprehensively reviewed by Joseph and Phillips (1984). In either situation, however, the bulk of the literature suggests that need for a synthesis of social and organisational approaches along with the traditional spatial perspective for the continued investigation of medical service systems.

Public utility services

By definition, the locational and operating policies of the public utility services are subject to direct public control, usually via a local government organisation. With the concentration of the population of developed countries into urban areas such services, particularly in the spheres of education, welfare, recreation and the provision of emergency facilities, have become increasingly important facets of urban life. These have been termed 'collectivised public services' by Pinch. Urban geographical interest in these services focuses on three major themes.

(1) Of primary interest is the size of the facility, their relative spatial locations and the extent of the areas they serve. Choices have to be made between a relatively small number of large units located far apart and a larger number of small units spaced closer together. The former tend to maximise accessibility, while the latter can offer higher degrees of specialisation. Hillman and Whalley in a study of sports and informal recreational facilities in urban areas argued against the development of a smaller number of large leisure centres because these disadvantaged the 'low mobility' younger age-groups and those without a car.

(2) A second line of interest centres on the operational implications of the alternative strategies in terms of the 'efficiency' with which the service is provided. Fire fighting and ambulance services, for example, need locations which allow them to reach the outer limits of their service areas within acceptable time limits. Access and related issue of the 'distance decay' of efficiency are of critical importance (Knox, 1982).

(3) The social implications of alternative strategies are also worthy of investigation. In the case of educational facilities, for example, interest has

focused upon the effects of alternative catchment-area strategies. Herbert draws attention to the adverse social repercussions felt by America's black urban communities of defining neighbourhood catchment areas for secondary schools and the development of policies designed to redress the disadvantages such as redrawing catchment-area boundaries, busing and compensatory education. Similar misgivings relating to social disadvantage have given rise to the definition of Educational Priority Areas in British cities, a theme which was subsequently developed by Kirby.

Clearly, the geographical analysis of public utility services has proceeded rapidly in recent years. A number of recent reviews demonstrate the wide literature in the social sciences relating to the provision and evaluation of public utility services and offer an assessment of the contemporary theoretical concepts of methodologies. They stress the need to integrate the social and spatial perspectives to maximise future geographical investigations of these services.

Summary

In the nineteenth century the unity of the wide array of commercial and public services was essentially spatial. Concentrations occurred in and around the edges of city centres, and functional segregation emerged both between and within service types in relation to the specifics of the physical and commercial opportunities offered by sites. Retailing gravitated to its various markets, finance retained its early agglomerative advantages of concentration, wholesaling and warehousing responded to changing transport technology, while the public service sector was displaced by peripheral locations. The changing circumstances of twentieth century urban development has, however, witnessed a major change from the central city concentration of services to a widespread suburban decentralisation. The inherent functional differences between the various types of services have been focused in quite different spatial patterns of adjustment. Thus, the spatial unity of the nineteenth century has been replaced by a spatial divergence by function, which is also reflected in the associated patterns of service utilisation behaviour (see Chapter 10). Retailing, for example, has demonstrated both hierarchic and anarchic responses, traditional wholesaling and warehousing is being replaced by transport-orientated systems of distribution, offices demonstrate the inertial aspects of central city concentration along with a degree of spatial fragmentation and suburbanisation, while the public utilities increasingly reflect public controls and considerations of locational optimality. As a consequence, in recent years the various urban services are being analysed in increasingly different ways. The basic methodologies, however, retain a degree of unity, while the analyses of all stress the need to integrate spatial and social considerations for maximum effect.

CHAPTER 9

The Residential Mosaic

Residential land-use incorporates all forms of housing accommodation within the built environment of the city and as such occupies about 40 per cent of urban space. This makes resident land the dominant user of space with twice the share of transport space which is the second largest user. A social geography of the city derives much of its content from the study of this residential land-use and initially from the fact that it is not uniform but is typified by strong patterns of segregation. The bases of residential segregation in Western cities are reasonably well understood and have been most commonly identified as socio-economic status, family status or stage-in-life cycle, minority group member-ship or ethnic status, and, in many cases, migrant status (Figure 9.1). These 'dimensions' emerge most clearly in North American cities where housing is allocated on market principles and have a common link with an economic basis of differentiation and the ability to buy or rent a dwelling unit which matches a household's position in social space. An orderly social geography relates both to the fact that similar households are exercising similar choices and also to the roles of the agencies of the housing market in providing a variety of types of dwellings as uniform clusters in specific spatial locations.

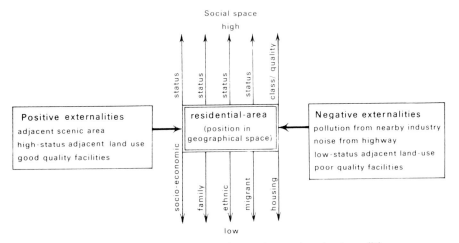

Figure 9.1 Bases of residential segregation and associated externalities

207

The notion of choice along any of the dimensions, however, requires considerable modification; constraints of some kind are always present and decisions are rarely entirely in the hands of individual consumers. Similarly, a view that economic bases produce the mosaic is seductive but only partial. Both individual dwellings and residential areas are imbued with social and symbolic values in addition to the economic rent they may command on the housing market, 'home' has acquired special meaning. Again, at any one point in time the city presents a 'time-layered' mosaic; its different parts have different ages, histories and morphologies, it is a multi-stranded rather than a single-stranded surface.

The discussion which follows focuses on residential segregation by neighbourhood but White (1984) notes the persistence of two other forms of separation in European cities. In parts of Southern Europe he shows residual evidence of middle classes occupying lower floors of apartment blocks with workers on upper floors giving vertical segregation. Again there was some evidence of segregation between fronts and backs of buildings with richer residents occupying the larger, airy dwellings overlooking the street.

The extent of residential separation

Attempts to establish the actual extent of residential separation have focused on the clearest ways in which social distinctions have found spatial expression; ethnicity is therefore a dominant theme. Such studies work within limits imposed by the quality of available data and the levels of spatial disaggregation for which they are available. Scale is a critical consideration. Most commonly a number of indices of segregation are used of which the Index of Dissimilarity is the best known; this is stated

$$I = \tfrac{1}{2} \sum_{i=1}^{k} (x_i - y_i)$$

or one-half the sum of differences between two population groups, x and y, for each of i spatial units in a given city. The two population groups may be minorities, such as blacks compared with Hispanics, or may comprise one minority group compared with the total population. Indices of dissimilarity fall within a range of 0 to 100 and form measures of displacement – the proportion of the total population of one specified group required to move residence in order for no segregation to exist. A score of 100 indicates complete segregation.

Generally, results of these analyses, particularly of ethnic groups, for Western cities reveal high levels of segregation. In the United States, for example, a study of cities in 1960 obtained a median index of dissimilarity between blacks and whites of 87.8 at the city-block level of spatial disaggregation, and of 79.3 at the census tract level; Rees calculated a segregation index for blacks in twelve American urban areas of 76.2. British analyses of New Commonwealth immigrants suggest that levels of residential segregation are increasing in the 1970s, and indices based upon 1971 census data range from 38 for Indians to 51 for Caribbeans, but in Coventry the Pakistanis with an index score of 70 proved the most segregated. A study of Belfast in the late 1960s produced an index score of 70.9 for street-by-street segregation between Catholics and Protestants; Keane (1985) showed that in public sector estates in the same city between 1969 and 1977, the index rose from 64 to 92. Doherty argued that levels of segregation varied from one part of Belfast to another and recorded an index range from 19.7 in Holywood to 72.8 in West Belfast.

Keane also used an Index of Isolation (P*) which has the advantage of taking account of the composition of the population group and gives some indication of probability of contact. This can be expressed as:

$$_xP_y^* = \sum_{i=1}^{n} \left(\frac{x_i}{x}\right)\left(\frac{y_i}{t_i}\right)$$

where: x is the total number in group X in the city; x_i is the number of group X in a census tract (or small area); y_i is the number of group Y in a census tract; and t_i is the total population of the census tract. An x P* y value of 0.4983 would mean that an average member of X group lived in an area where 49.83 per cent of the total population belonged to group Y.

Using this index, Keane showed that although the overall ID increased between 1969 to 1977 to show greater segregation, the likelihood of Protestant contact with Catholics also marginally increased from 0.13 to 0.17 reflecting the larger number of Protestants in the overall population. Studies of 'transactional' contact have shown that even in situations of complete residential segregation such links exist: Romann's study of Jewish-Arab relationships in Jerusalem revealed considerable interaction in economic, political and legal worlds.

There are other forms of residential segregation which can be measured. In a study of census tract data for eight American cities using occupational groups, Fine, Glenn and Monts found indices of 27 between professional and clerical workers, 50 between professional and unskilled manuals, and 36 between unskilled manuals and clerical workers; findings which seem, rationally, to indicate greater residential separation with increasing social distance. In a replicative study based on Australian data, Timms produced indices of 35, 46, and 32 respectively for the same groups. Duncan and Duncan brought together a large number of American studies and concluded that socio-economic status segregation was most marked at extremes of the hierarchy; In other words, the very rich and very poor were most segregated but there was less clear differentiation by residential areas in the broad middle band. This finding has some intuitive appeal but the problems of occupational definition, upon which status divisions are based, are greatest in this middle band. Studies of British cities reveal similar results but tend to show less marked segregation at the lower end of the socio-economic status scale (see Figure 9.2). They also suggested that socio-economic status segregation is higher in larger cities, particularly those in which there are high proportions of professionals and managers in the labour force.

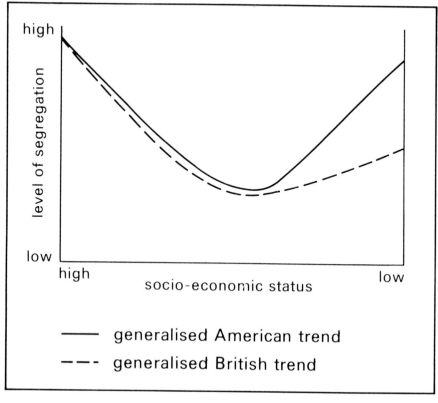

Figure 9.2   Residential segregation and socio-economic status in Britain and America

Analyses of segregation based upon demographic characteristics have obtained modest results. Most of these have focused on segregation of the elderly, a group for which age-segregation is thought to be increasing. Golant reports a study in which indices of dissimilarity ranging between 10.8 and 37.7 were calculated between population aged 65 years and over and the rest of the population for 72 American cities. For this subgroup studied over the 241 American SMSAs, Cowgill (1978) obtained an index range from 15.2 to 44.4. The elderly possess a level of residential segregation but this is not as high as that identified either for ethnic minorities or for socio-economic status groups. Of more general interest are the levels of lifecycle stage segregation and here the problem of data and measurement make calculation difficult. A lifecycle stage has no necessary close correlation with chronological age and is also affected by time-lags which may blur the link between change of stage and its expression in residential mobility.

These analyses of levels of residential segregation fall within what has been termed the 'dissimilarist' school, so called because of its common methodology in summarising patterns of distribution. Another strong line of research has been that concerned with the classification of residential areas within cities.

The definition of residential areas

The objective of delimiting different types of residential area has been pursued vigorously in social geography. In some ways it has its origins in earlier morphological studies which sought to identify urban subregions and to relate these to historical phases of growth. More properly, however, the early precursor of the line of research, referred to as *residential differentiation*, can be nominated as the natural area concept which was a product of the Chicago school of social ecology in the 1920s and 1930s. It was at this time that the emphasis on people rather than on the physical characteristics of the environments in which they lived first emerged. Residential differentiation studies since have had a number of consistent themes. Firstly, they seek to identify distinctive residential subareas within cities and to delimit their boundaries; secondly, they seek to characterise these residential areas in terms of their key features and qualities; and, thirdly, they test and examine the bases upon which residential separation is predicated and the persistence of these over time. As the methodology to achieve these objectives has developed, it has revealed a number of trends. Whereas early studies were largely intuitive and subjective, later studies have become much more quantitatively based. As systematic quantitative approaches evolved, the progression was from single-stranded techniques, involving diagnostic variables, to multivariate statistical procedures in which wide-ranging inputs of data can be analysed. The progressions in objectives and approaches will now be examined.

Natural areas

The natural area concept was developed by Robert Park and his associates in the Chicago school of social ecology. Although this school is better known for the concentric zonal model of Burgess, its main *spatial* generalisation, the natural area concept probably generated the most inspired empirical urban studies. The natural area was conceived as a geographical unit, distinguished both by its physical individuality and by the social, economic and cultural characteristics of its population. In contrast to the studies of urban sub-regions developed by urban morphologists, with their 'unpeopled' townscapes, the natural area was envisaged as an area of social as well as physical uniformity. The view of a total urban habitat in which particular relationships existed between the environment and population was part of the more general ecological theory of the Chicago school, and Park argued these relationships explicitly in his theoretical statements. It was in the monographs, mainly on Chicago, in which these broader theoretical statements on symbiosis were largely incidental, that the natural area concept found its clearest expression. Of these the best known were the *Gold Coast and the Slum* (Zorbaugh, 1929) and *The Ghetto* (Wirth, 1928).

The natural areas identified by Zorbaugh were delimited by the *de facto* boundaries of the urban environment: roads, railways, parks, lakes and rivers. The physical individuality of the natural area was accurately reflected by land values and rent, but Zorbaugh was at pains to stress that the natural area was not necessarily coterminous with community, as it was the result of economic rather than cultural processes. The attractiveness of Zorbaugh's study, however, lies less in any attempted justification of ecological theory than in his vivid portrayal of life in Chicago's Near North Side, a district of some 90,000 people close to the city centre. The Near North Side was an area of diversity, the main contrast being between the high-prestige district of the Gold Coast along Lake Shore Drive and the low-status district west of State Street (Figure 9.3). The latter district was itself a mosaic, containing the rooming-house district, hobohemia, little Sicily and other ethnic quarters, and the slum. The person-alities of these sections of the city were partly derived from the physical structure of which they are composed, but much more from their distinctive populations and ways of life. Zorbaugh emphasised the dynamic qualities which these districts possessed and described the territorial shifts as the invasion-succession process took place. Always regarded as less bounded by ecological theory, Wirth's attitude was reflected in his preface to *The Ghetto* (1928):

> Having started with the study of a geographical area, I found myself, quite un-wittingly, examining the natural history of an institution and the psychology of a people.

In his study, Wirth examined the evolution of Jewish ghettos in many European cities and described them as communities of interest, motivated by the need to preserve a religion and based upon the inner solidarity of strong family ties. His identification of the Chicago ghetto as a physical entity approached the concept of the natural area as closely as his ecological contemporaries. He identified the Chicago ghetto as a territory demarcated from adjacent parts of the city by environmental barriers such as streetcar lines and railway tracks. Within this territory, the natural area was a socially cohesive community with a distinctive personality. The natural areas which Zorbaugh and Wirth described were identified and defined intuitively from an intimate knowledge of the city, rather than by the use of statistical procedures. Zorbaugh, however, did make ex-tensive use of simple indicators to characterise his natural areas, such as persons listed in prestigious directories and those receiving welfare payments. This procedure initiated a useful technique which has continued utility. Some natural areas, particularly the ethnic districts, Zorbaugh described as closeknit communities whereas others were scarcely communities at all, and a feature of the Gold Coast was that 'one does not know one's neighbours'.

The original concept of the natural area was questioned along with other

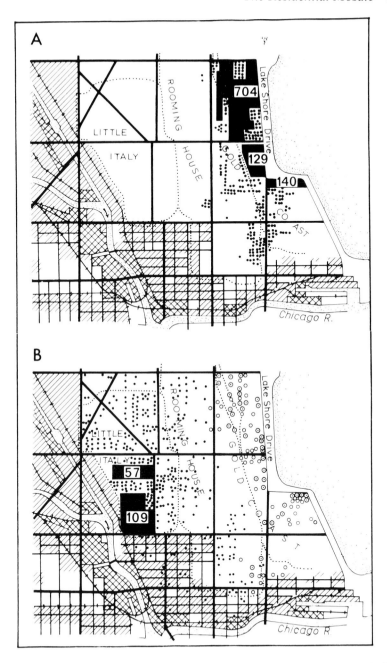

Figure 9.3 The Gold Coast and the Slum. (a) Each dot shows a person on the high-status social register, with some block totals. (b) Each dot is a recipient of welfare, each open circle a donator. Shaded areas show non-residential land use

(After Zorbaugh, 1929, *The Gold Coast and the Slum*)

aspects of urban ecology in the 1930s and an explicit reformulation was offered by Hatt (1946) in his study of Seattle. Hatt suggested that the natural area concept as developed by the ecologists had two interpretations: on the one hand the natural area could be regarded as a spatial unit, limited by natural boundaries and enclosing a homogeneous population with a characteristic moral order; on the other it was regarded as spatially united on the basis of a set of relationships analogous to the biological world. Hatt concluded that this latter interpretation should be rejected but that natural areas could be accepted as logical statistical constructs offering an excellent framework for further analysis. The eventual map of natural areas in Seattle was based upon a diagnostic variable, that of rental values, rather than upon the intuitive approach of ecologists. Though Zorbaugh and others had certainly been aware of their possibilities, Hatt explicitly used rental values as delimiting criteria for the first time, suggesting that one variable could be used to characterise different parts of the city.

The potentialities of such diagnostic variables of urban structure are now well recognised and their use has extended over a considerable range of problems. In a wider context there are studies using land values, notably by Hurd and Hoyt, which predate Hatt's study of Seattle while more recently statistical analyses of the determinants and correlates of land values have been completed. In the context of defining urban sub-areas, a number of more straightforward British studies have adopted measures of monetary value as diagnostic variables. One problem in studying British cities has been the fact that land values and rental values are difficult to obtain in a consistent form. Therefore rateable values (a form of local taxation), based on the physical characteristics of a property and its general location, have been used instead of land values or rents. A study by Herbert and Williams of Newcastle-under-Lyme is typical of the adaptation of this approach to define residential areas in a British town. Four categories of rateable value were mapped with the initial hypothesis that these would reflect differences in urban social structure. Similar uses of rateable values were made by Robson in Sunderland. Robson found that rateable values in the modern city had lost much of their usefulness because of the considerable amount of municipal housing, which could not be reliably correlated to these values.

The range of approaches to the definition of sub-areas in urban residential structure has been widened considerably by the availability of better census data for cities, both in the range of recorded information and their publication for small territorial units, census tracts in North America, enumeration districts in the United Kingdom, with equivalents in many other parts of the world. Small census areas of this type must be sufficiently small for a high level of internal consistency to be assumed, so that when scores are allocated they are the equivalents of point distributions which may be aggregated to form areal patterns. To a considerable extent, small census areas possess these qualities, but there are qualifications. The population size can vary considerably within one city; the range of census tracts in North American cities is from under 1000 to over 10,000 and of enumeration districts in British cities (which are smaller) from under 100 to over 1500. The areas are correspondingly divergent in size, although this is related to density, and the question of weighting procedures (Robson, 1969) is relevant. More fundamental questions concern the real internal consistency of small census units. Some censuses have defined boundaries only with reference to the needs of census-taking; in the British census, for example, the enumeration district is arbitrarily defined on mainly topographic criteria. The Canadian census states that census tracts are designed to be relatively uniform in area and population, and such that each is fairly homogeneous with respect to economic status and living conditions, qualities which fulfil the *desiderata* of small area statistics. This uniformity is inevitably less than perfect, however, and some research has developed techniques to accommodate heterogeneity in census districts.

Census data for enumeration districts have been used extensively in Britain, more usually to analyse individual variables than to form composite sub-areas. In his Belfast study, however, Jones used enumeration district data to delineate social regions on the basis of population density, social status and religious affiliations; the resultant map was judged to provide meaningful sub-areas of the city from which the main social regions of Belfast were easily recognisable and compact and summed up features both of the landscape and human geography. The approach had self-imposed limitations, but it provides a useful link between the natural area concept and subsequent procedures which have made increasing use of census data.

Social area analysis

The main statement on the methodology of social area analysis (Shevky and Bell, 1955) followed earlier empirical work in Los Angeles and San Francisco in which census tract differences were examined using three indices of social rank, urbanisation, and segregation. The methodology was important in its attempt to develop multivariate indices of residential differentiation to classify census tracts and, also, in its attempt to relate these indices to a more general theory of urban development. In the former of these objectives, the methodology attained considerable success, in the latter far less. Although the *theory*, as opposed to the *typology* of social area analysis, proved contentious the principle of establishing a theory of social differentiation and of initially recognising variations in social rather than in geographical space, set social area analysis apart from social ecology which had sought initially to identify natural areas as geographical territories and to study them in terms of their social characteristics.

Shevky and Bell viewed the city as a part of society as a whole and suggested that change over time would be mirrored in the city. They suggested that such change had three main expressions which could be described collectively as *increasing scale*, implying a continuum of change from traditional primitive to a more modern civilised style of life (Figure 9.4). The three expressions of the

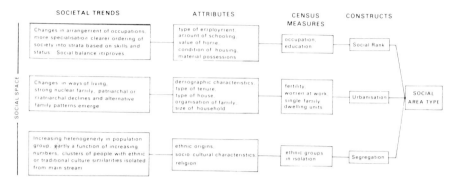

Figure 9.4   Social area analysis: derivation of constructs

increasing scale they summarised as constructs, each of which was a dominant temporal trend in social organisations. *Social rank* (economic status) described the tendency for society to become more precisely ordered into strata based on specialisation and social prestige. *Urbanisation* (family status) described a weakening of the traditional organisation of the family as the society became more urbanised. *Segregation* (ethnic status) suggested that over time the population group would tend to form distinctive clusters based primarily upon ethnicity. The alternative names for the constructs were proposed and used by Bell, the only difference in computational procedure being that high scores on urbanisation were the equivalents of low scores on family status. Having derived these constructs, regarded as being diagnostic of change, Shevky and Bell sought to measure them from the available census data. *Social rank* was measured by ratios of *occupation*, described as the total number of operatives, craftsmen and labourers per 1000 employed persons, and of *education*, described as the number of persons who had completed no more than grade school (eight years or less of schooling) per 1000 persons aged 25 years and over. *Urbanisation* was based upon three ratios: *fertility* measured by the number of children aged 0 to 4 years per 1000 women aged 15 to 44; *women at work* measured by the number of females employed in relation to the total number of females aged 15 years and over; and *single-family detached dwelling units*, measured by the number of single-family homes (a term which has a specific meaning in North American censuses) as a proportion of all dwelling units. Social rank and urbanisation were the main constructs of social area analysis and a large part of the computational procedure was concerned with their derivation. The third construct, *segregation*, was obtained as a simple percentage of the numbers of specified alien groups (mainly coloureds and all those of ethnic origins outside north-west Europe) as a proportion of total population.

These constructs and their component ratios were thus identified from social space but were obtained as statistical expressions from the available census data and combined in stipulated ways to form criteria for the definition of urban sub-areas. The operational procedure which leads to the eventual social areas can be briefly summarised:

(1) The scores on the individual ratios are initially simple proportions, but Shevky and Bell specify the additional step of transforming the ratios into standardised procedures to make comparisons more valid.
(2) The construct scores are obtained by finding the average of the ratio scores.
(3) The social rank and urbanisation scores are each given a four-fold division which in combination provides sixteen possible social area types.
(4) Segregation is added to this framework where the proportion of a census tract's total population which is in specified alien groups is above the average for the city as a whole.

The first applications of social area analysis, in Los Angeles and San Francisco, both provided some confirmation of the utility of the approach. It has become customary to regard a social area as a contiguous territorial unit, though its initial usage was to describe a cluster of scores in social rather than in geographical space. A typical set of results from an application of social area analysis to a North American city can be described from a study of Winnipeg, Canada (Herbert, 1972).

The metropolitan area of Winnipeg had a population in 1961 of 475,989 and was divided in to 86 census tracts with an average population of 5500; over half

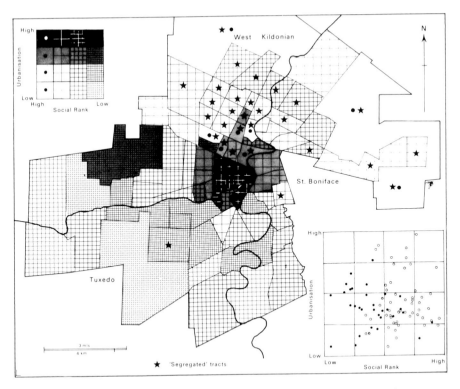

Figure 9.5 Social areas in Winnipeg 1960: with inset showing the social space diagram

the census tracts were between 3000 and 6000, with only three with less than 1000 and five with more than 10,000. The social space diagram for Winnipeg (Figure 9.5, inset) illustrates the classification of census tracts which was obtained. Each point on the diagram represents a census tract, the position of which is determined by its scores on social rank and urbanisation, with a separate symbol for segregated tracts. In this diagram, therefore, the position of each census tract is affected by its scores on the six component variables of the typology: occupation, education, fertility, women at work, single-family dwellings and ethnicity. The census tract in 4D, for example, has high social rank, with few people employed in manual occupations and few without advanced education. It is also high scoring in terms of urbanisation, with few children, high numbers of women in employment and a comparative absence of single-family homes. The census tract contains few members of specified ethnic groups and is in fact part of fairly high prestige residential district, pre-dominantly of rented apartments, in a central city location. Besides allowing the interpretation of individual tracts, this diagram also provides an overall im-pression of the social structure of the city: 63 per cent of the census tracts are within the two higher social rank categories and 25 per cent are in the two higher urbanisation categories; of the 31 tracts which are classed as segregated, only eight qualify as higher social rank. The analysis has so far allowed an insight into the social structure of Winnipeg by classifying the census tracts in social space.

Social area analysis, as a theory, specifies a set of relationships among its constructs and ratios which must exist if the procedure is to be valid in any case history. The theoretical rationale of these relationships has been questioned but the actual measurements can be tested by statistical techniques, the most straightforward of which is Spearman's rank order correlation coefficient. The results of these tests in Winnipeg are shown in Figure 9.6 together with the set of relationships which the theory postulates.

The specified set of relationships shown here requires that the ratios which make up the respective constructs should be independent. This requires high correlations between occupation and education and also among the three

Figure 9.6 Correlation scores for Winnipeg

Ratios	Occupation	Education	Fertility	Women at work
Education	+0.84*			
Fertility	+0.53*	+0.34		
Women at work	+0.03	+0.23	−0.53*	
Single-family dwellings	−0.07	−0.33	+0.45*	−0.68*
*Significant at the 0.1 per cent level				

		Specified set		
	Occupation	Education	Fertility	Women at work
Education	+			
Fertility	0	0		
Women at work	0	0	−	
Single-family dwellings	0	0	+	−

ratios which comprise urbanisation. The women-at-work ratio is held to have an inverse relationship with both fertility and single-family homes. The results for Winnipeg confirm the existence of the specified set of relationships in a way which has been typical of North American studies. An exception in the Winnipeg results, not without precedent in North America, is that the occupation and fertility ratios have a much higher correlation and the constructs are thus less independent than the hypotheses of social area analysis suggest.

The social space classification forms the basis for the derivation of social areas in geographical space. Contiguous census tracts with scores in the same categories may be aggregated to form social areas in the sixteen-class typology, with the additional segregation categorisation. Figure 9.5 shows the geographical patterns which can be interpreted in terms of the six component variables. Generalised patterns are most easily identified from the separate constructs and the high social rank scores: for example, the southern and western part of the city indicate the high-prestige residential areas. The more central parts of the city and the northern and eastern districts, which include the central slums and tenements and low-cost suburbs, are characterised by low scores. Urbanisation scores distinguish between the central city districts of low family status and the outer suburbs of strong family life; segregation indices demarcate the Ukrainian districts extending north along Main Street.

Applications of social area analysis outside North America have been less successful in establishing the validity of the approach either as a theory or as a classificatory procedure. Herbert found that whereas the social rank construct could be identified and its constituent variables held the hypothesised relationships, the urbanisation or family status construct could not. McElrath's study of Rome did identify the hypothesised relationships of variables with constructs but found that the constructs themselves were not independent. McElrath also studied Accra, Ghana and here found it necessary to add migrant status, as a fourth construct. For North American results only, it has been possible to form spatial generalisations from the results of social area analysis; these consistently reveal sectors of economic status, zones of family status and ethnic clusters.

Although social area analysis has been eclipsed in recent years by the development of multivariate procedures, the theory and its application have stimulated a good deal of academic discussion. In summary, social area analysis, despite its weakly developed theory, provided an important stage in the evolution of residential differentiation studies. Its typology, consistently verified in North America, accurately identified the key bases of residential separation in cities of a particular technological stage and in societies of specific characteristics.

Factorial ecology

The term factorial ecology has been used to describe those studies of urban residential areas which employ factor analysis as a technique. Social area analysis as used originally by Shevky and Bell has now been virtually replaced by this approach which allows more flexibility, no necessary adherence to a preformed theory, and potentially at least a high level of objectivity. Factor analysis is not one technique but a collective term which covers a set of alternatives. A first point to note, therefore, is that the results obtained from a study in factorial ecology may vary according to the particular procedure adopted and Davies (1978) has emphasised the need to establish the invariant quality of results across a range of factoring techniques. A second consideration is the form of input to factorial ecology as this again will strongly influence results. Input usually comprises a set of variables, commonly derived from census small area statistics and covering social, economic, and demographic characteristics, measured for a set of observations or small areas.

As it has been most generally used by geographers, factor analysis can be described as a summarising device which operates in terms of the interrelationships among the set of input variables and identifies, in the order of their significance, a series of factors which are diagnostic of the input and which account for measurable amounts of the initial variance. These qualities can perhaps be made clearer by drawing an analogy with social area analysis which, through deductive reasoning, identifies changes in society, transforms these into constructs and selects census variables or ratios with which to characterise them. Factor analysis, by contrast, derives factors which can be regarded as equivalents of constructs, by an objective statistical procedure. Three forms of output – eigen values, loadings, and scores – provide the means of interpreting the results obtained. The *eigen values* indicate the relative strengths of the factors and can be expressed as proportions of the total variance or variability in the initial input; the size of eigen value represents the ability of factor analysis

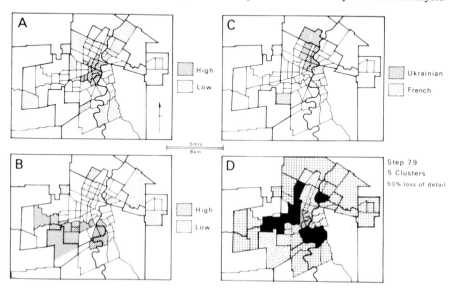

Figure 9.7 Factorial ecology of Winnipeg (1961). (a) Family status. (b) Socio-economic status. (c) Ethnic status. (d) A cluster analysis composite areas

to summarise a high proportion of this variability in a smaller number of factors or dimensions. A *loading* is calculated for each original variable against each factor or component and allows the 'nature' of the factor to be interpreted. Loadings range in value from $+1.0$ to -1.0. *Scores* are calculated for each observation on every factor and enable the spatial distribution of the characteristics of each dimension to be shown. The general qualities of factor analysis and its application to the study of urban residential areas as factorial ecology can be illustrated with reference to Winnipeg (Figure 9.7).

North American cities

From the 1961 Canadian census, 34 variables were calculated for each of the 86 census tracts in the urban area; this particular study used a components model with a varimax rotation. The results (Figure 9.8(a)) are useful in that they closely resemble a large number of studies of North American cities completed in the later 1960s and early 1970s. From the eigen values it is clear that the

Figure 9.8 Factorial ecology

(A) Winnipeg (1961): nature of factors

Factor 1 (housing style) (32.2 per cent)		Factor 2 (social status) (23.8 per cent)	
Variables	*Loadings*	*Variables*	*Loadings*
single family dwellings	$+0.91$	high school or university	$+0.93$
single person households	-0.89	males in managerial,	
		professional, technical	
owner-occupied households	$+0.89$	employment	$+0.92$
tenant-occupied households	-0.87	males primary, craftsmen	
		labourers	-0.91
		males salaries 6,000 or	
		more	$+0.88$

Factor 3 (ethnicity) (8.6 per cent)	
Variables	*Loadings*
French origins	$+0.98$
English language only	-0.97
Roman Catholic	$+0.89$

(B) Winnipeg (1971)*

Component 1 (family status) (21.5 per cent)		Component 2 (socio-economic status) (13.4 per cent)	
Variables	*Loadings*	*Variables*	*Loadings*
small households	$+0.90$	construction/transport	
		workers	$+0.86$
apartments	$+0.80$	manufacturing workers	$+0.76$
children	-0.98	graduates	-0.91
family size	-0.97	white-collar ratio	-0.88

Component 3 (migrant status) (10.6 per cent)	
Variables	*Loadings*
middle-aged	$+0.86$
low intermunicipal movers	$+0.84$
non-migrants	$+0.80$
new housing	-0.82
mature adults	-0.66

*1971 results obtained by Dr W. K. D. Davies

leading dimension accounts for almost one-third of the initial variance (32.2 per cent), and the leading three dimensions for almost two-thirds. A few leading loadings are shown for each of the main dimensions in order to characterise the factors. Factor 1 is described as a measure of housing style indicative of family status or stage-in-lifecycle: Factor 2 as a measure of socio-economic status, and Factors 3 and 6 ethnicity. These dimensions are clearly reminiscent of the constructs of social area analysis and most North American studies show very similar results. Figure 9.8(b) shows similar – though different – results from a 1971 analysis of Winnipeg; migrant status has replaced ethnic status and a family-status dimension is more clearly defined.

The last output from the analysis is that of scores, which are recorded for each factor for each census tract and allow patterns to be identified in geographical space. The spatial patterns of scores are shown in Figure 9.7. Factor 1 scores (9.7(a)) distinguish between the central city and the family suburbs; Factor 2 scores (9.7(b)) between the high-prestige districts of south and west and the low-prestige districts of north and east; Factor 3 (9.7(c)) identifies the French district of St Boniface, and scores from Factor 4 which are also included in this map identify ethnic districts which are principally Ukrainian in origin. Spatial generalisations of these scores could be described as zonal for Factor 1, sectoral for Factor 2 and clusters for Factor 3; these patterns conform with those identified by analysis of variance for social area scores and with the model suggested by Murdie for Toronto. A further expression of the spatial patterning of scores was obtained by a grouping procedure (see Figure 9.7(d)) which classifies census tracts on the basis of their similarity of scores for the first six factors. Potentially this last procedure has the capability of classifying census tracts into 'objective communities' of multiple similarities, though the reality of this outcome needs to be tested by other criteria.

The Winnipeg case-study provides an example of the use of factor analytical procedures and produces a set of results which are typical of North American application. Both those studies which have been designed as direct tests of the Shevky-Bell hypotheses, and those which evolved as independent investigations of the dimensions of urban-social space, have tended to confirm the existence of the three main constructs of economic, family and ethnic status. Studies of Canadian cities in the 1970s often identify a migrant status dimension, evidence of continuing inward movement and change; the black ethnic dimension remains strong in more recent American studies.

West European cities

White (1984) has reviewed the large number of factorial ecological studies which have been carried out on West European cities. Although the data bases of these are variable, they do reveal some of the main features which emerged from similar studies of North American cities. Social status in some form is always the first-ranking dimension though it is often linked with measures of

Figure 9.9   Nature of components in Leuven (Louvain), Belgium

Component 1 (socio-economic status)	
Variables	*Loadings*
small dwellings	+0.93
labourers	+0.78
businessmen	−0.85
large dwellings	−0.83
Component 2 (minority group)	
Variable	*Loadings*
students	+0.93
foreign-born	+0.85
substandardness	+0.61
Component 3 (family status)	
Variables	*Loadings*
single-person household	+0.93
no children	+0.91
two-person household	−0.94
children	−0.82

housing quality. Again some indices of familism are typical of the second dimension and are identified by a variety of demographic and life-cycle stage measures. An ethnic dimension is commonly the third-ranking dimension, very often associated with the presence of foreign migrant workers. A study of Louvain, Belgium nicely illustrates this kind of European result (see Figure 9.9). Attempts to generalise upon the spatial expressions of these dimensions have proved difficult and as White (*op. cit.*) suggests:

> ... ecological analysis leads to the identification of complicated patterns of social or residential areas based on the complex interaction of social class, life-cycle, and housing dimensions with urban space.

The old city core of Vienna, for example, was divided into a 'business' area with many middle-class professionals but a general admixture of population groups and an 'administrative' area with more managerial staff. A surrounding inner area was mainly occupied by older middle-class apartment dwellers with main modern working class areas on the southern edge of the city. This pattern does not fit easily into any spatial model and White's own generalised model for the West European city retains a historic core of associated high-status residence (see Figure 9.10).

Factorial ecologies of British cities fall into two main phases. Earlier analyses were dominated by measures of housing occupance, tenure and dwelling condition and in large part reflected the data input. Studies of Cardiff and Swansea, for example, produced leading dimensions of housing tenure and levels of substandardness. Factor scores from these distinguished between private and public sector housing areas and inner city/outer city housing conditions respectively. Later studies using more balanced input identified the more common dimensions of socio-economic status, family status and ethnicity. Davies and Lewis conducted a factor analytic study of Leicester, a city with a relatively high level of Asian immigration. What emerged was the familiar triad

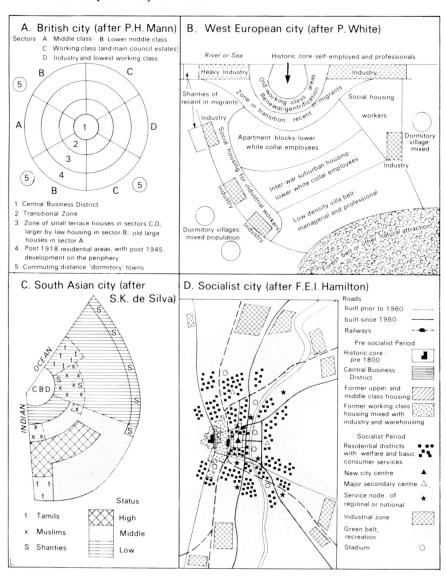

Figure 9.10   Models of the city

of social status, family status and ethnicity-migrants. Most factor ecologies of British cities have reported strong distorting effects on any zones, sectors or clusters, produced by the amount of public sector housing. This was true of Leicester though the distortion was thought to be less evident in that case.

Weclawowicz (1979) has provided a factorial ecology of a Socialist city. An initial analysis of Warsaw used 1930 data as input and identified results closely reminiscent of the western model. Leading factors were labelled social class or housing quality ethnicity (Jewish) and demographic or lifecycle. For 1970, after the change to a socialist state, a different set of results was obtained. Some residential separation by occupational groups did remain and could be identified spatially but this was limited to the specialised artist/intellectual group provided with special quarters in the central city and a small group of managers who appeared to have achieved some privilege in housing. The main feature, however, as revealed by the composition of Factor 2 was the lack of residential segregation amongst main occupational groups resulting from the policy of equalising housing opportunities. Apart from the central location of artists there were clear difficulties in generalising upon the spatial form of component scores, and Weclawowicz's phase 'mosaic spatial structure' reflects these. (See also Figure 9.10(d))

Figure 9.11   Variables used in the Colombo study

A.	Age	1.	Under 5 years
		2.	6–17 years
		3.	18–54 years
		4.	Over 55 years
B.	Ethnicity	5.	Sinhalese (x^2)
		6.	Tamils $(\log^{10})$
		7.	Moors/Malays $(\log^{10})$
		8.	Indian Tamils $(\log^{10})$
		9.	Burghers
C.	Religion	10.	Buddhists $(\log^{10})$
		11.	Hindus $(\log^{10})$
		12.	Christians $(\log^{10})$
		13.	Muslims $(\log^{10})$
D.	Size of household	14.	Less than two members
		15.	Three to five members
		16.	Six to eight members
		17.	Nine to eleven members
		18.	Over twelve members
E.	Shanty population	19.	Shanty population $(\log^{10})$
F.	Annual value of	20.	Less than Rs. 100
	residential unit	21.	Rs. 101 to 500 (x^2)
		22.	Rs. 501 to 1000
		23.	Rs. 1001 to 2000 $(\log^{10})$
		24.	Over Rs. 2001 $(\log^{10})$
G.	Access to services	25.	Individual services $(\log^{10})$
	(water and sanitation)	26.	Common services
		27.	No services
H.	Residential density	28.	Persons per 100 m^2 of residential floor area
I.	Size of residential	29.	Less than 15 m^2
	unit	30.	15–74 m^2
		31.	75–149 m^2
		32.	150–199 m^2 $(\log^{10})$
		33.	200–299 m^2 $(\log^2)$
		34.	Over 300 m^2 $(\log^{10})$
J.	Types of buildings	35.	Shanties $(\log^{10})$
		36.	Tenements (x^2)
		37.	Houses $(\log^{10})$
		38.	Non-residential $(\log^{10})$
K.	Sex ratio	39.	Sex ratio (x^2)
L.	Fertility ratio	40.	Fertility ratio (x^2)

NB Variables were tested for normality and appropriate transformations were applied as indicated for each variable.   (x^2 ... square; $\log^2$ ... log to base 10)

Non-Western cities

It is non-Western societies with considerable problems of data bases that factorial ecologies have been least developed. Two better-known early studies, of Cairo and Calcutta were affected by these problems revealed in the latter case by the large size of areas and in the former by paucity of variables. The leading Calcutta dimensions were labelled land use and familism, Muslim, and literacy. The first of these simply distinguishes between areas exclusively used for residential development from commercial or institutional land; the spatial pattern of scores on this dimension was concentric zonal with an increasing trend towards functional specialisation. Literacy measures in some ways related to socio-economic status and a sectoral form while the Muslim dimension was effectively ethnic. Literacy was similarly interpreted as an indicator of socio-economic status in the Cairo study.

A factorial ecology of Colombo, Sri Lanka (Herbert and de Silva, 1974) may be used as an example for a non-Western Asian city. For the 47 wards 40 variables were obtained (Figure 9.11) within the Colombo urban area and the analysis was conducted in stages through the use of a principal components model followed by varimax and promax rotations. Component 1 could be identified as a *social status* dimension, though mainly through indices of the quality, value and size of dwelling space (Figure 9.12). Some elements of

Figure 9.12   Nature of factorial dimensions (Colombo)

Component 1 (social status)			
Variables	*Loadings*	*Variables*	*Loadings*
residential density	+0.74	individual services	−0.69
low annual value	+0.72	houses	−0.69
fertility ratio	+0.64	high floor space	−0.69
low floor space	+0.64	high annual value	−0.56
common services	+0.45	burghers	−0.43
Component 2 (land-use differentiation)			
Variables	*Loadings*	*Variables*	*Loadings*
Six to eight member households	+0.88	aged 18–54 years	−0.83
percentage aged 6–17 years	+0.82	non-residential use	−0.79
houses	+0.38		
residential units	+0.37		
Component 3 (substandardness)			
Variables	*Loadings*	*Variables*	*Loadings*
low floor space	+0.46	shanty dwellers	−0.82
over twelve member households	+0.45	low floor space	−0.58
tenements	+0.39	no services	−0.54
common services	+0.34		
Components 4 and 6 (ethnicity)			
Variables	*Loadings*	*Variables*	*Loadings*
Tamils (4)	+0.90	Buddhists	−0.58
Hindus	+0.89	Sinhalese	−0.41
Christians	+0.73		
Muslims (6)	+0.69	Sinhalese	−0.62
Moors	+0.68	Buddhists	−0.35

familism were also linked with the dimension, especially through the association of high-fertility ratios and more children with the low-status groups. Component 2 was a measure of *land-use* and distinguished non-residential buildings from more purely residential space. Component 3 measures different types of *substandardness* from tenements at one end of the dimension to shanties at the other, and reflects the ubiquity of low housing quality. With both components 4 and 6 *ethnic groups* are recognised, showing the plural composition of society and its separate expression in residential space. These dimensions bear limited resemblance to those in Western cities and reflect the different bases of these societies. Spatial patterns can be identified in Colombo but are difficult to form into a composite picture. There is a large higher-status area in the south of the city but part of this area retains an admixture of non-residential land-uses. Districts of substandard housing occur through the urban area with some dominated by tenements, others by shanties. Clearest are the ethnic areas with highly segregated clusters of Tamils and Muslims set apart from the rest of the population.

Generalisations from factorial ecology

The large number of factorial ecologies completed during the late 1960s and early 1970s, and the rather fewer number since, allow some generalisations to be made upon their findings. Firstly it should be stated that greater awareness of technical problems and attempts to develop sounder research strategies have typified later studies; the early wave of analyses may well have been influenced by arbitrariness of data inputs and variability in technique as much as anything else. There is a general confirmation, however, of the three main dimensions of economic, family and ethnic status in all North American studies. The ethnic minority may vary in type and dimensions and may be superseded by more general migrant status measures, but the 'triad' remain remarkably consistent. Abu-Lughod (1969) stipulated the conditions under which the two most stable dimensions – economic and family status – would emerge. Her reasoning was that an independent socio-economic status dimension would occur where there was an effective ranking system in the society, distinguishing population groups according to their status or prestige, and where that ranking system was matched by corresponding subdivisions of the housing market (each prestige group lived in a particular type of residential area). Similarly, a familism dimension would occur where family types could be linked to specific stages of the lifecycle and where each stage was paralleled by available residential sub-areas. Socio-economic status and familism dimensions might be associated in social space but could still appear as geographically separate where a comprehensive housing market could cater for all lifecycle stages within each socio-economic status level. The necessary conditions for the two leading dimensions are, therefore, ranking by socio-economic status, clear stages of the lifecycle, a housing market structured to cater for each possible combination of these characteristics in distinctive sub-areas, and a population consisting of independent households mobile enough to use the possibilities. A factorial ecology in which the two dimensions failed to emerge could be explained in terms of the absence or limited expression of these necessary conditions. Abu-Lughod did not include ethnic status in her interpretation, but Rees (1979) views the dimension in the American context as a limited microcosm of the city as a whole. His argument was that there are constraints which limit minority groups, such as negroes, to particular sections of the city and that within these sections the relevant range of socio-economic status levels and lifecycle stage had to be incorporated. With reference to his Chicago study, Rees was able to identify this range within ethnic districts but owing to constraints of other kinds, mainly misallocation of resources between white and coloured people, it was never fully represented. The general milieu in which these conditions exist might be described as a free enterprise, pre-welfare state stage of capitalism, with the additional attributes of an advanced economic and technological development, and what might be crudely summarised as a non-traditional cultural context in which economic and functional forces dominate.

This rationalisation on conditions under which the key dimensions have emerged as bases of residential separation in North America, provides some guidelines for the interpretation of factorial ecologies in other parts of the world. The analogy must be handled with care as superficial similarities may result from sharply contrasted societal forces but some comparisons are possible. The clarity of an ethnic or migrant dimension will relate to the extent to which a significant minority group exists within society or to the contemporary levels of residential mobility. On a broader front, stratification may be real enough in social terms but may not find clear spatial expression either through the inadequacies of the housing market or from the preferences of those able to exercise choice. In Third World societies we are considering situations in which in addition to the non-economic bases of many preference patterns, concepts such as residential area and housing market have different meaning. Cities are often non-urban in character, infrastructures are grossly inadequate, and basic needs of shelter precede any other considerations. Though studies of Third World countries suggest cities in transition as 'modernisation' diffuses through the urban and social system, there is great diversity between larger and smaller urban areas, between one part of the Third World and another. Again, in Europe, there are differing levels of public sector intervention which have sharp effects on the social geography of the city. In Britain it has been summarised as a 'distorting' effect in which the general spatial generalisations remain but in heavily modified forms; in socialist societies as key bases of separation are removed, so the utility of any Western model is diminished.

From the available evidence a couple of broad generalisations may be offered. Firstly, there is some support for a type of stage-model in terms of which cities can be seen to possess particular social geographies at particular 'stages' in their development. Secondly, there is what might be termed a 'social formation' model which suggests that different types of societies will be typified by contrasted urban factorial ecologies. Free-market capitalism is one type of 'social formation', socialist societies form another, welfare states a third, and less appropriately, the Third World countries can be placed in a very broad fourth category. Generalisations of this kind are clearly sweeping and vulnerable to detailed analyses. Factorial ecologies, however, have produced evidence which gives them some level of credibility; their findings have given insights both into the nature of social stratification and its expression as residential segregation in cities.

Ethnic areas

Ethnic residential segregation is often the most pronounced form of segregation within urban areas; it possesses a high level of ubiquity across contrasted types of society and can often be detected in an incipient form in the very early stages of city growth. Boal (1978), in a review of the concept of ethnicity and its manifestations in urban social geography has provided useful definitions and guidelines. The bases for ethnic categorisation can be racial, religious, or national; its recognition may rest on distinguishing physical characteristics, on cultural traits such as language or custom, or on a group identity obtaining from common origins or traditions. Greeley summarised this last characteristic as a 'human collectivity' based on an assumption of common origin, real or imaginary. Most research on ethnic groups has focused upon minorities in any given society. Ethnic minority groups have varying levels of residential segregation which appear related to two key features. The first of these relates to the migrant status of the group. Virtually all ethnic minorities are initially immigrants both to urban areas and also to the wider society; the recency of migration and their migration history are clearly important considerations. The second feature is the 'social' distance which separates the ethnic minority from the 'charter group' or host society which forms the dominant matrix into which it is inserted. For those immigrants whose differences with the charter group are small, separate identity may be of only temporary duration; for those whose differences – either real or perceived – are great, separation in both society and space is likely to persist. These two factors clearly interact. New migrants, regardless of ethnic status, will be distinctive at least in social characteristics; long-term migrants, however distinctive they have remained, will have acquired some of the characteristics of the new society.

Assimilation: choice and constraint

The maintenance of the ethnic minority group as a distinctive social and spatial entity will depend on the degree to which assimilation occurs. A distinction is normally made between *behavioural* and *structural* assimilation. The former describes the process whereby members of a group acquire the attitudes, values and mores of the charter group and are 'acculturated' into the new society. Structural assimilation refers to the ability of migrants to compete successfully in the system of stratification within that society – principally its occupational, educational, and housing markets. Both types of assimilation have to be seen in a temporal context but whereas behavioural assimilation is normally attainable by all types of immigrants, structural assimilation is typically much more difficult to achieve. The rate at which behavioural assimilation takes place can vary from one ethnic minority to another – some groups may purposely seek to retain their distinctive characteristics and thereby delay assimilation – but a common estimate is that by the third generation a migrant group has substantially acquired the behavioural traits and values of the host society. Time taken to achieve structural assimilation will vary and the type of ethnic minority is again significant; the key factor, however, is the attitude of the charter group. Whereas West European immigrants to the United States, for example, will normally achieve almost immediate structural assimilation, i.e. they will fit into existing systems at a level appropriate to their skills and qualifications, black minorities in American cities continue to occupy lower-paid jobs and low-cost housing after well over a century of in-movement. Most research in the social sciences has been concerned with those ethnic minorities for whom the constraints upon assimilation and levels of discrimination are greatest. These groups are often racially distinct, set apart by inherited physical traits such as colour of skin.

It is for these latter groups that membership of a minority is most likely to lead to residential segregation as an expression of spatial separation from the host society and also to residential deprivation as an expression of subordinate status. The ethnic areas typical of many cities at many points in time have often been initiated and maintained by attitudes of a charter group which continues to discriminate and restrict and has the effect of creating both this separation and disadvantage. Not all of the forces which promote ethnic segreation, however, emanate from the charter group. There is strong evidence that choice operates in the maintenance of ethnic group segregation; for minorities who wish to retain some level of group cohesion, the ethnic area offers an obvious instrument to that end. Boal (1978) has nominated a number of functions which the ethnically segregated area fulfils. The *defensive* function enables the isolation of members of an ethnic minority to be reduced and an organised defence to be developed within a clearly defined area. As the term 'ghetto' (from the island of Geto in Venice) was first applied to Jewish compounds in European cities, it has this kind of meaning. In that situation locked gates kept one group in and other groups out, circumstances which have subsequently been replicated in principle if not in practice. An *avoidance* function emphasised the self-supportive roles of ethnic residential segregations. Avoidance is more clearly seen in the context of recent arrivals to an established ethnic area. The area serves as a place of initiation and familiarisation in which retention of traditional values and customs makes these processes easier to accomplish. Ethnic minority areas often have institutions, such as those of religion or welfare, which may be in part designed to provide sustenance at earlier stages of contact with a new society. Chain migration has frequently been recognised by which earlier migrants maintain flows of information and aid to those who follow; social networks developed in this way form part of the avoidance function. *Preservation* functions offer the most positive choice bases of ethnic segregation. Here the aim is to preserve and promote at least central features of the ethnic group's cultural heritage such as language, religion, and marriage customs. Wirth, in his classic study of the ghetto, suggested that for Jews the geographically separated and socially isolated community seemed to offer the best means of preserving the traditional facets of their lifestyle. There is considerable evidence that Asian communities in Britain hold the preservation function very high on their list of priorities. Finally the *resistance* function involves the use by an ethnic group of a particular territory as its power-base for action against the wider society. At times during the late 1960s and 1970s the Black Power movement in the United States aspired to use the ghettos for such purposes; the Catholic 'no-go' areas in Northern Ireland had this fairly explicit function, and in many parts of the world urban resistance movements have used parts of the city in this way.

These four functions of ethnic areas could in some ways be classified as choice mechanisms but they could also be regarded as responses to constraint. Whereas both choice and constraint operate to produce ethnically segregated areas, they are invariably interwoven and explanations are rarely single-stranded. Whatever the mechanisms which produce ethnic areas, high levels of segregation – as already illustrated – typify many minority groups in Western cities. In studying these segregations a number of issues need resolution. Firstly, the scale of analysis needs to be stated as different levels of spatial resolution will produce different results. These *caveats* are well known and researchers have experimented with a variety of scales. Peach has shown that high levels of segregation can occur even where the minority is numerically very small. In that group of American cities with small proportions of non-white population, ranging from 2.1 per cent to 7.0 per cent, indices of dissimilarity of 60.4 to 98.0 were still obtained. A second issue involves the extent of dominance by one group within an ethnic area. Immigrant areas were being defined in British cities, for example, when it was still rare for immigrants to form more than 20 per cent of the population in any one area; Ford and Griffin report that white Americans may regard an area as ethnic if it is 25 per cent black. Whereas black Americans would regard it as integrated if it was 25 per cent white. A third issue, arising directly from this, concerns the drawing of boundaries to delimit an ethnic area. Most researchers have adopted arbitrary thresholds; Ford and Griffin, for example, defined ghettos as areas with at least 50 per cent black or 70 per cent minority group (blacks, Hispanics, Asians). A problem with the second part of this definition is that such minority group may segregate within the ethnic area and there is ample evidence to show that this does occur. Again, it is well to remember that as ethnic areas are often dynamic with fluid boundaries, notions of core and periphery may be appropriate.

A typology of ethnic areas

Boal (1978) suggests ways of classifying ethnic areas which provide a useful conceptual typology although the 'form' may not vary significantly. He uses the term *colony* to describe an ethnic area which is temporary in character. Its main functions are to provide a foothold in new societies for groups who are likely to have little difficulty in achieving either behavioural or structural assimilation and are motivated towards both those ends. An *enclave* is an ethnic area which is likely to persist over time but is primarily based on choice and a preservation function in particular. The term *ghetto* is reserved for ethnic areas which persist and are based largely upon constraints and the discriminatory action of the charter group. Figure 9.13 suggests some ways in which these three spatial forms might emerge and are based upon Boal's examples. *Colony* provides an initial cluster which disappears over time as the minority group participates successfully in assimilation processes; an example of this is the Dutch immigration into Kalamazoo. *Enclave* need not differ significantly in spatial expression from ghetto, the indicators are found in the ways in which it functions as a social organisation. As Jewish groups in Winnipeg adjusted their spatial positions and in part moved to another district of the city, they remained clustered together and moved their cultural institutions to the new locations. *Ghettos* in American cities are best exemplified for black populations. Their relegation to the most substandard and lowest cost inner-city districts is a reflection of their inability to achieve structural assimilation; their subsequent restriction to limited sectors of cities for expansion indicates the barriers presented by charter group attitudes and discriminatory practice in the housing market in addition to the obstacle of cost. Cater and Jones (1989) argue that ghetto results from a one-sided and seemingly perpetual black-white conflict which essentially relates to race. They invoke the black nationalist concept of ghetto as 'internal colony' occupied by an underclass for whom separation and non-acceptance is acccompanied by disadvantage and oppression.

It is possible that different spatial generalisations can be made about the ways in which enclave and ghetto expand, though the arguments are not convincing. There is some credibility to the suggestion that the ghetto typically expands in a sectoral form, so formed by constraints which eliminate large proportions of urban space and force ghetto expansion in specified directions. Again there is some evidence that Asians in British cities are forming discontinuous concentric zones in response to a 'fabric effect', that is, the location and availability of the type of housing to which they aspire. These spatial generalisations have some merit but they are less significant than the socio-spatial processes which work to maintain and enlarge ethnic areas.

Ethnic areas in American cities

The subject of ethnic minorities in the United States, and especially of black

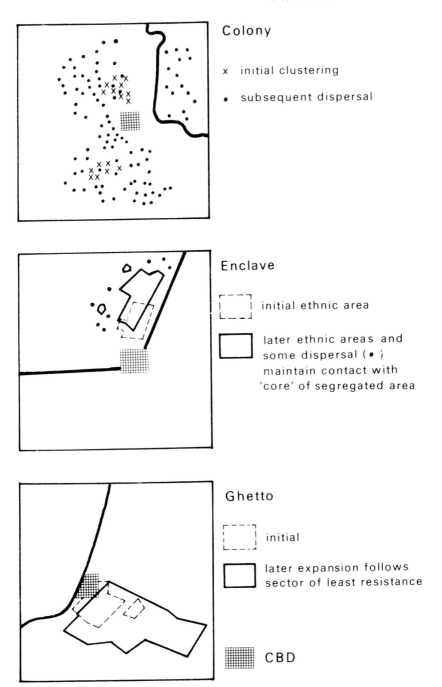

Figure 9.13 Types of ethnic area

early southern

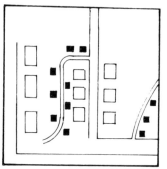

spaces behind masters' houses

classic southern

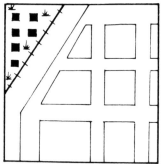

'other side of the tracks'

early northern

foothold in inner city

classic northern

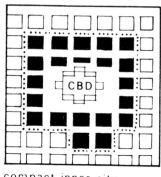

compact inner city

'new city'

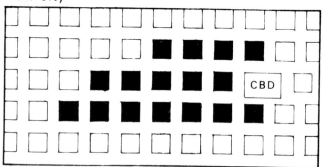

sector growth towards suburbia
ethclass range within ghetto

Figure 9.14 A typology of black ghettos in the United States

(Derived from information in Ford and Griffin, 1979)

ethnic groups, has attracted a great deal of research attention. Studies have focused on the early development of immigrant areas, on the spatial ecology of slave cities, as well as on modern processes of ghetto formation. Ford and Griffin (1979) offer a useful typology of black ghettos in the United States (see Figure 9.14). In the *early southern* ghetto, as found for example in antebellum Charleston and New Orleans, blacks typically lived close within white neighbourhoods – for which they served domestic roles as servants or gardeners – but occupied alleys and backstreets in small dwellings. In the *classic southern* ghetto the newly free blacks were placed in purpose-built housing on unwanted land, such as near railway tracks – 'the other side of the tracks' – or on badly drained areas. As southern States experienced considerable outmigration of blacks, neither of these types of ghetto had potential for growth and tended to stagnate or disappear.

The *early northern* ghetto was the product of intense competition for space in the early twentieth century. Its tenements and row-houses, especially in large north-eastern cities, are occupied at high density with chronic shortage of space and high levels of poverty and substandardness. *Classic northern* ghettos are more recent and much more extensive in scale. As the 'white flight' from the central city gathered force, so large areas of land and housing were left to an expanding black population. The term ghetto has the implication of enforcement and segregation was legally enforceable in the urban north and rural south until a Supreme Court hearing of 1948. Even after legal changes, discriminatory practice continues to have its effect. This type of ghetto, the classic northern, is also found on the west coast in its 'older' large cities. Black south-central Los Angeles, for example, extends to 40 km (25 miles) from near Beverly Hills to Long Beach. Within these vast areas of this type of ghetto are enormous tracts of vacant land, dereliction and abandoned properties. Ford and Griffin (1979) argue that although this is the dominant image of the black ghetto, the reality is being modified by the emergence of a '*new city*' type of ghetto in those parts of the United States which are currently experiencing significant urban growth.

As typified by San Diego and other cities like Denver and Phoenix these ghettos extended from the inner city to rural-suburban fringes. The gradient from poverty and poor environment at the inner city end of the sector to affluence and good environments on the fringe is contained within the black community. 'Ethclasses' or social stratifications within the ethnic group find separate spatial expressions within the ethnic sector; there are segregated socio-economic status groups within the black community. Although the emergence of this fifth type of ghetto suggests structural assimilation amongst some sections at least of the black population of the United States, there are no signs that the ghetto is dispersing. Fears and prejudices rooted in generations of segregated residential areas will take many years to dissipate.

This discussion has focused on black ethnic groups in American cities but there are of course others, and in many southern and south-western cities the rise of Hispanic minorities has been the feature of the last decade. Clark (1984) showed a rapid rise of Hispanic children in Los Angeles elementary school enrolments against a sharply falling white and a slowly declining black population. By 1980, 55 per cent of enrolments were Hispanic. The school enrolments indicator reflects more general demographic trends; Hispanics by 1980 formed a group of 816,076 in the City and 2,144,022 in the County of Los Angeles. The Hispanic population forms some clusters, as in Alhambra and East Los Angeles, but is more dispersed than the blacks.

Immigrant and ethnic areas in British cities

Although there were ethnic minorities in the United Kingdom before the 1950s, they were – apart from the Irish who occupied the nineteenth century 'ghettos' – insignificant in numerical terms. The influx of immigrants from the New Commonwealth during the 1950s and 1960s gave substantial ethnic minorities, and their behaviour in residential space has been closely monitored. The main immigrant groups, from the West Indies, India and Pakistan, have followed classical patterns of immigration. They arrived with many disadvantages associated with lack of employment skills and education, and have found these exacerbated by the early discriminatory practices of the host society which has made structural assimilation a very difficult process. As a generalisation the *replacement* theory is most relevant to understanding the niche which they occupy in both social and geographical space. They found employment in those types of jobs which either through low pay or unpleasant conditions the native British worker did not want; they obtained housing in those substandard parts of the inner city which had experienced population decline through out-migrations over a long period of time. Certainly in the earlier years, choice mechanisms did function in the initiation of segregated areas. Avoidance and preservation have been powerful roles which persist.

Studies based on 1961 census data showed that some segregation did exist but that the new ethnic minorities were relatively small elements of population in poor environments which they shared with the low-income British population and often the long-established Irish communities. Evidence from successive later censuses is that levels of segregation tend to increase, that ethnic minorities tend to become the majority group within some areas, and that the various minorities are occupying different ethnic areas. Whereas part of the segregation, of an order 10 to 15 per cent, can be explained by socio-economic characteristics it is clearly an *ethnic* basis of separation which is occurring.

Detailed case studies have been conducted in the city of Birmingham where in 1971 the coloured minority of 92,632 comprised 9.3 per cent of the total population. By 1961 a distribution of ethnic minorities had emerged which broadly conformed to a concentric zone at 1 to 1.5 kilometres outside the city centre. Within this zone densities of immigrants were low but they were locating in response to a *fabric effect* – these were the pre-1919 terraced-row, low-cost housing districts – and to a *replacement model* in that these were also districts from which local people were moving out. By 1971 the continuing combination of demographic circumstances – out-migration of whites, in-migration and natural increase of immigrants had consolidated this zonal concentration at much higher densities. Levels of immigrant representation within the clusters in 1971 had reached 38 to 51 per cent; for smaller areas the levels were higher and processes likely to produce ethnic areas of American dimensions were ongoing. A feature of the 1970s has been the tendency for different ethnic groups to cluster separately in different parts of the zone, with Pakistanis, for example, centred on parts of south Birmingham, such as Saltley and Small Heath.

Since 1971 the picture of changing levels of segregation is more complex than hitherto when it could be said that South Asian segregation was increasing and West Indian segregation, now locked into council estates, is relatively stable but there is much more variation among South Asians. Segregation for this latter group decreased in Wolverhampton from 1961 to 1981 but increased in Cardiff; in Blackburn it increased to 1974, decreased to 1981 and then stabilised. A point made by Cater and Jones (1989) relates to scale and suggests that despite low scores on indices of dissimilarity, 'immigrants' may be far more sharply divided from their white neighbours than has been acknowledged.

A significant factor in British cities is the role of the public sector in the housing market. Although this sector has a traditionally strong welfare role, there was evidence in the 1960s that municipalities were exercising discrimination in their allocation policies against immigrant households of a kind which was also evident in the private housing market. The recency of most immigrant residence in a city was counted heavily against them; where they had to be rehoused, a series of expedients, such as deferred renewal areas, improved terraces, or old inner-city estates, was used. By 1971, however, aided by national legislation, the situation had improved; the percentage of black households – mainly West Indian – living in public housing had risen to 19 per cent compared to a 32 per cent figure for the total population. Municipalities were now adopting positive rehousing policies in relation to the black population occupying the most substandard sections of the urban housing market, though those policies have been sources of conflict in some cities. Public sector housing has also been a factor in increasing the degree of residential separation and 'social' position among the various ethnic minorities. West Indians are most amenable to rehousing and there is some limited evidence that their levels of segregation are decreasing; for other immigrant groups, however, these trends ar far less obvious.

Asians have progressed through a number of housing situations with stages which Robinson summarised as early pioneer, lodging-house era and family-reunion with more recent evidence for trends towards suburbanisation and municipalisation. Whereas some basic points have to be acknowledged, such as the fact that the Asian 'community' comprises a considerable number of ethnically different groups and that there is evidence of change over time, recent research suggests the strong influence of a 'myth of return' or the belief that their British residence is temporary. Because of this myth of return, Asians may reveal an unwillingness to assimilate or to assume ties or commitments with British society. Choice forms a strong factor, therefore, in their segregation and even where moves to private suburbs or council estates occur, they tend to remain relatively close to the 'enclave' which houses the majority of the ethnic group and in which its cultural traditions and institutions are maintained. A trend which has become significant in the 1980s is the suburbanisation of elements of the south Asian population; in Manchester there is a gradual outward drift in specific sectors of the city and Leicester shows similar trends. A new phenomenon is the appearance of ethnic minorities in towns outside the 'traditional' centres such as Basingstoke and Milton Keynes. South Asians are achieving some social mobility (with more in white collar jobs) and this is being reflected in changing residential status: it is the main part of the West Indian population which is in danger of being left behind.

Whereas no British coloured ethnic minority shows clear signs for dispersal, there are variations from one group to another and the social processes underpinning the contemporary situation may vary significantly. The overall balance of evidence remains such as to suggest that in British cities ethnic areas have emerged and are consolidating. Whereas severe constraints have an instrumental role in this process, it is clear now that the choice mechanisms are also there and public policies, traditionally set towards integrationist goals, are now being modified. The city of Birmingham eventually adopted a rigid dispersal policy in its public sector housing allocations, intended to maintain an immigrant element on any one estate at a low level, but this had to be replaced owing largely to West Indian opposition in favour of higher levels of clustering. Cullingworth, in a government-sponsored report, stressed the positive effects of ethnic concentration, and public policy since has developed a much stronger regard for the choices and preferences of the minority groups. Such a policy which would allow the continuity of ethnic areas and outmovement based only on choice has a number of critical qualifications. First, as a longer-term goal, the disadvantages which ethnic minorities suffer through the inequalities present in society and its mechanisms must be eliminated. Structural assimilation must be a clear and real possibility. Second, in the short term, it should be recognised that ethnic areas are frequently disadvantaged now in terms of quality of environment, resources and facilities; the positive discrimination and area-enrichment policies already initiated must be developed. Third, where a preference exists to live outside an ethnic area, it should be made possible and on this point there is some reassurance from the lack of problems which Asian professionals experience in residing in white middle-class areas.

Conclusions

The focus of attention in this section has been upon ethnic minority groups in western societies and the residential segregation which they typically reveal. Throughout many Third World countries where plural societies are much more common, the issues are more diverse and complex. Residential segregations on ethnic grounds have strong religious and language connotations and are often reinforced by extensive kinship networks and internally organised social systems. The nature of these segregations will differ within the Third World and will reflect both the societal organisations of the various countries and the stage of urbanisation which they have reached. In south Asian cities, such as Colombo, the traditional societal divisions drawn on ethnic lines are strongly represented in segregated ethnic areas in cities housing Tamil and Muslim groups. In Malaysian cities such as Penang and Kuala Lumpur there are distinct and tightly segregated Chinese districts. Clarke reflected on the plural nature of West Indian society with marked segregation of whites and to a lesser extent of Hindus but more general mixing. Ethnic divisions and ethnic areas, in their diversity of forms, typify cities in many parts of the world and maintain their distinctive imprint on urban life.

Residential mobility

The term 'residential mobility' is normally reserved for migration of house-holds within the same city. Urban populations have always been characterised by high levels of mobility but these overall rates disguise significant differences among the various groups. Lawton showed that in the later nineteenth century in English cities, between 40 and 60 per cent of recorded population were still in residence between decennial censuses. A study of Liverpool at this time showed that the highest levels of persistence, or no change, were in the high status areas. It was in the low-income districts of the inner city that rates of change were greatest. Moore examined American cities where modern rates of population change have been put as high as 25 per cent a year. Here it was found that mobility was highest in the rooming house districts of the inner city, 70 per cent a year, and lowest in more established suburbs, 5 per cent per year. An estimate based on the 1981 Census in Britain showed a population change rate of nearly 9 per cent over the previous twelve months. Over half (54%) of these moves had taken place within the same local authority area and gave an indication of the level of residential mobility as opposed to other forms of migration. Where total households had moved, 46 per cent of these were owner-occupiers, 30 per cent were council tenants and 24 per cent were private tenants. This last group is typically over-represented among movers. High rates of residential mobility are common to the central areas of all West European cities; in Amsterdam the peak turnover rate in 1977 was 334 movers per 1000 population and occurred in a privately rented area.

Housing markets and residential change

A number of approaches has been employed to study the housing market and the process of residential mobility. These various strands can be recognised as parts of the same overall framework:

(1) Attempts to model the urban housing market using a small number of basic variables and the principles of neoclassical economics.
(2) Studies of the factors and agencies involved in the supply of housing and urban development in general; these studies had a more explicit concern with the decision-makers in the supply side of the urban housing markets, with the allocative systems which are involved and the 'gatekeepers' who manage them.
(3) Analyses of residential change with a focus upon the consumers in the housing market who, within recognised constraints, are making decisions on where to live.

Discussion on each of these themes is developed below but initially two further contextual statements need to be made. Firstly, several significant attempts have now been made to see the development of the urban housing market in Western cities against a framework of broader societal change. Vance has examined the emerging housing market as Western cities moved from pre-capitalist to capitalist to post-capitalist stages; his argument also emphasises the contrasted attitudes of American and West European governments to the provision of low-cost housing in the twentieth century and the effects which this difference has had. Both Walker in a historical context, and Roweis and Scott with closer reference to the modern urban housing market, relate outcomes to the structural imperatives of the capitalist system. Badcock (1984) argued that an understanding of the residential assignment process 'who lives where' and in what kind of accommodation, involves knowledge of the institutional frame-work behind housing provision and the related political and economic forces. In a similar way, Mellor stated that the housing market process could only be understood as part of a national allocation of resources, and not as the outcome of demand from individual households. Secondly, many geographers were drawn to an analysis of the housing market as a consequence of their preoccu-pation with residential patterns and in an attempt to understand the processes which produced those patterns. An early dominant feature of this thrust was the study of movers themselves, the consumers whose decisions on where to live were the underpinnings of the urban mosaic. This research was typically over-concerned with those limited sections of society which possessed the ability to move and who exercised choice and preference. More recently the balance has been redressed and emphases have shifted from the study of the overt processes of residential change to the forces and mechanisms within society which strongly influence them. This shift has also involved much greater recognition of the constraints and limits within society and the fact that many consumers are in no position to exercise choice.

Micro-economic models

Micro-economic models of the housing market are in a sense a product of their time which rest upon simplifying assumptions and attempts to generalise upon the distribution of house prices, housing supply, and densities over urban areas. The approach has long heritage and can be identified, for example, in Hurd's early study of urban land values; many studies were completed in the 1960s as the regional science school of urban studies developed. The working bases of these models are found in the economics of supply and location and the neo-classical theories of household behaviour merged into a general equilibrium framework. The model typically makes a number of limiting assumptions such as perfect competition, a unidimensional product, invariant tastes and a single-centred city; the market process is a mechanistic one in which individual households, maximising satisfaction, distribute themselves according to income, accessibility needs and space preferences. Suppliers seek to maximise profits in the manner in which they develop new units for the housing market.

Outputs from micro-economic models are typically a set of relatively simple generalisations (see Bourne, 1976). Population density, for example, decreases from centre to periphery, whereas housing-lot size tends to increase as does income of householder and house-buying ability. This set of models demonstrates the contribution of positive science to an understanding of land-use patterns, including residential land use in cities. The basic 'trade-off' mechanism states that each household's utility is maximised by trading off consumption of space against commuting or travel costs. Each household finds:

> . . . its optimal location relative to the centre of the city by trading off travel costs which increase with distance from the centre, with housing costs which decrease with distance from the centre, and locating at the point at which total costs are minimised. (Evans, 1973).

Although these models can be refined, the simplifying assumption tends to distance them from reality and give them limited practical value. The assumption of a single-centred city is diminished by decentralisation which locates employment opportunities in peripheral locations. Again, as Badcock (1984) has noted, the heavy reliance of the trade-off model on utility theory with its pretentions of free consumer choice makes it an 'ideological sham'. Similarly assumptions about the mobility of capital and perfect competition are confounded in a complex housing market.

These micro-economic models of the urban housing market developed at the apogee of the influence of positive science. Subsequently they have been disregarded on the grounds that they are *mechanistic* and fail to recognise human diversity, that they are *ideological* and serve to nurture and legitimise market capitalism and that they *ignore issues of welfare* and the inequalities of social conditions within society. As with other applications of positive science, this approach has added considerable technical ability to urban analysis. Its scope is severely limited, however, by the restrictive assumptions upon which it is typically based.

Agencies in the housing market

The suppliers

Bourne (1976) well summarises the alternative framework within which the supply side of the housing market needs to be studied; it is not, he argues,

> ...as assumed in most micro-economic models, characterised by optimal decision-making within a uniform and unconstrained environment. The housing industry itself, and the various private and public agents responsible for the provision of housing, are not homogeneous in character or behaviour.

It is in this complexity of a hierarchy of decision-makers operating within the framework of a particular society and interacting with broad market trends of supply and demand, that some of the main determinants of the changing residential geography of urban areas are to be found (see Figure 9.15).

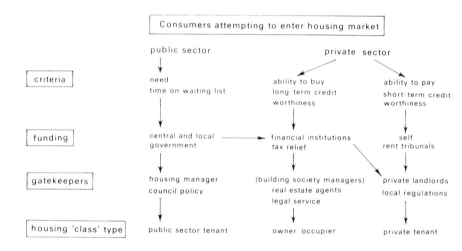

Figure 9.15   Consumers in the housing market: choices, constraints, and urban managers

Housing classes

New residential development is added to the housing stock of the city and the individual consumer is faced with three main routes into this market. These are summarised in Figure 9.15 as renting in the public sector and buying or renting in the private sector. In Britain during the 1980s the right to buy has created a new category of buying in the public sector; an option exercised to date by some 1.2 million former local authority tenants. Which route a household takes into the housing market is largely determined by its position in society and it is here that the concept of housing classes is of value. Rex and Moore (1967) used

Weberian theory to argue that households fell into distinctive 'housing classes' which reflected their ability, or lack of it, to compete in the housing market. Their original typology ranged from outright owners of whole houses to tenants of rooms in a lodging house. There is no simple alignment of housing class with form of tenure. Whereas owner occupiers of good quality suburban housing are highly placed, so are tenants of expensive inner-city apartments. Again the tenant in a desirable public estate may be better off than the owner of a rundown terrace in the inner city. Cater and Jones (1989) suggested as a modified typology of housing classes:

1A owner occupiers of legitimate housing (suburban or gentrified)
1B renters of legitimate public sector housing (usually suburban)
2A owner occupiers of low-grade property (usually inner city)
2B tenants of undesirable public sector housing (often high-rise)
3 private renters

All classifications can be questioned and it could be argued, for example, that category 3 is capable of sub-division. Whereas 'housing class' as a concept with notions of class struggle is questionable, the idea of groups, between which households can move, is useful.

Managerialism and the 'gatekeepers'

The basic thesis of managerialism states that between the producer and the consumer of housing there is an intermediate level of decision-makers concerned with the allocation process. Pahl argues that whatever form society takes, resources will always be scarce and procedures to effect their distribution will always be necessary, consequently specific agents will ultimately control and allocate such resources. Once housing is constructed and becomes available for sale or rent, the more explicit gatekeepers of the housing market are involved.

In the public sector (see Figure 9.15) the key gatekeepers are the local housing manager and housing committee policy. The first obstacle is that of qualifying for public housing. Municipalities often require some years of residence in the area and evidence of housing need. Once qualified the potential tenant is placed on a waiting list which may be operated in terms of date-order, a points system, special needs or a combination of these. There is competition for desirable estates and those with the ability to wait have some advantage; in Swansea it was shown that households were prepared to wait up to ten years for attractive estates. Cater and Jones (1989) make the point that not all public sector housing is a desired resource, it ranges from the desirable to the disgraceful. Gate-keepers can therefore decide who qualifies and also who goes where within the local authority housing sector. Difficult-to-let estates are occupied by the losers in this segment of the housing market. As the 'Right to Buy' is exercised in desirable estates, some areas and their occupants become increasingly marginal-ised.

In the private sector, the capital and credit-worthiness of consumes are of critical significance to the gatekeepers. Easiest routes to private accommodation are in the rented sector where large landlords and property companies often adopt allocation rules which favour childless, professional households which cause fewest management problems. Landlords and tenants are controlled by codes of practice, legislation and local regulations. In the United Kingdom, with a rapidly shrinking private-rented sector and its increasing confinement to least-desirable properties, the members of this 'housing class' are commonly among the least competitive in the housing market. They have least security, poorest living conditions and the lowest chance of real accumulation of capital. For the consumer with both the ability to buy and recognised creditworthiness, the options are more real and this group forms the most privileged housing class. Choice is possible, good living environments are likely and ownership of property carries advantages such as the appreciating value of the asset.

The key issue now is the way in which the 'gatekeepers' mediate in the private housing market and some examples of their activities will be discussed. Firstly,

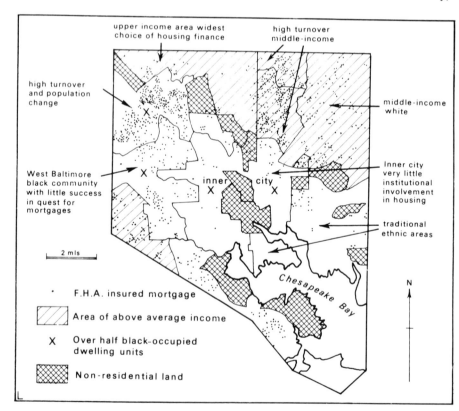

Figure 9.16 Institutional funding and the Baltimore housing market

(After Harvey, 1977, in Harloe (ed) *Captive Cities*; reproduced by permission of John Wiley and Sons Ltd.)

however, some general points need to be stated. Managers or gatekeepers function as individuals within the frameworks of the larger organisations which they serve. In many respects they merely conform to policies laid down elsewhere or work to a few simple rules – such as maximising profits or lending money with least risk. There is also evidence, however, that they interpret rules in an individualistic way and that judgements are tempered by local considerations and issues. The evidence for the independence of gatekeepers is ambiguous, but their roles are real enough. A key problem in using the concept of managerialism is that of theorising their roles and defining the rationalities upon which they are based.

Managers of financial institutions are key figures in the private housing market as their decisions on the lending of housing finance – 'to whom' and 'where' – have profound effects. Harvey's study of Baltimore (Figure 9.16) showed that prospects of house-ownership in different parts of the city were strongly influenced by the varying willingness of different agencies to lend money. Within Baltimore, submarkets could be distinguished within which the prospects of housing finance and the availability of alternative institutions varied considerably. In the inner city, for example, what little financing existed was obtained through private sources; the ethnic areas depended upon small-scale, community-based savings and loans societies or, in the middle-income black district, on federal sources. It was in the affluent white suburbs that greatest choice of financing was available. Harvey's main concern was to relate the outcomes in the Baltimore housing market to the macro-structures of society through which financing flowed, but he also recognises the significance of 'taps and regulators' in the allocative system.

A study of Sacramento (Dingemans, 1979) utilises the material assembled by financing companies in response to the US Home Mortgage Disclosure Act of 1975 in order to examine patterns of mortgage lending in the city. Dingemans was especially concerned with the issue of *red-lining* as the practice of defining area in the city within which lending is regarded as high risk; occupants of such areas are therefore discriminated against. A number of alternative hypotheses was examined – for example, that red-lined districts are declining anyway and have a low demand for mortgages – but the statistical analysis showed a strong positive association of mortgage lending with socio-economic status and a negative association with non-white residents and ages of property – even when influence of new housing units was eliminated. Of the sample neighbourhoods examined, the upper middle-income white suburb received far more loans than any other, though the direct evidence for red-lining policy in ethnic minority areas was not convincing. Other evidence, however, more emphatically asserts the reality of the practice of red-lining ethnic areas.

British studies of mortgage-lending behaviour have identified similar features. In Newcastle-upon-Tyne, mortgage lending within the inner parts of the city was minimal, even from the municipal authority. Consideration of risk appeared dominant amongst building societies and profiles of successful mortgage borrowers revealed a strong bias towards professional and managerial groups with above-average incomes. A leading building society was quoted as admitting that it was reluctant to lend money on properties, which though acceptable in themselves, were in environments of declining status and depreciating values. Local authority loans seem to follow similar guidelines and the least advantaged areas remain starved of investment. Back-street finance tends to develop in such areas and a study of Saltley, Birmingham revealed that only 7 per cent of mortgage holders paid the normal rates of interest. These examples show how discriminatory lending practices appear to depress housing areas and inhibit home ownership within them; the Islington study showed how building societies responded to a 'gentrification' process by progressively increasing their investment levels in that part of inner London. Whereas in 1950 virtually all major building societies were not lending money in Islington because of its perceived lack of stability and high risk clientele, by 1972 all but one of the major societies were lending in a rapidly appreciating residential district shifting from low-income private renters to high-income owners.

Real estate agents (realtors) form another group of managers or gatekeepers in the urban housing market. In some ways they provide a better example of managerialism in that most realtors are local businesses rather than elements of national or regional organisations. The real estate agent is the intermediary in the housing market between the buyer and the seller; as housing markets have developed there are increasing ties between the realtor and the financing, legal, and other professional services – typically the realtor acts as 'broker' for all of these. Rising house prices favour the realtor as his income normally rests on a percentage ratio of sale price; a high level of transactions in the housing market is clearly also in his interests. A number of studies of American cities suggest that realtors have very positive roles and in some ways seek to push residential area change in specific directions. A study of New England in 1953 showed that realtors were using principally ethnic criteria to direct clients away from some areas and towards others. A New Haven study in 1968, after civil rights legislation, showed that the same pattern existed and was rationalised by realtors on the grounds that it fitted in with the preferences of both black and white clients and also with the investment policies of financial institutions. The overt tactics of 'blockbusting' and 'lily-whiting' have been used by realtors to direct and control the growth of black areas. *Blockbusting* involved the use of scare tactics to increase white turnover – such as advertising a house for five dollars – and bringing hordes of blacks onto the street (Ford and Griffin, 1979); *lily-whiting* involved realtors steering white buyers away from any area that had even a few blacks, thereby ensuring ghettoisation.

Palm used a set of four hypothetical household profiles sent to a sample of realtors in San Francisco, to examine the way in which realtors organised the housing market. Generally there was an attempt to make a judgement on the purchasing power of the client but there was also evidence that realtors were actively attempting to change the pattern of the housing market in some areas. The high-income household was often directed to neighbourhoods rather below its private expectations, the low-income households to neighbourhoods rather above. The interpretation was that both recommendations would lead to higher turnover and more buoyant housing markets as the former neighbourhood upgraded and attracted more high-income occupants whereas the latter downgraded and prompted present incumbents to move out. In his study of gentrification in Islington, London, Williams saw realtors as holding key roles in the process of upgrading; they were the 'agents' of change who by actively promoting the improvement possibilities of this part of Georgian London created higher levels of transactions and residential change. The urban gatekeepers exist and fulfil critical roles in the housing market. Even as mere interpreters of societal rules their activities deserve close scrutiny, and it is likely that within the varying limits of discretion available to them, the 'gatekeepers' interpose some independent effects.

Residential change

Aggregate studies

There are two scales at which geographers have studied residential change within cities, aggregate and individual, and of these the former has the longer tradition. Aggregate analyses focus on movement of groups or areas over time or seek to establish trends and relationships from area statistics. Hoyt established the study of high-status residential areas and their typical processes of temporal change as part of the development of his sector theory of neighbourhood growth. His basic proposal – that high-status areas originate near the centre of the incipient city and migrate along specified sectors to the peripheries in alignment with urban growth – has been tested and verified in many places. Hoyt also suggested a number of laws governing the direction in which such movements occur and although the concepts are dated they retain some general validity. Figure 9.17 shows some patterns of movement identified by empirical studies; the sectors are often not unambiguous because of the variegated nature of landscape over which movement occurs, but can be recognised. Jones emphasised the significance of social values attached to space in interpreting the sector pattern in Belfast; an emphasis given increased credibility in later studies. The Swansea example shows a progressive migration of the core area of high-status residence from the inner city out west towards the scenic coastal and industry-free periphery over a century of urban growth. Similarly conceived studies of ethnic area change have already been discussed and Figure 9.17(c) shows the gradual expansion of San Diego's black ghetto over the period 1950–75.

Studies of neighbourhood change provide further examples of aggregate analyses of the residential mobility process. The literature is replete with examples of this process, dating perhaps from Burgess's orginal statement of the invasion-succession process and Zorbaugh's consequent Chicago monographs depicting community character and change. Firey's analysis of land-use

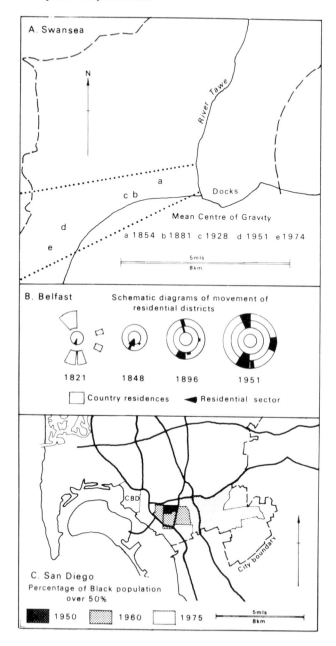

Figure 9.17   Movements of residential areas over time. (a) Shifts of high-status residences in Swansea, 1854–1974 (after Victor, 1975). (b) Changing high-status residential areas in Belfast 1821–1951 (after Jones, 1960, *The Social Geography of Belfast*). (c) Movement of the black ghetto in San Diego, 1950–1975 (after Ford and Griffin, 1979)

in central Boston provided graphic examples of neighbourhoods reacting to pressures for change in different ways. Whereas some Boston residential districts showed gradual declining status over the years as higher-income groups moved out, one or two districts, principally Beacon Hill, showed greater persistence – explained by Firey in terms of the sentiments and symbolism attached to place – and remained a dominantly higher social status in composition of its population. The Beacon Hill case tends to be regarded as the exception and more generally the 'filtering' model can be applied whereby high-incomes households continually move to new housing and leave vacancies which lower-income households fill. In this way housing stock passes 'down the social hierarchy' and there is an allied process of neighbourhood change. Gentrification is a significant form of neighbourhood change in many cities which can effectively reverse this process of filtering. It involves the improvement and upgrading of older property, the movement out of low-income tenants, and the inflow of high-income owner-occupiers. Washington's Georgetown is a well-known example of this phenomenon, and the case of Islington in inner London has already been described. Cybriwsky describes the example of Fairmount, a low-income Philadelphia neighbourhood, which having successfully withstood infringement from the black community, has subsequently been affected by a gentrification process. This process, which began in 1970, has typically involved young couples or single people, usually well educated and professional with 'cosmopolitan' attitudes, who constitute up to 20 per cent of the neighbourhood population. This change has raised new sources of conflict and has weakened the stability and cohesiveness of the community. Large-scale examples of these problems have become evident with the regeneration of docklands areas, notably in London. In some ways this is less gentrification than urban redevelopment though the effects tend to be similar. Gentrification can be explained in behavioural terms as selected groups express preferences to live more centrally or in structural terms as investment capital is directed towards those parts of the older city in which returns can be realised.

Individual studies and the behavioural approach

The shift in intra-urban mobility studies to behavioural approaches and the individual scale was highly significant. Wolpert's conceptual statement had considerable influence on later work and Brown and Moore's framework for research aided this shift in perspective. Central to this approach to the study of mobility is the focus on the individual household as a decision-making unit, on the way in which the decision itself is made and becomes operative, and on the behaviour in space of individual households which leads to the emergence of orderly social areas. As suggested earlier, this research was essentially concerned with how those with choices behaved and the existence of constraints was severely understated, but it did add an important new dimension to residential change studies.

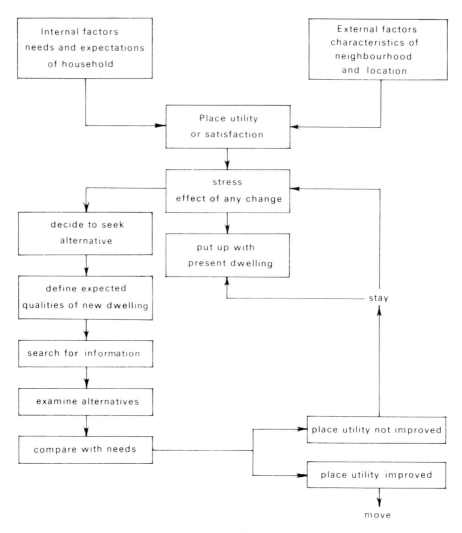

Figure 9.18   Residential mobility: a model of the decision-making process

Figure 9.18 summarises the steps in the decision-making process which leads to a residential move; several of these have provided research themes in their own right. The concept of *place utility* summarises the level of satisfaction which a household experiences with its present residence – a satisfaction which is affected both by the internal characteristics of the household and by the features of the external environment in which the residence is placed. It is change in either internal or external factors which may lessen place utility, generate stress and lead the household into the mobility process. An extra child, for example, may render a house too small, an influx of black neighbours may render the neighbourhood undesirable. Key issues for geographers have been

Figure 9.19   Reasons for residential moves

(A)	**Nationwide**	*per cent citing as a main reason*
	lifecycle (marriage, family size, space needs)	53.5
	design of dwelling	9.8
	access or neighbourhood quality	11.1
	changing personal status	14.5
	other reasons	11.1
(B)	**Philadelphia**	*per cent citing as a main reason*
	dwelling space	51
	dwelling design	50
	other dwelling features	16
	costs	19
	access or neighbourhood quality	41
	other reasons	23

(Source: Rossi, 1980, *Why Families Move*)

this central decision – why families move – and the ways in which search behaviour and mobility itself find expression in space.

Rossi's study of Philadelphia provided early guidelines which have not been significantly modified in subsequent research. He distinguished involuntary moves, such as urban renewal outcomes or tenant evictions, as a separate category, but it is the larger category of voluntary moves which can be related to Figure 9.18. Rossi's basic findings on reasons for intra-urban moves was that a stage in lifecycle was the main cause. As family size and space requirements change at various stages of household lifecycle, so moves are made to find the appropriate qualities of dwelling design and space. A typology of lifecycle stages might be marriage, pre-child, child-bearing, child-rearing, child-launching, post-child, and widowhood, and some stages, such as child-bearing and post-child, are likely to correspond with residential moves. A good deal of subsequent research has confirmed the importance of life-cycle stage and Figure 9.19 summarises some response patterns on reasons for moves; some research, however, has questioned the interpretation of changing space needs as a life-cycle factor. The point has some qualifying value in relation to the lifecycle argument; other factors such as career advancement may lead to an aspiration for a larger dwelling. Again, there may be a desire for more space for its own sake or for a larger property as a form of investment. Rossi did not rate social mobility highly as a reason for residential change but his measure may well have understated the level of career advancement *within* professions.

At the point at which a decision to move is made other behavioural concepts are invoked. *Awareness* of housing opportunities within the city and *preferences* for specific areas affect the kind of *search* behaviour involved in looking for a new home. There is now a good deal of evidence to suggest that search behaviour is neither exhaustive nor systematic. Many households appear to rely only upon casual and informal sources of information to instruct them on the number and locations of existing vacancies. Households limit their search to specific segments of the city which interest them and within those chosen segments typically examine only a small number of options. Most households tend not to enjoy the process of searching for a home and curtail it as much as they can. Rossi's general finding on search behaviour supports the existence of a haphazard process with only limited use of professional and formal sources of information such as estate agents or newspaper advertisements; there is variation by socio-economic status and movers in low-cost housing areas appear to consider very few alternatives before arriving at a decision.

Several generalisations are possible on the spatial forms which the individual moves take. Firstly, movers clearly operate within closely defined *submarkets* the limits of which are strongly influenced by general factors of cost and location. Secondly, there is a strong *neighbourhood factor* which has some generality but which may be especially relevant at the lower end of the market. This factor suggests that moves will be made which keep as many elements as possible constant while enabling the household to achieve the difference in dwelling characteristics which prompted the move in the first place. By moving to a larger house in the same neighbourhood, for example, a family may obtain its extra rooms but will retain established access facilities, such as use of the same schools, and social networks of neighbourhood friends, with which it has no dissatisfaction. Thirdly, there is a *sectoral bias* to moves which again may be general but available evidence suggests that it is typical of the upper end of the

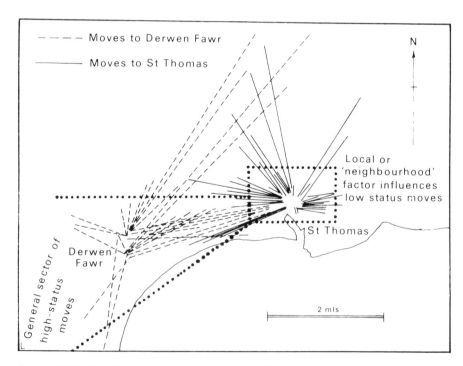

Figure 9.20   Residential moves to two areas in Swansea: corresponding to high status sectoral movement and low-status neighbourhood factors

housing market. The suggestion here, which conforms with the rationale of spatial generalisations on patterns of residential areas already described, is that households will move within specified status sectors and typically these follow a centre to periphery direction. Figure 9.20 contains some evidence of both the neighbourhood and the sectoral factor influences on directional traits.

White (1984) offered three generalisations on moves within West European cities. Firstly, movement out of the inner city is to suburbs on the same side of the city centre; secondly, many moves are extremely local; thirdly, moves within suburbs are extremely complex with many lateral exchanges. The first two of these can, broadly, be accommodated under the categories of sectoral and neighbourhood change respectively.

Some statement can be made relevant to moves in public sector housing in Britain; there is a hierarchy of estates which tends to mirror the general social geography of the city and is indicated by initial preferences, requests for transfer and exercise of the Right to Buy. Least desired estates are often inner city, high-rise and old; more desired are smaller, newer and more suburban in location.

Conclusion

As residential differentiation studies identified patterns in space, so studies of the housing market have revealed the processes. Within these processes are macro-structures, controls, constraints, agencies and consumers, all of which contribute to our understanding of changing residential areas.

CHAPTER 10

The City as a Social World

Introduction

As the industrial city developed in the nineteenth century, the focus of interest was upon the economic activities with which it was associated and the industries which were its driving force. Manufacturing activities dominated the industrial city at this time both in terms of its essential functional features and land use. Large industries often occupied large tracts of central city space, emerging patterns of social geography were closely linked to the location of places of employment, power structures were aligned to industrial interests and the city was most sharply differentiated from rural areas because it was the concentration of industry and commerce. As the post-industrial city has emerged in western societies, the character of the economic institution has undoubtedly changed – from manufacturing to service dominance – but there is also evidence that the social dimension has become the most significant feature of urban life. Urban economic activities are now more dispersed and variegated. They remain important but the simple view of the city as an economic entity is no longer valid. The social dimension to urban life is complex and difficult to specify; older ideas of urbanism and urban/rural differences have proved difficult to maintain and are indeed hardly relevant. More important perhaps is the fact that as large cities have developed they have become the encapsulation of 'modern trends' which have profound effects upon lifestyle, quality of living, and levels of deviance in contemporary society. Over the next two chapters some of these issues will explored. For this present chapter the emphasis will be upon social institutions and social behaviour in the city, topics for which recent work on behaviouralist and humanist perspectives has particular relevance. The next chapter looks more generally at urban problems but emphasises the social issues which have become most acute in the latter part of the twentieth century.

The social institutions of the city are multifarious. They include easily defined institutions such as family but also less clear concepts such as 'neighbourhood' and 'community'. Informal social behaviour such as visiting friends and neighbours has to be seen in context with more formal and regulated forms such as the voting process in political elections. These types of behaviour are different, though not necessarily discrete, from those described in chapter 3; they are more voluntary than involuntary and they are affected by the personalities and preferences of those involved. As a starting point, concepts of environment and behaviour are introduced. One of the city's distinguishing features is that it actually creates an environment on a scale unprecedented in other forms of settlement. Built environments are the dominant environments for city dwellers; they become reference points for behaviour and the extent to which they act as independent sources of influence upon attitudes and activities needs to be considered.

Urban environments

The built environment comprises the morphological framework of streets, buildings, and open spaces which is the setting for urban behaviour. Values are attached to the elements of this framework, social as well as economic. These social values – the meanings attached to space and place – which were recognised in earlier writings, may have special significance. With the focus upon 'built' rather than 'natural' environments, none of the well-known conceptual problems disappear. Questions on the independence of the environmental variable and its definition remain along with issues such as the generality of people-environmental relationships and the nature of intervening variables. A major difference associated with studies of environment and behaviour in cities is that built environments are constructed and therefore modifiable. If environmental effects exist they have been created by architects and planners, sometimes intentionally. Of the two architectural approaches to urban design, one emphasises *visible form* and is aesthetic and abstract in its language; the other is concerned with *social usage* and with the behavioural experience of people in different types of designed environment. Both approaches are relevant to an understanding of the interaction between people and environment; though the latter has a direct role. The *built environment* with its buildings, structures, design features and plan, spaces and alignments of streets and paths poses questions. Do high-rise apartment blocks engender particular types of attitude and behaviour? Is population or building density a critical variable in understanding social pathology? Again, the *urban* environment is more than the *built* environment. People occupying space give it meaning and the idea of a *social* environment within the city is relevant. Herbert suggested that the *social* environment could be usefully subdivided into *impersonal* and *personal*. Impersonal social environments are objective and can be measured by census indicators of demographic structure or social class; *personal* social environments are subjective and rest on values, attitudes and forms of behaviour. Urban environments, variously defined, form a backcloth against which people live their lives. How individuals will react to it relates to their individual differences and the diversities of their past experience. Any attempt to postulate simple associations of behaviour with environment is confounded by this diversity among the population.

Michelson makes a useful distinction between mental and experiential

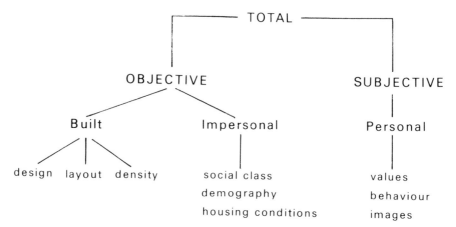

Figure 10.1   A typology of environments

congruence between people and environment. Mental congruence exists if an individual *thinks* that a particular environment will successfully accommodate his or her personal characteristics, values, and lifestyle; experiential congruence exists if the environment actually accommodates the individual. The extent to which people adapt to new environments and achieve satisfaction is therefore related to the extent to which mental is equivalent to experiential congruence. A further distinction in terms of environments came from Stokols, who suggested the need to distinguish between *primary* and *secondary* environments. The former are those in which the individual spends most time and congruence is therefore critical; for secondary environments, however, which are used only in a transitory way, it is less important. This brief discussion is perhaps sufficient both to indicate the complexity of the concept of urban environment *per se* and also to indicate some of the *caveats* in attempting to isolate an environmental influence. Figure 10.1 offers a simple typology of environments. The total environment is composed of elements which relate in different ways to different people – there is a variety of scales as well as types. The built environment, which is the focus of the next section, has to be seen in context with the social environments formed by the people and activities which occupy space. Whatever the objective qualities of these two facets of environment – built and social – they have to be seen through the filters of people's subjective awareness, understanding and appreciation of the space they occupy. Objective conditions such as overcrowding or unattractiveness have meaning only in terms of the cognition of the population involved.

Built environment and behaviour

There is a strong mythology on the relationship between built environment and behaviour, much of which assumes a strong and positive effect. Many of the problems of inner-city slums in the early part of this century, for example, were attributed to the physical conditions under which people lived. Whereas some of these myths have been exposed, others persist and there is still an absence of sufficient controlled research experiments to allow firm statements on causes and effects. A number of propositions are relevant to any examination of environment and behaviour, and prominent among these are the suggested effects of design, of distance, and of density. Research has been unable to establish that any one of these effects has independent status but they continue to show links with some facets of human behaviour.

The best-known starting point for an analysis of built environment and behaviour is the study by Festinger, Schachter, and Back (1950) of two housing projects at the Massachusetts Institute of Technology, called Westgate and Westgate West. The former consisted of small, prefabricated single-family and detached homes, grouped around courtyards and facing away from access roads, and the latter of two-storey apartment blocks with five apartments in each storey. Festinger examined the extent to which environmental influences affected friendship patterns and attitudes. In Westgate, the strongest influences appeared to be the physical distance between the front doors of the housing units; most friendships were formed within courts and among near neighbours of courts. The localised friendship networks also seemed to foster attitidinal stances and commonly held views. Isolates from Westgate friendship networks were typically the occupants of end-houses facing access roads rather than interior courts, or were households where working wives did not participate in the local interaction patterns. Physical distance appeared, therefore, to be a key ingredient in the Westgate friendship network. For Westgate West the critical factors seemed to be the lines of movement from dwelling-unit to exit – functional rather than physical distance. From this study it seemd possible to argue that the physical matrix within which the occupants of the project lived – through both residential proximity and channels of contact – exerted heavy influence on the way in which friendships were formed and attitudes developed. Mercer (1975) suggests that two assertions arise from this classic study. Firstly, that friendships can be determined by physical proximity and, secondly, that groups however established exert influence over members through friendships. For Mercer, the latter is the more significant finding.

An acknowledged shortcoming of the Festinger study was the fact that the study-group drawn from one institution possessed an artificially high level of uniformity. They were all students and had similar backgrounds and ages. Not all studies of environmental effects have been based on institutions. Kuper studied residential districts in Coventry in which the dominent house-type was a semi-detached dwelling unit with paths between each set of houses. The placement of doors was found to bring people together and enable neighbourly contact to turn into more meaningful relationships. Kuper did, however, stress that although proximity and functional distance could bring about contact and interaction, this could have both positive and negative outcomes. Whyte (1957) also studied estates and recorded social activity patterns in the Park Forest area at two points in time with an intervening period of three years. Proximity seemed to affect interaction markedly, and although residential change occurred over the three-year period, the same 'homes' were grouped in activity sets. Whyte made a number of observations:

(1) Children had key roles in establishing contacts.
(2) People in corner plots were most likely to be isolated.
(3) People in central locations had the highest levels of involvement.

Whyte's sample population was not a controlled institutional group but did contain relatively high levels of uniformity. A new housing development tends to attract people of similar social status, aspirations, and lifecycle characteristics. The significance of uniformity is recognised:

> We emphasize . . . that where the community is heterogeneous one would expect the ecological factors to have considerably less weight than they do in communities where there is a high degree of homogeneity and common interests among the residents. (Festinger, Schachter and Back, 1950)

The significance of this qualification, often ignored by critics of this type of study, is stressed by Mercer (1975) as an essential footnote to an earlier quotation which is often taken as a clear statement of architectural determinism;

> The architect who builds a house or who designs a site plan, who decides where roads will and will not go, and who decides, which directions the houses will face and how close together they will be, also is, to a large extent deciding the pattern of social life among the people who live in these houses. (Festinger, Schachter and Back, 1950)

Most criticisms of environment and behaviour research have suggested a neglect of factors such as age, stage in life cycle and shared interests. Gans (1972) argues that planners overestimate the influence of design; buildings – he argues – are of secondary importance in comparison with economic, cultural and social factors and although bad design can hinder relationships and good design can aid them, design *per se* does not shape human behaviour significantly. There are counter-arguments. Lee (1971) argues that although built environments may well influence behaviour, it 'moulds' in a manner which provides choices and possibilities. Clearly, there is a middle ground between the extremes of architectural determinism and design irrelevance; the polarities may indeed be a convenient figment of the critics' imaginations rather than the intentions of the practitioners. Built environment is a context but intervening factors are invariably acknowledged:

> In short, spatial proximity often based on the position and outlook of doors may determine interaction patterns, but this normally only occurs under conditions of real or perceived homogeneity in the population and where there is need for mutual aid. (Michelson, 1970)

Design factors have consistently been introduced into new projects as attempts at social engineering. The *neighbourhood unit*, first introduced as a planning device in Radburn, New Jersey in 1929, was an explicit attempt to create 'communities' through physical design. A set of principles involved in these neighbourhoods included size, boundaries, services, and traffic layout intended to create a physical identity and a social sense of belonging. The 1944 Dudley Report, for England and Wales, adopted the neighbourhood unit principle though with some modifications in detail. Mumford was a staunch supporter of neighbourhood planning, which he viewed as a means of recovering the sense of intimacy and locality which has been disrupted by the scale of urban growth. The evidence for the utility of neighbourhood planning is not unambiguous, however, and some research suggests that the neighbourhood unit is at best neutral and at worst antipathetic to the development of an integrated community life. Some versions of neighbourhoods continue to appear in city plans, basically because residential areas have to be arranged in 'unit' form with some local facilities. The thrust is now, however, towards flexibility in planning design, as exemplified in the plan for Columbia in Maryland. Basic needs and contacts are available in localities but lines of movement are designed to maximise choice and enable interaction over a range of distances.

A further example of social engineering through design mechanisms is provided by policies to develop 'socially integrated' housing schemes. Early attempts in British new towns proved unsuccessful as mixtures of social class led to local fragmentation and crystallisation of groups rather than integration. Berry suggested that progress towards racially integrated housing in the United States had met continued resistance and had limited success. The ideal of integrated neighbourhoods remains elusive.

Much research into design influences on behaviour has been stimulated by the

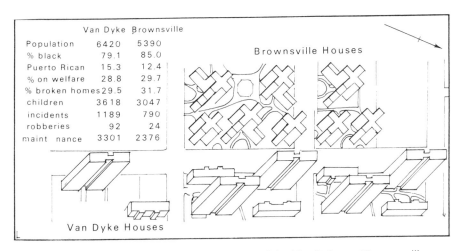

	Van Dyke	Brownsville
Population	6420	5390
% black	79.1	85.0
Puerto Rican	15.3	12.4
% on welfare	28.8	29.7
% broken homes	29.5	31.7
children	3618	3047
incidents	1189	790
robberies	92	24
maint nance	3301	2376

Brownsville Houses

Van Dyke Houses

Figure 10.2 Defensible space: a comparison of the Van Dyke and Brownsville public housing projects in New York

(redrawn from Newman, 1972, *Defensible Space*)

apparent vulnerability of some types of built environment to urban problems. Newman was interested in the high crime rates typical of particular high-rise sector housing projects in New York and developed the idea of *defensible space* as a set of primarily design principles aimed at the reduction of these rates. Newman compared projects of contrasted crime rates and found them to have different design features (Figure 10.2). Features which seemed to heighten vulnerability included upper storeys of high-rise buildings, corridors and stairways which were not well observed, and open spaces which served only to separate buildings. An extreme American example was the St Louis development of Pruitt-Igoe which became so badly affected by crime and accelerating vacancy rates that it was eventually demolished. Newman argued that design principles could be introduced which would help make such environments more livable, and therefore reconstituted as 'defensible space':

(1) Territories must be defined and delineated. Barriers should be used to identify open spaces as extensions of the living block; amenities for a project should be located within the defined territory.
(2) Windows and doors in particular should be so designed that they enable surveillance by residents, who could overlook public spaces and detect strangers.
(3) Quality of built environment should be improved with avoidance of featureless walkways and tiled walls.

Newman's defensible space concept has been replicated (Coleman, 1985) but has also provoked much criticism, principally on the grounds that it understated social factors, but its broad aim was to create a local sense of identity, to increase safety and the quality of life; it sought to place

> ... greater control within the hands of the community and coincidentally, but just as importantly, allowed the underlying cohesiveness of the community to be articulated. (Mercer, 1975)

High-rise buildings and flats or apartments continue to attract research interest and Fanning compared families in self-contained houses with those in three to four storey apartments and found morbidity rates to be 50 per cent greater in the latter. Findings of this kind are common but can rarely be isolated as an independent effect of high-rise buildings. There are some people for whom high-rise apartments pose problems – mothers wishing to supervise young children, old people finding difficulty with stairs or lifts – and opportunities for casual interaction may be limited. Still it is difficult to assert any direct causal link between high-rise living and social problems. Another hypothesis is that levels of crowding and residential density affect human behaviour. The general supposition is that overcrowding creates stress affecting behavioural and physiological functions but research is not conclusive and:

> ... those who draw firm conclusions about density and behaviour are either speculating or making astounding inferences from flimsy evidence. (Fischer, Baldassare, and Oske, 1975)

The point is made that whereas population density is a measurable, objective state, overcrowding is an experiential condition relevant to a particular time and space. These relationships are clearly complex, privacy may appear a 'good' goal but isolation may not; how individuals react may vary widely. As Boots suggests, crowding should be considered as a multivariate phenomenon resulting from the interaction of physical, social, and personal characteristics; the main reactions, where they occur at all, are likely to be psychological rather than physiological.

Summary

Research such as that discussed in this section does not produce conclusive proof that built environment, through its content of quality and design features, affects human behaviour in predictable ways. There are far too many other sources of variation at work for such a finding to emerge. Neither, however, does it dismiss the built environment as irrelevant. The built environment has basic functions to perform such as shelter, safety, and access which are sources of satisfaction among its occupants. Built environments can be engineered in such ways as to improve the probabilities of social interaction, safety, or access, but design is no guarantee of such outcomes. Whereas local physical arrangements are not irrelevant to ways in which individuals or groups behave, they are rarely the *main* determinants. Statements on the extent to which urban environments affect people need to be partial and prudent if they are to have any lasting value and credibility.

Local social interaction

Whereas geographers have an established tradition of research in many types of interaction such as shopping trips and journey to work, social interaction has not figured at all prominently in the literature (Irving, 1978). One hindrance to the analysis of social interaction is the fact that terms and definitions and even the concept itself provide innumerable difficulties of classification. The notion of 'friendship' poses significant measurement problems, issues of kin and non-kin relationships remain unresolved, and there are several *caveats* concerning the assessment of the quality of relationships and the validity of currently favoured ideas such as that of a social network. A further problem for those geographers interested in a spatial analysis is that some of the central assumptions of many spatial interaction studies do not apply. Unless analysis is narrowed to use of a key 'social' institution, for example, such as community centre or church hall, there is no point of conflux, no single destination to which people are drawn. A study of social interaction must consider large numbers of origins and destinations, flows which are not necessarily reciprocal, and a highly fragmented and compartmentalised web of relationships albeit with

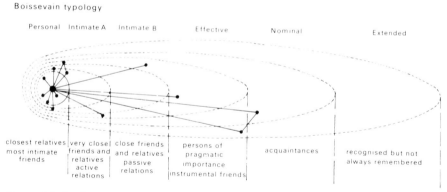

Boissevain typology

Figure 10.3   A typology of informal relationships

(After Boissevain, 1974)

overlaps and subsets. Any attempt to demonstrate a simple spatial effect such as distance-decay will have very limited value – even if proven – and traditional concerns with space and distance need to be wedded more firmly within a complex of social factors.

Allan (1979) defines a sociable relationship as one which an individual enters into purposefully and voluntarily for primarily *non-instrumental* reasons. This type of relationship excludes any kind of business or contractual arrangements, and focuses upon systems of exchange and upon emotional and affectional ties and the social environments within which they are placed. Boissevain (1974) used social network analysis to study patterns of friendship and though his empirical studies are of somewhat specialised groups, such as Sicilian and Maltese, whose social relationships have an untypical 'conspiratorial' quality, he does highlight several concepts of greater generality. Firstly, his research uses a methodology which has received considerable support over the past two decades. Secondly, he devotes explicit attention to the different *roles* which invoke varying levels of social interaction. Some of these roles are separate from each other, others overlap and each contribute to the 'multiplexity' of social relationships which form bases for interaction. Thirdly, within the key roles of kinship and friendship, he offers a typology of relationships which has some general utility (see Figure 10.3). It is in the personal and the intimate cells of this typology that Allen's non-instrumental relationships are most clearly contained. These issues are important but there are several other conceptual questions which tend to bedevil literature.

A majority view now seems to be that although kin and non-kin may fulfil very similar roles in some forms of social interaction, they are more generally different in kind and warrant separate analysis. Among non-kin relationships in particular the values and meanings attached to the term 'friend' have proved elusive to measure and define. Allan argues that research should acknowledge the distinction between those human bonds which can be made and unmade at will and those which cannot. The extent to which people will use opportunities for social interaction will vary enormously; some people are highly active and are involved with numerous contacts in a diversity of settings; others are, through choice or circumstance, extremely isolated. The extreme contrast is between what Irving terms the social 'lions' and the social 'recluses'. Within this range of levels of involvement and activity, patterns of sociability reflect more general leisure proclivities.

Faced with problems of definition and conceptual accuracy, there has been a variety of responses to the problem of studying social interaction. Allan adopts the definitions of social relationships which are held by the participants themselves, governed only by some imprecise 'rules of relevance'. Clearly there is some justification for this type of approach as friendship is a personal and subjective form of relationship, but most studies have attempted to form objective indices. Irving, in particular, has devoted a considerable amount of attention to the development of indices of social interaction. *Intensity* indices are designed to measure the value and meaning of social interactions and tackle the central conceptual problem. Frequency and duration of contact can be measured and scaled in a variety of ways and Irving added a measure of *spread* to indicate the extent to which relationships were centred upon a small number of key inter-

---

A Irving

Interaction types	Durational features	Frequency features
1. Low intensity	Half-day or less	Less often than once a week
2. Long frequent	Whole day or more	Less often than once a week
3. Middle range	One hour or more	Once or twice a week
4. Short, frequent	Half-day or less	More often than twice a week

B Raine

1. Acquaintance	Pass time of day if we meet, but never been in house
2. Quite friendly	Chat in street if we meet, but rarely, if ever, go in house
3. Friendly	Always chat when we meet, only occasionally go in house (1/month)
4. Very friendly	Chat regularly in street, frequently visit home (1 or 2/week)
5. Very close friend	Chat daily, regularly visit home (4/week)

C Irving

Index of Localisation

Local	More than two named interactors were local
	if 2 to 4 named, then two local,
	if one named, one local
Middle	Two interactors named as local
	if 2 to 4 named, 1 local
Non-Local	No named interactors local

N.B. Local if residence within half mile of each other (but this may vary with context)
Each respondent limited to 5 named interactors

Figure 10.4 Classification of measures of social interaction

(After Irving, 1978; Raine, 1976; reproduced by permission of the authors and John Wiley and Sons Ltd.)

actions. A classification of four interaction types (see Figure 10.4(a)) is designed to combine the basic characteristics of duration and frequency to give a simple working typology. A similar classification by Raine, which does attempt to add an indication of the content of the interaction, is also shown (Figure 10.4(b)).

Irving needed to accommodate the fact that kin and non-kin relationships were different from each other yet are not necessarily exclusive. His *kin-orientation* index was an expression of the proportion of total social interaction which involved kin. In a discussion in which the significance of space and environment was assessed, he also developed a *localisation* index designed to demonstrate the extent to which social interaction is contained within a home area or neighbourhood. This particular index has relevance to studies of 'community' (Figure 10.4(c)). Finally, Irving's *network* index was intended to characterise the overall form of the pattern of social interaction of which each respondent was part. Its measurement was concerned with degrees of connectedness within networks which could range from looseknit, where the contacts of individuals were not known to each other, to closeknit, where such reciprocity exists in an integrated system. This index is one example of a methodology which has become strongly influential.

Barnes introduced the idea of a network in his study of a Norwegian island parish and Bott developed the concept in her study of conjugal roles and family relationships in London. Central to the social network approach is the notion that it is possible to view the social relations in which every individual is embedded, at one level of abstraction, as a scattering of points connected by lines. The points are persons and the lines represent social relationships, so that each person can be viewed as a *star* from which lines radiate to other points, some of which are connected to each other. In this personal network, persons in direct contact are in the primary (personal) zone but these persons are also in contact with others whom the initial 'star' individual may not know but could come into contact with via others – these are the 'friends of friends' within the secondary (intimate or effective) zone and the network can be developed sequentially in a similar way. Applying social network analysis poses key issues. 'Boundedness', or the limits of the network, is one such issue; without constraints the points in the network make it unmanageable. Most studies overcome this problem by taking a fixed number of people, by giving each individual a set number of contacts or by restricting links to within the primary zone. Another issue concerns the weighting of links; some are very strong, others relatively weak, and the content of a relationship needs specification.

Despite reservations of this kind, social network analysis has valid research roles. It offers an organising framework in which to study social interaction, ensures that individual relationships are seen within the broader context of a social environment:

> Coalitions, groups, classes and institutions are formed of people who, in different ways are bound to each other, Together they form the constantly shifting networks of social relations that we call society. (Boissevain, 1974)

Geographers have examined the extent to which patterns of social interaction vary amongst different groups of people. Social class differences are clear and generally working-class people rely more upon kin and local social interaction than do professional groups. This generalisation understates the complexity of the real world and Irving, for example, suggests that class is a telling but complex influence. Whereas his middle-class respondents tended to have less localised patterns of relationships, they attached more significance to duration of contact. They had less dependence on kin but it was argued that the independence of the nuclear family was greatest in classes which could afford it. Raine (1976) suggested that middle-class relationships were sustained by regular if not very frequent exchange visits. Allan (1979) acknowledges critical class differences but argues that comparisons of middle-class and working-class are blurred by conventional definition of sociability and the roles of kin and non-kin. Although working-class sociability is often kin-orientated, the significance of non-kin relationships may be underrated because they are limited to specific contexts. Working-class friendships may be very strong but are typically tied to specific situations such as workplace or club and may lapse if those situations are changed. Middle-class friendships have greater ability to 'broaden' and are less tied to 'contexts'. Among working-class people, kin has a strong pervasive influence and is often part of their everyday lives; the fact of geographical dispersion makes the roles of kin for middle-class people less active but nonetheless important. Many comparative studies of working-class and middle-class sociability may have proved fallible because of the definition used of interaction. Proportions of respondents recording no visits with spouses to homes of friends, for example, were 24 per cent among middle-class groups and 72 per cent in the lowest working-class group. Visiting, however, may be a particularly middle-class form of sociability and other approaches might have shown different patterns.

Age, or more particularly stage in lifecycle, has consistently been shown to be an influence upon levels of social interaction. Stages containing most constraints are generally thought to be those of child-rearing and retirement. Young children present constraints in the sense that they tie parents to the house but they can also facilitate social interaction by drawing parents together. Among working-class people, young children can cement the bonds of kinship as they are normally involved in family sociability. Irving recognises the influences of age but argues that it is not consistent; Raine views children mainly as catalysts in the generation of friendship among his middle-class housewives and dependence on neighbourhood as a source of friends tends to increase with the birth of children. If people are geographically mobile at particular stages of their lives this has an effect upon social interaction. Friendships, even among the middle-classes, rarely survive residential change in contrast to kin relationships. Movement to a new housing estate in the early stages of family life may correspond with a strong impetus towards sociability as a new community emerges and its members find common issues. Class, age, family stage are all examples of factors which may affect levels of social interaction but these are personality dimensions which confound neat generalisations.

The role of locality in forming and maintaining patterns of social interaction is a key interest for geographers and it is clear that distance and proximity have significant relevance. Allan acknowledges that when people move, relationships developed in one locality are gradually replaced by those created in another and many friendships grow out of local contacts. One approach is to compare friendship patterns in contrasted residential areas. Irving (1978) compared a high-status with a low-status area in Hull and found extremely localised social networks, involving both family and friends, to be much more typical of the latter.

Local community

It is at the point at which geographers seek to relate social interaction to places within the city that the issue of local community becomes relevant. Research shows that it is possible to classify residential areas in the city along several dimensions – to what extent do these match local images and activities, is there a mosaic of social worlds? The concept of 'community' is elusive and Hillery identified 94 different definitions in relatively common usage in the literature. Community can be applied to forms of human association which are based on shared interest and values and have no necessary spatial organisation but of Hillery's 94 definitions, 70 included a criterion of place or territory, which ranked with common ties and social interaction as the three main determinants of community. Geographers are centrally concerned with community as place and the term local community is more appropriate. There are other terms. Lyman and Scott (1967) suggested a four-part typology of human activity spaces which they labelled *body territory* or an individual's personal space; *interactive territory* or small group transactional space; *home territory* or the local setting for social ties outside the home; and *public territory* or wider settings with which a person has general familiarity only. It is home territory which is closest to the idea of local community and British Community Attitudes Survey did in fact use the term 'home area' in its examination of public views on community. As the typology proposed by Lyman and Scott shows, the term 'territory' is another which is relevant. This term has symbiotic meaning and Ardrey defined it as an area which a single animal or group defined as an exclusive preserve. Social geographers have translated this into human terms and people's sense of territoriality.

Suttles showed in his study of the Addams area of Chicago, how a relatively small segment of urban space of less than a square kilometre (half a square mile) in area, was subdivided among a variety of ethnic groups into well-recognised territories. Each territory could further be associated with distinctive social orders which had a very localised frame of reference and behaviour. Teenage groups have often been shown to possess particularly strong territorial associations and 'turfs' which are resolutely defended from outsiders. Ley and Cybriwsky demonstrated how such gangs in inner Philadelphia occupied territories which were sharply demarcated by graffiti which has the additional quality of representing the 'imprints' of specific groups. With greater proximity to the edges of a group's territory, the graffiti becomes more strident and abrasive in its assertions. Boal studied territoriality in Belfast and used a number of approaches to demonstrate the relatively sharp divisions between Protestant and Catholic communities, Clonard and Shankill, 99 per cent Catholic and Protestant respectively, and separate patterns of spatial inter-action with very little overlap. Since the late 1960s the continuing situation of conflict in Belfast has given territories an even sharper distinctiveness and a more intense meaning. Constraints and the heightened need for group co-hesiveness or security often exaggerate the need for territory considerably; the greater these constraints, the more completely contained within territories the group activities will be.

Studies of territory and home area are valuable but it is the concept of *neighbourhood* which most closely matches the geographer's definition of local community within the city. The term 'neighbourhood' suggests not only an identifiable territory to which individuals feel some attachment but also some sense of cohesion as a group. Queen and Carpenter defined a neighbourhood as an area in which there is the habit of visiting one another, of exchanging articles and services and, in general, of doing things together. Others have arrived at similar definitions of neighbourhood:

> . . . a territorial group the members of which meet on common ground within their own area for primary school activities and for spontaneous and organized social contacts. (Glass, 1948)

Definitions such as these are demanding in that they not only require clear identity of a bounded area but also spatial cohesion within that area. Does this combination of circumstances commonly exist? Geographers have tackled this question in various ways. One approach is to recognise that the urban area does fall into *physical units*, such as a housing estate built at a particular time, and these often correspond with *residential groups*, such as a middle-class suburb which has social and demographic homogeneity, but these are not necessarily *neighbourhoods* in which regular social interaction occurs. One solution then is to suggest typologies of neighbourhood types which reflect such situations. Figure 10.5 is an example of one such approach. A *recognised area* is no more than the term implies, a loosely-defined place which has a name; a *morpho-logical unit* has physical uniformity, it is a segment of the built environment; *social areas* are given identity by population characteristics and are homo-geneous residential groups; *local activity systems* suggest local services and patterns of movement around them; whilst *true community* may incorporate all of these things but adds the vital ingredients of local social interaction, common ties and shared values. Other kinds of typologies are possible. Taking these key indicators of levels of social interaction, strength of common ties, identity with place, etc. a classification from *loose-knit* to *close-knit* neighbourhoods could be formed. This raises other questions. Why should some neighbourhoods be

Neighbourhood type	Qualities	How defined
Recognised area	spatial identity legibility	images of city mental maps
Morphological unit	Physical definition common design features recognizable limits	observation morphological mapping
Social area	social homogeneity demographic unity	social area analysis census indicators
Local activity system	local social interaction local nodes or points of conflux	activity studies trip patterns
True community	sense of belonging social cohesion identify with place	cognitive maps social interaction common bonds 'communion'

Figure 10.5   Types of neighbourhood

'loose-knit', no more than groupings of people with no social cohesion? Is a neighbourhood dynamic, can it change over time? Bell and Newby's (1978) distinction between *community* and *communion* offers a key perspective. Community, it is argued, involves an implicit sense of belonging in a taken-for-granted situation, any social area with recognised boundaries can thus constitute a community. Communion rests upon a form of human association which refers to affective bonds, it implies an active and involved group rather than one which is passive and apathetic. Community can at any time be transformed into communion by an event such as an issue which affects the neighbourhood as a whole or by an 'activist' who launches an innovative idea or activity. The issue may often be some threat such as closure of a local school or a road-widening scheme which affects the place and the people who occupy it, the latent group can become an active association.

The question of neighbourhood boundaries has attracted geographical interest and each component of the typology in Figure 10.5 offers its own solution. Morphological units have physical, visible boundaries, the point where one house type ends and another begins often marked by a physical barrier such as main road or open space. Social areas rest on census indicators and have the boundaries of the building blocks of which they are composed, census small areas or tracts. Boundaries of local activity systems can be defined by point of origin of 'consumers'; catchments of local schools or neighbourhood shopping centres and local social networks. True community again can include these features but needs some extra dimension which marks out the *place* to which allegiance is held and researchers have experimented with cognitive mapping techniques to tease out the 'image' of neighbourhood.

Lee's study of Cambridge neighbourhoods involved housewives sketching boundaries on maps. The result was a wide range of boundaries although 80 per

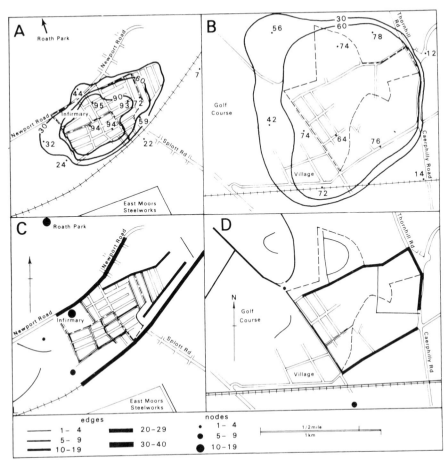

Figure 10.6 Images of neighbourhood in Cardiff: (a) Low-status area isopleths (surface); (b) High-status area isopleths (surface); (c) Low status area edges; (d) High status area edges

cent of his respondents felt able to delineate their neighbourhood. Herbert and Raine (1976) developed techniques to identify images of neighbourhood in Cardiff. Respondents in six different parts of the city were asked to categorise a list of sites in relation to their neighbourhood and also to name the locations at which their neighbourhood ended. Marked differences were apparent among types of residential district. A high-status area (see Figure 10.6) was defined in an extensive way, with little more than 60 per cent consensus at any one point, a low-status area was intensively defined with a much higher level of consensus, often over 90 per cent. Boundaries were often formed by environmental features such as railway lines or main roads but key landmarks, such as parks and hospitals, were frequently nominated. Large local authority estates, sometimes designed as neighbourhood units were in fact segmented into smaller, more manageable units in the images of their inhabitants. As another aggregate device to define neighbourhood, the standard deviational elipse was used and although this produced idealised shapes it did indicate the compactness and directional biases of subjective neighbourhoods.

Geographers have retained their belief in the reality of local communities or neighbourhoods within cities but the concept has had a more chequered history in the social science literature. Wellman (1978) suggested a triad of community lost, community saved and community transformed to describe the various schools of thought on the local community idea. The *community lost* position dates from Tonneis' idea of *gesellschaft* and Louis Wirth's urbanism as a way of life. Both involved the break-down of face-to-face primary relationships within the city and the erosion of any sense of belonging to a local community. Webber's notions of the diminishing significance of locality and proximity in the city as society became increasingly mobile and footloose fits into this school of thought. *Community saved* was the counter-argument that neighbourhood remains a real part of urban life. Examples of this view are found in Gans' study of urban 'villages' in Boston and Jacobs' essay on neighbourhoods as sources of vitality in American cities. Within neighbourhoods it 'was argued, primary face-to-face relationships characterised by emotional cohesion, depth and continuity persisted'. The roots of the 'community saved' school can be traced to the early part of the twentieth century and the still extant neighbourhood unit principle. Advocates of planned neighbourhoods claim to replicate one of the better elements of natural or 'organic' city growth. Mumford found ample evidence of neighbourhoods in the European cities of Paris, Venice and Florence, 'quarters' typically formed around focal points such as church or square and possessing some level of local organisation. Following its precursors, the Garden City movement, social settlement schemes, and garden suburbs, the planned neighbourhood unit principle found its clearest expression with the work of Perry and the working example of Radburn, New Jersey (see Figure 10.7). Radburn as a planned neighbourhood incorporated ideas on population size, boundaries, provision and location of open space, local stores, institutions and an internal street system. At the centre of the neighbourhood unit was an elementary school intended to act also as a community centre, shops were peripherally located and population size – 7500 to 10,000 – was related to the catchment of an elementary school. With modifications on design, size and internal organisation, the basic principle of neighbourhood planning was incorporated in many urban developments in several parts of the world including the British new towns.

Much time and effort has been spent in establishing the details of design for neighbourhood units, but perhaps of greater importance are the purposes and underlying assumptions of neighbourhood planning. There was clearly an idealism among some early writers who viewed neighbourhood as a device to improve the quality of life and obtain some return to rural standards. The aim was to introduce physical order, to encourage face-to-face relationships, to promote local togetherness and feeling of identity, security and stability. Any measurement of the success or failure of neighbourhood units has proved an

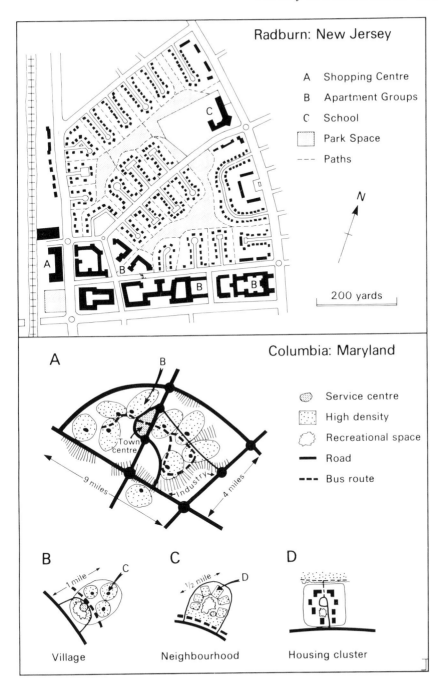

Figure 10.7 Planned neighbourhoods. The Radburn plan (1927) was perhaps the original neighbourhood unit but Columbia in the 1970s retains neighbourhoods in a more flexible city structure

impossible task. Judged by the criteria of 'true community' they have no significant claims to success, but measured by their success in creating acceptable urban environments in which to live which provide opportunities for local interaction, their case is much stronger. Sociologists continue to dismiss neighbourhood planning:

> The problem with the neighbourhood unit idea is not, therefore, that it cannot be shown to coincide with the existence of a local system, but that it misinterprets the nature of this system. (Bell and Newby, 1978)

In Bell and Newby's judgement, the role of a local basis of human relationships is overstressed, it confuses a sufficient with a necessary condition. Territory often leads to close human bonds but is not an essential ingredient for 'community' to develop. Despite these reservations, planners retain faith in neighbourhood units and Banerjee and Baer (1984) suggest:

> The pervasiveness of its influence and use, despite professional reservations and intellectual repudiations, suggest the power of the neighbourhood unit as a construct.

Between the extremes of 'community lost' and 'community saved', some middle ground is both possible and desirable. 'Community transformed' represents this third group who view urban communities as moving throughout a phase of adjustment rather than one gradual decline; local place continues to provide the context for some, occasionally new, forms of activity, community action and identity. With the passage of time and the advent of more mobile, intercommunicative societies, the 'tyranny of space' has obviously been reduced. As C. J. Smith argues, whereas 'true' communities may have only existed in the imagination of a few people who witnessed exceptional neighbourhoods, such as Boston's North End and London's Bethnal Green, it is reasonable to observe that even in very large cities, people are not 'placeless'. People certainly have more choice about where to interact; many will have almost 'aspatial' behaviour but for a large majority locality will remain a significant context for social interaction. The notion of incorporating choice and flexibility into urban design while retaining 'locality' is evident, for example, in the American new town at Columbia, Maryland. Here housing cluster, neighbourhood and village are elements within the city available for local interaction in an overall structure which allows movement and accessibility (see Figure 10.7). As neighbourhood units remain significant elements of planning strategy, so neighbourhoods or local communities remain important in urban life. Many observers have noted a rebirth of localism with the emergence of groups seeking some level of political decentralisation. Neighbourhood associations and community councils have expanded in the 1980s and locality-based action groups have responded vigorously to urban environmental issues. Neighbourhood assumes new roles and C. J. Smith among others has sought to identify these. Neighbourhood has *locational* roles acting as a base for household activities. These may focus on a local institution, such as church or community centre, or fit into a social network of friendships. Neighbourhood as location determines the quality of available local services and the concept of externalities or services outside the home becomes relevant. The *structural* qualities of neighbourhood involve built environment and composition of the residential group, both of which give the neighbourhood its character. Neighbourhood as *place* in the humanistic sense involves a sense of belonging to a home area. In this sense neighbourhood can act as refuge or haven within a large city and is a social world with which its residents identify closely.

If these are the roles of neighbourhood, the remaining question is whether they can be used in constructive and positive ways. At a general level the humanistic place neighbourhood can contribute to human welfare. Neighbourhood planners have for decades used neighbourhoods in attempts to achieve a better quality of urban life. Smith is concerned more narrowly with neighbourhoods as providers of care. His concern is particularly with mental health in which a number of deinstitutionalisation policies, prompted both by fears of rapidly rising demands for hospital beds and by genuine doubts on the value of prolonged institutional care, has the effect of returning mentally ill people to residential neighbourhoods. Community-based services require resources and organisation, but as important may be the informal set of relationships which neighbourhood provides. It is this which may provide the individual with a protective envelope against the stresses of personal and civic life.

People and space: activity patterns in urban settings

Mobility *per se* has received a great deal of attention in the geographical literature (Daniels and Warnes, 1980). The purpose of this section is to summarise some of the recent issues concerning the analysis of activity patterns in cities. These are varied and complex:

> Each individual has a moving pattern of his own, with the turning points at his home, his place of work and his shopping centre during the week and his recreation grounds on a holiday or a Sunday. (Hagerstrand, 1971)

Some activities, such as work and school, are fixed in place and time and evoke regular patterns of movement at constant frequencies; others, such as shopping and recreation, may involve a great deal of variability. Kofoed describes travel patterns as responses to activities; they are affected by the characteristics of the urban system and the quality of physical channels of movement.

Many earlier studies are concerned with aggregate forms of movement such as migration and journey to work, and generalisations upon such well-defined 'rhythms' remain relevant. Regular flows along particular channels at particular times and similar flows of children to schools tend to impose order upon movement within the city. Beyond generalisations of this kind which are relevant to 'prescribed' movements, it is diversity rather than order which is typical. As the variety of 'voluntary' movements and activities has become more obvious, geographers have turned increasingly to aspects of the behavioural sciences both for descriptive tools and explanations.

Classifications of types of spaces have been one outcome and follow the behavioural rationale that the total urban environment contains subsets within which interaction occurs. *Awareness space* is that portion of total reality which is known to the individual either through direct experience or by communication from others, and can be enlarged purposefully. *Action space* summarises an individual's total interaction with and response to environment and is both known by experience to individuals and also has been evaluated by them.

Action space is a subset of awareness space in the sense that the latter is held as an image, but the former is capable of being ascribed values, preferences, and place utilities. *Activity space*, or all urban locations with which the individual has direct contact as a result of day-to-day activities, is that part of action space which involves direct contact between individuals and their social and geographical environments. Jakle, Brunn and Rosemann (1976) differentiate between activity space and action space by limiting the former to actual movement and enlarging the latter to include communication.

The activity space of an individual will vary with roles. The roles of family member, neighbour, worker, student, club member and holiday-maker, all involve different forms of movement. Roles of family member and neighbour in particular involve small spatial orbits and frequent contact; the activity spaces associated with these roles are circumscribed but intensively used. Jakle, Brunn and Roseman (1976) suggest that activity space for the typical individual is dominated by:

(1) Movement within and near the home.
(2) Movement within and near the sites of regular activities such as work, schools and shops.
(3) Movement between these places and home.
(4) Movement involving the use of specialised services which are used on an irregular basis such as holiday sites and conference centres.

Individual characteristics will influence roles and also the distribution of activities over the various types of spaces. Housewives with young children, the elderly and the immobile are all likely to have highly localised activity spaces. The more roles an individual adopts, then the more diverse are the activity spaces used. Spatial generalisations in terms of activity spaces are of limited value but an inverse relationship is generally thought to be held between frequency of participation in an activity and distance travelled.

Research into relationships between time and geographical space has added a new dimension to the study of activity and movement. Time has always been an implicit component of activities research and urban planners have been investigating the time-budget qualities of urban living patterns for some time.

Most researchers seem to agree that analysis must begin at the individual scale with *routines*. Once regularities in behaviour are understood at the micro-level, horizons can be expanded to all individuals in the community and generalisations attempted in a wider social context. Figure 10.8 shows the displaced peaks of sleep, work-trips and social trips with the former involving movement

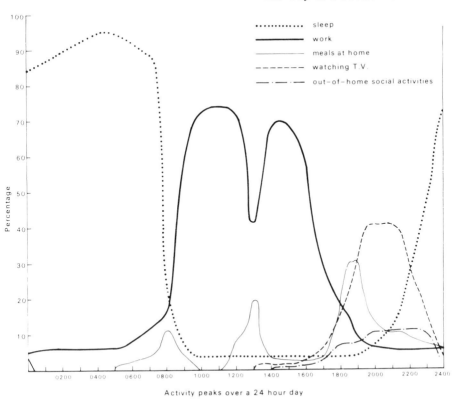

Figure 10.8   Time-rhythms of activities over a 24 hour day

in morning and early evening, the latter occurring at midday and in late evening. Shapcott and Steadman emphasise the constraints which lead to the generalising of time and space, movement and activity. Figure 10.9 demonstrates this with some activities set in particular locations, many of which are fixed, but also constrained by the times during which facilities are available. Shops have flexibility within fixed hours of opening, social interaction has greater flexibility within the convention of 'reasonable' hours of visiting. The rhythmic patterns of availability of facilities or opportunities are not all independent of each other, they in fact form a highly integrated and coordinated structure within which individual life-patterns must be contained. There is a simultaneous timing of many people's hours of work – imposed by the needs of industry, commerce, and administration – which has strong effects on those not directly involved such as retired people and housewives. Despite recent attempts to produce variations, such as flexitime, most work movements continue to be placed within narrow time bands. For future studies linking time and space in activity patterns, some guidelines on research frameworks are emerging. Firstly, there is a 'structure' of traditional routines and practices which effectively pose constraints; secondly, there is a physical framework of facilities

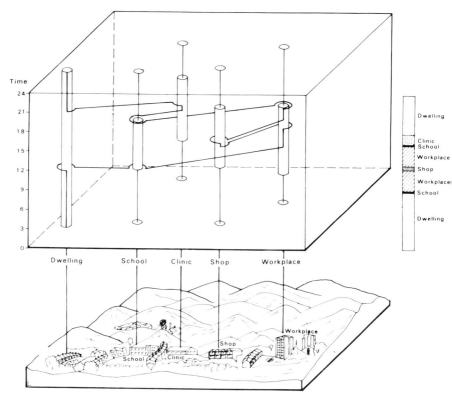

Figure 10.9   Time and space: a schematic representation of a working housewife's spatial activities in a temporal setting

which needs to be synchronised in both time and space; thirdly, the basic building blocks for further research must be individual households and the daily and weekly routinised rhythms around which their activities are patterned.

Consumer behaviour

Of necessity, there is an interactive relationship between systems of consumer services and the spatial patterns of behaviour of the urban population. A close and predictable relationship, however, does not exist between the location of services and ways in which they are used. As the development of systems of services responds to a wide range of formative influences, so too are patterns of behaviour similarly complex. To develop a better understanding of the characteristics of the systems of services in the city, this section focuses upon studies of consumer behaviour.

The normative models: central place theory and spatial interaction theory

There have been attempts to derive *norms* from *a priori* reasoning to model spatial behaviour. *Central place theory* has been concerned primarily to provide a deductive theoretical basis for the development of hierarchical systems of service centres. A consumer is expected to use the nearest centre offering the good or service required. From this expectation the 'nearest centre assumption' or the 'movement minimisation hypothesis' is suggested as the basic behavioural tenet of central place theory.

However, a considerable amount of information now exists which demonstrates that this axiom is a serious overstatement of behavioural realities. Shoppers have been shown to respond to a wide range of additional factors reflecting their social characteristics, the availability of transport, the types and combinations of goods and services required, and the availability and knowledge of alternative shopping opportunities. Similar findings have been reported widely for the use of medical services (Joseph and Phillips, 1984). In fact, as urban consumers have become more mobile and the range of service facilities more complex, the behavioural assumption of central place theory has been demonstrated consistently to explain between only a half and a third of trips. Thus, at best, central place theory, provides a partial explanation of service utilisation behaviour at the intra-urban scale. Nevertheless, it has in the past provided a useful introduction to the study of consumer behaviour, while the partial explanatory value of the nearest centre assumption attests to the continuing significance of the 'friction of distance' for spatial behaviour in the city.

Spatial interaction theory aims to provide a more precise prediction of consumer behaviour, again originating in deductively derived norms. Based upon Reilly's early 'law of retail gravitation', Lakshmanan and Hansen (1965) postulated a probabilistic reformulation of the gravity model considered more appropriate for the intra-urban situation. Alternative service facilities were considered likely to be used by the residents of an area with varying degrees of probability – varying in direct proportion to a measure of the relative attraction of the centre; in inverse proportion to a function of distance between the centre and the residential area; and all in inverse proportion to the competition exerted upon the earlier relationship by all other centres in the system. A model was designed to estimate the shopping expenditure flows between any residential area (i) and shopping centre (j) in a system, from which it would be possible to predict the turnover of any shopping centre (Figure 10.10).

The three assumed determinants of intra-urban shopping behaviour patterns – the attraction of centres, the disincentive of distance, and the competition of alternative centres – all appear to exert a strong influence on shopping behaviour and no significant additional factor has yet been consistently identified. Thus, it is not surprising that increasingly sophisticated variants of this model have been used widely to predict shopping and other service utilisation behaviour. Notable in this respect has been the entropy-maximising approach of Wilson.

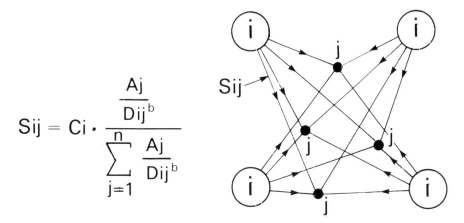

$$S_{ij} = C_i \cdot \frac{\dfrac{A_j}{D_{ij}{}^b}}{\displaystyle\sum_{j=1}^{n} \dfrac{A_j}{D_{ij}{}^b}}$$

Where:–

S_{ij} = the expenditure flow from area i to centre j

A_j = the size (or index of shopping attraction) of centre j

D_{ij} = the distance from area i to centre j

b = an exponent empirically calibrated using known origin–destination data to express the distance disincentive function operating in the system

C_i = the total shopping expenditure of residents in area i

Figure 10.10   The intra-urban version of the gravity model, based upon Lakshmanan and Hansen, 1965

The prediction of consumer behaviour at the intra-urban scale by models of this type is, however, not without difficulties. These centre on the issue of obtaining data sufficiently refined for the rigorous demands of the model. Measurements of attraction for the large numbers of shopping centres in urban areas require expensive data collection exercises, as do the derivation of distance matrices and shopping interaction data with which to calibrate the model for a base date. Similarly, the extrapolation of the parameters of the model forward to predict consumer responses in a rapidly changing and possibly quite different behavioural situation is problematic. For these reasons developments of such models have tended to focus on technical refinements rather than practical issues, although versions are available which provide approximations of the complex patterns of behaviour between residential areas and a range of service facilities. In recent years, the refinement and eventual critical re-evaluation of the early models has resulted in the development of a wide range of alternative methodologies for the analysis and prediction of consumer behaviour. These promise to provide a greater precision to the understanding of shopping and related service utilisation behaviour in cities.

The behavioural approaches

Alternative behavioural approaches provide additional insights into consumer behaviour in the city. Here emphasis is upon *inductive* research methods through the analysis of survey data obtained from individual respondents. A considerable amount of information relevant to the evaluation and improvement of the existing theories of consumer behaviour is provided which also has shorter-term practical value for planning purposes.

Trade area studies of specific stores or centres use information from shopper surveys, while *aggregate surveys* investigate random samples of consumers drawn from city-wide residential areas. Both yield consistent and similar results for Western cities. For traditional shopping centres there is a strong tendency, due to the friction of distance, for shopping centres of all hierarchical levels to draw the greatest proportion of their customers from nearby areas, and the higher the hierarchical level of the centre the wider will this area be. There is also a significant tendency for trade-areas to overlap both within and between hierarchical levels. These findings suggest behaviour consistent with the intra-urban version of the gravity model, and a similar situation has been indicated for the use of medical facilities in the USA.

The trade areas of shopping centres in Greater Swansea demonstrate these effects (Figure 10.11). The CBD acts as a regional shopping centre for an area with a hinterland extending beyond 20 miles. This contrasts markedly with the more locally significant Aberafan district shopping centre. However, it is also of interest to note that the new shopping environment offered by the car-orientated Enterprise Zone Retail Park has a trade area similar to the CBD despite a fourfold size differential. Clearly, the modern out-of-town shopping centres are not functioning like traditional shopping centres, and this highlights the difficulties involved in the calibration of the sorts of models of behaviour mentioned in the previous section.

More specific studies of the *factors influencing consumer behaviour* highlight behavioural variations associated with the social characteristics of respondents.

Figure 10.11   Trade areas in Greater Swansea (% respondents)

Miles travelled	Swansea CBD 1988 (139,000 m)	Aberafan District Centre 1978 (22,000 m)	Enterprise Zone Retail Park 1985 (35,000 m)
0–1	15.1	44.4	15.2
1–2	18.6	28.4	13.8
2–3	13.0	8.2	13.5
3–4	13.8	3.1	12.9
4–7	17.3	8.8	19.8
7–9	6.3	0.8	9.9
10–20	6.0	5.6	8.1
20+	9.8	0.0	6.2
No. of respondents	905	258	676

In Britain, most research has focused on the combined influence of income, social status and personal mobility. Broadly consistent results emerge from a wide range of studies. For convenience foods, significantly higher percentages of the higher status groups travel to a number of middle-order centres outside their immediate residential areas than their lower status counterparts, although the effect does not extend as far as the CBD. This reflected the higher levels of car availability and usage of the high status groups. By contrast, the lower status groups were significantly more restricted to the lower order neighbourhood facilities, except for a small percentage of trips to the CBDs by public transport. These findings suggest that an increasingly mobile population is likely to require a wider choice of convenience goods than is normally available at the neighbourhood level, but falling short of the specialisation offered by a CBD. For higher order durable goods, however, the CBDs continued to dominate irrespective of variations in socio-economic status and mode of transport. The latter situation seems poised for change if the trend towards the development of larger retail parks or regional out-of-town facilities continues. The only other factor which has been investigated significantly to date is the effect of age-structure. The literature suggests the constraining influence of imbalances of families with pre-school children or for those over 60 years old. For these groups there are unexpectedly high allegiances to local facilities for convenience goods, although the evidence is both sparse and inconclusive.

Equivalent studies have been undertaken in the sphere of medical services. In an early introductory review Knox indicates that while proximity is an important determinant of visits to family doctors in Britain, there are major deviations from the nearest centre assumption. Alternative influences, such as proximity to workplace or shopping centres or hours of opening were suggested. Similarly, social barriers, such as perceived 'hostile territories' *en route* to surgery, or psychological barriers such as a limited knowledge of the transport network or of the location of potential alternatives might be important. Finally, a range of other factors such as the personal attributes of the doctor or the inertial effect of a patient's former home might be significant.

Phillips provides evidence for patterns of surgery attendance in West Glamorgan. Behaviour is as complex as that for convenience shopping trips, despite the supposedly invariant quality of service offered. Where several practices were accessible, the high status groups used local surgeries, but not necessarily the nearest. The 'local variable' attendance pattern reflected personal choice in combination with high levels of car availability. By contrast, the low status respondents conformed to a 'dual attachment' pattern. Either they were restricted to the nearest surgery, or, if a convenient public transport route existed, they travelled to a practice in the city centre, almost invariably near to a former residence. The latter 'relict pattern' effect was important since it accounted for between a third and two thirds of the attendance patterns of the low status groups.

The behavioural variations associated with particular social groups have in recent years suggested that for some sections of the community *'constraints'* are more important determinants of consumer behaviour than '*choice*'. Specifically, the lowest social classes and ethnic minorities are restricted to whatever local services exist due to a combination of low income and low levels of personal mobility. Policies affecting service distribution have largely ignored the needs of these groups, and this has given rise to the notion of the '*disadvantaged consumer*'.

These circumstances are considered significant for both shopping and medical facilities. In Britain, decline has dominated the recent experience of small independent convenience stores in the inner city and the peripheral council estates, reflecting a combination of the competition of superstores and outmoded premises and poor locations. Centralisation of general practitioner services into larger group practices and health centres has also resulted in decline in accessibility. In both cases, however, the remaining facilities in the inner cities appear to have retained a reasonable measure of accessibility for the resident population. Hallsworth *et al.* demonstrate this effect for convenience retailing in Portsmouth, which is replicated in Jones and Kirby's study of general practitioner and dental services in Reading. By contrast, in both situations the peripheral local authority housing estates were found to be spatially disadvantaged.

The situation is exacerbated by variations in personal mobility. Currently in Britain approximately 65 per cent of households have access to a car. This figure, however, obscures considerable variation. Many middle and upper status residential neighbourhoods exhibit ownership levels of 85 per cent, while the low status housing areas still rarely exceed 40 per cent. Furthermore, low levels of personal mobility are most marked for mothers with young children and the elderly; in effect those most likely to require easily accessible shopping and medical facilities. Hillman and Whalley (1977) suggest that this restriction is not necessarily redressed by public transport since, although 84 per cent of the population lives less than five minutes walk from a bus stop, bus services are considered poor by at least a third of users due to unreliability and a third of both mothers with young children and the aged reported significant difficulties with using the services. Also, the alternative of walking more than a quarter of a mile poses considerable problems, particularly if the trip involves the purchase of bulky goods. Benwell estimates that the elderly and infirm experiencing problems of access and mobility constitute around 10 per cent of the adult population of the UK. If to these are added the unemployed and school-children, restrictions on mobility are considered to adversely affect nearer 30 per cent of the population.

Investigations of disadvantage relating to these circumstances are, however, singularly sparse, and their findings are equivocal. With regard to shopping, for example, new convenience store chains have emerged in recent years to provide a more versatile range of services in accessible locations in residential areas and along main roads leading to the suburbs. These have partially redressed the decline in accessibility for the less mobile sections of the community, while at the same time offering a supplementary 'top-up' function for the remainder.

The 7-Eleven chain and the group purchasing partnerships between independent retailers and wholesalers such as VG and Spar are notable cases. Similarly, Guy's (1985) study of the grocery shopping of unemployed and retired adults in Cardiff concluded that their attitudes and behaviour were like those of a control group, except that superstores were used less and shorter distances were travelled. On a note of caution, however, the equitable situation of 1982 appeared poised for deterioration with the progression towards larger out-of-town stores, and there was a 'cause for concern about the future choice of opportunities available to disadvantaged shoppers'.

Such concern led to the initiation of the experimental Gateshead Shopping and Information Service by Tesco, the Borough Council and Newcastle University (Davies, 1984). Attention focused on the infirm, the elderly and mothers with young children and investigated a micro-computer based ordering system available at branch libraries and via a telephone link to the Social Sevices Department. The orders were subsequently delivered to the consumers homes by the superstore. For convenience goods, however, it seems likely that this or similar forms of tele-shopping will be viable only as a heavily subsidised service for the housebound due to its labour-intensive characteristics.

A second category of studies is concerned with constraints upon the spatial behaviour of ethnic minority groups. These groups have low income and mobility but also have some culture-specific consumer demands and preferences, particularly for convenience goods and services. Initially, the structure of shopping facilities in such areas tends, like the other parts of the city, to reflect the nature of consumer demand and a particular sub-system of shopping facilities can be identified. A familiar pattern of small inefficient shops, high prices, low quality goods, fewer services, upwards of 25 per cent of outlets catering for culture-specific products and a general air of dilapidation resulted. However, in Britain this situation has not persisted universally. In some of the largest areas of immigrant concentration the economic and social progress of the community is reflected in environmental improvement and the emergence of a rich variety of quality goods and services. The Southall shopping area, central to the Asian community in Middlesex, is a notable example of this trend.

Bearing in mind the scale of variations of the socio-economic characteristics of neighbourhoods in Western cities and the trend towards the centralisation of services into fewer locations, the existence of the spatially disadvantaged consumer is intuitively likely. As yet, however, few detailed investigations of the notion exist. It is, therefore, not possible to judge whether the disadvantaged consumer is merely inconvenienced by restrictions on choice or represents a significant minority experiencing severe hardships. The exploratory evidence suggests the latent importance of an issue which warrants further investigations.

At a more micro-scale of analysis patterns of *shopping behaviour within centres* have also been investigated. The detailed manner in which shoppers use a centre can have a considerable influence upon the commercial viability of particular sites. The lack of integration of pedestrian flows, transport termini and shop locations in either old centres or comprehensive redevelopment

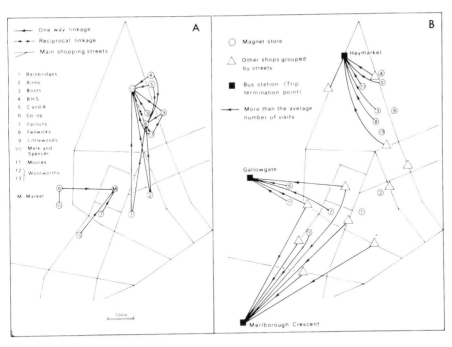

Figure 10.12   Factors affecting shopping behaviour patterns within a central area: Newcastle-Upon-Tyne. (a) Shopper linkages between 'Magnet' stores (greater than 25%). (b) Shopper linkages with selected Trip Termination Points

(Source: Bennison and Davies, 1977; reproduced by permission of Department of Geography, University of Newcastle-Upon-Tyne)

schemes can result in 'dead space' and virtually unlettable shop units. Such a result has a highly detrimental effect on commercial or public investment, while at the same time creating adverse environmental problems. Attention has focused on the identification of the determinants of recurrent patterns of behaviour, the attitudes of shoppers to varying spatial arrangements of facilities and the definition of principles which might result in the most efficient and satisfying spatial organisation of function.

The most comprehensive example of this approach was provided by Bennison and Davies (1980) for Newcastle-upon-Tyne (Figure 10.12). Pedestrian flows were analysed and these were complemented by a questionnaire survey of shoppers interviewed in a variety of locations. The functional linkages between stores and shopping streets were illustrated to determine the main influences upon shopping behaviour. These suggested the primary importance of large 'magnet' stores on recurrent behaviour patterns and the secondary, but significant importance of trip termination points at bus stops and car parks. These sorts of findings offer a base from which general principles designed to improve circulation patterns in city centres could be developed.

Similar methods were adopted by Bromley and Thomas (1989) in the more spatially diffuse environment of two unplanned retail parks. Despite the predominance of car-borne linkages between stores, recurrent patterns of behaviour emerged. These reflected a combination of the *functional characteristics* of the stores and their *relative spatial proximity*. The influence of 'comparison' and 'complementary linkages between alternative furniture, furnishings, clothing and footwear outlets was evident. Significant 'spinoff' shopping linkages originated from the superstores and DIY stores, while differences in the social profiles of 'discount' stores and the 'upmarket' outlets suggested the importance of 'market segmentation' considerations for shopping linkages. Spatial proximity was also identified as a positive generative force, irrespective of the functional characteristics of stores, while the adverse trading implications of a peripheral location were demonstrated. The positive commercial advantages of a spatially compact form were highlighted. This offered the advantages of proximity, centrality, the minimisation of internal car-borne traffic, and the maximisation of pedestrian linkages; while the problems of peripherality would be avoided.

Thornton *et al.* (1987) have provided a comprehensive critical review of the variety of methods for investigating patterns of shopping behaviour within centres. These included the traditional pedestrian counts, questionnaire surveys and pedestrian tracking ('stalking') approaches, but also offered insight into the opportunities offered by developments in aerial photography, video-cameras and time-lapse photography. Time-lapse photography was the preferred method used to obtain flow of pedestrians and their associated social profiles in an exploratory study in central Nottingham.

Clearly, some interesting findings are emerging from the study of shopping behaviour within cities. This is providing information relevant to the planning and design of shopping centres and is likely to influence developers' and planners' decisions on pedestrianisation, layout of malls and balance of selling space, and the optimal locations of public transport and car parking facilities.

The focus in this section has been upon shopping behaviour but as the references to use of health-care facilities shows, some of the main principles have more general application to consumer behaviour in the city. The growth of leisure facilities has prompted similar patterns of movements. Some leisure facilities are neighbourhood-based and act as points of conflux for localities; as schools assume general community use out of teaching hours they fulfil these roles. Other leisure facilities need more central locations and the growth of multi-purpose leisure centres has been a feature of British cities. Again there are specialist facilities such as playing fields and athletics tracks which require space in location but which generate their own patterns of movement. Whereas the young are the main consumers of sports and recreation the widening range of activities is matched by broader demographic range of participants.

Voting behaviour

With some forms of behaviour, geographical study has been less concerned with the idea of movements over space than with the nature of the behavioural process itself and related spatial outcomes. Voting is a form of behaviour which occurs at long intervals, has compulsion in some countries, and is increasing in frequency with new tiers of government and use of referenda. The principle of one person/one vote is now virtually universal but there are several types of electoral system, and which one to use remains contentious. In the widely used *plurality* system, the candidate (or candidates) who polls most votes in a given constituency, regardless of the form of the majority, is elected. *Proportional representation*, in which voters rank-order the candidates, has the general aim of allowing the overall distribution of votes for each party to have some effect. Dail Eirean, for example, the Irish parliament, has 144 deputies drawn from multi-member constituencies by a proportional representation system of single transferable votes. Whereas the plurality system often produces a majority government with a minority of the overall vote, proportional representation often leads to fragmentation and the lack of a clear winner.

The most explicit geographical input to voting behaviour is the spatial frame-work of areas for which representatives are elected. All facets of these areas, including their size, shape, composition, and stability are clearly critical determinants of the outcomes of voting behaviour. The possibilities of using these criteria as determinants have been understood since at least 1812 when Governor Gerry of Massachusetts earned himself a place in history by author-ising a rearrangement of constituency boundaries designed to produce a particular electoral result. The process of 'gerrymandering' has since been widely used and Cox (1973) describes the forms which it takes. One strategy, for example, is to seek out *districts of strength*, for instance, place all white middle-class voters in one constituency; another is the *excess vote* strategy which concentrates as much of the oppostition vote as possible in a small number of areas where massive majorities produce only a few successful candidates; a *wasted vote* strategy disperses opposition votes over a large number of constitu-encies so that they always remain insufficient to achieve a majority; and the *silent* gerrymander involves not changing electoral districts to coincide with population change. The silent gerrymander in particular has led to an over-representation of rural and under-representation of urban areas, a situation which reapportionment and the redrawing of boundaries has tackled in the 1960s. For British parliamentary constituencies, reports of a Boundary Commission recommending substantial changes are emerging in the early 1990s. A result will be a decline in inner-city and an increase in suburban representation as boundaries seek to match redistribution of population. Main guidelines in the British case are equality of electoral size (set at around 63,000 for England), compactness and avoidance of irregular shape, conformity with major local government units, and awareness of the issues concerned with uniformity or heterogeneity within areas.

The constituency spatial framework is a highly influential factor in deter-mining the outcomes of the electoral process. Although redistricting by an overall body, such as the British Boundaries Commission, strives to be impartial and objective, this is very difficult to achieve in practice and there are inevitably tradeoffs which have some partiality. Political parties and indi-vidual candidates are faced with an imperfect set of constituencies at any one point in time, the exact form of which is critical especially in plurality electoral systems. In terms of party competition, votes for some people in some places are more important than others. Parties may concentrate 'vote-buying' in some constituencies whereby large funds are spent on promoting a particular candidate or issue. Johnston suggests that the 'allocation of political money...is spatially biased by the electoral geography of the relevant territory'. The vote-buying model as an explanation of voting behaviour has some support, in other words, the more spent on a campaign, the more votes a party receives. The forms of 'vote-buying' are various. Patronage may involve the allocation of public funds into specific areas or causes.

There are other considerations which affect voting behaviour. A general assumption in Western societies is that political activity in the form of beliefs, values, and actual voting behaviour is class-based. As classes tend to be spatially segregated, there is a geography of elections which reflects these biases. In the United Kingdom, working-class districts like the Rhondda produce Labour representation, whereas professional and 'county' areas produce Con-servatives. In the United States, the most likely sources of Republican support are in rural conservative districts and suburban municipalities, whereas Democratic allegiance is traditionally higher in industrial regions and inner cities. In addition to the actual way in which people vote, there is some suggestion that high socio-economic status produces high turnout and therefore greater support for 'non-working-class' parties. In the United Kingdom, where voting is not compulsory, a major objective of parties is less to convert marginal voters than to get their own voters out. Canvassing is a major factor here and is normally concentrated in areas in which known support exists. The 'party-effect' or class allegiance is general but there are other factors, and specific issues at times of election may become highly influential.

Ways in which information or recommendations on a particular issue reach individual voters are thought to influence voting responses. Pieces of inform-ation which are partisan to the extent that they represent advocacy of a particular issue or person are sometimes termed 'cues'. Cues originate from the parties themselves, from trade unions or pressure groups, from the media and from the whole network of acquaintances which an individual may possess. Cox argues that a voting response is conditional upon receiving cues from politically relevant sources. The extent to which a cue is accepted is in part a function of the credibility of its sources, the force of the argument, and the pre-disposition of the recipient. The significance of cues is affected by several kinds of bias which include geographical distance, general acquaintance circles and more intimate social networks.

Several 'effects' have been identified in an attempt to understand the extent to which cues are accepted. A *relocation* effect occurs where an elector moves into an area of marked partisan bias and eventually, through the influence of aspir-ations and attitudes accepts the majority point of view. A *neighbourhood* effect is used to explain the fact that the consensus view in a particular area may influence the voting behaviour of all residents, even though some of them may be otherwise aligned in terms of class, race, religion, or some other criteria. Individuals may be affected by informal arguments and greater flows of information of a particular type and – particularly where their formal party commitment is not strong – a neighbourhood or contagion effect affects the way they vote.

A 'friends and neighbours' effect describes the situation in which the candidate receives higher than average support in a district in which he or she is very well known, such as birthplace, school, home or place of work. Attempts to attach a quantitative measure to this effect have not shown it to be very significant. In the 1968 Christchurch City Council elections it was found that 85 per cent of the spatial variation in a candidate's support could be accounted for by a 'party effect', 12 per cent by a random element, and only 3 per cent by a friends and neighbours effect. A territorial protection effect is suggested where residents of an area perceived an imminent threat to their interests and vote for a party most likely to protect them. An uncharacteristic swing towards the right and the Conservative party in the 1964 election in selected West Midlands constituencies, at a time when the national swing was 3 per cent in the opposite direction, reflects a fear of the growth of immigration and coloured communities. In local elections, issues relating to externalities, which party will produce a new school or block a new highway, are common.

The right to vote concerns a special form of behaviour, often achieved in embattled circumstances, but at the present time frequently typified by apathy and low electoral turnouts. A recent trend which promises to reverse this, although only on localised and diverse bases, is the growth of pressure groups outside the party system designed to campaign on specific issues which may eventually enter the political arena. At a neighbourhood level, Christensen has documented the emergence of pressure groups to protect the Covent Garden district of London and other residents' associations have performed similar roles. Ecological and environmental lobbies have become of increasing significance and the growth of the 'green' parties is a major factor in European politics. Local community action is increasingly evident and demands for greater accountability may become a key factor in the government of cities.

Behaviour in the city: are there special cases?

Most statements on human behaviour are general and assume applicability to all groups. Statements on residential mobility, for example, are made in terms of households as collective units. There are of course group differences which form topics of special study – the elderly have special characteristics as do some ethnic minorities and social classes. The neglected dichotomy in many ways is that of gender and the 1980s has been typified by a strong surge of interest in the study of women and the ways in which their 'geography' differs from that of men in what are normally 'male-dominated' societies. The neglect works both ways. Whereas there has undoubtedly been a failure to recognise the special features of women in cities, there has also been a tendency to forget that some of the mainstream research areas, notably perhaps the study of shopping behaviour, are in fact studies of women's behaviour.

Women in the city

The place of women in society still varies dramatically from one part of the world to another. There is a so-called 'liberalisation' of women in many Western societies but this is in sharp contrast to the place women occupy in, for example, Islamic societies. Even within countries such as Britain the differences are great between groups such as recent Asian immigrants and native British population. The 'women's movement' would argue that we are looking at degrees of male-dominance but there are significant trends for change evident in most societies. Two fundamental changes are the growth of married women workers and the changing nature of family life and household composition. In 1950 in Britain, 38 per cent of women in the workforce were married, by 1970 this had risen to 63 per cent. In terms of the total labour force there was a process of 'feminisation' (Lewis and Bowlby, 1989) with women forming 45 per cent by 1985. The labour market still posed some major problems for women – unequal wages, limited access to higher level jobs, dominance of 'service' types of employment – and they were also more liable to comprise the 'flexible workforce' of those on part-time or short-term contracts. In a situation in which 60 per cent of women aged 18 to 60 now do paid work, the place of women in the labour force has changed dramatically. There has also been change in family composition. If one takes the narrow definition of a traditional family in which the husband works, the wife stays at home, they have two children and have always been married to each other, only 4 per cent of households fall into this category. There are in fact more single-parent families. Taking a broader definition of married couples with one or more dependent children captures 29 per cent of households. These are indicators of change but the outcome is that:

> ...most women's lives no longer conform to the pattern of unpaid married women living at home, caring for children, and doing the housework while the man goes out to earn the money. (Lewis and Bowlby, 1989)

Despite these salient facts, the average women still spends 75 per cent of her adult life in marriage and the burden of domestic and child-care roles has attracted research attention. Even women in paid work undertake 300 per cent more hours of housework than do men; the traditional roles of wife and mother have not changed that much. As Harman argues, long hours of paid work discriminate against women by creating norms of employment they find difficulty in meeting; patterns of employment need to be modified to meet the needs of women.

Some research has focused on the particular problems of women, especially those with out-of-home employment, in allocating time to a range of domestic roles. Palm and Pred argue that women's activities in the city are inhibited by difficulties of arranging work schedules to conform with domestic 'duties' and access to public service facilities. Shapcott and Steadman, in their Reading study, devoted considerable attention to housewife time-budgets and the variety of constraints upon their time; cooking and food preparation controlled and dominated a large part of the day and care of young children could consume large amounts of time. Households with young children allocated three to four hours each day to basic child care whereas the demands of older children, involving for example the need to convey them to and from activities, were not inconsiderable. Sex roles discriminate against women, there is a *gender role* constraint. The term *gender relations* is used to signify the social relations between men and women which lead to male dominance, the differences are of social construction rather than biological determination.

Allan (1979) placed particular emphasis upon the gender differences affecting social interaction and the distinctive qualities of women's roles in a male-dominated society. One result of this is that a range of leisure pursuits is more readily available to males, many settings for sociability are male preserves, and female sociability tends therefore to be more constrained. Peterson, Wekerle, and Morley argue that male dominance is over the 'larger'-scale components of society whereas women's 'dominance' is typically restricted to neighbourhood and home. Neighbourhood may be an arena of action for women, but because of their limited personal mobility and the demands of a child-centred family existence their range may be no greater than that of a small child. As women spend more time at home, it is they who have to cope with household emergencies, lack of play space in the neighbourhood, inadequate services etc. As public and welfare services have contracted in the 1980s, it is women who have felt the effects.

Women have problems of access, about one-third own cars and only half the women in car-owning households have regular access to the family car. There is a reliance on public transport and yet as Figure 10.9 shows, the multiple roles of worker, mother and housewife may make more demands on daily travel. In the Reading flexihours scheme, all of the men, but only 50 per cent of the women, had access to a car. Palm and Pred noted the findings of a San Francisco survey in which 42.5 per cent of all females aged 19 years or over lacked personal access to a car compared to 18.7 per cent of males. It is clear that the macro-structure of social-economic time-rhythms is set on traditional male-female roles; many of the difficulties of the working wife arise from the dissonance between the demands of the job, family commitments and this macro-structure. Societal rhythms of time allocated for sleep, work, and school have changed more slowly than female availability for paid work; there are societal differences with, for example, greater female involvement over a wider range of occupations in the United States. Working wives have to use early evenings and weekends, what might 'normally' be regarded as leisure time, for household chores.

It has been argued that women are 'invisible' in studies of human behaviour; recent research has moved some way towards remedying this situation and illuminating the special features of women in the city.

The child in the city

Many children grow up in cities, their world is an urban world which enlarges from home, to locality, to city as they move from childhood to adulthood. This spatial learning experience of children has attracted a considerable amount of research which often draws upon the four-phase developmental framework of Piaget and Inhelder (1956);

(1) The **sensorimotor** stage (up to 2 years of age) is that during which the child defines his or her place in the world in terms of actions operative through tactile senses and the manipulation of objects.

(2) In the **pre-operational** stage (between the ages of 2 and 7 years) children may acquire awareness of a few topological properties of space such as proximity, separation, enclosure, surrounding and order; recognise home as a special place with strong emotional attachment and develop elementary notions of territoriality. This phase represents the transition between the stage of intuitive thought and behaviour and later stages which contain clearer evidence of organisation.

(3) The **concrete operational** stage (between ages of 7 and 11 years) is marked by a maturing of the abilities to represent environment and to recognise interrelationships of the topological properties in an integrated system.

(4) The **formal operations** stage (from 11 years of age) is marked by an increasing ability to use abstract spatial hypotheses which involve the use of symbols and transformations. Topological transformations, for example, involve rules of proximity, separation and sequence, geometrical transformations involve metric relationships which coordinate space with respect to a system of outside reference points.

This 'constructivist' approach which holds that spatial learning is based on experience has been widely adopted by geographers.

Piché (1977) analyses the geographical understanding of children between intuitive and systematic approaches to spatial learning. Her findings were broadly in accord with Piaget's scheme of development and the view that the child progresses from an egocentric confusion of self and environment, with space defined entirely in terms of personal actions, to a practical apprehension of Euclidian space in which objects, including self, have positions. Piché's experiments with children show how they begin to analyse routes into segments and imagine directions at the intuitive stage. The children did, however, refer to landmarks and displacements within their own intuitive representations and could not construct overall cognitive schemes with flexibility or reversibility. Older children in the sample often failed to close the network but were able to represent it and to predict shorter routes. Other research on routes has points of interest. Stea asked children to draw routes from home to school and found that the youngest children drew straight lines whereas older children show changes in direction. Jakle, Brunn and Roseman (1976) recount the ability of a child to find the way home but only by orientating along a familiar route. Shemyakin argues that 6 to 8 year-olds define routes without reference to other roads, 8 to 12 year-olds depict other roads as offshoots, but after that age the interconnectivity of routes begins to be shown.

Cognitive mapping

Spatial learning processes form a basic means of understanding spatial behaviour but have not yet been adequately researched by geographers. Much behavioural geography has focused on notions of urban imagery and cognitive mapping and refers to the earlier writings by Boulding (1956), who argued that human behaviour depends upon images or the pictures of the world which we carry around in our heads. Boyle and Robinson (1979) are critical of this over-reliance on Boulding and the tendency to conceive the image as synonymous with subjective knowledge. The older psychological tradition has its roots in the nineteenth century when there was already a prevalent view that humans had an innate sense of spatial orientation, comparable to their senses of smell and taste. Trowbridge used the term 'imaginary maps', Lewin's concept of life space had subjective qualities and the ideas of social space developed by de Lauwe involved consideration of space as perceived by members of particular groups. Buttimer (1969) summarised the primary value of de Lauwe's work as the connection postulated between the internal subjective order (attitudes, traditions, and aspirations) and the external spatial order within an urban milieu.

Although the possibilities of identifying cognitive maps which depict an individual's subjective view of environment rather than total reality has a great deal of appeal to geographers, the concept, as Boyle and Robinson (1979) point out, is difficult and ambiguous. Hart and Moore use the term cognitive map to imply a visual image which has some of the properties of the conventional cartographic map – 'the internalised reconstruction of space in thought'. This narrow view, analogous to Tuan's 'mental map' and Canter's cognitive cartography is also preferred by others:

> It is an internalized, predominantly visual structure, and it is dissociated conceptually from affective connotations. (Boyle and Robinson, 1979)

This view of the cognitive map can be related to Down's threefold typology of approaches to the study of geographical space perception. Of his 'evaluative', 'preference' and 'structural' approaches it is the last, concerned with the identity of space perceptions and the mental adjustments of space users, which most resembles the Boyle and Robinson interpretation of the cognitive map:

We accept that cognitive maps play only a minor and intermittent role in effective thinking and that it is misleading to impute to them any great significance in the co-ordination of our spatial activities. (Boyle and Robinson, 1979)

The argument suggests that mental maps have little place in routine activities, which dominate normal patterns of urban living and when special activities, such as a visit to a new shopping centre or search for a new home, arise, they prompt particular responses which may include consulting maps or some formal information-seeking. Subjective images of the city which are generally held may be influential but are not likely to be relied upon in a detailed way. Given this line of argument, mental maps have some intrinsic interest but are of limited use in explaining behaviour; much of the geographical literature on cognitive mapping has to be regarded in this qualified way.

The task of identifying the cognitive maps which people hold, especially in some conventional graphical form, has raised a number of measurement problems. Measurement can be based upon verbal responses and some success has been achieved by this method; more generally, however, researchers have aimed at 'graphic' responses and people's ability to draw their images of the city. Lynch demonstrated the potential of sketch maps which gave some insight into the form which spatial awareness of Boston took. Other ways of identifying cognitive maps have involved completion tests in which respondents are presented with an incomplete cartographic stimulus and are requested to add detail. Lee presented Cambridge housewives with a standard 1: 10,560 map and asked them to draw a line around their neighbourhood. Cloze procedure involves the superimposition of a grid upon a map from which some cells are subsequently deleted. Respondents are then asked to add detail to the blank cells. Size of grid and density of detail on the original map are clearly critical factors and these procedures, which require people to use maps, do introduce new sources of error. Sketches in part reflect an ability to draw and to represent things in graphical form, cloze procedures involve ability to 'read' maps and use the information which they contain. Individuals have these abilities to varying degrees and it is noticeable that many experiments have used groups, particularly students, with 'controlled' levels of ability. Boyle and Robinson (1979) compare the maps of Sunderland constructed by correspondents with sharply contrasted catrographic experiences. Whereas one drew a conventional map with places and routes in relative positions, the other could only construct a long transect route from home to city centre.

Other procedures rely less upon abilities to draw or interpret maps. Herbert presented each of his respondents with a list of sites and asked if they were or were not parts of their neighbourhood. This involved some control in that sites were preselected but did allow aggregate cognitive maps to be derived. Similarly, Klein presented respondents in Karlsruhe with a total of 24 cards bearing the names of well-known streets and landmarks with a request that they select those which were part of the city centre. Other researchers have used photographs in place of named sites but here the quality and content of the photograph became critical variables. Ranking or scoring places in terms of desirability has been a common approach. Such exercises can be conducted at an intra-urban scale – preferences among residential neighbourhoods or shopping centres – or national scale – preferences among regions of a country. Such exercises have some interest but are of limited value. There are typically local preferences, which affirm the preference for present place of residence, and a general tendency to opt for aesthetically more attractive places with amenable climates or unspoiled environments. Preferences or choices made in an unfettered way without necessity to account for costs or other practical constraints, are unlikely to reveal more than fairly obvious idealistic attitudes. Lynch's seminal work on Boston provided some systematic ways of approaching the measurement of urban images and his typology of paths, landmarks, nodes, edges, and districts has been widely adopted. More generally the attempts to identify images of the city has received many replications. De Jonge compared the images of Rotterdam, Amsterdam and The Hague, using small groups of residents from each city. Amsterdam proved the most 'legible' city with its distinctive morphology oriented around the concentric canals and well-known landmarks such as the Royal Palace and the Dam Square. Francescato and Mebane investigated the images of Milan and Rome and found them both to be highly legible but in different ways. The Milanese emphasised work, activity, dynamism, active recreation and sport; the Romans saw their city in terms of its art, culture and history and most frequently mentioned its monuments, buildings, and museums.

Conclusions

The themes which have been discussed in this chapter all relate to the 'social dynamic' in urban life and also, in various ways, to the influence of behaviouralism in human geography. One can find examples of both behavioural tendencies with, for example, the spatial learning processes of children, and of more subjective humanistic interpretations of space, place and urban territories. Some of these research strands, such as that concerned with urban neighbourhood, have practical relevance. However, the continuing need for urban geography to develop its applied qualities and relate to public policy can be exemplified by those recent studies which have become centrally concerned with identifying and understanding the problems of the modern city.

CHAPTER 11

Urban Problems

Introduction

For most societies the emergence of problems and problem areas has been especially associated with urbanisation and the growth of cities. It can be argued that this association is an inevitable consequence of the scale and dimensions of the urban phenomenon, and therefore that society's problems are *merely manifested* in intense form within the city, but there is also an argument that some problems are *particularly urban*, there are differences of kind as well as of degree. At least to a large extent, however, the city is the mirror-image of the societal context of which it forms part. If a society engenders gross inequalities, these will find sharp expression in urban areas; if the technological base of an economy produces hazardous by-products, these may well accumulate in urban areas; and if rising material and social aspirations are not being matched by essential forms of change and broadening opportunities, the diverse forms of evidence for these 'failures' will occur most clearly in cities. The focus in this chapter is upon some of the problems manifested in cities which can be taken as evidence of inequality, disadvantage and the hazards of urban life. Some of these problems are as old as cities themselves, others are of recent emphasis if not of origin. The issues of inner cities and the crises of city government have long roots but only recently have they become regarded as critical. As with most phenomena, therefore, urban problems have to be viewed in a time-place-social context continuum.

The selection of problem-focus for analysis of the city does pose issues in itself. A focus on problems, it can be argued, diverts attention from society itself and its structures and to surface manifestations rather than causes. Questions of *definition* are also critical. The 'problems' most commonly studied are those which are defined as such by official agencies and the statistical returns which they generate. There is a growing literature in the social sciences which questions the existing assumptions, traditions and biases upon which agencies and their official statistics work. Data from which social problems may be defined are neither neutral nor absolute facts, they have been defined by the data compilers and involve subjective judgements which have no theoretical bases. More pragmatically, data bases are often incomplete and may also be unrepresentative.

A further criticism of a problems-approach is that it has a strong tendency to be reformist and ameliorative in its prescriptions: the most common focus is upon the remedying of visible effects with what are termed 'welfare policies' rather than upon addressing the deeper source of inequity. The approach followed in this chapter is one which accepts the need to place problems within the context of societal structures and to ask real questions of data and problem definition, but which still focuses most attention upon ways in which problems find expression within cities. Despite the conceptual inadequacies of definition and origin, these are *real* problems which affect the lives of many people in significant ways. We should be more concerned with the *fact* that people are dying and suffering rather than with getting the concepts straightened out. Similarly, ameliorative reform may do little to change, perhaps something to enable, the persistence of basic sources on inequality, but in the short term at least, as part of a wider strategy, it can help those in need. Some problems, such as the living conditions of old people, are more susceptible to short-term measures, others, such as inner-city unemployment, require more radical change. A focus on problems has value as a basic inventory, as a portrayal of the extent of human misery, and as one stage in a broader strategy for change.

From the range of urban problems, a selection has to be made. The chapter begins with a discussion of the current crises of the inner city – crises which clearly find their origin in wider contexts. The associated issue of urban government is related to inherited patterns of fragmentation and political interaction in large metropolitan areas. Most urban problems are economic, social, and political but the hazards of environment – both natural and manmade – are assuming larger significance. A thrust towards social indicators and analysis of the quality of life has provided much recent research interest and this is discussed. Finally, some specific problems – ill-health, crime and the disadvantages attached to old age – will be isolated to demonstrate ways in which geographical research has focused upon contemporary issues.

Defining the inner city and its problems

Through the many centuries when cities took a 'pre-industrial' form, and even during the nineteenth and early twentieth centuries when urbanised areas were compact and of limited spatial dimensions, there was no real sense of the division between 'inner' and 'outer' cities which has come to typify many modern metropolitan areas. Clearly there were divisions within these older forms of urban area, as previous discussion has shown, but their scale and organisation was such as to function as one city, at least in a *de jure* sense. The notion of an inner city in these terms is a function of the modern Western metropolis and often had some kind of legalistic definition such as the separate municipalities in the United States, metropolitan boroughs in London and *départements* in Paris. Research which begins with the need to define the inner city usually adopts these legalistic definitions or else constructs an amalgam of administrative units on an *ad hoc* basis. For example, Berry suggests that a good definition of the American inner city is that part constructed before the Great Depression. Inner cities have a number of common characteristics. They are the oldest parts of the urban fabric and hence contain the historic buildings in addition to the most outmoded morphology. They typically accommodate the main institutions of government and culture in addition to the central business district; within their confines are both traditional forms of economic activity and the residual areas of high-density residential districts built to house workers in the industrial city.

There is nothing new about inner-city problems; they have been features of the industrial city over several stages of its evolution. A consistent problem, which may even predate the industrial city, is that of the congestion and over-crowding of people and activities into a limited amount of central space. As transportation routes focused in a radial manner on a central location so the conditions for convergence were set; as industries demanded easy access to cheap labour, the need for high-density housing was created. A technology which only permitted a basic infrastructure of services and facilities in the nineteenth century, promoted the compact city. These basic problems of central overcrowding were not restricted to large industrial cities in the Western world. As the 'metropoles' (McGee, 1967) of the Third World have struggled to cope with the sheer weight of urban populations, so their levels of inner-city congestion have reached new dimensions which show few signs of abatement. Industrial cities of the Western world have adapted to this basic problem in a number of ways. The processes of concentration and centralisation which dominated earlier stages of industrial city growth, were replaced by deconcentration and decentralisation as people and functions began a long process of dispersal towards the periphery and thus initiated the transformation of the compact city.

These processes were tied to an evolving transport technology which enabled the process of urban growth to occur, albeit in a selective way; to the availability of space on the urban periphery – though initially in limited amounts in some cities; and to the space preferences of the owners and managers in the new urban society. The ongoing dispersal process, filtering downwards through society, has been a dominant trend during the twentieth century and has allowed some measure of control over problems of congestion in the inner city. Many cities continue to experience considerable problems of traffic congestion, shortage of car-parking space and pressure on public transit systems; the 'new' twentieth-century cities of the United States are conspicuous for their alternative urban forms with less reliance upon highly centralising radial transport systems. The dispersal process has affected retailing, manufacturing, and office functions as well as population; in some ways the congestion of the inner industrial city has been replaced by vacua in modern metropoli. Decreasing population densities are reflected in the changing gradients from centre to periphery.

For Western cities, central densities have remained relatively high but the gradient has become shallower with a more gradual change to lower densities on the extended urban periphery. For non-Western cities densities have risen in both central and more peripheral locations with highest densities in inner city tenements and lower but still relatively high densities in the 'suburban' areas.

A second problem of the inner city over time has been its role as a locale for the concentration of poverty and deprivation. Initially, in its pre-industrial form, the central city was the focus of wealth, affluence and power in prestigious buildings and the vestiges of this system may persist in residential quarters or morphological heritages. As the wealthy progressively used their prerogative to divorce workplace and residence, the inner city began to acquire more uniform characteristics of a different kind. The industrial proletariat became the occupants of inner-city residential space, tied to workplace and living in crowded, often polluted environments. The homogeneity of this condition – the Victorian slum – must not be overstated but notions of poverty and sub-standardness in the inner cities of western Europe were marked by the mid-nine-teenth century. Added to these features were social problems such as ill-health and crime and an emergence of ethnic minority districts which sometimes created their own form of tension. There are many graphic accounts of the inner-area problems of nineteenth-century cities ranging from the con-temporary observations of Mayhew and Booth to the retrospective analyses around congestion and overcrowding on the one hand and poverty and depriv-ation on the other, both set in ageing and progressively inadequate urban environments.

Recent trends in the inner city

The inner city is therefore no stranger to problems, and the processes of social separation towards the suburbs in Western cities – in many ways a reaction against those problems – have been ongoing for long periods of time. During the 1970s and 1980s however, awareness of inner-city problems in Western urban areas increased dramatically. It is unlikely that any emergence of new problems underlies this change, but a number of precipitating conditions can be classified. Firstly, there has been a continuing *decline of population* in inner-city areas. Between 1966 and 1976, Liverpool lost 22 per cent of its population, Manchester 18 per cent; and Hall, Thomas, Gracey and Drewett showed that in the 1960s the 'cores' of British urban areas were decentralising in absolute as well as in relative terms, and similar trends are observed in European cities. Over the period 1951 to 1981 the six largest cities in the United Kingdom lost over one-third of the populations of their inner areas; the inner city of Paris saw a population loss of 300,000 between 1968 and 1975; and in Rome, 1963 to 1971, the loss was almost 200,000. As this outward movement is selective, the result is to give special compositional features to inner city populations. Champion, Green, Owen, Ellin and Coombes argued that the inner city areas have in-creasingly become the repository of people with the least economic 'clout' in our society, thereby undermining the quality of life there by creating a situation of multiple deprivation. This is one view. Well worth noting however is White's view (1984) that West European inner city populations have a tendency towards polarisation with an accentuation of representation of the highest and lowest levels of the social hierarchy.

In American urban areas, Berry suggests unprecedented population losses from central cities with 30 out of 50 larger cities showing losses since 1970. The most affected cities are those in the old manufacturing belt. Inner Cleveland lost 15 per cent of its population in the first half of the 1970s, Buffalo and Pittsburgh lost 12 per cent; elsewhere St Louis lost 16 per cent and Atlanta 12 per cent.

The image of the American city has changed from one of a high-density and congested but vital centre in which face-to-face relationships could still exist, to that of an ageing, polluted, crime-ridden vacuum typified by declining services and employment bases and escalating taxes. In both European and American cities there have been compensating population flows but these have added to the changing character of the inner city. Foreign immigrants from less developed countries – often former colonies – have moved into inner cities in Britain and in Europe; these sometimes started as seasonal labour migrations but they have tended to acquire permanence. In the United States the black population has gradually moved to numerical dominance over large areas of the central city. Major Koch of New York estimates that the large majority of the million people who left his city in the 1960s were middle-class and white, while the large majority of those who moved in were black, Hispanic, and poor (*Firing Line*, 1979). Indeed, in 1989 Mayor Koch was replaced by the first black incumbent of the post. This accelerating ethnic distinctiveness of inner-city populations, particularly in American but also in British cities, was at the roots of civil disorder in the later 1960s and early 1970s and forms one powerful reason for a heightened awareness of inner-city problems. It became clear that the disadvantage under which inner-city residents lived – with its discriminatory connotations – required at least ameliorative action. One other compensating flow into central cities warrants mention. Gentrification of selected neighbourhoods in particular cities has allowed the localised return of middle-class population, and some evidence – such as at Capitol Hill, Washington and parts of London – suggests that it is increasing. Gentrification, however, is selective both of the conditions under which it can occur and the population it can attract; there is no evidence that it has affected the residential preference patterns of the majority of urban populations.

Population change is one recognised inner-city problem; another, already discussed in Chapter 4, is that of job loss particularly in manufacturing industry. In 1989, Gordon reported unemployment rates of twice the national (and London) average in inner London boroughs such as Hackney and Tower Hamlets. The job-loss problem is not new as industries and businesses have been migrating out to peripheral highway-based locations for some decades, but closure rather than transfer, and the attendant total losses of jobs, has become a feature since the later 1960s. A series of studies of the British inner city has pinpointed the nature and dimensions of these job losses. Lomas showed that between 1966 and 1973 there was an overall loss of 200,000 jobs from inner London, 140,000 of these in manufacturing and the rest in services. Gripaios, in a more detailed study of south-east London, suggested that 69 per cent of closures resulted from 'deaths' of firms rather than transfer. A Manchester study discovered that 85 per cent of the total employment decline 1966 to 1972 was due to deaths and transfers and most of these were actual closures. Districts within inner cities with an above-average reliance on traditional industries were particularly affected; Canning Town in London and Saltley in Birmingham suffered job losses of 24 and 14 per cent respectively between 1966 and 1972. Hausner showed that between 1951 and 1981 the inner cities of the six large UK conurbations lost over one million manufacturing jobs, one half of those which they held in 1951. From these British studies, several generalisations can be made:

(1) The inner-city manufacturing sector is sharing a downturn in fortunes and viability with the total urban and national economy.
(2) Inner-city firms of a traditional kind are proving particularly vulnerable because of their small size and high costs.
(3) Some transfers from inner city to outer city (and within the inner city) are occurring, but most losses are associated with total closures.
(4) Urban redevelopment schemes have had adverse effects on small firms through displacement and higher costs.

These economic downturns and their adverse effects on inner-city employment are also evident in American metropolitan areas. Growth industries are increasingly being dispersed towards the peripheries or the manufacturing belt cities, older slow-growth industries remain as the former core. From 1969 to 1977 the manufacturing belt in the United States on a whole lost 1.7 million industrial jobs; New York City is estimated to have lost 600,000 jobs between 1968 and 1978. Although there were compensating flows in other sectors, of the 500 large industrial corporations surveyed by *Fortune Magazine* in 1965, 128 had New York headquarters, by 1975 this has declined to 90.

The third aspect of the inner-city problem as it emerged during the 1970s can be summarised as the *low quality of life* which it appeared to present to the vast majority of its permanent residents. These conditions, as discussed earlier, have long records but in some ways have worsened despite formidable planning machinery in Western societies. Physical environments in the inner city remain substandard with residual low-quality tenements and other urban fabric elements, high densities and overcrowding and an increasing amount of derelict land. Berry argues that with the expansionist activites of construction industries on the edges of American cities, 27 million new dwelling units were added between 1963 and 1976 at a time when household expansion was only 17 million. As 'filtering' occurred and older housing was passed down the line, 'abandonment' began to occur in the inner city and dereliction spread. People spend their lives in these kinds of environments and, as Knox argues, it is part of the con-

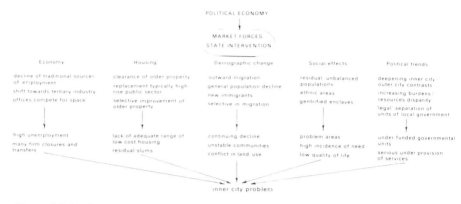

Figure 11.1   Sources of the inner city problem

ventional wisdom about cities that most of the disadvantaged, vulnerable and victimised are concentrated in inner city areas. There they form an 'underclass' of:

> ... persons who lack training and skills and either experience long-term unemployment or have dropped out of the labour force altogether; who are long-term public assistance recipients; and who are engaged in street criminal activity and other forms of aberrant behaviour. (Wilson, 1985)

Knox shows that for the one-hundred largest US inner cities poverty is disproportionately the lot of the black and Hispanic population. In Washington 25 per cent of the white population lived in inner city poverty areas but 72 per cent of blacks and 46 per cent of Hispanics. There are poverty areas in manny inner cities with characteristics reminiscent of American patterns. Recent immigrants, often forming ethnic clusters, typify European cities; Merlin identified 400,000 immigrants and 400,000 elderly persons in inner districts of Paris. The poverty areas often become typified by multiple deprivation and Figure 11.1 summarises these characteristics. It should also be noted however that the inner city as a whole cannot be classified as a deprived area and as Smith and others have shown, the inner city itself is a mosaic with some districts of advantage and status close to others of real poverty (Figure 11.2). Inner city problems are general but do vary with size of city and in some ways with type of city. Inner city problems are most acute in the larger, old industrial cities where the inherited urban fabric has deteriorated *in situ*.

Something of the variety of inner-city problems has been revealed by the research studies of the 1970s in the United Kingdom. Three government-sponsored studies of London, Birmingham and Liverpool revealed strong common strands but also significant variations in quality and emphasis. Whereas the loss of manufacturing jobs in inner London was causing several problems for the 'traditional' labour force, there were also significant issues arising from the pressures for growth. Demand for office space – often speculative – remained high and construction in areas such as Southwark played

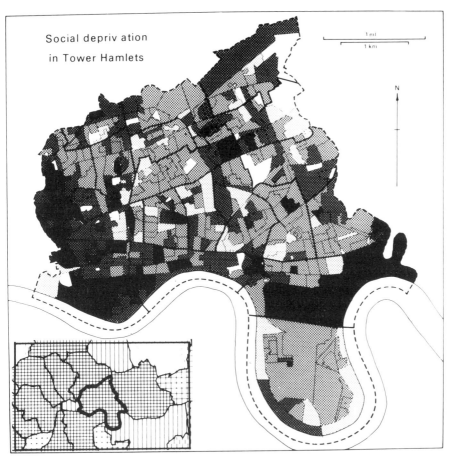

Figure 11.2 Deprivation and the inner city. Inset shows: Tower Hamlets as a deprived borough within London. Main map shows: variations of deprivation within Tower Hamlets. In both cases, most intense shading shows highest rates of deprivation on a composite index

(After Smith, 1979; this modified version is produced with the author's permission)

active roles in reducing the amount of space available for low-cost housing. Offices generated a demand for labour but this was met by suburban commuters rather than by the indigenous labour force with its more traditional skills. Birmingham's traditional role as a base for traditional industries on a small scale of enterprise was sharply affected by the economic decline of the 1970s, and the city's role as a reception area for immigrants had led to profound changes in the social geography of the inner city. Liverpool's industrial structure was generally vulnerable but the inner city was a 'waste-land' still suffering the consequences of overzealous clearance schemes, and unimaginative redevelopment remains a powerful image. Liverpool's traditional Catholic component makes it, along with Glasgow, one of the few mainland cities in which religious conflict has any meaning. Further evidence of this variety was provided by Hausner. He showed that between 1971 and 1981, Glasgow, Tyneside and West Midlands were among the twenty British cities which experienced most rapid decline affecting the whole urban area and not just the inner city. Whereas London had been successful in attracting advanced business services, Glasgow, Tyneside and West Midlands were still dominated by traditional activities.

European cities have less publicised inner-area problems though some trends are discernible. Drewett has identified those European cities which have experienced decentralisation from the core and the trends are often reminiscent of American experience. The 'city' of Paris, at the centre of the metropolitan area, has been losing population since the 1950s through decline in household size and reduction of housing stock. During the 1970s, the city and its inner suburbs lost manufacturing jobs at a rate of about 40,000 per year with closures and intra-regional dispersal responsible in roughly equal degrees. Of new industrial building 70 per cent is now in the outer suburbs with offices concentrating in the inner ring of Haut de Seine; at a time when manufacturing employment declined by 3 per cent, service employment grew by 16 per cent in the Ile de France. The features are reminiscent of British and American cities, but in Paris the suburbanisation of manual workers has allowed them to escape the consequences of decline in the inner-city employment market. There are inner-city housing problems in Paris but they are restricted to certain sectors and communes and are associated with foreign immigrants. Sectors of this kind are common in West European cities and are occupied by a transitory population of students, young single adults, immigrant labourers and the very poor. Yet White (1984) was able to describe the overall inner city in West Europe as an area of steady population decline but of rising social status though with sharp social polarisation. Clearly, there are variations over time and place and some contrary trends can be discerned, but the generalisation that inner cities contain problem areas has some credibility.

Problem estates

Whereas the notion of the inner city as a problem area has become well-known, such areas are not necessarily restricted to the inner city. Public sector housing programmes have led to the phenomena of problem estates which may be on urban peripheries yet are often typified by deprivation and disadvantage. The Liverpool Inner Area Study stated that concentrations of people at risk were to be found in many outer council estates such as Speke and Cantril Farm. Similarly, it was noted that the scale and concentration of deprivation was increasing in Glasgow's peripheral estates. The inner city then has no monopoly of poverty and deprivation and the 'problem estate' is a feature of many British cities. Such estates acquire unenviable reputations in terms of social behaviour and become 'difficult-to-let' in housing tenancy terms. Taylor and Hadfield claimed that some of the local authority housing on estates was disgraceful and degrading; Cater and Jones (1989) included a category of undesirable council property typified by overcrowding, lack of amenities and disrepair and often suffering from poor service provision and above-average levels of unemployment. Ideas on the emergence of problem estates will be discussed below but the significant point here is that pockets of deprivation can occur throughout the urban area and are most commonly linked with larger-scale public housing projects.

Urban ecological crises

During the 1960s and 1970s there has been a strong surge towards greater environmental awareness and the need to monitor and protect the ecological habitat. Although many of these habitats are in non-urban locations, they primarily serve urban populations and many country parks and reserves have been 'developed' with urban needs in mind. The city itself, however, despite its predominantly man-made qualities, is also an 'ecological habitat' and its condition in these terms has become a matter of increased – though by no means new – public concern. Historically, concern was with the squalid conditions of streets, services, and houses at particular stages of urban development, such as the industrial cities of nineteenth-century Europe. Contemporaneously in modern cities of Europe and North America, this concern focuses on the quality of goods and services emanating from cities and on the ways in which urban areas threaten natural environmental qualities.

There are perhaps three main headings under which the ecological issues posed by and within cities can be grouped. Firstly, there is the role of the city as a *generator of waste*. Urban populations, by the fact of their concentration in space, are typified by concentrations of the by-products to the smoke emissions of industrial plants. Secondly, there are the roles of cities in *modifying the local environments* in which they are placed, and both climatic and hydrological conditions can be affected in highly significant ways. The growth of urban-industrial societies has been coincident with the types of hazard termed 'quasi-natural' in which the 'urban effect' added to the natural phenomenon produces a malevolent output such as 'smog'. The third group contains the roles of cities in relation to more purely *natural hazards* or elements in the physical environment harmful to people and caused by extraneous forces. Here it is the built form of the city and the intensity with which it occupies space which places its population at high risk to natural phenomena such as floods, hurricanes, tornadoes and earthquakes. Figure 11.3 lists some of the main ecological hazards in cities. Some hazards are entirely manmade, such as traffic noise, others are purely natural, such as tornadoes, but most draw some influence from both sets of agents. The emissions which constitute air pollution are manmade but a set of natural conditions – presence of temperature inversions, lack of ventilation – are necessary before they constitute a major hazard.

Type of problem		Pollutants sources	Nature of damage	Indicators	Treatment	Recent trends
Man-made	Air pollution	sulphur oxides nitrogen oxides carbon oxides hydrocarbons	health hazard loss of amenity	indices show concentrations of pollutants	ban on fuels emission control	sources decline with more control on fuels and emission increase in small particulates
	Water pollution	industrial commercial waste sewage	health hazard polluted waterways aesthetic problems	biological oxygen demand P.D.I. index	emission control water processing	increasing sources several irredeemable outcomes
	Solid waste	industrial domestic building rubble packaging	fire risk health hazard aesthetic deterioration disrupted ecosystem	visible environment weight collected	collection disposal recycling	increasing problem technology available re-cycling
	Noise and heat	highways industries airports	physical and mental property value	decibels noise exposure index	noise shield land use planning	increasing problem more attempted control
Natural	Fogs	particulates urban climates	traffic hazard safety stress health	visibility		
	Floods	drainage condition flood plain	threat to life and property	water level frequency	channels flood control	greater control higher losses
	Special events earthquake hurricane drought	geological or climatic conditions	life, property urban system	frequency vulnerability	basic precautions warning systems	greater disasters increased vulnerability

Figure 11.3 Ecological hazards and cities

Similarly, periods of torrential rainfall may produce flood conditions but the high runoff rates of urbanised surfaces and interventions into natural drainage conditions produce large-scale flood hazards. The list is by no means complete, but it does provide a set of major categories with which to assess the reality of urban ecological crises.

Social problems

There are – as argued earlier – social and economic problems which find expression both as problems *in* the city, implying that they are found throughout society but surface more dramatically in urban areas with their concentrations of both people and activities, and as problems *of* the city, implying that the particular form they take is a product of the urban environment *per se*. One significant role of urban geography during the past decade has been that of presenting an accurate portrayal of the extent of these problems, both singly and in association with each other, and of demonstrating the intensity within which they occur in particular urban areas. Rates of unemployment, of substandard housing, of ill-health, deviance and many other persistent urban problems can be shown to be highly clustered in specific parts of the city which often show features of multiple deprivation. Having made this point, it is as well to note that large cities have no monopoly of such problems; unemployment and poverty are just as likely to occur in rural areas or small towns – it is the size and density of the city which principally sets it apart. The further qualification is that economic and social problems are both culturally and historically specific; deprivation in its various forms is a relative rather than an absolute concept.

Figure 11.4   Alternative criteria of human well-being

---

(1) *UN components of level of living*
     Health, including demographic conditions
     Food and nutrition
     Education, including literacy and skills
     Conditions of work
     Employment situation
     Aggregate consumption and savings
     Transportation
     Housing, including household facilities
     Clothing
     Recreation and entertainment
     Social security
     Human freedom

(2) *Criteria of social well-being in the United States*
     Income, wealth, and employment
     The living environment
     Health
     Education
     Social order
     Social belonging
     Recreation and leisure

Extracted from Herbert and Smith (1979) *Social Problems and the City*, Table 2.3; reproduced by permission of authors and Oxford University Press.

Territorial social indicators

The phase during which geographers developed an interest in social indicators was paralleled by the emergence of the relevance issue; the shift from studies of residential differentiation to the use of the similar methodologies to identify 'problem' residential areas was a simple and logical step. As geographers developed their research, they focused upon the particularly spatial implications of social indicators research. D. M. Smith (1973) defined territorial social indicators as quantitative measures of the incidence of given types of social problems in each of a number of spatial subdivisions. Successive emphases in geographical analyses were on the provision of better spatial recording units for spatial statistics, greater disaggregation to give a finer mesh, and upon more consistency of spatial units over time and place to allow comparability; the outcome was a surge of investigations into the numerical measurement of social conditions in cities, using terms such as level of living, social well-being and quality of life. Figure 11.4 shows the criteria used by the United Nations to measure level of living and by David Smith (1973) to measure social well-being.

The use of territorial social indicators is subject to several caveats. It is often difficult to find appropriate data at the required spatial scale; in particular normative data which can be measured on a range of good to bad or high to low. Again a term such as quality of life will have different meanings to different people, it is in a word 'subjective' and research has begun to use indicators based on the feelings and values of people involved. This raised questions of

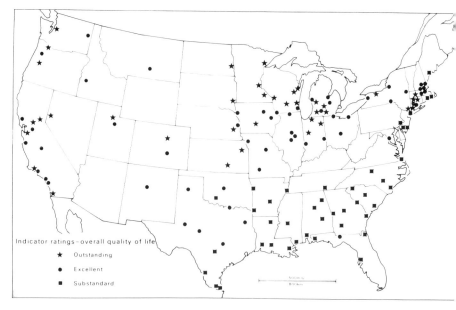

Figure 11.5   Overall quality of life in American cities

(Based upon information derived from Liu, 1975 and Northam, 1979)

measurability as for example in Dalkey and Rourke's finding that love, caring and affection were rated highly as quality of life attributes. These are very real qualities but how can they be measured?

Comparisons among cities

At an inter-urban scale there have now been several attempts to classify American cities according to the quality of urban life. D. M. Smith (1973) used a form of factor analysis to classify metropolitan areas according to a range of social indicators whilst Liu (1975) used five broad classes of social indicator – economic, political, environmental, health/education, and social, with sets of indicators being used to measure each class. Figure 11.5 shows Liu's classification of American cities on the economic and social components. Larger metropolitan areas generally tend to score highly on the economic component with Dallas, Houston and Portland in the south and west, a cluster of manufacturing metros in the mid-west, and emerging clusters of smaller cities in 'sunbelt' states such as Texas. On the social component, the high-scoring metropolitan areas are found in the Rocky Mountain states and on the west coast, together with the 'newer' urban areas of the plains and broad west. By contrast, the low-scoring metropolitan areas are found east of the Mississippi and in older urban America.

Theory	Source of problem	Characteristics of problem	Perpetuating features	Main outcome
Structural class-conflict	Social formation	unequal distribution of power maintenance of disparities	organisation of labour class distinctions	inequality
Institutional management	allocative system	uneven distribution of resources inefficient bureaucracies weak communications/ awareness	maintenance of elitism low welfare inputs non-sharing of opportunities	disadvantage underprivelege
Cycle of deprivation	social group residential area	few opportunities limited access to social mobility transmission of poor attitudes disadvantaged environment	sub-cultural norms lack of positive interventions	deprivations low aspirations low achievement
Cycle of poverty	individual inadequacies family background	group apathy inherited deficiencies	fatalism failure of welfare services	retardation poverty

Figure 11.6 Theories of poverty and deprivation

Patterns within cities and the theories of poverty

At an intra-urban scale, territorial social indicators have most commonly been used to identify problem areas, to monitor change over time. and to compare the spatial incidences of various types of problem. Individual indicators can be used to identify distributions of particular problems, to serve as diagnostic measures of a more general malaise, or more typically several criteria may be combined into a composite indicator which measures multiple deprivation. In all of these approaches, however, research into territorial social indicators is vulnerable to the criticism that it is focused upon the spatial manifestation of problems – and has little to offer in terms of explaining their origins. Some consideration of the concepts of deprivation and poverty *per se* and of the 'theories' which have been developed to explain them throws some light on this issue.

Both deprivation and poverty pose definitional problems. Many societies define poverty levels, usually in terms of income, below which households are recognised as poor or deprived. The 'levels' however, will vary from one society to another according to some *internal* standard of assessment and point to the relative nature of the concept. Perceptions of poverty are similarly internalised. The poor American may appear affluent in comparison to the Bangladeshi peasant, but his points of reference are not in the Third World but in middle-income America. With this qualification of the relative nature of poverty and deprivation in mind, some theories can be discussed and Figure 11.6 summarises these.

Structural class conflict theories suggest that poverty and deprivation arise out of particular social formations and the capacities for inequality which they promote and perpetuate. Capitalism, it is argued, invariably produces inequality as it allocates differential rewards in a competitive society; whereas in-

Competitive markets and social indicators

	Employment	Housing	Education
Problem	Failure to find work Failure to find job with good rewards or high satisfaction	Inability to obtain mortgage or to own house Inability to qualify for good local authority house	Failure to obtain good educational qualifications Inability to obtain access to educational opportunities
Outcome	unemployment low-skill job low-paid job	substandard housing overcrowding lack of privacy	no educational qualifications few usable skills poor attitudes to schooling
Indicators	percent unemployed percent low-skill workers	percent without household facilities percent overcrowded or sharing percent private rented furnished	percent leaving school without O levels percent leaving school at minimum school leaving age

Figure 11.7   Competitive markets and social indicators

equality need not imply the existence of poverty in absolute terms the critical relative conditions are established. If this source of deprivation is recognised, its remedy clearly requires a considerable change in societal structure and attitudes. *Institutional* sources of deprivation develop from the inability of the allocative systems of government and of private institutions to channel goods and services in ways effective enough to reduce or eliminate disadvantge. There is evidence that the failure of bureaucracies to promote awareness of welfare, for example, can lead to unnecessary incidence of deprivation; administrative or investment policy failure may divert resources and reduce the ability of the system to eliminate poverty. Although the *cycle of deprivation* thesis has received detailed scrutiny the evidence remains inconclusive. The thesis suggests that children born into deprived households and (typically) into deprived areas may consistently be faced with fewer opportunities to advance because of their limited access to alternative paths and possibilities. A 'cycle' is perpetuated as children go from deprived homes to schools which they share with similar children, acquire few qualifications, usable skills, or different sets of values, and in adulthood find themselves as uncompetitive in employment or housing markets as their parents were. This concept calls for positive intervention into home, school, and neighbourhood in order to compensate for inadequate aspirations, attitudes, and behavioural norms. Finally, the *culture of poverty* thesis provides a more individually based theory with some genetic connotations. It also, however, suggests a general group attitude in which low-key aspirations and fatalistic assessments of low achievement and norms are typical. Again this theory calls for more individual treatment and for positive intervention through educational and social work systems.

Although these different theoretical approaches are available, most earlier studies were essentially empirical and took little cognizance of these. The Liverpool 'malaise' study analysed a large set of data, others have selected more limited sets of indicators though still in a largely intuitive way. Edwards argued that the choice of indicators could be related to failure to compete in competitive markets (see Figure 11.7). This conceptual framework allows the systematic

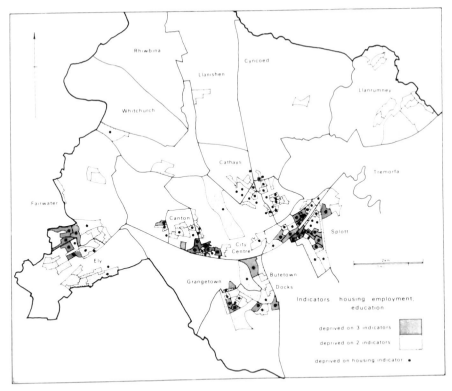

Figure 11.8 Deprived areas in Cardiff, 1971

choice of key indicators and Figure 11.8 demonstrates the application of the procedure and its outcome as the definition of deprived areas in Cardiff. The map shows a cluster of deprived areas in the inner city, though there is variation and some inner city areas are not deprived, and it also shows that housing substandardness occurs in older public sector estates such as Ely. The more general message from this study is that although public policy has improved housing conditions, social deprivation remains even on new estates, such as Llanrumney, on the urban periphery.

Studies involving the use of territorial social indicators of the type described here have been widely used as policy instruments, particularly in the development of positive discrimination and area policies. This link is contentious, as will be discussed later, but has found some support in many analyses. Holtermann argued that in order to give priority treatment to 61 per cent of Britain's deprived households, positive area policies would need to be allocated to 15 per cent of the enumeration districts. Boal, Doherty, and Pringle showed that in Belfast the ten worst-off areas contained 10 per cent of the households, 19 per cent of the unemployed, 27 per cent of the children in care, 19 per cent of delinquents, 19 per cent of illegitimate births, 14 per cent of infant mortalities and 22 per cent of the incidence of bronchitis. This Belfast example illustrates both the diverse set of indicators used and also the extent to which some areas have a disproportionate share of disadvantage. Knox shows how the 'poverty areas' of the hundred largest American cities contained over 60 per cent of the poor population and over 80 per cent of the poor black population. Given these concentrations, policies focused on 'poverty areas' as identified by social indicators would clearly reach a very large number of those in need. Policy issues will be discussed later but critics argue that deprived areas do not contain *all* of those in need, neither do they consist wholly of a disadvantaged population. Agnew argues that policies should be directed at people in social rather than locational contexts, Ottensman shows that there are major differences in types of poor people living inside and outside poverty *areas*. Whereas in American cities the poverty areas contain disproportionate shares of blacks, Hispanics and female-headed families, they do not have such shares of the elderly. There is a trend for the 'feminisation' of poverty with a striking increase in the proportion of poor people accounted for by women.

The use of subjective indicators remains exploratory and Knox and Maclaran have shown broad correlations between objective conditions and subjective feelings, though on average inner city residents *felt* less deprived than their objective circumstances would have suggested and the elderly tended to feel less concerned about poor living conditions.

A study of Fresno, California showed some social 'class' bases for variation in subjective assessments of life quality. Over the six survey dirticts and 2500 residents in the sample, there was some general consensus on the significance of health-care cost and drug addiction levels to their personal wellbeing, but whereas flood hazards and the number of people on welfare became issues from residents in the affluent north, it was access to health care and jobs which dominated priorities in the low income areas. As Smith (1979) argues,

> ... what constitutes a social problem in a city depends, then, on who you are and where you live, at least to some extent.

Some specific social problems

Studies of deprivation have covered a wide range of circumstances and conditions under which urban problems occur. Each 'condition', though, may constitute an issue in its own right and a sample of these may be selected for detailed analyses.

Ill-health

The association of ill-health with particular types of urban environment and with specific districts within cities has been studied over long periods of time. There are significant global and regional variations of illness and disease which have generated a considerable literature, but published work at the intra-urban scale is sparse. One of the best-known early examples of the spatial ecology of disease in a Western city was provided by Snow's study of cholera in mid-nineteenth-century London. In establishing a link between a contaminated water supply and the residences of cholera victims, Snow established a basic procedure which has endured over time. In this instance the causal link between environment and illness was clear, and studies of other cities at this time were able to demonstrate that districts of substandard housing, water and sanitation services were breeding places for disease. Rowntree's 1901 survey showing a relationship between poor physique, poverty, and malnutrition in the inner city was of similar *genre*. The overall effect was to give distinctive spatial concentrations of ill-health where disease and high infant mortality accompanied bad living conditions. As improvements in medical science and basic living conditions have taken place in Western cities, so absolute standards have been raised.

Relative concentrations of ill-health remain however. Coates and Silburn described children in the St Ann's district of Nottingham in the early 1960s as generally being in a poor state of physical development, noticeably smaller and less well developed than children from suburbia. The Belfast study showed a disproportionately high concentration of infant mortality in the most deprived areas of the city. Outside Western societies, close correlations are postulated between ill-health and those living in areas which are badly served in terms of water supply and sanitation. Lakshmanan and Chatterjee (1977) have estimated that nearly 250 million urban dwellers occupy districts without safe water or sanitation in unserviced 'settlements' and these are growing by 12 million persons each year. This type of problem appears to be reaching crisis proportions in less-developed countries and in Calcutta 79 per cent of households occupy a single room, 1.8 million live in slums in which latrines are shared among 30 to 50 people and 63 per cent have no regular water supply. De described cholera as endemic in the bustees or squatter settlements – life is often brief and brutal. As already noted, infant mortality rates among Cairo's *zabeline* population have been put as high as 60 per cent.

More recent studies of physical ill-health in Western cities have confirmed the existence of distinctive spatial concentrations. Shannon and Spurlock hypothesised 'environmental risk cells' within cities in which urban inhabitants are exposed to above average health hazards. They argue that both 'structural' health hazards and communicable diseases are distributed differentially across urban landscapes. and individuals are at risk both by area of residence and activity patterns which may involve contact with such environmental risk cells. Those ecological hazards – air pollution and contaminated open water – already discussed are major factors and numerous epidemiological studies suggest links between atmospheric pollution and several types of morbidity and mortality. Gastro-intestinal and respiratory complaints are common in most cities and often assume debilitating forms.

Epidemiological studies based upon the social characteristics of population groups have also produced significant results. There are clear demographic correlates. Propensity to most diseases increases with age but for particular diseases there are specific age-groups, lifecycle stages, and sexes which have above-average vulnerability. When demographic variables are controlled, socio-economic status consistently appears to have a strong inverse relationship with ill-health. One major exception appears to be AIDS which recognises no social barriers and according to Dutt, Monroe, Dutta and Prince is the bubonic plague of the twentieth century. American AIDS was initiated in the three metropolitan areas of New York, San Francisco and Los Angeles which between them contained 67 per cent of all cases in 1983 though it has since diffused to other urban areas. The spatial clustering of AIDS has been in districts with large numbers of homosexual men. Other diseases have shown regular links with poverty and a tendency to cluster in 'poor' environments within the city. Pyle and Rees identified three ill-health dimensions which they labelled 'poverty', 'density', and 'respiratory'; these showed correlations with low income, overcrowding, and adjacency to open water surfaces respectively. Each dimension had a specific spatial form with the main poverty syndrome revealing the strongest central-city concentration. Haynes showed that highest lung cancer rates in Britain occurred in inner urban areas – Hammersmith and Fulham in London and Knowsley in Liverpool.

Many contagious diseases have temporal as well as spatial dimensions and diffusion techniques have proved useful exploratory tools. Pyle examined measles epidemics in Akron, Ohio, for four periods of outbreak between 1965 and 1970. The clusters of high rates were consistently in central and south-eastern parts of the city despite the fact that numbers of children at risk were greater elsewhere. A diffusion process could be traced from the poverty area in the south-east to the inner-city transitional districts, to some suburbs and eventually back to an area near its point of origin. There was some evidence that in the low-income areas, where most of the outbreak was contained, preventive measures were not fully adopted. It appears, therefore, that despite the general improvements in living conditions during the past few decades, vulnerability to some kinds of disease remains high in specific urban districts.

Mental illness

Mental illness as an urban problem bridges a gap between physical disabilities and forms of behaviour which might be categorised as deviant. Geographers' interest in mental illness research have broadened considerably in recent years from earlier emphases on epidemiology and spatial ecology. Faris and Dunham (1939) provided one of the best-known early studies with data collected for the city of Chicago. Using 120 community areas within the city as data-recording units, incidence rates of new cases occurring within a given population group over a specified period were calculated and spatial distribution patterns derived. The schizophrenic sample of 7253 cases revealed a regular gradient from incidence rates of 1195 per 100,000 near the city centre to 111 at the urban periphery. Other disorders such as senile and alcoholic psychosis showed similar patterns but others – notably manic depression – did not. Manic depression was randomly distributed and drug addiction had peripheral as well as inner-city concentrations. Over a majority of types of mental disorder, some districts of the inner city – rooming house areas, transient quarters, and some low-income ethnic communities – had marked spatial concentrations. More recent studies have produced similar patterns, but Levy and Rowitz suggested that significant changes have occurred since the early ecological analyses of the 1930s.

Studies outside the United States have produced inconsistent evidence for the spatial 'model'. The several Liverpool surveys conducted during a 40-year period, showed a clear centre-periphery gradient in 1931 and 1954 but a more diffuse pattern in 1973. Timms and others have shown the several forms of neuroses seem to cluster in peripherally-located public sector housing projects. The step from observations of patterns to an understanding of processes has proved difficult. Earlier studies of Chicago were concerned with a 'breeder' hypothesis which suggested that local environments played a significant role in mental illness and a 'drift' hypothesis which suggested that the mentally-ill moved into particular environments after they had been affected. A density link has been argued, though never conclusively and as Ley (1983) has argued, the statistical connection is clear enough but its interpretation is controversial. Statistical associations offer guidelines on the ecology of mental disorder, but do not offer causal explanations. Causality in this field is clearly a complex feature and needs to account for individual and genetic as well as environmental precipitating conditions. Some forms of mental illness are clearly inherited and the role of 'environment' as home, community and neighbourhood is to cushion the individual against both its manifestations and implications. In this sense, ecological studies are identifying the environments which are least successful in those roles. Other mental disorders emanate directly from environmental 'stresses' which either accumulate or are related to a specific traumatic event. In this category, studies may seek to identify the environments in which stress is most likely to occur and these tend to be low-income, higher density and disadvantaged. The important point is that mental illness is a collective term which covers many very different conditions; some of these conditions cluster in space and correlate with environmental indicators, others do not. Facility location has attracted research interest as facilities for the mentally-ill are typically regarded as undesirable by residents in the areas in which they are placed. Studies show an increase in tolerance towards facilities with distance removed in a classical distance-decay effect. De-institutionalisation, or the involuntary return of many mentally-ill patients to the community, has meant an unprecedented impact and considerable conflict in mental health-care. This conflict derives from two sources: the *assignment* problem or matching client to treatment setting, and the *siting* problem or fitting facility form to community context. Communities resist both facilities and the mentally ill and new forms of spatial segregation arise from (i) neighbourhood resistance to facilities; (ii) planners' tendency to locate aftercare facilities in downtown or central city locations of least resistance; (iii) informal filtering towards transient rented areas of the mentally ill. All of this points to the fact that the cycle has come full circle and the 'unwanted' mentally ill may once again be clustering in specific inner city areas. Substitution of community for institutional care is proving illusory and close family provide the only real haven for the mentally ill unless the State re-assumes its responsibility for mental health care in a more catholic way.

Substance abuse

As with many other forms of malaise, substance abuse tends to be a particularly urban problem. As a category it covers the many forms of illegal drugs and also alcohol which though legal is often harmful. Drug abuse increasingly is a major urban problem and both in itself and in terms of the kinds of behaviour which it stimulates, it poses an enormous burden upon those concerned with social control in the city. Heroin is a major drug which though illegal and controlled has become widely available in Western cities. Prior to the 1940s, heroin was virtually unknown in Britain and was limited in North America to groups who generally lived outside the law. Pearson argues that the abuse of heroin can be likened to a contagion model in which its use spreads by contact and shows a strongly localised effect in particular areas because of its reliance on a local, largely hidden, network of suppliers, pushers and users. By the 1980s, heroin was a national problem in the United States, often linked with crime, and was known to be prevalent in specific parts of cities such as east and central Harlem in New York. In Britain there was a three-fold increase in known addicts between 1979 and 1983; heroin was thought to be cheap and plentiful in major cities such as London, Manchester and Glasgow and its use had begun to show correlations with social deprivation and there seemed to be some localisation on run-down council estates.

   Although drug abuse, of which heroin is but one example, is a major problem, C. J. Smith (1989) points out that ten times as many die from someone abusing alcohol as from all drugs combined. Data constrain most analysis to a regional scale but Smith and Hanham show the highest American rates for alcoholism to be in the south-western and north-eastern states along with other 'high-spots' in the mid-west, Great Lakes and Florida. Smith shows that in 1983 there were over 12,000 alcohol related car accidents in New York and over 2000 deaths from other forms of alcoholism. Alcohol-related admissions accounted for over one-million patient days in New York hospitals. Alcohol abuse is most widespread in cities and is focused on places of entertainment; in both the United States and Britain there are strong regulatory powers on land-use and the location of outlets and also times of sales and constraints on groups such as juveniles. Although alcohol abuse is widespread, the poor tend to fall victim and early views on the escapism provided by alcohol and the 'macho' image of the drinker, remain relevant. Smith (1989) reviews the relevant theories: a *disease* model which sees drinkers as 'different'; a *social integration* model which views drinking as an acceptable form of behaviour but recognises problems linked with excesses; and a *public health* model which aims to reduce consumption. Against this last objective is the fact that alcohol, like tobacco, is a multi-million pound industry and the pressures to boost consumption will be inevitable.

Urban crime and delinquency

One of the most consistent findings of analyses of official crime statistics has been the association of crime rates with urbanisation and the growth of cities. Crime rates over a range of offences seem to increase with urbanisation and despite the fact that some societies are well-known for 'rural crime', within any country rates tend to be higher for urban than for rural areas. Evidence to support this contention has been available from the early nineteenth century with the statistical mapping exercises in France and of social reformers such as Mayhew, and continues to receive confirmation from a variety of contemporary sources. In addition to this link with cities *per se* there are striking regional variations in crime rates and Harris has demonstrated this fact in the United States. Perhaps the best-known American pattern is that which depicts the 'violent south' with high rates of crimes of violence in the southern states. In 1975, the southern region had 42 per cent of the nation's homicides and 75 per cent of its prisoners under sentence of death, both statistics suggestive of distinctive regional characteristics. Harries and Brunn discussed some of these characteristics and summarised them as a 'traditionalistic political culture' which in some way 'nurtures' both violence itself and a set of related attitudes.

Although there can be little doubt that associations of crime with cities and with particular regions are real enough, criminologists stress the need for caution in the use of official statistics. There are problems of the completeness of data, of the extent to which they may contain biases, and of the ways in which 'definitions' of offences are arrived at and interpreted. Crime and delinquency are defined as such by the societies in which they occur – or at least by the law-makers – and reflect their particular traditions and value-systems.

Most Western societies have experienced increases in crime in general over recent years, a fact which has aroused both concern and a closer scrutiny of effective policies of policing and sanctions. There are marked differences among societies. From 1957 to 1976 the crime rate in the United Kingdom quadrupled and between 1972 and 1976 there was a 50 per cent increase in crimes of violence. These are dramatic relative rates of increase but United Kingdom rates remain undramatic in comparison with those from the United States. In 1975 there were 493 recorded homicides in the United Kingdom but in the same year the American total was 18,780 and New York alone had 1622 homicides, followed by Chicago with 814, Detroit with 633, and Los Angeles with 501. As Oklahoma City's homicide rate passed 100 in 1979 it was described in the local press as 'entering the big league'. As national crime surveys, involving detailed questioning of households, are carried out, they offer a much clearer picture of the reality of crime. The 1983 British Crime Survey showed a total crime estimate of 7.5 million; a figure which was 10 per cent higher than the 1981 estimate. At a more localised level, the Islington Crime Survey, London showed that over a twelve-month period a staggering one in two households could expect to fall victim to some form of crime.

Evidence for the spatial concentration of crime and delinquency in specific parts of the city has been available for some time. Nineteenth century observers noted the existence of 'crime areas' within cities which act as breeding grounds for criminals. These 'rookeries' were located in parts of inner London, Manchester and other large cities, places occupied by 'the lowest grade of thieves and dissolute people'. Later much of this work was formalised by the systematic studies of Shaw and McKay (1942) in Chicago. They identified both delinquency areas and regular crime gradients from city centre to periphery (see Figure 11.9).

This 'model' for the spatial patterning of known crime rates within cities has some generality and some persistence over time. Some qualifications are necessary:

(1) The model is most applicable to North American cities and mirrors a social geography in which the least advantaged occupy inner city areas. Even in the United States there is recent evidence, however, that inner city/suburban crime rate differentials are narrowing selectively as low-status suburbs show high rates of crime.

(2) Where interventionist housing policies transfer poorer people to peripheral estates, high crime rates tend to become more typical of those estates. Social class appears to be the key to much crime rather than age of housing.

(3) Crime patterns in geographical space take different forms if they relate to known offenders as opposed to offences; the former will correlate with social environments, the latter with opportunity environments.

(4) There are many types of crime and these will in turn have different geographies; most robberies tend to occur in central city commercial areas, most burglaries in residential districts.

(5) Known crime is not all crime and white-collar crime in particular is under-represented in official statistics.

Analyses of spatial patterns of crime have included attempts to explain those patterns. Shaw and McKay measured the statistical association between rates for delinquency, adult crime, recidivism and truancy and a set of social indicators for the various spatial units. The findings revealed high levels of association between deviance and substandard housing, poverty, foreign-born population and mobility. Shaw and McKay argued that these correlates had no specific causal significance in themselves but were symptoms, along with delinquency and crime, of some underlying social condition. Their theory of social disorganisation expressed this condition and suggested that in the absence of a

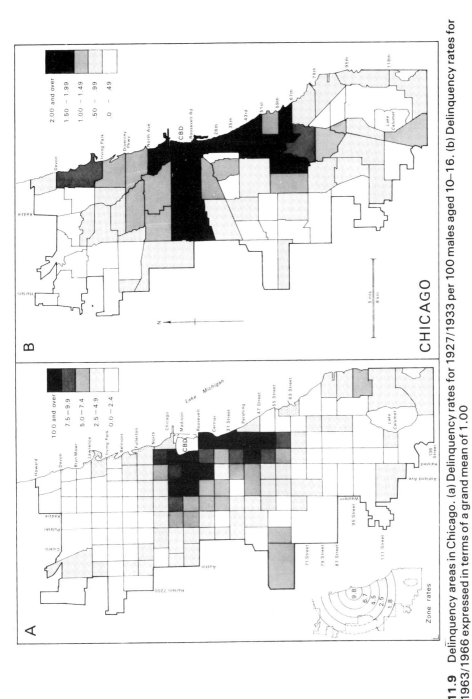

11.9 Delinquency areas in Chicago. (a) Delinquency rates for 1927/1933 per 100 males aged 10–16. (b) Delinquency rates for 1963/1966 expressed in terms of a grand mean of 1.00

(From Shaw and McKay (1942); reprinted by permission of the University of Chicago Press)

stable form of society, with legalistically-based codes of behaviour and established norms and values, precipitating conditions for deviance would exist. Subcultural theory suggests that crime or delinquency areas correspond with groups within which particular sets of values, beliefs and behavioural norms prevail which condone some forms of illegal activities. There are in fact many theories which seek to explain crime though none have achieved anything like universal acceptance. The range includes *structural* theories which locate the roots of criminal behaviour in the inequalities that have been created in the capitalist system, *genetic* theories which regard some forms of criminality as inherited, and *environmental* theories which look towards the social conditions from which deviant behaviour emerges. Both social disorganisation and subculture belong to this last group which has been the main focus of geographical study. Most consistently there is a *poor environment* hypothesis which suggests that most known offenders are drawn from disadvantaged localities which can often be identified by social indicators such as housing substandardness, unemployment, low socio-economic status and weak family life. This focus does not negate structural arguments, they are still there underpinning the poor environments in the first place but all macro-explanations such as inequality, poverty etc. suffer in that they do not explain all criminality, some disadvantaged individuals turn to crime, many do not. Macro-explanations set the broad parameters but they need to be refined by individual and local circumstances.

Within the broad category of the *poor environment* hypothesis there are more specific ideas:

(1) The 'housing class' hypothesis derives from the Sheffield study and suggests that offender rates are lower in owner-occupied rather than in rented housing areas. In Cardiff this could be verified with lowest offender rates in owner-occupied areas and highest in private rented areas and in some council estates.

(2) Social disorganisation, or the idea that more offenders are·found where stabilising conditions are absent, is an old idea sometimes discarded but supported in the Sheffield study.

(3) The poor social environment hypothesis comes from the work of Herbert in which he described a study of Cardiff in which six districts were selected for detailed investigation in a controlled area-sampling framework. Areas were controlled for objective characteristics, such as demographic structure, socio-economic status, and tenure type, and also in terms of delinquency rates. Two districts, for example, were low income, inner city, but one of these had a much higher delinquency rate; three public sector housing projects were included but two had high and one low rates of delinquency. Within this framework, the objective was to investigate variations in the subjective environments of the selected districts. Evidence was found to be supportive of the hypothesis that deficiencies in the subjective environments of some districts were associated with above-average delinquency rates. In the 'delinquency areas', parents made more use of physical punishment,

were less dedicated to the educational prowess of their children, and had 'weak' or blurred definitions of the differences between right and wrong. This set of characteristics typified both the inner-city delinquency areas and the peripherally located 'problem estates'. The evidence here pointed towards a subcultural effect in which residents of delinquency areas appear to hold *some* sets of values which condone deviant behaviour.

This last example explores the idea of *delinquency areas* and there are other studies which examine such distinctive parts of the city. Ley examined the distribution of teenage gangs and their alignment with segments of inner city space or 'turfs'. Ley and Cybriwsky mapped gang graffiti in inner Philadelphia and showed how graffiti was used as a boundary marker which asserted the territorial claims of the group. Rowley has written on the 'skid-rows' of North American cities or 'any dilapidated section of town where petty criminals, degenerates and derelicts hang out'. Skid-rows are amongst the most unambiguous deviant or delinquency areas, others are less obvious and need careful mapping of social indicators to identity. There are other nuances, a delinquency area in Glasgow or Detroit is likely to be of different dimensions to its equivalent in Swansea or San Diego; the inner city has no monopoly over such districts as studies of British cities have shown.

The facts of deviant areas can be established and their internal characteristics can be examined; there are remaining questions however, on the emergence and persistence of such areas. The first of these questions is often difficult to resolve as historical evidence may not be available. Common locational features may typify skid rows or red-light districts but detailed studies of their origins are rare. A more recent problem area in British cities is the 'difficult-to-let' estate in the public sector of housing. As they are relatively recent, the opportunities to understand ways in which they acquired bad reputations are more realistic. When Baldwin reviewed the problems of problem estates, he cited high rates of tenant turnover, paucity of recreational facilities and some evidence that local authority housing managers had followed a practice of 'dumping' problem families in particular estates. The issue is contentious but a significant number of studies do attribute key roles in the creation of problem estates to the managers who control the allocation of housing as a resource. Gill (1977) for example, scrutinised housing officials' records of tenants of the Luke Street area of Liverpool and found them liberally sprinkled with phrases such as 'not suitable for new property', 'suitable for the Dock area only', and 'not suitable for the Corporation to rehouse'.

> It was local planning and housing department policy that produced Luke Street. (Gill, 1977)

Others such as Wilson have argued that there is a strong self-selection process operative among potential residents of problem estates which is related to the image of the estate, levels of rent, proximity to family and friends, and expectations of the quality of housing and estate life. On problem estates the tenant with any kind of social aspiration was attempting to leave, those who stayed were either indifferent to the estate's reputation or were desperate for housing. Labels given to problem estates are influenced by the initial occupants and in their Sheffield study, Bottoms and Xanthos showed how one estate was used to rehouse a number of notorious gang-leaders and their associates in the 1950s whilst another was tenanted by people displaced by slum clearance. In Cardiff an estate was given distinctiveness by the fact that its occupants were largely Roman Catholic. Once labelled, estates have reputations which are difficult to change even if actual behaviour no longer matches up to expectations. Damer studied Wine Alley in Glasgow, a place labelled by municipal officials as being typified by rent arrears, vandalism, crime and socio-psychiatric problems. His enquiry pointed strongly to the negative effect of a labelling process which was based far more upon past rather than present events. (Figure 11.10 summarises factors which may 'produce' a problem estate).

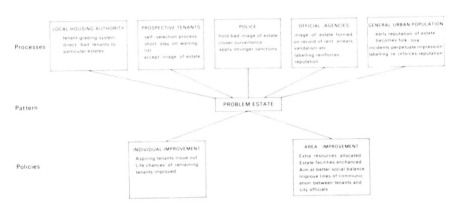

Figure 11.10 Problem estates: factors contributing to their emergence and possible policies

Environmental criminology

Environmental criminology is an approach to the geography of crime which focuses on criminal events and the places at which they occur, the thrust is the offence rather than the offender. One assumption is that many crimes are reactions to opportunities in the local environment; it is the assemblage of targets, access, low surveillance, weak control or poor security which makes some places more vulnerable than others. Newman pursued this approach with his idea of 'defensible space'. From surveys of housing projects in New York, he suggested that housing would be well defended if it was visible, if a community spirit is fostered to control space, and if private territory was clearly identified. Principles of defensible space involved the development of good design and

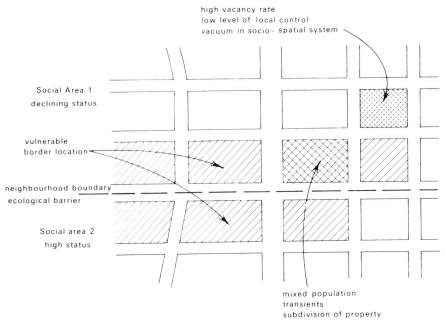

high vacancy rate
low level of local control
vacuum in socio- spatial system

Social Area 1
declining status

vulnerable
border location

neighbourhood boundary
ecological barrier

Social area 2
high status

mixed population
transients
subdivision of property

Figure 11.11 Some characteristics of the vulnerable area

management of space to reduce vulnerability. Coleman applied similar ideas to public sector housing in London and her Index of Disadvantage was a measure of the extent to which different parts of the city suffered from defects in the design and quality of the built environment.

Geographers working within the environmental criminology approach have developed a number of hypotheses to explain why some residential districts are vulnerable to burglary and offences against dwellings:

(1) The offender-residence hypothesis suggests that areas become vulnerable if they contain many offenders or are close to where offenders live. This is based on the fact that most offenders travel only short distances to commit crime.

(2) The border-zone hypothesis suggests that the edges of well-defined neighbourhoods are more vulnerable than their cores which benefit from clearer neighbourhood identity (see Figure 11.11).

(3) The local social control hypothesis suggests that well-integrated neighbourhoods where residents share a sense of place are the least vulnerable.

(4) The area variability hypothesis suggests that mixed areas are more vulnerable, though the kind of mixture is contentious. Mixture which implies transience in housing occupants and juxta-position of relative wealth and poverty appears the most relevant.

Fear of crime has been strongly highlighted by national crime surveys and the

Islington survey revealed that over half the women interviewed avoided going out after dark. Fear of crime is often translated into fear of places and Ley showed how perceived unsafe areas in Philadelphia were carefully avoided. Smith argues that fear of crime is heightened among those who are on the 'margins' of society, either in economic or social terms. Research shows that real and perceived levels of vulnerability are often in tandem and those who live in vulnerable areas respond by showing a stronger security consciousness. On the other hand it must be said that wealthier people invest more in security and ensure lower vulnerability. A detailed study of Swansea showed a close relationship between fear of crime and dissatisfaction with residential area.

Most geographical research into crime and delinquency has been concerned with offenders and offences and the local environments in which they occur. There is however a growing interest in the criminal justice system and with the rule-makers rather than the rule-breakers.

(1) There are issues of policing strategies – how are these organised territorially and what effects do they have on crime? Mawby argues that differential policing did not affect local crime rates but there is contradictory evidence.

(2) Are there crime prevention policies which can be applied effectively? Neighbourhood watch involves residents in surveillance and reporting and is often claimed to reduce local crime rates. If this occurs does it reduce crime or merely displace it to less well-protected neighbourhoods?

(3) Shumsky and Springer provided a useful example of the geography of offences changing in response to varying interpretation and enforcement of the law. In a study of San Francisco's red light district between 1880 and 1934, they noted the movements of both brothels and prostitutes over time, and argued that there was an indisputable relationship between the changing spatial distribution of prostitution and legal attitudes. As the laws or the areas within which anti-prostitution laws were enforced were changed, so prostitutes moved their places of activity in order to avoid being arrested. This move in turn relocated the zone of prostitution. It was the actions of the rule-makers which led to this changing geography of crime.

(4) At a regional scale, Harries and Brunn have shown that there are wide variations within the United States in sentencing levels, court procedures and use of judicial discretion.

Old people in the city

Within most societies there are minority groups, unified on the basis of one or more characteristics, which can be distinguished from the rest of the population. Best-known and most closely studied of these are the ethnic minorities, some of whom have already been discussed but there are other groups made distinctive by religious beliefs, cultural backgrounds and also by demographic features. There is growing evidence, principally from western societies but also from parts of the developing world, that the elderly are emerging as a group with distinctive social and spatial characteristics. As a consequence of better health-care and living conditions, increased longevity is a feature of many societies and old people, usually defined as people aged over 60 or 65 years old, form increasing proportions of total populations. In the United States in 1900, 4.1 per cent of the population was over 65 years of age, in 1970 it was 9.9 per cent. Many states exceeded this figure by a wide margin with Florida heading the list with 16.4 per cent followed by Arkansas with 13.2 per cent. To give some idea of actual numbers of people involved, one survey counted 28.4 million Americans aged 62 years or over in 1976 and this was expected to rise to 36.1 million in 1991. For other Western societies the trends are similar. The population of pensionable age in England and Wales was 9 million in 1981 and was expected to rise to 10.8 million in 2021; for northern Europe in 1980, 19.6 per cent of the population was aged 60 years or over. The situation in less developed countries is different, only 4.3 per cent of East and West African population was aged 60 years or more in 1980; Warnes (1987) points out the potential for change and suggests that whereas demographic ageing continues *diminuendo* in the United Kingdom, it is now entering a phase of *crescendo* in many less developed countries. One projection shows that by 2025, 14 per cent (or 1.135 million) of the world's population will be aged 60 or over and that of these 71 per cent will be in less developed countries.

For many elderly people, increased deprivation is an inevitable consequence of growing old. Retirement from employment means a significant loss of income and a higher level of dependency may arise from greater disability or immobility. Such facts are self-evident but as Warnes (1989) argues, the elderly do not, simply by definition, constitute a social problem; in Western societies no more than 5 per cent of the elderly live in institutions and most remain self-supporting and socially active. Nonetheless, particular problems do arise. In 1976 in England and Wales, 30 per cent of the non-institutionalised elderly lived alone, including half of the women aged 85 years and over but only 14 per cent of the men aged 65 to 74. Warnes (1987) reported a survey showing that 28 per cent of elderly people aged 65 to 74 (and 53 per cent of the men aged 75 years and over) 'never dreamed they could be this lonely'. If the elderly become marginalised in economic and social terms, they begin to form part of the range of social problems in cities.

Not all old people are 'trapped' in urban environments unsuited to their needs and preferences. There is clear evidence that significant numbers of old people migrate to more amenable environments for their retirement years. American migration is to the 'sunshine states' such as Florida and Arizona which attract large numbers of retired people, in Canada the west coast and Victoria in particular have similar roles. British retirees migrate to coastal districts such as North Wales and the south coast of England and also to parts of Southern Europe such as Spain and Portugal. Such migration flows are of interest but for the large majority of old people such choices are not available and they are likely to spend their old age in the cities where they have spent the latter part of their working lives. There may well be real constraints in this decision but Warnes (1989) emphasises that although quality of housing may vary, British cities are not uniformly hostile environments for the elderly. They can offer a wide range of accessible services and facilities and often have well-developed public transport and social welfare systems. 'Accustomed places' will also contain established networks of neighbours, friends and relatives. Questions on quality of housing for old people in cities arise from studies such as that by Eckert who estimated that many of the 6.8 million elderly who live in American inner cities occupy single rooms in cheap hotels and rooming houses in areas that are often scheduled for renewal or redevelopment. Problems are especially acute among ethnic groups such as black Americans and British West Indian migrants who do not qualify for full pension rights. Evidence is not consistent from one large city to another but central Paris appears to be one case in which the elderly are becoming more represented in the population make-up. Central districts of Paris in 1954 were relatively youthful in their demographic composition when compared with the rest of France but by 1982 housed about one-third more old people than the national average. Golant estimated that 34 per cent of America's elderly lived in central cities where they formed 11 per cent of the total population.

In American cities a diversity of dedicated housing arrangements for the elderly has arisen in response to market demands for small, cheap dwellings, congregate settings or care facilities (Warnes, 1987). These can range from converted obsolescent hotels and low-grade mobile home parks to purpose-built and well appointed life-care facilities. Clustering of old people in American urban areas arises in part therefore from the form of housing provision whether it be in retirement residences, trailer villages or low-rent public housing. By the later 1970s in London a new phenomenon was the fact that over 30 per cent of new public housing was dedicated to the elderly (Warnes, 1989) and similar trends were evident in other British cities. The surge of private and housing association building for the elderly in the 1980s reflects awareness of growing demand. In summary, the forces which lead to clustering of old people in geographical space may arise from selective migration which either takes the elderly to targeted retirement areas or leaves them as residual groups in central cities. Clustering also arises as the housing market, both public and private, creates opportunities for old people in specific locations.

One qualification which needs to be made consistently with reference to the elderly is that they do not form a uniform group, there is considerable diversity within the group which could be designated as elderly on the basis of chronological age. Variables such as health and morale are involved with implications in both biological and psychological terms. The principal theories of ageing are essentially social theories though they must take some account of biological change. Disengagement theory states that old people will tend to turn inwards psychologically, a process which may be closely linked with key events such as retirement or loss of spouse. This kind of psychological disengagement is followed by social disengagement in which the old person moves into new and qualitatively different relationships with society which 'withdraws' from the old person. An extreme stage in terms of this theory would be a 'subculture of the elderly'. *Activity theory* suggests that old people will attempt to prolong the pattern of middle-age for as long as possible despite the process of chrono-logical ageing. Roles will be maintained even though substitutes may be found for those which are lost. Palmore found some support for activity theory with the suggestion that men and women who are most active in organisations and who engage in more physical activity are more likely to age successfully. *Continuity theory*, unlike disengagement or activity theory, does not have a developmental basis. Its principal statement is that a person will generally wish to maintain familiar roles but will adapt and substitute these as need be, giving the individual a never-ending capacity to change. None of these theories has achieved universal acceptance but they offer useful insights into current research on the ageing process.

Geographers have studied the ways with which the elderly cope with their urban environments against a general background of lessening mobility and in-creasing vulnerability. One study showed that in Florida 89 per cent of the adult population is licensed to drive but only 39 per cent of those aged over 75 years. As Birren (1970) points out:

> ...the old become discouraged by environmental obstacles which would not inhibit the young – high bus steps, the need to cross wide busy streets to catch a bus, fast-changing traffic lights, high curbs, and inadequate building labels. The aged may do without banks,...services, dentists, shops, lawyers and parks because of the time it takes to get to them.

The *environmental-docility* theory in its original form postulated declining competence to deal with environmental problems, this and other conceptual positions are based on the assumption that ageing involves a decreasing ability to cope with 'normal' urban environments; old people therefore face diminish-ing life-space, limited activity patterns, and 'stresses' in environment which do not concern other demographic groups. This is an assumption which has found a high level of support from empirical research; the Swansea study confirmed that increasing age usually involves greater limits of movement and interest, though it did also show that an individual's state of health and morale provide important sources of information.

The quality of life enjoyed by old people is in large part related to their indi-vidual ability to cope with the processes of ageing and much geographical research has been guided by this principle. Although, as Warnes (1987) argues, most elderly people remain self-supporting and socially active for many of their retirement years, they do have minimum requirements such as convenient access to services and to social networks. The problem of measuring levels of satisfaction among the elderly has attracted research attention. Rosow and Breslau measured elderly morale with indices of stress, boredom and satis-faction; Connors, Powers and Bultena found that quality rather than quantity of relationships was crucial. There have been studies of the activity patterns of old people which show that trip frequencies are lower, and total distances travelled are less than those of other age-groups. Declining ability to drive cars leads to an increasing reliance on public transport and an American survey calculated thresholds at which dissatisfaction with services became dominant. For a bus-stop the threshold was placed at three blocks from home, for a grocery a quarter-mile, for a restaurant a half-mile, and for a drugstore one mile (1.6 km). In Swansea, Herbert and Peace found distance to be a major constraint and few respondents claimed an ability to walk more than a quarter of a mile in each direction. Community facilities were used in inverse proportions to the distances that individuals were removed from them, and any organised activities needed to provide transport.

Studies of the images which the elderly hold of the environments in which they live suggest cognitive maps which are constricted in both content and dimensions. Reignier (1974) shows that old people have a strong sense of neighbourhood and delineate its 'core' to produce an image over which a high level of consensus is evident. More active old people with high socio-economic status tend to have more extensive images, and other contributory variables are good health, long residence and participation in specialised activity interests. In Swansea, elderly respondents in two areas were asked to delineate their 'neighbourhood' graphically and identified 'core' areas which were commonly perceived (see Figure 11.12); results pointed to a strong sense of place and well-defined images of locality.

Rowles (1978) made significant contributions to the geographical study of the elderly. He recognised the increasing constraints which environments place on the elderly:

> The elderly gradually become prisoners of space. Certainly some individuals remain active and mobile into their advanced old age ... for many older persons physiological decline, economic deprivation and traumatising effects of rapid societal change, herald physical, social and psychological withdrawal. This withdrawal, it is implied, is accompanied by progressive construction of the individual's geographical life-span and associated intensification of attachment to the proximate environmental context. (Rowles, 1978)

Rowles also stressed that physical activity amongst the elderly has to be considered in relation to their mental activity; the pleasure which they derive from observing the activities of others, and the ability to draw upon reservoirs of memories and life experiences are highly significant facets of their wellbeing. Home area, surveillance area, neighbourhood assume greater significance, other parts of the city merge with distant places. His notion of 'fantasy' stressed the role of remembered places which, though no longer visited or seen, have great meaning for the elderly. He argued that 'the old may be prisoners of space but it can also be a jail without walls' (Rowles, 1978).

Studies have been able to demonstrate spatial clustering of the elderly at regional and local scales but do not support the idea of a 'geriatric ghetto'. Many who are able to change residence on retirement do so, but the large majority have to spend old age in the same environments in which they have

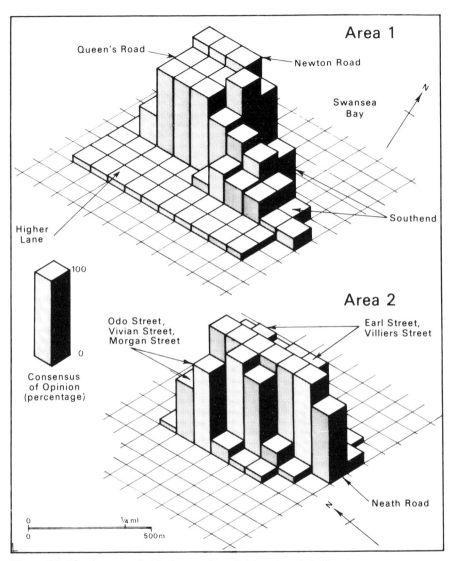

Figure 11.12   Images of elderly people: neighbourhoods in Swansea

(After Herbert and Peace, 1980, in *Geography in the Urban Environment* VI. 3)

lived for many years. The problems they face are therefore those of the population at large but these assume greater proportions and meaning for old people. In this context the increasing numbers of old people occupying inner-city areas is a cause for concern. A range of special services is being developed and this may help the elderly to cope. Examples are reduced bus fares, better design of buses, careful location of services, mobile facilities such as meals-on-wheels, in addition to the increasing range of types of residential accommodation. Present policies favour de-institutionalisation and a greater reliance on community services, trends probably in line with preferences held by the elderly. One estimate suggests that five per cent of old people live permanently in institutions but 20 per cent spend *some* time there during their post-retirement years. As the emphasis shifts away from institutions the need to provide community services and attitudes which ensure the right environment for 'successful' ageing becomes an imperative.

Summary

This chapter has discussed a number of urban problems, some of which are a consequence of the wider and ongoing process of urbanisation, others are directly or indirectly manifestations of societal conditions which find expression, often in exaggerated form, within urban environments. As the urbanisation process continues and as individual cities grow larger, so the visible evidence of urban problems will become more apparent. Urban geographers have for many years been concerned with research which is 'relevant' to real problems but during the 1980s this concern has become more sharply focused. The emphasis in this chapter has been upon research which seeks to enhance our *understanding* of urban problems.

Postscript

This text has discussed many of the traditional concerns of urban geography and has also sought to indicate the ways in which the subject continues to develop with new topical areas and conceptual positions which provide new insights into the nature of cities. The large city is now a global phenomenon and whereas there are features of both the process of urbanisation and its spatial outcomes which are recurrent, there are also special characteristics which mirror the kinds of societies in which those cities are placed and the need to understand the structural imperatives which underlie these differences is now fully accepted. Much of the literature of urban geography has been concerned with the developed world and the expressions of urbanism in advanced capitalist societies. For these studies the new forms of the urban phenomenon have prompted terms such as 'counter-urbanisation' and attempts to identify regional scales of megalopolitan development. Economic factors are still seen as the driving force of urban change though the political dimension receives increasing attention. Notions of world cities, urban systems and the post-industrial cities relate to these underlying processes. Whereas research continues to focus on Western urbanisation, it is acknowledged that the Third World is experiencing the most dramatic and innovative forms of urbanism as the scale and pace of urban growth runs well ahead of the ability of those societies to provide adequate infrastructures and to cope with the mass of people.

In virtually all these urbanising societies, the State at its various levels is compelled to assume an increasingly interventionist role. The level of intervention varies from the total control of command economies to the limited roles of State in some free market societies. Even in the latter group however the interventionist role increases as the need to manage urban growth becomes apparent and unavoidable. Urban policies are needed to control urban development processes and the use of land, to impose and maintain minimum standards, to manage traffic and to protect environments. Beyond these basic policy needs are a host of others and the government of cities becomes a major issue.

One theme throughout this text is that urban geographers have a professional expertise which can contribute to this need for effective policies. Such expertise and its attendant methodologies can be drawn from the the various perspectives extant within the discipline. The value of positive science and spatial analysis is evident in optimal location procedures and in techniques of regionalisation, some of the methods of territorial social indicators research are derived from the same source. It is in the studies of spatial inequality and territorial justice that the welfare concern of urban geographers show through most strongly as geographers have tried to influence who gets what, where and how. Area policies have similar bases in the research literature of urban geography and the debate over the balance between place policies and people policies is well founded in the discipline. As general political change in the 1980s has been seen to exaggerate disparities between urbanised regions and between rich and poor within society so the welfare component in urban geography has sought to respond. This response is reflected in concerns for the inner city, for the deprived estates and for the various forms of problem area. Research has no longer been prepared to confine itself to the roles of locating and portraying the problems but has striven to comprehend the processes involved and to contribute towards their amelioration. It is in the study of local community, community care and perhaps some forms of community action that the modern 'humanistic' face of urban geography shows through. Place has reassumed its central role in urban geography and focuses the special qualities of the geographers' art.

Urban geography has changed dramatically in the last part of the twentieth century. It is now more deeply involved in the development of theories and ideas than it ever was before. These competing theoretical interpretations have led to tensions which become explicit in what is euphemistically termed 'the urban question'. Despite these tensions urban geography remains definable, dynamic and capable of producing students well grounded in their understanding of the processes of urbanisation and the various forms of cities which result from these processes. In this its widest definition urban geography is concerned both with the wider urban system of cities in space and with the particularities of that real and tangible object, the city as place.

References

Abu-Lughod, J. L. (1969) Testing the theory of social area analysis: the ecology of Cairo, Egypt, *American Sociological Review*, **34**, 198–212.

Ahmad, Q. (1965) *Indian Cities: Characteristics and Correlates*. Research Paper No. 102. Department of Geography, University of Chicago, Chicago.

Allan, G. A. (1979) *A Sociology of Friendship and Kinship*, George Allen and Unwin, London.

Badcock, B. (1984) *Unfairly Structured Cities*, Basil Blackwell, Oxford.

Banerjee, T. and Baer, W. C. (1984) *Beyond the Neighbourhood Unit: Residential Environments and Public Policy*, Plenum Press, New York.

Beavon, K. S. O. (1977) *Central Place Theory: A Reinterpretation*, Longman, London.

Bell, C. R. and Newby, H. (1978) Community, communion, class and community action: the social sources of the new urban politics, in D. T. Herbert and R. J. Johnston (eds.), *Social Areas in Cities*, Wiley, London, pp. 283–301.

Bell, D. (1974) *The Coming of Post-Industrial Society*, Heinemann, London.

de Bell, G. (1970) *The Environmental Handbook*, Ballantine, New York.

Bennison, D. J. and Davies, R. L. (1980) The impact of town centre shopping schemes in Britain: their impact on traditional retail environments, *Progress in Planning*, **14**, 1–104.

Berry, B. J. L. *et al.*, (1963) *Commercial Structure and Commercial Blight*, Research Paper, University of Chicago, No. 85.

Berry, B. J. L. (1973) *The Human Consequences of Urbanization*, Macmillan, London.

Berry, B. J. L. (1978) Comparative urbanisation strategies, in L. S. Bourne, and J. W. Simmons (eds.) *Systems of Cities, Readings on Structure, Growth and Policy*, Oxford University Press, New York, 502–510.

Boal, F. W. (1978) Ethnic residential segregation, in D. T. Herbert and R. J. Johnston (eds.), *Social Areas in Cities*, Wiley, London, pp. 57–95.

Boissevain, J. (1974) *Friends of Friends: Networks, Manipulators, and Coalitions*, Blackwell, London.

Boudeville, J. R. (1966) *Problems of Regional Economic Planning*, Edinburgh University Press, Edinburgh.

Boulding, K. (1956) *The Image: Knowledge in Life and Society*, University of Michigan, Ann Arbor.

Bourne, L. S. (1976) Housing supply and housing market behaviour in residential development, in D. T. Herbert and R. J. Johnston (eds.), *Spatial Processes and Form*, Wiley, London.

Bourne, L. S. (ed.) (1982) *Internal Structure of the City*, Oxford University Press, London.

Bromley, R. D. F. and Thomas, C. J. (1989) The impact of shop types and spatial structure on shopping linkages in retail parks: planning implications, *Town Planning Review*, **61**, 45–70.

Carter, H. (1972) *The Study of Urban Geography*, Edward Arnold, London.

Carter, H. (1983) *An introduction to urban-historical geography*, Edward Arnold, London.

Cater, J. and Jones, T. (1989) *Social geography: an introduction to contemporary issues*, Edward Arnold, London.

Castells, M. (1977) *The Urban Question*, Edward Arnold, London.

Chance, J. K. (1975) The colonial Latin American city: pre-industrial or capitalist? *Urban Anthropology*, **4**, 211–228.

Cheshire, P. C. and Hay, D. G. (1989) *Urban Problems in Western Europe. An Economic Analysis*, Unwin Hyman, London.

Chorley, R. J. and Haggett, P. (1967) *Models in Geography*, Methuen, London.

Clark, W. A. V. (1984) Judicial intervention, busing and local residential change, in D. T. Herbert and R. J. Johnston (eds.) *Geography and the Urban Environment*, John Wiley, Chichester, 245–281.

Cox, K. R. (1973) *Conflict, Power and Politics in the City: A Geographic View*, McGraw-Hill, New York.

Cox, K. R. and Johnston, R. J. (1982) *Conflicts, Politics and the Urban Scene*, Longman, London.

Dalkey, N. C. and Rourke, D. L. (1973) *The Delphi Procedure and Rating Quality of Life Factors. The Quality of Life Concept*, Environmental Protection Agency, Washington, DC. ii, 209–21.

Daniels, P. W. and Warnes, A. M. (1980) *Movement in Cities. Spatial Perspectives on Urban Transport and Travel*, Methuen, London.

Davies, R. L. (1984) *Retail and Commercial Planning*, Croom Helm, London.

Dawson, J. A. (1983) *Shopping Centre Development*, Longman, London.

Dingemans, D. (1979) Red-lining and mortgage lending in Sacramento, *Annals, Association of American Geographers*, **69**, 225–239.

Doxiadis, C. A. (1968) *Ekistics. An Introduction to the Science of Human Settlement*, Hutchinson, London.

Evans, A. (1973) The location of headquarters of industrial companies, *Urban Studies*, **10**, 387–395.

Eyles, J. and Woods, K. J. (1983) *The Social Geography of Medicine and Health*, Croom Helm, London.

Faris, R. E., and Dunham, H. W. (1939) *Mental Disorders in Urban Areas*, University of Chicago Press, Chicago.

Festinger, L., Schachter, S. and Back, K. (1950) *Social Pressures in Informal Groups*, Stanford University Press, Stamford.

Fischer, C. S., Baldassare, M. and Oske, R. J. (1975) Crowding studies and urban life, a critical review, *Journal, American Institute of Planners*, **31**, 406–18.

Ford, L. and Griffin, E. (1979) The ghettoization of paradise, *Geographical Review*, **69**, 140–158.

French, R. A. and Hamilton, F. E. I. (eds.), (1979), *The Socialist City: Spatial Structure and Urban Policy*, John Wiley, Chichester.

Friedmann, J. R. (1978) The urban field as a human habitat, in L. S. Bourne and J. W. Simmons (eds.) *Systems of Cities. Readings on Structure, Growth and Policy*, Oxford University Press, New York, pp. 42–52.

Friedmann, J. and Wolff, G. (1982) World city formation: an agenda for research and action, *International Journal of Urban and Regional Research*, **6**, 309–344.

Friedmann, J. and Wulff, R. (1976) *The Urban Transition, Comparative Studies of Newly Industrializing Societies*, Edward Arnold, London.

Fujita, K. (1988) The technopolis: high technology and regional development in Japan, *International Journal of Urban and Regional Research*, **12**, 566–594.

Gilbert, A. (1982) *Urbanization in Contemporary Latin America: Critical Approaches to the Analysis of Urban Issues*, John Wiley and Sons, New York.

Gill, O. (1977) *Luke Street*, Macmillan, London.

Gottmann, J. (1976) Megalopolitan systems around the world, *Ekistics*, **243**, 109–113.

Guy, C. (1985) The food and grocery shopping behaviour of disadvantaged consumers: some results from the Cardiff consumer panel, *Transactions, Institute of British Geographers*, **10**, 181–190.

Hagerstrand, T. (1966) Aspects of the spatial structure of social communications and the diffusion of innovations, *Papers and Proceedings of the Regional Science Association*, **16**, 27–42.

Hagerstrand, T. (1971) cited in L. S. Bourne (ed.) *Internal Structure of the City*, Oxford University Press, New York, p. 244.

Haggett, P. (1965) *Locational Analysis in Human Geography*, Edward Arnold, London.

Hall, P. (1984) *The World Cities*, 3rd edition, Weidenfeld and Nicholson, London.

Hall, P. (1989) *London 2001*, Unwin Hyman, London.

Harris, C. D. and Ullman, E. L. (1945) The nature of cities, *Annals, American Academy of Political and Social Science*, **242**, 7–17.

Harvey, D. (1973) *Social Justice and the City*, Arnold, London.

Harvey, D. (1975) The political economy of housing in advanced capitalist societies: the case of the United States, in G. Gappert and H. M. Rose (eds.) *The Social Economy of Cities, Urban Affairs Review*, **9**, Sage Publications.

Harvey, D. (1985) *The Urbanization of Capital*, Basil Blackwell Ltd., Oxford.

Harvey, D. (1985) *Consciousness and the Urban Experience*, Basil Blackwell, Oxford.

Hatt, P. K. (1946) The concept of natural area, *American Sociological Review*, **11**, 423–427.

Herbert, D. T. (1972) *Urban Geography: A Social Perspective*, David and Charles, Newton Abbot.

Herbert, D. T. and Raine, J. W. (1976) Defining communities within urban areas, *Town Planning Review*, **47**, 325–338.

Herbert, D. T. and de Silva, S. K. (1974) Social dimensions of a non-western city: a factorial ecology of Colombo, *Cambria*, **1**, 139–158.

Herbert, D. T. and Smith, D. M. (eds.) (1979) *Social Problems and the City: Geographical Perspectives*, Oxford University Press, Oxford.

Herbert, D. T. and Smith, D. M. (eds.) (1989) *Social Problems and the City. New Perspectives*, Oxford University Press, Oxford.

Irving, H. (1978) Space and environment in interpersonal relations, in D. T. Herbert and R. J. Johnston (eds.), *Geography and the Urban Environment*, Vol. 1, pp. 249–284.

Jacobs, J. (1969) *The Economy of Cities*, Random House, New York.

Jakle, J. A., Brunn, S. and Roseman, C. C. (1976) *Human Spatial Behaviour: A Social Geography*, Duxbury, New York.

Jackson, P. and Smith, S. J. (1984) *Exploring Social Geography*, George Allen and Unwin, London.

Jakobson, L. and Prakash, V. (eds.) (1971) *Urbanization and National Development*, Sage, Beverly Hills.

Johnston, R. J. (1980) *City and Society: an Outline for Urban Geography*, Penguin, Harmondsworth.

Johnston, R. J. (1982a) *The Local State*, in *Geography and the State*, Macmillan, London, pp. 187–260.

Johnston, R. J. (1982b) *The American Urban System. A Geographical Perspective*, Longman, London.

Joseph, A. E. and Phillips, D. R. (1984) *Accessibility and Utilization. Geographical Perspectives on Health Care Delivery*, Harper and Row, London.

Khodzhaev, D. G. and Khorev, B. S. (1973) The concept of a unified settlement system and planned control of the growth of towns in the USSR, *Geographia Polonica*, **27**, 43–51.

Knox, P. L. (1982) *Urban Social Geography*, Longman, London.

Lakshmanan, T. R. and Chatterjee, L. R. (1977) *Urbanization and Environmental Quality*, AAG Resource Paper, 77-71, Washington.

Lakshmanan, T. R. and Hansen, W. G. (1965) A retail market potential model, *Journal of the American Institute of Planners*, **31**, 134-144.

Lamarche, F. (1976) Property development and the economic foundations of the urban question, in C. G. Pickvance (ed.), *Urban Sociology: Critical Essays*, Tavistock Press, pp. 85-118.

Langton, J. (1975) Residential patterns in pre-industrial cities: some case studies of the seventeenth century, *Transactions of the Institute of British Geographers*, **65**, 1-27.

Lewis, J. and Bowlby, S. (1989) Women's inequality in urban Britain, in D. T. Herbert and D. M. Smith (eds.), *Social Problems and the City: New Perspectives*, Oxford University Press, Oxford, pp. 213-231.

Ley, D. (1977) Social geography and the taken-for-granted world, *Transactions, Institute of British Geographers*, **NS, 2**, 498-512.

Ley, D. (1983) *A Social Geography of the City*, Harper and Row, New York.

Liu, B. C. (1975) *Quality of Life Indicators in United States Metropolitan Areas, 1970*, US Environmental Protection Agency, Washington.

Lord, J. D. (1988) *Retail Decentralization and C. B. D. Decline in American Cities*, Institute for Retail Studies, University of Stirling, Working Paper No. 8802.

Lowenthal, D. (1961) Geography, experience, and imagination: towards a geographical epistemology, *Annals, Association of American Geographers*, **51**, 241-260.

Lyman, S. M. and Scott, M. B. (1967) Territoriality: a neglected sociological dimension, *Social Problems*, **15**, 236-249.

McGee, T. G. (1967) *The South-east Asian City*, Bell, London.

McGee, T. G. (1971) *The Urbanization Process in the Third World: Explorations in Search of a Theory*, Bell, London.

Mayer, J. D. (1986) International perspectives on the health care crisis in the United States, *Social Science and Medicine*, **23**, 10, 1056-1065.

Mayer, H. (1954) Urban Geography, in P. James and C. F. Jones (eds.), *American Geography: Inventory and Prospectus*, Syracuse, New York.

Mellor, J. R. (1977) *Urban Sociology in an Urbanized Society*, Routledge and Kegan Paul, London.

Mercer, C. (1975) *Living in Cities*, Penguin Books, Harmondsworth.

Michelson, W. A. (1970) *Man and his Urban Environment*, Addison-Wesley, Reading, Mass.

Mogridge, M. J. H. (1987) The use of rail transport to improve accessibility in large conurbations, using London as an example, *Town Planning Review*, **58**, 2, 165-182.

Moser, C. A. and Scott, W. (1961) *British Towns: a Statistical Study of their Social and Economic Differences*, Centre for Urban Studies, Report No. 2, London.

Muller, P. O. (1976) *The Outer City: Geographical consequences of the urbanizaton of the suburbs*, A. A. A. G. Resource Paper, No. 75-2, Washington.

Murphy, R. E., Vance, J. E. and Epstein, B. J. (1955) Internal structure of the C. B. D., *Economic Geography*, **31**, 24-40.

Myrdal, G. M. (1957) *Economic Theory and the Under-Developed Regions*, London.

Northam, R. (1979) *Urban Geography*, John Wiley, New York.

Ottensman, J. R. (1981) The spatial dimension in the planning of social services in large cities, *Journal of American Planning Association*, 167-174.

Pacione, M. (1983) *Progress in Urban Geography*, Croom Helm, Beckenham.

Park, R. E., Burgess, E. W. and McKenzie, R. D. (eds.) (1925) *The City*, University of Chicago Press, Chicago.

Piaget, J. and Inhelder, B. (1956) *The Child's Conception of Space*, Routledge and Kegan Paul, London.

Piche, D. (1977) *The Geographical Understanding of Children aged 5 to 8 Years*, unpublished doctoral thesis, University of London.

Pooley, C. G. (1977) The residential segregation of migrant communities in mid-Victorian Liverpool, *Transactions, Institute of British Geographers*, NS, **2**, 364–382.

Radford, J. P. (1979) Testing the model of the pre-industrial city: the case of ante-bellum Charleston, South Carolina, *Transactions, Institute of British Geographers*, NS, **4**, 392–410.

Raine, J. W. (1976) *Social Interaction and Urban Neighbourhood*, unpublished Ph.D., University of Wales (Swansea).

Ratcliff, R. V. (1949) *Urban Land Economics*, McGraw-Hill, New York.

Rees, P. H. (1979) *Residential Patterns in American Cities: 1960*, University of Chicago, Geography Research Paper 189.

Reissman, L. (1964) *The Urban Process: Cities in Industrial Society*, Free Press, New York.

Relph, E. (1976) *Place and Placelessness*, Pion, London.

Rex, J. A. and Moore, R. (1967) *Race, Community and Conflict*, Oxford University Press, London.

Roberts, B. (1978) *Cities of Peasants*, Edward Arnold, London.

Robson, B. (1988) *Those Inner Cities*, Clarendon Press, Oxford.

Rodwin, L. (1970) *Nations and Cities, A Comparison of Strategies for Urban Growth*, Houghton, Mifflin, Boston.

Rossi, P. A. (1955) *Why Families Move*, Free Press, Glencoe, Ill.

Rowntree, B. S. (1901) *Poverty, a Study of Town Life*, Macmillan, London.

Saunders, P. (1980) *Urban Politics*, Penguin, Harmondsworth.

Saunders, P. (1981) *Social Theory and the Urban Question*, Hutchinson, London.

Scott, P. (1970) *Geography and Retailing*, Hutchinson, London.

Seamon, D. (1979) *A Geography of the Lifeworld: Movement, Rest and Encounter*, Croom Helm, London.

Sharpe, L. J. (1976) The role and functions of local government in modern Britain, Layfield Report, *The Relationship between Central and Local Government*, HMSO, London, pp. 203–220.

Shaw, C. R. and McKay, H. D. (1942) *Juvenile Delinquency and Urban Areas*, University of Chicago Press, Chicago (revised edition, 1969).

Shaw, M. (1977) The ecology of social change, Wolverhampton 1851–71, *Transactions, Institute of British Geographers*, NS, **2**, 332–348.

Shaw, M. (1979) Reconciling social and physical space, Wolverhampton 1871, *Transactions, Institute of British Geographers*, NS, **4**, 192–213.

Shevky, E. and Bell, W. (1955) *Social Area Analysis*, Stanford University Press, Stanford, California.

Short, J. R. (1984) *An Introduction to Urban Geography*, Routledge and Kegan Paul, London.

Short, J. R. (1989) Yuppies, yuffies and the new urban order, *Transactions, Institute of British Geographers*, NS, **14**, 173–188.

Simmons, J. W. and Bourne, L. S. (1978) Defining urban places: differing concepts of the urban system, in L. S. Bourne and J. W. Simmons (eds.), *Systems of Cities: Readings on Structure, Growth and Policy*, Oxford University Press, New York, 28–41.

Smith, C. J. (1989) Alcoholism and alcohol control policy in the American city, in D. T. Herbert and D. M. Smith (eds.) *Social Problems and the City: New Perspectives*, Oxford University Press, Oxford, pp. 323–341.

Smith, D. M. (1973) *The Geography of Social Well-being in the United States*, McGraw-Hill, New York.

Smith, D. M. (1979) The identification of problems in cities: applications of social indicators, in D. T. Herbert and D. M. Smith (eds) *Social Problems and the City: Geographical Perspectives*, Oxford University Press, Oxford, 13–32.

Soja, E. (1971) *The Political Organization of Space*, Association of American Geographers, Washington, Resource Paper No. 8.

Taylor, G. (1949) *Urban Geography*, Methuen, London.

Thomson, J. M. (1977) *Great Cities and Their Traffic*, Victor Gollancz Ltd., London.

Thornton, S. J., McCullagh, M. J. and Bradshaw, R. P. (1987) *Shops, Pedestrians and the CBD*, Department of Geography, University of Nottingham.

Vance, J. E. (1966) Housing the worker: the employment linkage as a force in urban structure, *Economic Geography*, **42**, 294–325.

Vance, J. E. (1970) *The Merchant's World*: The Geography of Wholesaling, Prentice Hall, Englewood Cliffs, NJ.

Vance, J. E. (1971) Land assignment in pre-capitalist, capitalist, and post-capitalist cities, *Economic Geography*, **47**, 101–120.

Vance, J. E. (1977) *This Scene of Man*, Harpers College Press, New York.

Victor, C. R. (1975) *The Changing Location of High Status Residential Areas on Swansea, 1854–1974*, unpublished B.A. Thesis, University College of Swansea.

Walmsley, D. J. (1988) *Urban living: the individual in the city*, Longman, Harlow.

Ward, D. (1971) *Cities and Immigrants*, Oxford University Press, New York.

Ward, D. (1975) Victorian cities: how modern?, Journal of Historical Geography, **1**, 135–151.

Warnes, A. M. (1987) Geographical location and social relationships among the elderly in M. Pacione (ed.) *Social Geography: Progress and Prospect*, Croom Helm, London, 252–294.

Warnes, A. M. (1989) Social problems of elderly people in cities, in D. T. Herbert and D. M. Smith (eds.) *Social Problems and the City: New Perspectives*, Oxford University Press, Oxford, 197–212.

Wheatley, P. (1963) What the greatness of a city is said to be – reflections on Sjoberg's pre-industrial city, Pacific Viewpoint, **4**, 163–188.

Wheatley, P. (1971) *The Pivot of the Four Quarters*, University of Chicago Press, Chicago.

White, P. (1984) *The West European City: A Social Geography*, Longman, London.

Whitehand, J. W. R. (1967) Fringe belts: a neglected aspect of urban geography, *Transactions, Institute of British Geographers*, **41**, 223–233.

Whyte, W. H. (1957) *The Organization Man*, Anchor Books, New York.

Wilson, W. J. (1985) The urban underclass in advanced industrial society, in P. E. Peterson (ed.) *The New Urban Reality*, Brookings Institute, Washington, 129–160.

Yeates, M. (1975) *Main Street: Windsor to Quebec City*, Macmillan, Toronto.

Zipf, G. K. (1949) *Human Behaviour and the Principle of Least Effort*, Addison-Wesley, Reading, Mass.

Subject Index